ALSO BY KATE SIMON

NEW YORK: *Places and Pleasures*

NEW YORK (with Andreas Feininger)

MEXICO: *Places and Pleasures*

KATE SIMON'S PARIS

KATE SIMON'S LONDON

ITALY: *The Places In Between*

ROME: *Places and Pleasures*

ENGLAND'S GREEN AND PLEASANT LAND

KATE SIMON

England's Green and Pleasant Land

ALFRED · A · KNOPF   NEW YORK   1974

1784286

/09252/2

THIS IS A BORZOI BOOK
PUBLISHED BY ALFRED A. KNOPF, INC.

Library of Congress Cataloging in Publication Data:

Simon, Kate, date.   England's green and pleasant land.

1.   England—Description and travel—1971–
—Guide-books.   I.   Title.
DA650.s58   914.2'04'85   74-7258
ISBN 0-394-46826-0

Manufactured in the United States of America

FIRST EDITION

For Sasha and Nila

CONTENTS

Acknowledgments   xi

Foreword   xiii

Prepare and Be Prepared For   3

NEAR NORTHEAST   11

East Anglia   13

*East Bergholt, Hadleigh, Sudbury, Long Melford,
Lavenham, Ickworth House, Bury St. Edmunds,
Freston, Woodbridge, Framlingham, Dunwich,
Walberswick, Blytheburgh, Southwold, Belton, Great
Yarmouth, Norwich, Wroxham, Thetford, Grime's
Graves, Swaffham, South Acre, Castle Acre, King's
Lynn*

Lincolnshire   58

*Grantham, Belton House, Lincoln, Tattershall Castle,
Horncastle, Louth*

South from Lincoln   75

*Nottingham, Coventry, Warwick, Compton
Wynyates*

NORTHEAST   83

York   85

Yorkshire Rides   107

*Rievaulx Abbey, Beverley Minster, Ilkley, Otley,
Harrogate, Ripon Cathedral, Fountains Abbey,
Newby Hall, Grassington, Haworth*

Durham   122

Into Northumberland   129
  Raby Castle, Hexham

Northumberland   136
  Alnwick, Warkworth Castle, Seaton Delaval Hall,
  Washington Old Hall

NORTHWEST   147

Lake District   149
  Muncaster Castle, Gosforth, Whitehaven,
  Cockermouth, Keswick, Grasmere, Sizergh Castle,
  Levens Hall

SOUTH   165

Surrey, Kent, and Sussex   167
  Guildford, Losely House, Comptom, Petworth House,
  Shere, Polesden Lacey; Chartwell, Knole, Penshurst,
  Hever Castle, Ightham Mote, Wrotham, Mereworth,
  Cranbrook, Sissinghurst Castle, Biddenden,
  Headcorn, Wye, Chilham; Lewes, Glyndebourne,
  Burwash, Etchingham, Bodiam

The Momentous Coast   191
  Rye, Winchelsea, Battle, Wilmington, Alfriston,
  Ditchling Beacon, Sompting, Fishbourne, Bosham

SOUTHWEST   199

Dorset   201
  Dorchester, Maiden Castle, Stinsford, Higher
  Bockhampton, Tolpuddle, Bere Regis, Cerne Abbas,

Sherborne, Blandford Forum, Badbury Rings

Devon and Cornwall   213

Honiton, Paignton, Totnes, Moretonhampstead,
Bickleigh, Cadbury, Cullompton, Tiverton, Dunster,
Exford, Bideford, Clovelly; Morwenstow, Boscastle,
Tintagel, Delabole, Launceston, Lanhydrock House,
Trethevy Quoit, Port Isaac, Padstow, St. Colomb
Major, St. Agnes, St. Ives, Zennor, Porthcurno,
Veryan, Mevagissey, Fowey

Westward   240

Odiham, The Vyne, Winchester, Romsey, Salisbury,
Wilton House, Marlborough, Avebury, Lacock,
Malmesbury, Corsham Court, Bradford-on-Avon,
Bath, Claverton Manor, Wells, Glastonbury, Longleat

NEAR NORTHWEST   273

The Other Cotswolds
and North to Chester   275

Fairford, Bibury, Northleach, Cirencester, Sapperton,
Whiteway, Painswick, Stroud, Bisley, Nether Lypiatt,
Minchinhampton, Berkeley Castle, Cheltenham,
Stanway, Deerhurst, Tewkesbury, Kempley,
Ross-on-Wye, Leominster, Croft Castle, Shrewsbury,
Battlefield Church, Oswestry, Offa's Dyke, Chester

And Be Prepared For   309

Index   *follows page* 311

Acknowledgments

Many thanks to Mr. Raymond Hewett of the British Travel Authority and to the helpful staff of the London Library. Many affectionate thanks to my friends for their interest, suggestions, skillful, patient chauffeuring and hospitality, especially Aida Young, Esther Freedman, Leila Nash, Joan Morse, Brigadier-General and Mrs. Eric Forster, Angela Forster, and Harry Goss.

K. S.

FOREWORD

The allure of England to English, European, Oriental, and American is not the drama of countryside, although there is drama in the Lake District, on the northern moors, the coast of Cornwall. Switzerland is more dramatic, America more varied, Yugoslavia more showy. It isn't the art treasures; nothing can match the opulence of Italy. Except for a dozen cathedrals and several overstated mansions, there is little of the magniloquence of medieval French churches and later chateaux. The charm is the lack of exaggerations, the subtlety of contrasts, the clinging to patterns that reflect and join the solid worth and probity of the English people, reasonable in abstract considerations of needs for change, slow to countenance the actuality. There is much more to say about the English, and in all languages (including Tamil, Mandarin Chinese, and Swahili) it has been said. A few of their endearing old charms have been sprinkled and buttered over various pages of this book, but that which is generally, consistently most conspicuous, after the politeness and kindliness, is the opposition to change, the adherence to tradition and habit. The fact of numerous eccentrics, of great innovators in the sciences, geniuses in literature, movers and shakers in government, does not necessarily contradict the general inclination. Opposition to change is strengthened by stubborn fortitude, a quality universally admired in the conduct of the English under German bombing, a quality that marked the endurance of the poor farm worker, the women who wore their lives away at looms, and the children who wasted in mines. There were, as everyone knows, peasant revolts and revolts of apprentices, early attempts at unionization, and associations of agricultural workers, but the mass endured in the ancient tradition as expressed in an Anglo-Saxon lament: "That which they [others trapped in misfortune] have endured, I can too."

The reluctance to change dictates immutable styles—the worthy shapeless coat with strong buttons, the plain-spoken felt hat, the countless new industrial estates that repeat rowing, cricket matches, concerts, tours, theatre, and so on, in each of their sitting rooms. The redoubtable stubbornness is often a challenge to the tourist. He finds himself reluctant to stumble around one more Roman, Saxon, or Norman tower

until he notices an old English lady on a cane nimbly negotiating every pile of old stone in sight. He feels he cannot face
another Lely lady and finds himself in a group that includes
a man carefully describing each portrait in the drawing room
of a stately home to a blind friend. Nothing can stop Englishmen (or Englishwomen especially) in their habits and convic-
tions, and little can budge them out of their steady, stalwart
ways.

Along with this national characteristic and the universal
civility, there are minor regional differences. The north will
never enter a hotel breakfast room without saying "Good morning" to the general assemblage; the south is cooler and lazier
in these matters. Cornwall, proud of its tradition of individ-
ualism, clasps you to its bosom and then turns its back on you;
you never know. There are communities that strive to stay the
fading strains of morris dance music, keep the pensioners in
their almshouses in sixteenth-century cloaks and caps, conduct
town ceremonies in Middle English. Others dress some of their
citizens in doublet and hose and farthingales at the drop of a
tourist while the opposition hibernates, during the tourist season, with book and telly, muttering with Deor of the Lament,
"This, too, will pass."

The towns inhabit different moods. Guildford is well fed,
energetic, and smiles politely; York is well fed, beamish, and
affectionate; Salisbury is an aristocrat, Tewkesbury a hoyden;
Winchester walks gravely, Lincoln bounces; Durham Cathedral glowers, Beverley Minster is merry.

The search for legendary rural England, as the search for the
truly rural anywhere, becomes increasingly difficult. Farm
lands are abandoned, leaving drowsy fields to the elderly;
empty cottages are bought and refurbished as weekend houses
by prosperous townies. A surprising and gratifying amount
still remains, though, and this book attempts to give you samplers of it attached to the towns and show pieces of several
regions. A glance at the map will show how densely peppered
it is with names, how closely villages abut on each other, how
near each other the towns must be in an old country that can
be traversed north to south or east to west in a day . . . a har-
rowing idea. Consequently, trips here have been designed in
clusters and loops, sometimes overlapping, occasionally changing direction; many more than the traveler can make in the

accustomed vacation time, but enough for a selection on which to base suitable home-made itineraries, best by car, but many possible by bus, train, and bus tours out of the larger towns. There is no attempt here at "the complete England" book, no large industrial cities, no exploration of London. It is assumed that many travelers will take, or have taken, trips to Canterbury, to Ely, to Oxford and Cambridge, and to great houses not far from London, during a stay in that city. The purpose of this book is to introduce possible new places, grouped, generally, in various directions from London.

Out of this grab bag, try to pick up a town that enjoys a famous cathedral, a medieval quarter, and a university, a felicitous combination that makes a joyous spirit, as in Norwich and York, for instance. Add to that a castle, a ruined abbey, and a historic house not too far away. Then work out other combinations, always including a few villages. Their measure will be a quiet, modest comeliness, made of venerable houses, a remade church on an antique base, and gardens and gardens. The village design in any one area may appear repetitious, but it is the very peaceableness of the repetition that is so attractive to travelers from more restless lands. The villages are usually very pleasing . . . and who would be satisfied with one oyster when there are a dozen on the plate?

ENGLAND'S GREEN AND PLEASANT LAND

Prepare and
Be Prepared For

First, avail yourself of the information offered by your local British tourist office, or, before setting off from London, visit the British Tourist Authority, 64 St. James's Street, off Piccadilly, for information and pamphlets. They should be able to guide you to bus tours, farm houses at which to stay, where to hire a boat for canal crawling. Detailed regional maps can be had at any good-sized bookshop which also stocks books listing sights, houses, hotels, pubs and inns, guest houses, and restaurants throughout the country; books about camping, hiking, cruising the waterways, and the railroad schedules book, should you need it. Some of these are also available at hotel news and magazine stands and stalls on central thoroughfares in London. The publication *In Britain* includes, among its descriptive essays, lists of the when and where of festivals of all kinds, racing and boating events. Many towns tell of local racing, cricket matches, concerts, tours, theatre, and so on, in their Tourist Bureau listings.

Prepare to be patient with old towns and their ancient streets. Their shapes were not made for the automobile, nor, it appears, were the occasionally erratic schemes devised to keep traffic flowing.

Unless you have a year to do it in and Olympic enthusiasm, you must content yourself with a few of the innumerable fortresses, castles, manor houses, mansions, palazzi and palais— and regional museums—that sit on almost every slope of the countryside. The consolation is that, unless your taste for these is inordinate, you will find a ceaseless trek from house to museum to castle a trifle boring, in any case.

Every Englishman has at least three favorite stately homes, one for its veins throbbing with history, one for its swollen size and majestic fittings, one because it is the manor house, the closed castle of his childhood (real or imagined or experienced in the cinema) that ushered mounted red coats tearing through the field and Daimlers rocketing up the High Street. Listen, but judge carefully since it requires ingenious planning and mobility to see even a few of them. The most generous periods of opening are the summer months; stately homes go into hibernation, to poke their public heads out only now and then during the darker months; some are open six days a week, some two afternoons. To plan a house itinerary one needs the detailed maps mentioned that usually pinpoint locations, and the indispensable *Historic Houses, Castles and Gardens*, published annually in paperback and available in all bookstores, which lists them by county, giving times of opening and short descriptions. Not always up to date, particularly when owners substitute family craftsmanship or modern family shrines for sequestered treasures, the information is generally still quite reliable.

Stately homes can be cool and rational, amiably eccentric, enterprising jumbles, or remote classical blocks. Prices of admission vary, too, on a rather mysterious scale. Thirty pence can buy foot-burning vistas of ancestral portraits and Italian marquetry; 50 pence and a box that suggests tips (not common) buys only linenfold paneling and topiary art. By and large, though, and at any price, one must always be prepared for a vast population of curly gentlemen and pearly ladies painted by Lely and Kneller, usually outshone by a Reynolds, a Gainsborough, a Lawrence; for forests of heavily carved Jacobean furniture, marble-topped, intricate Italian; solid, hand-embroidered English coverlets; and extensive spreads of English china in gleaming rows.

There is a feeling, treacherous for a respectable Englishman to express, felt nevertheless, that there are too many great houses with the same repertoire and that the money might well be used in other ways. But then, what would happen to the ladies who guard, one per room, the properties of the National Trust? The ladies who speak with pursed mouths and immobile brows and the jolly ladies who let one linger a few moments after closing time, "Don't worry, dears. Enjoy yourselves. It would be a pity not to see all the lovely things."

With so many to choose from, the determining factors for the traveler must be available time, or proximity to an imposing cathedral or beguiling village; or a taste for the vigors of the Tudor, the frozen wastes of the neo-classical, the reverberations of the classical, the golden tinkle of Adam. Whichever you choose or pass by, be assured that an English friend will accuse you with, "You didn't see Wickley Welfoot Hall, or Meechly Meekly Abbey?" A thunderous pause. Then, "Well never mind. It can't be helped now, can it?" in the tone of controlled rebuke that often wings in and out of the famous English politeness. With enough luck and English friends this will happen a good many times and the sheer multiplicity of accusations should cancel out the guilt over tourist duty neglected.

Country hotels, particularly in the north. The big halls and stairs are enlivened by chipped busts of the English equivalent of Old Black Joe, a hawk or a falcon under glass, copper and brass bowls of heroic diameter, and trays like primitive shields. Already unfortunate singles are further punished by being entombed in maids' rooms that stem from a time when limp, meager curtains, or none, scarred old furniture, and thorough tattiness in no space was good enough for the help. Ask for a double if you can possibly afford it, or go on into the nearest town, hoping for better.

"Ye Olde" inn hotels, where Mr. Pickwick or Dickens or Elizabeth I or the Venerable Bede or Alfred the Great stopped, are naturally alluring, particularly to Americans whose buildings have a lifespan of twenty-five years. "Ye Olde"-s have public rooms of deep chairs, fireplaces, polished bars, copper warming pans, and brass tankards and, a requirement, beamed walls and ceilings; very nice and as comforting as a warm bath after a long, dank walk. Often the rooms upstairs, joined by short flights up and down and a maze of fire doors to rooms in adjacent houses—acquired over the years—have been refurbished livably. Sometimes an inn is so enchanted by antiquity that it refuses to touch a beam and they threaten your head, cut up space, crowd the beds awkwardly, and leave no room for luggage. In addition, these authentically old rooms usually face a street that once enjoyed the occasional muted sounds of hooves at night and, in the morning, the creak of market wagon wheels. Now they top the ceaseless traffic of the High Street. Look, admire, breathe in the atmosphere, and ask for a non-beamed room in the back.

A later bygone, or compendium of bygones, is the Edwardian merchant's house converted to hotel. These are rarely expensive and as rarely look normal or act normally. Your £5 will buy breakfast, double bed, a doorless shower, and a toilet down the hall; a call system implores the attention of people who never, never answer; the great hall raises a silent and un-tenanted bandstand. The path to the bedrooms is through fancy souvenir china, a caseful of international dolls toppling over each other, a Sicilian cart, virile beer pulls, and lustrous black Victorian ladies holding lamps, Florence Nightingales, if you can imagine it, in déshabille. And watching everyone and everything, a big boss of the size and immobility of Sidney Greenstreet at his most inscrutable. Not bad, all this; just a shade odd.

At some time, out of exhaustion or the Englishness of it, you may decide to sleep in the rooms over a pub on a market square. It will be plain and cheap, noisy until eleven and, if a local soldier is back on leave from hazardous Belfast, the celebration will move out into the streets to stay for long hours. Use ear plugs or join the party, and hug to your sleepy bosom the next day the realization that such pub-inns will soon be rare anachronisms, disappearing to reappear as tarted-up bar-restaurants, workers' clubs with entertainment, and dancing-girl saloons.

For other types of entertainment—usually concerts—find out what the local Trust House hotel is offering, at reduced week-end rates, in the off-seasons. And don't forget to ask English friends about their favorite, self-effacing country inns, hidden in forgotten dells.

Everyone knows about the collapsible dollar, and everyone knows about soaring prices in England as well as Italy, the United States, France, and almost everywhere else. Rural England will, of course, be cheaper than London, but for meals and hotels with pretensions of decency be prepared to pay more than the bargain rates you hoped for. Bed and breakfast accommodations, snack bars, farm-house hospitality for tea alone or total keep may be chancy but cheaper. And it must be kept in mind that all quoted prices are deceptive unless you add a service charge of 10 or 12½ per cent and the 10 per cent Value Added Tax (VAT), which increases a stated price by one-fifth or more. Between the time of research and writing and the time of publication, prices will have increased sub-stantially and probably will continue to do so. Therefore, specific costs have not been quoted; they would be misleading. Instead, you are offered categories that range as follows: "Modest" would cover £3–5; "moderate," up to £10; "high" goes beyond, and there are, fortunately, comparatively few country hotels that ask that much for accommodating two people for a night.

Study your maps carefully, to the point of memorizing your next route, if possible. Indications to major highways are at times lost in local signs, while country lanes, rather profusely signposted, will frequently tell you the names of hamlets after you've passed the turnoff to them. If fog blankets your chosen area, spend your time reading, listening to and watching the highly educated, omnivorously informative BBC on radio and TV or, if you must, creep slowly along secondary and tertiary roads. Leave the big, shrouded highways for the jaunty suicides.

The best literary foraging in remote places, and reporting them vividly, has been almost a monopoly of English writers; a reliable lot, except when let loose on their native heath. Writers of earlier centuries, Defoe, Celia Fiennes, Cobbett, were hard-minded and independent enough to dismiss a town or a region with a sharp *mot juste*. Later writers, particularly those who re-explore the places of their youth, incline to see them through tinted lenses of nostalgia, love for Mum and the kindly vicar. Every day is sunny, every brick caressable, every pub a warm, golden egg, every patch of grass an emerald, every tree a kindly giant. Read them, if you like, with pleasure (as you will) and a pinch of salt.

When to travel, assuming job and child commitments allow a choice? Possibly early September, when the Bank Holiday crowds have retreated to work and home and the long, golden summer light blazes the haystacks, then lingers on the fields through a slow twilight. Spring is a good time for explosions of buds and blossoms but be prepared for occasional tricks. The summer will usually give you clement weather and festivals—and, unfortunately, crowds. Even for those equipped with thermal underwear and an indifference to cold, the winter time is not highly recommendable. Show towns and hotels are not likely to be crowded—an advantage—but daylight puts in a brief appearance and by 5:30, after the shops have closed, there is very little life on the streets; it has scuttled toward hearths, telly, and soon-to-be-opened pubs.

Most towns of size or fame have Information Centres that supply pamphlets of local interest and maps for nothing or little. The attendant will be pleased to point out where you are and to circle places of interest so you will have some idea of directions and distance.

English food isn't all that bad, nor is it particularly good. London and other big cities can feed you well and there are country inns and pubs—exhaustively documented in numerous books—that try and often succeed. The dinner in a highly regarded rural hotel can be worldly or countrified: huge helpings of "roast duck," for instance, which has been boiled and soggily browned, mounds of chips in addition to potatoes in another style, what was once two or three kinds of vegetable with their own distinctive tone of green and clean shape reduced to one discouraged gray mass. And you will have to fight to keep mock gravy off the roast beef and the custard off the apple pie. The best present advice is to buy and follow one of the good food guides, usually reliable and their recommendations symptomatic of general improvement.

Rural service will almost always be "with a smile," the smile sometimes readier than the service. The regular waitress may have decided to take her children on a Women's Institute picnic and the elderly, nice hostess may have trouble locating the pats of butter, nor does she know how to tell the bewildered Maltese dishwasher to clean a couple of glasses, quick. Your waiter may be Spanish or Italian, just arrived to make a few pounds and learn Eengleesh. (Incidentally, it helps to know some Spanish and Italian, not only for restaurants but also in hotels where the mop-and-broom and bedclothes ladies are almost exclusively Mediterranean.) The most disconcerting smile is that on the face of a fresh, bovine girl who absent-mindedly takes the order, ambles back to the kitchen, and stays there, maybe dreaming herself out of the Cinderella role into marriage with Prince Charles, maybe ruminating on the movie she saw last night on telly. Someone dislodges her, in time, from her dreaming stool in the kitchen and she returns with the wrong dishes. In fairness, one must mention her cousin, a country girl too, who listens carefully, whose quick eye examines your table for imperfections, who wants you to eat promptly and comfortably, who brings the salt and a glass of water before you ask for them and, best of all, seems to be enjoying herself like a great hostess and lady.

The only non-smile service lives in Chinese and Indian restaurants, the Chinese brisk and efficient (after the manager has translated your order), and that is all a customer should ask; the Indian usually wrapped in mysticism or gloom.

A recent development in dining presents "medieval" dinners in the halls of stately homes. The entrepreneurs hang banners on honorable walls, stamp the men's toilet "Lords," and serve at long, convivial tables high mounds of substantial food and vats of drink. Waitresses, often housewives of the neighborhood, dress up as "wenches" in tight, low-cut bodices, and patiently allow their behinds to be pinched, the essential purpose of a wench. A king of misrule and an assisting clown or two may keep the pinching and the laughter and the beer going with an energetic stream of jokes. What with safari parks, art lessons, train and boat rides, children's shelters and zoos, tea shops and garden shops, and now big, boozy meals, the stately homes may be on the way to becoming complete popular pleasure palaces, like Tivoli in Copenhagen or the entertainment parks that were, and still may be, the people's pleasure grounds of Singapore.

Please give a minute or two to flower arrangements in churches. They are the loving work of local women and are invariably beautiful.

If you intend to hike in the Pennines, make sure of the potentials of your terrain. It can be rough going here and there. And if you intend joining a trailer camp near a popular coastal area, try to arrange it well in advance of a summer trip. Places are often spoken for by April.

And fill your pockets with traveler's checques. Inflation has hit England, as other nations, staggeringly. Prices cited herein may, therefore, have changed since this writing.

NEAR NORTHEAST

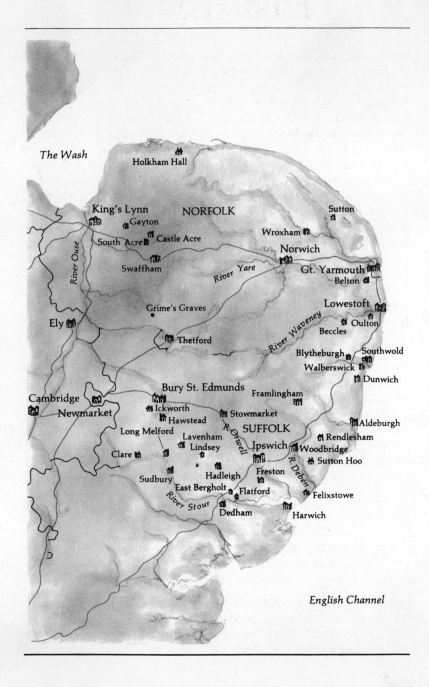

The Wash

Holkham Hall

NORFOLK

King's Lynn
Gayton
South Acre • Castle Acre
Swaffham

Wroxham
Norwich

River Yare

Sutton

Gt. Yarmouth
Belton

River Ouse

Grime's Graves

Lowestoft
Oulton
Beccles

Ely

Thetford

River Waveney

Blytheburgh   Southwold
Walberswick
Dunwich

Cambridge
Newmarket

Bury St. Edmunds
Ickworth
Hawstead
Long Melford
Lavenham
Lindsey
Clare

Framlingham

Stowmarket

SUFFOLK
R. Orwell
Ipswich

Aldeburgh
Rendlesham
Woodbridge
Sutton Hoo
R. Deben

Sudbury
Hadleigh
East Bergholt   Flatford
River Stour   Dedham

Freston
Felixstowe
Harwich

English Channel

East Anglia

Londoners will tell you that East Anglia—the combination of Norfolk (north folk) and Suffolk (south folk)—is a place apart, different. Though it abuts on Cambridge and Ely, not far from London, inland East Anglia is not frequently explored. A bus tour to pink, ladylike Lavenham, a concert or two at the festival organized by Benjamin Britten in **Snape** near **Aldeburgh**, a boat on The Broads, a visit or short stay in a shore cottage or hotel, a meager pilgrimage of devotees to Constable country around East Bergholt or to Saxon towers, usually does it. The flat immensities are calming to some for a week or so but they would not choose to live in such silences, the emptiness of fields and villages in the late afternoon when the peal of a church bell swells infinitely, floating over the long, wide somnolence. (The picture may have changed somewhat in the avid search for country cottages, anywhere, everywhere.)

The palpable quiet, the sense of abandonment, are variously attributed to the wind, to the character of the people, to its history and hardworking marginal living. V. S. Pritchett: "the lazy and forgotten country of slow-talking Suffolk people who had been stunned by the east wind." Early statistics in the Domesday Book prove East Anglia to have been one of the most populous regions in England at the time of the Conquest. Modern statistics point out that depletion still goes on at the rate of about 30,000 people a year, who leave the pigs, the barley, the beets and beans to work in eight-hours-a-day-and-at-least-one-day-off factories. In his remarkable *Akenfield*, Ronald Blythe quotes Suffolk people whose statements suggest reasons for the abandonment, the separateness, the silence:

> I want to say this simply as a fact, that village people in Suffolk in my day were worked to death. It literally happened. . . . They are so private. They talk about beets, holidays and telly, but never about personal hopes or worries. . . . They look solid, their faces are Celtic. Eyes are seeing things in a world of their own, like sailors' eyes.

In stressing boundless, evocative somnolence—often very beautiful—the marriage of secretive land and dignified, polite, unyielding people, there is some danger of neglecting towns and villages surprisingly assorted in mood and dress, and places where trees and flowers stretch in luxuriant gesture. Houses chatter at each other with painted or not plasterwork daisies and tendrils; bricks, bored with the eternal horizontal, take to herringbone and straying in any direction; terra-cotta tiles invite green or yellow moss. In damp mist, the sharp steeples become immense furled umbrella signs made of isinglass. Where church pavements have lost stones, flirtatious little angels, neatly carved into boxes, smile up at the visitor to counter the turned-down mouths of miniature bishops on lecterns and pulpits. Away from the marshes, wheat spreads a golden sea around islands of windmilled villages that have no wish to travel, to come out of their serenity. The music that accompanies the love of the undisturbed traditional is the church bell, the preoccupation of dozens of societies all over England and particularly active in Suffolk. You may find yourself, on entering a church in a small village, confronted and surrounded by an elderly gentleman and his young trainees asking, eagerly, if you've come for learning to pull the ropes in their arcane combinations. The church may not be prepossessing except for the warmth of welcome and enthusiasm for bell ringing but, at a distance, its flint held in Gothic stone has the nubbed glow of dark Baroque pearls.

One of the green, frondy places is **East Bergholt**, on the border with Essex to the south. John Constable was born here in 1776 (the house has disappeared), went to school in the next village, **Dedham**, and later painted his way between home and school in "The Cornfield." His "Hay Wain" plods through the shallow waters of the River Stour to reach the cottage, once the property of his younger brother, at adjoining **Flatford** where the lock and mill that belonged to his father still stand and which he painted in one of his numerous studies of the countryside. Besides its Constable connotation and shadowy peaceableness, East Bergholt has a singular bell arrangement, a slatted sixteenth-century hut that uses no ropes or pulleys but requires that the bells be pushed by hands, strong hands. The substantial church shelters Maria, Constable's wife, and in the yard lie his parents, Golding and Ann Constable. In the center aisle, a brass of a thirty-year-old seventeenth-century cavalier as stylish as only a cavalier can be, and in the south aisle a Constable sketch. A recess in the north wall still carries a fifteenth-century mural and the west door delightful early carving, but most of the rest that meets the eye are monuments, and those queer, or dour, or both. To return to *Akenfield* for a moment: "They are Strict Baptists who have descended from part of the fiercely unconforming East Anglians who helped to settle New England." Of the children, "They're all a lot of little puritans . . ." And back to the church, admittedly Establishment, yet the clock warns "Time passeth away like a shadow"; near the plaque for a "beloved schoolmaster" who was "Unfortunately shott" (no explanation), a stone that warns that this too you shall be, "despised wormes and putrid slime, then dust forgot and lost in time," and so on at vengeful length. Not quite so dour the memorial to Edwarde Lamb, arranged in two lines beginning with his initial letters. The list of "E" for Edwarde strings out as "Edwarde, Ever, Envied, Evil, Endured, Extremities, Even, Earnestly, Expecting, Eternal Ease," a tricky country fancy of an era when there was time for such slow games.

The River Stour which waters many Suffolk villages sends a tributary to **Hadleigh** of wavy medieval houses, staunch half-timbered Tudor and Georgian houses, decorated with bow windows, with heads, brave overhangs, many-faceted windows, and garlands around the dates of houses. Stop at the Spinning Wheel on the High Street for tea or shelter for the night and especially to see the use of dark, crooked, heavy beams as an effective screen to divide a large copper-glinted room.

Out of its faint tristesse, with little topographic drama to excite its views, Suffolk yearns for color and uses it with passion. Pale pink elsewhere turns to shocking in Suffolk; a stone house in Hadleigh will sport a purple door, a half-timbered elder will wear a beauty patch of bright orange. A barn on a narrow country road puts on a dress of black, a vest of orange turning to vermilion and, as a shawl, panels of pale beige—a stunning hippie costume or, if you prefer, a notable abstract painting. The trendy barn sits in a country land that rises and turns through tree-bound fields to reach **Kersey**, the ravishing ghost of a once important wool town, that holds in its lap a spit of river which your car must ford. At its crest a now over-imposing church, on one haunch a row of half-timbered houses with outside steps that purportedly housed Flemish weavers. Kersey was so eminent a weaving village that it gave its name to a sturdy cloth for men's wear, as its neighbor, **Lindsey**, was remembered as the source of the softer linsey-woolsey. Both have sunk into the passive roles of historic witness and appealing points in the twists of Suffolk lanes.

Remember the ride of Paul Revere and the instructions "One if by land and two if by sea" signaled to him by a lantern in a church tower in Boston? It was flourished by a Thomas Dawes, one of the "fiercely unconforming East Anglians" who migrated in considerable number to build fiercely uncompromising Puritan New England. His town was **Sudbury**, once the leading wool town of Suffolk and, although it has had to diversify into other industry, still a weaving town, now limited to silk. Unlike other wool towns, Sudbury does not tiptoe about dressed in the veils and ribbons of nostalgia. Its market-place church, St. Peter's, which charges into the stalls like a ship in full sail, has been declared "redundant," the commonly used polite word for "fired." No hint of regret on Gainsborough's statued face in front or on the faces of the elderly who sit on the benches at its door to pleasure themselves in the brouhaha of the market without being jostled. The market (Thursday and Saturday) is as go-ahead and practical as the flat description of the death of an unregretted church; it is noisy, bright, and as shrewdly opportunistic as a market should be. Itinerant station wagons spill their gaud—last year's Carnaby Street gaud—onto planks and sidewalks, next to the classic market miscellany of watch bands, flashlights, shaving cream, cans of cocoa and syrupy fruit picked up cheaply in close-out sales and carried from town to village to town. Eggs broken in the transporting are never discarded but emptied into jars for carrying away to make omelettes and cakes. Vegetable crates with provocative Italian names serve, when empty, as trays for local flowers or to burn when the wind blows in cold and damp from the North Sea. Sudbury's practicality gives it the most magniloquent public library in England. They took their Corn Exchange—gravid with ocher-gold bunches of wheat on classic columns, volutes and gold dolphins, big arches and iron-bound skylights—and hung modern wood and glass library structures inside it. Odd combination as it is, the result is a roomy, well lit, well functioning, and popular library.

Market Street is faced with amiable, undistinguished houses

painted in tones of red, off-white, and several shades of blue in the Suffolk manner, then descends to the house where Gainsborough was born, on the street named for him. It is an airy, unassertive house that shows a few paintings, mainly as copies, furniture which belonged to the family or the period, a case of old books; not too much that is revealing since the painter's rich glamour days were spent away from the home town, in Ipswich, in Bath. The bedroom is cut open in one area to show an antique style of housebuilding, slats and branches crisscrossed to hold clayey filler. The lower rooms hang the works of local artists in changing exhibitions and swell toward a vivid garden whose springtime pansies are as broad and deeply colored as lordly shields marching under a tree in crimson blossom. Farther down the street, a group of ancient houses whose gray wood bears softened carvings of capitals on the slender pillars, on heavy supporting beams; wooden tatting around the windows; men, animals, and flowers cavorting dimly in the silvered wood. The Friar's Restaurant near the Corn Exchange has similar wayward beams and the dark amber patina of carved wood in its doorways.

Suffolk fatalism expresses itself near All Saints' Church, whose scaffolding bears a sign: WATCH OUT FOR FALLING MASONRY AND FLINT, less a warning than inviting banner to young women pushing prams on the way to the market via the perilous green short cut. The church holds discreetly decorative sections of carved screen; an inventive range of figures and foliage among the pew carvings; a sturdy oak pulpit supervised by a solemn angel; and an extraordinary number of brooms and pails for keeping the church pristine. The Church of St. Gregory fills part of its simple cambered ceiling with good openwork ornaments and, feeling this insufficiently luxurious for the section above the altar, fills that portion with red bands interlaced among stars and doodles on a blue field. Better, more indigenous, are the fine ironwork patterns on lamp posts, the busy hamlet of misericords ("pity" for old and ailing monks in the form of half-seats), an extraordinary font cover whose long thin spires and lancets rise up and up to meet a pole from the ceiling that holds it erect. Not so many brooms and pails here but a Lady Chapel that stores chairs and little else, certainly not Marian worship. No more than Sudbury is a churchly town is St. Gregory a churchly church, although one of its founders, Simon Tybald, was Archbishop of Canterbury in the reign of the enigmatic Richard II and one of the spurs of the Peasants' Revolt. His zeal for grinding agricultural workers into starvation poverty with a series of suppressive measures implemented by the king cost him his life. When the Wat Tyler rebellion marched on London in 1381 he hid in the Tower, but they found him and chopped his head off. Awe and the necrophilia which filled mountains of reliquaries brought the head back to its church where, purportedly, what is left of it remains. No urgent need to search for it; the market place and library are now the living and lively essences of Sudbury.

One soon enters bus-tour Suffolk. **Clare** and **Cavendish** fold subtly swelling hills around thatched houses, some Georgian, some Victorian, some ebulliently plastered, some showing gashes of old carving; inexpensive snacks and tea rooms. In all the narrow front lawns brilliant flower borders and, spilling into the road, falls of blossoms. The ebullience calms to a roof or two of elaborate lacing, knotting and hair-cutting of thatch, rough slats on barns the color of hard winters, and a village unlike any other, the aristocratic, don't-touch-me **Long Melford**, named, it is said, from a combination of words for mill and water. Other conjecture gives it the meaning of a long purse closed by a ring, the kind Shakespeare's courtiers wing across the stage, heavy with ducats, to their servitors. The shape of the village better answers the latter description.

From a carved bench near the church, the vast long banner of green tacked to its side by great trees. At one side, small Victorian and Georgian houses and at the other the octagonal towers of Melford Hall and beyond, long farm houses that hug the earth under their sharply scalloped hats of thatch. The almshouses built on a bequest of the lord of Melford Hall, Sir William Cordell, still house in small Elizabethan units several old people who now live with all mod. cons., a matron and TV, at a pittance per year. Their neighbors are the church and a line of swaying houses whose bow windows force their way through thick ivy.

By the end of the fifteenth century, the export of wool had diminished but gave way, in several large areas, to the manufacture of cloth, which created a new prosperity and splendid "wool churches" like this one of Long Melford. Built in the late fifteenth century (the tower is much newer), its walls are of flint held in stone that shapes the long slender arches, the geometric and stylized designs, the quatrefoils holding shields that characterize the Perpendicular style. Its size was a matter of money and pride, meant to provide space for everyone in the parish on high ceremonial occasions. The Clopton Chantry of little niches, pierced stone around shields, the sedilia (seats for the clergy), and the piscina, the basin for washing the vessels of the Mass, afford closer details of the style. More naïve, folkloric aspects of late-fifteenth-century decoration rest in the ceiling, painted with scrolls and stars in green and red and rows of in-decipherable holy poems in medieval Latin. The accustomed chantry inhabitants appear: the colored stone shields of a stone bed to support a knight in armor with his little dog at his feet and, under shreds of rug, brasses of ladies in a fashion show of headdresses, a mustachioed man whose pillow looks like a headdress as well, and a sign that says one must pay 50 pence (and prices fly upwards, one must always keep in mind) per rubbing. Before you settle to the soothing—except to the knees —monotony of endlessly passing a wax stick over paper over brass (hardly a creative act but it makes some people feel that they are palpably touching antiquity), look for two distinctions of the Chantry Chapel. The one piece of glass is a Crucifixion on a lily, a medieval linkage of Christ with his mother's sym-bolic flower and to the modern eye a surrealistic flower paint-ing. At the entrance to the chapel, a long-hidden flooring panel, rescued in the eighteenth century and now believed to be a fourteenth-century piece of an earlier church. A supernaturally long, calm Virgin sits propped up on an unusually comfortable couch, even for manger accommodation. At her feet, tired Joseph leaning on a crutch; in her lap the Child, already capa-ble of standing; the three Magi—one in the act of lifting off his crown—holding their gifts at the side of the couch and, peering out from under the bed, the heads of a donkey and a cow. The Lady Chapel is a light, welcoming room ringed by an indoor cloistered walk, its wood of a soft, pale color and skill-fully carved. Behind the altar, silk that was woven for West-minster Abbey to enhance the coronation of the present queen,

and a huge black "Act of Parliament" clock picked out with
chinoiserie, a very useful object when a tax was put on watches
in the late eighteenth century. Back inside the church proper,
a piece of glass over the north wall presents a lightweight
enigma; it shows three rabbits so clustered that though each
appears to have two ears, only three show, each single ear act-
ing for two rabbits. Is it, as churchmen say, a symbol of the
Holy Trinity (the name of the church) or an expression of a
craftsman's playfulness? It might easily have been both.

In a stillness disturbed only by an occasional truck and the
shrill of a bird, walk along the assortment of modest houses
behind the Black Lion and, by way of the small turreted and
ivied conduit structure on the green, down to the sturdy old
houses—probably the homes of wool merchants, now inns and
restaurants resplendent with gleaming windows and carved
beams and broad fireplaces—that line the main street. Across
from the Bull Hotel, a brooding house in dark red and deep
black-brown wood whose funereal mood is echoed in the dour,
outraged faces of an Elizabethan gentleman and lady who support the deep-gabled porch. Relief is around the corner from
the Rose and Crown, whose Bridge Street opens to contented
thatched houses on serene fields dotted with a few serene cows.

Melford Hall was the property of Sir William Cordell, the
wool merchant of the immodest tomb in the church, the Mae-
cenas of the almshouses, functionary and host to Queen Elizabeth I, who appears in stained glass in one of the windows. The
first building you may see is the engaging Pavilion, bright light
pouring in from its octagonal sides, extraordinarily tall finials
on the eight gables, so exaggeratedly Tudor as to be almost a
fancy. Beyond, imposing red brick walls turn as octagon turrets, sharpen as gable, and rise as firm chimneys. The house, a
not uncommon display of truncated banqueting hall, big vases,
Oriental ivory figures, things Georgian, things Regency, things
Victorian, ushers one out into gardens and topiary birds and
animals. A drunken hedge, a small wooden bridge lead into the
rural poetic of a few fruit trees and ducks among the reeds of a
marshy pond. On the other side of the road, topiary figures to
surround the red brick school; still ponds turned to flowing
stream, swans meandering with the river beside green paths
among wildflowers, and frail young trees sheltered by older,
taller trees that weave a canopy of birdsong.

NOTES

HOTELS AND RESTAURANTS: Long Melford has several reputable ones, a few quite splendid and pricy. To stay at the Bull in the summertime one must book well in advance, as also in one or two of the more lustrous restaurants. For simpler tastes, decent bed and breakfast at a modest cost, try the Rose and Crown or the hardworking, solicitous Black Lion, which boasts weekly jam sessions by young Suffolk combos nostalgic for Jelly Roll Morton's New Orleans and boasts, too, a tunnel from the church—dug out, they say, for safety from Cromwell's soldiers. Keep in mind that these and their peers are pubs with a few rooms upstairs and there may be no space for you. Proprietors and customers, invariably courtly, will point you, after detailed considered discussion, toward a pub or hotel in another village. Asked about a house or farm that may provide bed and breakfast as do other sections of the country, East Anglia answers out of its staunch, knotty pride: "Oh no, we don't do that here. That's in the south," meaning soft, effete Kent and Surrey.

Lavenham's overhead wires have been hidden underground, it has been scraped and scrubbed and propped up and painted "to be the least spoilt example of an English medieval town." Medieval town it isn't; nostalgic illusion, a fantasy of untroubled times that never existed, it is. Sets of clean, and as always centrally placed, "public conveniences" have obliterated the medieval stench of sewage and slops. The paths that swerve, rise, and loop among the restored overhung and timbered houses lost their authentic mud and horse dung a long time ago. The soft-spoken tea rooms and gift shops are a far cry from the raucous shouting of medieval wares. The good tourist doesn't cavil; he acquiesces in his host's version of reality and enjoys the village for its deluded, ingratiating self. He stands at the Market Place and admires the combined charm and worn might of the Guildhall; he explores its neighbors whose bulges, swelling in several directions, are corseted in beams as strips,

as arches, as narrow wings, as diagonal sketching, or scored
with blithe geometric doodles; he enjoys the ladylike tipsiness
of Lady Street, a soft pink jumble of rectangles and roofs. He
enjoys the position of the virile church as it dominates the
village, the wayward streets that shoot up to views of hills and
trees, and wonders only a little about the predominance of
pink as the color for medieval houses, or is this an acknowl-
edgment of rosy vision?

The shops and houses of the High Street slip to the uncertainties of the old Swan Hotel, to the Wool Hall, somewhat
steadier on its carved supports. Water Street opens with a
Tudor Shop, goes onto the narrow slopes and diagonals of
Oxford House and the tottering pink of fourteenth-century
weavers' cottages, the oldest in Lavenham. The Post Office and
its supporters sway a bit, and so do the antique and weaving
shops that supply this tourist mecca and so does, one begins to
imagine, every house including the perfectly thatched Old Tea
House out on Church Street and the Angel Inn (possibly once a
guildhall) and the rows of twinkling windows on Shilling
Grange. A gentle restlessness of swelling and retreating, leaning
forward, pulling back, affects all the streets.

The Guildhall is the historical and architectural quintessence
of the town. Like most guilds of its time, Corpus Christi, which
built the hall, used it for business meetings and for religious
ceremonies, often linked in processions with the church. The
cloth trade began to fall apart simultaneously with the suppression of the religious aspects of the guild, and the carved door
posts and exterior beams then welcomed civil functionaries
and petitioners into the newly established Town Hall. The rest
is downhill. A prison from the late seventeenth century to the
late eighteenth, with whipping post and stocks outside and
inside, wind and cold that came through the gaping walls. The
stronger escaped through the breaks before they could be held
by thumb screws sent in as deterrents. From prison to work-
house, to almshouse, to wool storage, decaying all the way. It
was restored by a private owner and the local Preservation Society and turned over to the National Trust about twenty years
ago. Now open to visitors, it shows its massive oak, Tudor
arches, what is left of linenfold paneling, a great fireplace or
two, and a small, informative museum which cannot resist a
few cases of "bygones"—the common repertory of glove

stretchers and old irons and Victorian children's clothing—
though it concentrates mainly on wool and weaving. It demon-
strates the wool of several breeds of sheep in various stages,
gives place to a big loom and carpeting of wool, hangs
sweaters, and piles up colorful pyramids of knitting wools;
among the bygones, a brush for the horsehair woven at home
after the decline of wool.

Northwards, toward the town with the majestic medieval
name of Bury St. Edmunds, a signpost points to **Hawstead**,
then into deep woods, fancy thatch on black-browed Gothicked
houses, and hairy old trees like those in Flemish drawings. A
lonely small church, no string of path visibly attached to it,
sits shrouded in isolation. Screened by a tall hedge and taller,
broad dark trees, a peculiar, secretive house whose arches ape
the Norman and whose windows of roundels and arabesque
speak the tongue of the Victorians. Hawstead's pub bounces
one back to now with a children's playground in its yard and
then, with a glimpse of seclusive paths and another lonely
church tower, sends one on to the eccentricities of **Ickworth
House**, near Bury St. Edmunds.

Too large and presumptuous to be the usual folly—often gleeful improvisations that seem to have risen from the fumes and
bubbles of light wine—Ickworth is yet, by its pretensions, its
dream of transporting a vast, undigested mass of the Italianate
in art and culture to the edge of a small town in Suffolk, a folly,
an extraordinary piece of foolish vanity and that on the part of
a bishop. The major identification of the bishop was, however,
as the fourth Earl of Bristol, the scion of a lusty family, owners
of large estates, makers of scandal and money. The earl before
him was a bishop in Ireland who made a good thing of it,
amassing a sizable fortune on top of the comfortable packet
he already had. He strewed some of his money, and charm, and
enthusiasm for Irish nationalism around Ireland, then left it
for long periods of Grand Tour, leaving memories and the
name of the hotels "Bristol" one still frequently finds on the
Continent. He liked designing and building, an interest his heir,
our Ickworth bishop, inherited along with the lands and
princely incomes. His first foray into the "nobiltà" of Italian
architecture was begun in Ireland and never finished. The
major opus on similar lines, much bigger than the first and so
literally, exaggeratedly Palladian as to miss Palladian grace and

harmony altogether, was Ickworth, planned with the support of a simpatico architect, Francis Sandys. The house was hardly begun, in the last years of the eighteenth century, when the bishop took himself off to the Continent to shop for other art treasures to hang and pedestal in his outsize villa. The building itself remained a lively preoccupation, expressed in letters to friends: "I flatter myself that my architectural ideas are Pure and Noble. . . . I wish to make it quite classical, to unite magnificence with convenience and simplicity with dignity. . . ." In another letter he discusses the problems of applying bas-relief according to the injunctions of "dear Canova." The bishop-earl never saw his house or England again. Absorbed in purchasing miles of marble and mosaic, important Renaissance "name" paintings, and—unusual for his time—Italian primitives which included Giotto and Cimabue, he was oblivious to the winds of change and found himself in an Italian prison, his treasures taken, when Napoleon marched into Italy in 1798. In under a year, the bishop was released and instead of fleeing to the arms of his mother country, continued his shopping trips in Italy. There he died a lowly death in the barn of a farm worker who would not take a heathen Anglican into his house. Ultimately Ickworth was finished, ultimately much of the estate and villa and arts were turned over to the government in lieu of taxes (a phrase one sometimes sees attached to art and precious objects in the New Acquisitions Room of the Victoria and Albert) and put in the care of the National Trust.

There is no slow becoming accustomed to Ickworth, no distant view that can be encompassed, no long space for the eye to absorb the ballooning rotunda and long extending of wings. Hidden by bright gardens and sweeping, aspiring trees, the villa presents itself full and startlingly panoplied. The earl-bishop had intended to cover it with the imperishable stucco used by "dear impeccable old Palladio," but whatever was put on as cover has run to dun-colored stains and blotches. After being accosted by the immensity of the rotunda, the visitor is soon challenged by large family portraits (one lady to be respected for having borne seventeen children, and her husband, the first earl, for having fathered the brood—and this was his second marriage), and a vehement group borrowed from classical statuary, Bernini out of Michelangelo by the English Flaxman. By way of chandeliers, Chinese vases, and classical busts on foamy tables, into a yellow-pillared library, gilt-scrolled, silken, classicked, and curving with the rotunda. The neat rows of books in finely bound sets seem too real to be readable, the little chaises worked in the most petit of petit-point not exactly styled for a good, long comfortable evening's read, and the affectionate couples in Canova's marble fireplace distracting. Elsewhere, an aristocratic genre piece-cum-family portrait of the third earl, vice-admiral and Don Juan, taking leave of his family for yet another assault on sea and boudoirs. In the drawing room, the plump, balding earl-bishop beams placidly at his painter, Madame Vigée-Lebrun, in spite of threatening Vesuvius behind him. That lady pictures herself prettily on the wall of a set of curved rooms and corridor surrounded by lightly sentimental female portraits, a particularly interesting group that of Mary, Lady Harvey, an ornament in the court of George II, here double-chinned, shrewd-eyed in plump middle age, among her four daughters. Near sections of bibelots, an expression of the ideals of the house, the Pompeian Room, painted in the then fashionable chalky imitations of the colors of Pompeii: a round, waxy goddess and cavorting putti, one so tired of flying around ceilings and walls through so many countries and centuries that he plunges downward to suicide.

It cannot honestly be urged that the traveler make a great effort to see Ickworth, singular as it is for the luxurious show dressed in classic worship. It is, though, a close neighbor (as mentioned) of **Bury St. Edmunds**, a delightful town, a statement hard to believe as one approaches it through new raw housing and the scraped red of the late nineteenth century. A few minutes of suspended disbelief, then Georgian Crown Street rising to the ruins and churches and towers that were the core of the medieval city dedicated to St. Edmund and one of the most engaging centers an English town now enjoys. The Angel Hotel, a tavern in the Middle Ages, later host to Mr. Pickwick, now leading inn and guardian of too many parked cars on Angel Hill, looks across to the Abbey Gate which leads into the court of the abbot's great palace. The present gate, showing crenellations and steel fortress teeth, was built in the mid-fourteenth century to replace an older gate destroyed by irate citizens. The saints are gone from their slender niches, but not the slots from which to send arrows into the flesh of hoi polloi below.

Inside the now tamed gate, rose gardens established and maintained by the profits from a book called *Suffolk Summer*
written by an American, John Appleby. A ruined church pillar
reminds one that it was at St. Edmund's altar in the gone abbey
church, on St. Edmund's Day in 1214, that the barons vowed to
wrest from King John the freedoms he finally ceded them in
1215 with the signing of the Magna Carta. Tracing the reflections of the ancient arches of the Abbot's bridge, imagining
among the grasses extensive abbey vineyards, trying to rebuild
of bare broken stone the ancient buildings, then skirting a
newer church, and leaving by the awesomely strong and direct
Norman tower that was another entrance to the abbey, one
begins to discern its full size and importance.

No abbey without a saint, no saint without an abbey, says
ecclesiastical history. Ergo, Edmund, a ninth-century king of
East Anglia and a Christian, was defeated by the invading
Danes, or willingly relinquished his life to save his people, or
was pressed to repudiate his religion and would not (the history
which is early mythology is comfortingly open). To earn martyrdom he was set up against a tree, filled with arrows like
St. Sebastian, and then beheaded. A wolf which appears in representations of his story guided friends to the body—some say
head—of the dead king. Head or body, or, miraculously, the full
ensemble, came to rest in a chapel in the town, to be moved a
century later to London when the Danes came again. One story
says that the holy relics were returned to St. Edmundsbury, as
the town was earlier called, and there remained through the
building of a large church and still larger. Another story has it
that in the struggle between John and the barons, the latter
supported by the Franch Dauphin after the Magna Carta was
renounced, the saint was carried off to France. There he remained until rescued by a Duke of Norfolk who took the bones
to Arundel Castle much later. The fact that they were the true
bones was established only about a dozen years ago. Civic literature in Bury disregards these trans-Channel wanderings and
prefers to dwell on the expansion and importance of the abbey,
the contributions of King Canute and later kings, the power of
its abbots, the luster of its learning, and the masses of pilgrims
who came to pray with their saint in the magnificence of the
Norman buildings.

Wander back—it is a pleasure worth repeating—first looking

at the red brick Tudor building with intricate chimneys and at the back of St. Mary's Church in its skirt of frail green trees, then to the little square at the side of the Cathedral and the broken spurs of abbey softened by flowering trees and shrubs, on to the shapely gardens and at the gate, ghosts of vaulting, fine Gothic tracery and two Gothic Stars of David high on the façade.

The present Cathedral was the parish church of St. James until 1913, most of it spanking new and fresh from major renovations in the last century. Sir Gilbert Scott redid the roof in the Suffolk peasant-art manner of simple arches curving to brightly painted angels. The colors are repeated in the geometric patterns of the choir ceiling, very new (notice the well-designed modern hanging lights), including the shields that reproduce those of the thirteenth-century barons and skillful wood carving. The nave is cool and neat, and the 1,000 kneeling cushions made by local women, each of its own unique design, rigidly displayed when there is no service, emphasize the coolness. Cathedrals need dim corners, inexplicable shafts and spurts of stone, the faint echoes of plain chant, and lost wisps of incense, and these St. James unfortunately and utterly lacks.

The Church of St. Mary lives in another, mellower, more fragrant, more mysterious universe. Though older fabric was used and later rearranging and shoring up of elements became necessary, the church, in toto, is of the fifteenth century, the time of prosperous God-fearing merchants in a booming wool town. John Notyngham, a grocer who died in 1440, could afford to build the attractive north porch with an interesting ceiling and, lest one forget, stamped it with his name and that of his wife. A contemporary clothier, John Baret, appears to have been responsible for the angels that soar above the nave, and Jankyn Smyth, who died in 1481, was rich and generous enough to build much of the chancel area. (The church still holds an annual special service in his honor, an observance that has lasted five hundred years and joins him to the semi-saints, the learned abbots and misty early hero-kings, in the national subhagiography.)

The big ceiling angels, now repainted as they were in the beginning, surge decorously from their brackets, completely aloof from scholars' controversies: do they or do they not represent the Mass processional? are two of their pairs, or not,

the non-angelic, ruthlessly ambitious Margaret of Anjou and the
bewildered Henry VI (who might have been happier and more
efficient as a learned monk)? The ceilings are not, fortunately,
uniform. One tawny stretch is pierced for starlike lights and
banded with strong lettering, the chancel ceiling burred and
prickled with satirical figures rather like those found on misericords. Your opera glasses should define the figures on stone
corbels and, in the aisle roofs, angels and saints, King Edmund's
handsome head held in a sling by two angels, warning demons,
and a pelican plucking at her own breast to feed her young, a
symbol of the boundless solicitude of the Church. Folk figures
and medieval mythology inevitably join the exalted. A depressed
monkey is chained and burdened with a big vase which may be
a chamber pot, a fox clamps his jaws on a goose, a mermaid
with flat dugs and the boiled face of naïve carving—hardly
Heine's "schönste Jungfrau"—combs her long twist of hair with
a large comb. Someone has dressed a chained bear in bikini
panties and cast the dread basilisk, whose glance could turn a
man to stone, as an abnormal chicken. A blacker entertainment
is the tomb monument of John Baret, which shows him already
deep in decay, a popular medieval fancy stressed with "He that
will sadly beholde me with his ie may se hys owyn merowr and
lerne for to die," the whole confection designed and carved
while the incumbent was still alive. One more memento mori—
the tomb of Mary, the sister of Henry VIII and wife of the
Duke of Suffolk, was moved here (the only one that was) from
the abbey church during the Dissolution. Here and there, usually protected by rugs, a number of respectable brasses, and
then you are free of details to admire the total ensemble, the
seignorial eighteenth-century almshouse for a dozen old people
who had "lived with credit and reputation," and the very carefully kept churchyard, not one blade of grass out of place.
Akenfield, once more: "They spend hours tending graves and
they are also very concerned about the state of the churchyard. . . . Generally speaking, the God of the Suffolk country-
man tended to live outside the church, which was a building
near the graves, and thus holy."

Across the street—across any street—refreshment at one of
the many old pubs and by way of the Georgian houses on
Chequer Square to the Athenaeum, a Palladian structure by the
Francis Sandys responsible for Ickworth, built around fragile

plasterwork in chandeliered ceilings, slender columns, and refined festoons, ordered for exclusive assemblies and now used for public entertainments of a more democratic nature. Follow shopping bags behind the Angel to the big irregular market place, alert, conversational, and closed to traffic, blazed with signs that point out toilets, taxis, and, as usual, the public library. Surrounding the foods (in overflowing abundance on Wednesdays and Saturdays), those lifegivers Boots, Woolworth's, Marks and Spencer's, Smith's, and cohorts. On the narrow Traverse stands the late-seventeenth-century Cupola House, with full cornice, dainty balconied bow windows, and an air of soundness in mind and body. On Cornhill, the town hall, and the unabashed big portico and statued pediment of the Corn Exchange; where Cornhill becomes Guildhall Street, the medieval Guildhall, still busily used in modernized sections, still entered by a thirteenth-century, churchlike doorway and a fifteenth-century porch with heraldic medallions in the ceiling. Take Westgate, College and Hatter (thought once to be "Heathen" for the Jews who lived here), Abbeygate and its Georgian houses, Lower and High Baxter—any or all of these off-market old streets—and return to Boots to absorb the Victorian "Tudor-Italian" confection that presses down on the hot water bottles and baby foods with a weight of black beams, bowed and mullioned windows, plaster grapes, grotesques and festoons and niches for Agricola, St. Edmund, Edward I, and Edward VI. Eye-boggling. Near this exuberance, the Adam town hall in which there was a theatre in the eighteenth century, now symbolized by plaques bearing musical instruments and dancing satyrs. A muddier, earthier sound of men's voices and sheep comes out of the big late-August sheep market not far off.

Lay history is accumulated in a sharp-peaked Norman house, that of the Jew Moyses, now used as the city museum. True, it gives room to the usual local bygones, and flints chipped by shaggy cavemen ancestors, muskets and swords used by soldiers now lying in peace; but this is Bury, where one feels patient and good-natured and, besides, there are a few items one shouldn't pass by. First, the house itself, low vaults and lightly pointed arches springing from robust columns, a broad hearth, and a firm, responsible stairway built in the fifteenth century. Among the pipes and fans and Toby jugs and musical instruments, try to pick out the glowing copper vats sized for measuring according to standards set by the city; pattens on metal rings designed to keep milady's feet from the mud; a backscratcher joined with a rapier. From a local house, a post carved in the fifteenth century and, of a later house, a beguiling yellow child's cart. Archeology, paleontology, and natural history greet one on the upper floor, then bow out for the Romans, who in turn leave to give space to an interesting collection of medieval coins, keys, pottery, ornaments, and displays with sophisticated additions—the small wax portraits, for instance —from succeeding centuries. When the abbey lived and breathed strongly, it had a window, in copy here, that was obviously meant to be a potent lesson. To us it is an entertaining example of anti-Popery sentiment that appeared at least as early as the excommunication of King John, which meant that the whole country was denied rites or ceremonies—every Englishman damned. When John repented and the all-powerful Pope Innocent III gathered him back into the fold, revoking Magna Carta in the process, a mighty band of barons and their cohorts took over the anti-papal field. The window pictures the "True and False Church," the false, this time, not the popular symbol of fox in priest's robe preaching to stupid geese but a gorgeous Pope receiving gifts from a church multitude. Around his head a banner that repeats "Antichrist"; below, grinning skeletons rising from their coffins, a demon emerging from one dessicated mouth. The true faith is preached by a simple "Helias" but his audience is asleep, bored, or giggling. If they don't look sharp the Pope may get them, seems to be the lesson.

Bury can be "done" in an intensive, energetic day, but that would be unfair to both viewed and viewer and there might be something going on in the Cattle Market, raffish entertainment at the refined Athenaeum, an extensive collection of clocks and watches (the John Gershom Parkington Memorial Collection) at Angel Corner to see, and more streets to stroll. Consider the possibility of having a lordly spread in the thirteenth-century cellar of the Angel Hotel and a bed in the high-moderate range, about the same at the Suffolk and somewhat less at the Everard. The Borough Offices, near the watches, supplies a list of cheaper accommodations and restaurants, including the expected Anglified Chinese.

. . .

The detailed map that includes the **Ipswich** area should lead you to a road marked PRIVATE and, at the end of a path, toward a large, decayed farm house and lazing pleasure craft on the river. Here is a solitary tower called **Freston** for a Lord de Freston who built this early red brick folly at the time of Henry VIII. He was an advanced man who wanted his daughter Ellen to become a well-educated woman and, in the zeal of his cause, built the several-storied structure—touched here and there with bits of balcony, a truncated little tower at the top—as rooms of study for her. The story goes that she started at the bottom at seven in the morning, maybe with mathematics, and progressed upward through Latin and Greek, fine needlework, and possibly sight-singing of madrigals or astronomy at the top, by this time certainly gazing longingly at the free-flowing twinkling waters. There seems to be no easily available knowledge of what happened to Ellen. Did she run off with a stable boy? Marry a titled gentleman and die, like many of her contemporaries, in childbirth? Whatever wit, wisdom, and accomplishments her father hoped for do not glitter in the pages of English blue-stocking history.

Woodbridge completes a varied trio: Long Melford, as long, cool, and unapproachable as a Gainsborough lady; Lavenham dimpling, flirtatiously demure; Woodbridge clear-eyed and candid, not given to twitching her skirts or sweeping them disdainfully from your path. With luck and care the town has preserved an unusual integrity of design, never slavish to a period nor entranced with its "picturesque" image, yet careful to fold its new housing into the old in a reasonable, tasteful manner. From the central Market Place an easy slope becomes Seckford Street, named for Thomas Seckford, an Elizabethan gentleman whom we shall meet again. The street opens with a timbered, swaying old inn whose beams are carved with heads that grin peculiarly through their cracked wood. Above, the Seckford almshouses, rebuilt and expanded from Elizabethan origins and now a stately red Victorian compendium of arches, overhang, stained glass, and scored plaster. Across the street, a silken field descends and rises to stop at playground and trees; at the side of the field, simple, well-spaced, scattered new houses flowing with the hill to the shelter of trees, a far cry from the bald, embryonic rows that afflict many towns. And these meld

well with the tall mill a short distance above and, on the gentle
turn below, the fifteenth-century flint-covered parish church of
St. Mary's (whose tower swings wildly when its bells are rung,
they say), enclosed in an echo of priory and a Tudor-style
school. Church Street, Cumberland Street, and the Thoroughfare and their tangents are comfortably Georgian touched up
with Victorian and beams and bulges of old inns and a sixteenth-
century house now inhabited by the Post Office. The Bell and
Steelyard Inn still sports a high overhang which held a mechan-
ism that weighed wagonsful of grain and hay.

At its prosperous times, Woodbridge was very prosperous,
drawing income not only from wool but from its business as a
port on the River Deben, a link to the sea. It countered the
decline of wool with shipbuilding, which ultimately declined
too, confining itself now to pleasure craft. The riverfront is
oldish and newish, abandoned here, reviving there. The elderly
railroad station bound in slender ironwork looks down on a
mélange of sandpit, tanks, a tiny ramshackle movie house, and
several tall, narrow, windowless buildings, one of which may be
the relic of a twelfth-century mill. The new is an attractive walk
at the side of the water, a bicycle path that swings into treed
rises in the distance, and families loading lunches and the kids
to take them for a sail.

Thomas Seckford returns with the gift of the Shire Hall on
Market Hill, restored but not ruined except that the openings
for wagons to reach the Corn Exchange under the hall are
bricked up. It is nevertheless good-looking and worthy of its
company on the hill: low, smiling houses whose gables meet in
a line of subtle waves; modest, calm shapes which break out in
triumphant shouts of purple trim on sea blue, tones of green
on sharp blue, a lively tutti to sing one out of a satisfying town.

NOTES

Seckford Hall, the country house of Sir Thomas, once entertained Elizabeth I and now behind its ivy-covered brick
and gleaming windows entertains paying guests amid
paneled and carved woods. Bed, a full breakfast, a newspaper, free bath salts, and careful, near-affectionate service
at moderately high cost per night and worth every decayed

dollar of it. (Book well ahead for summer travel and, if no space is available, try Melton Grange, also a big old country house; though not as splendid or expensive as Seckford, quite reputable.)

There is nothing much to see in the neighboring villages of **Rendlesham** and **Sutton**, but they may help place you in one of the geographical-historical slots that often deepen the pleasure of a trip. The former was the place from which the earliest kings of East Anglia ruled and the latter is edged by the burrows of **Sutton Hoo.** Several of these burial mounds, possibly those of dead kings and dignitaries, were excavated in recent years to yield the famous ship heaped with a treasure of Anglo-Saxon jewelry, gold, coins, implements, and ornaments now in the British Museum.

A zigzag northward and seaward by way of plain, contained farmland villages stops for a pause at **Framlingham**, a poor, courageously painted village coiled at the feet of its castle and church. Planned as triple fortification rings on a mound, the general scheme is too battered to discern clearly, but there is entertainment in walking through the inner yard equipped with a map sold at the castle. It guides you to the site of this and that vanished building: the chapel, the kitchen, the halls. Round stone shafts indicate the presence of chimneys, one or two topped by the brickwork with which Tudor builders showed off their skill and fancy. Huge fireplaces in the redone hall recall the odor of boars turned on spits and the thump of flagons of mead on thick plank tables. From the walk on the walls, one looks down on spurs of ruins, rounded arches in the yard which narrow to slitlike openings on the vulnerable outside. Moving from tower to tower, changing outer views that open long, smooth fields rimmed by trees, a ditch or moat cut centuries ago, village roofs and the church spire springing above them.

The fortress is one of the earliest in England, built first in the twelfth century and rebuilt (after some trouble with Henry II, who ordered it demolished) in the beginning of the thirteenth century, its style suggested by the castle-fortresses in the East whose architecture came to Europe with the returning Cru-

saders. To breathe life into the ruin, try to imagine King John
invading the castle to take half a hundred of his rebellious
citizenry or, above the Great Hall merriment, the distant
shrieks of men closed in the prison tower outside the keep. Of
the many families which owned Framlingham Castle, one of the
most prominent was the Howards, Dukes of Norfolk, who held
it from the fifteenth century to the seventeenth, well and inter-
estingly represented in the Church of St. Michael in the company of pale, primitive paintings and a font held by Suffolk
woodmen (or wodemen or wildmen). Near the door, the universal request for repairs and rebuilding, donations collected
in a pipe organ. The rest is grand monuments of Howards
lucky and unlucky. A high white tomb is that of Thomas
Howard, third Duke of Norfolk, who was accused of high
treason by Henry VIII. His son Henry, Earl of Surrey and a
gifted poet, was accused as well and they were both taken to
the Tower for execution. The son was beheaded first, but the
night before the father came to the block the king died and he
was released at 2 A.M. on the day of execution by Mary Tudor.
The son's body was interred in the Tower and not freed for
entombment until the reign of James I, when *his* son built
him a fine painted alabaster sepulchre. The shadow of the ax
returns to hang over the fourth Duke of Norfolk, the eldest
son of the Earl of Surrey. He was married three times; all three
women died in childbirth. Only two lie here, with a space
between them for Mary, Queen of Scots, who was to marry
the duke after he, she, and co-plotters pushed Elizabeth off
the throne. His plans agley, he was beheaded. Happier, more
progressive matters at the neighboring pub, which uses plastic
gloves to serve fried chicken, and in **Saxtead**, whose green lifts
a tall windmill, and in villages smothered in frolics of roses
or sitting shyly in stilled time.

Dunwich—reached by sandy, scrubby patches of marsh grass
where hares and pheasants shelter and banners of red wheat—
is a ghost that haunts the coastal waters of the North Sea.
When the Conqueror's accountants surveyed Dunwich they recorded a fairly large population which supported itself well
by fishing, a little piracy, a little smuggling. Off the treacherous
sliding dunes there are said to be many vestiges of that city—
the Saxon, probably Roman, and certainly a major fourteenth-
century port with a sizable number of churches and at least

one important monastery. A booklet distributed in the minute remaining community tells the history of the lost town, opening with a list called "Milestones in the Dunwich Story." Most of the items speak of disaster: "1328, fort choked by the sea. 1347, a great part of the Town and more than 400 houses, shops and windmills devoured by the sea. 1385, Sts. Leonard, Martin and Nicholas lost," and so on at close intervals—port choked, church down, road washed away—until only flotsam and legends were left. Because it was apart from town and sea, the leprosarium was left to be devoured by time, which spared some stones and arches of its chapel wall. A far gate of a Franciscan monastery still frames empty sky. A small museum records the duties of officials and obligations of merchants and fishermen and, for those who couldn't sign documents with their names, the marks of their trade, a comb to represent a thatcher, shears for a shepherd. Standing on the saddened coast under the concealing cliffs, one can hear the sounds of the drowned town and the peal of its church bells, the suggestible say. It is not a difficult fancy to submit to as one stares along empty coastline, threatened by the voracious cliffs.

Walberswick, which once shared its neighbor's profitable pleasures of smuggling and waylaying nonindigenous boats for booty, was not drowned (though threateningly washed) by the seas, but by Wolsey and Henry VIII. Because business affairs were controlled by the Church, town and church were depleted by the Dissolution, to survive as a watery artists' colony, with loose wide greens, comfortable houses, and studio-shacks on stilts, standing like the other stilt-legged birds in grassy marsh gliding toward sea.

Across a dappled patchwork of sea and marsh sits **Blytheburgh**, raising a church that speaks of a larger community. It is airy and spacious, with the vividly painted angel roof of the region, carvings in the seats of explicitly depicted Deadly Sins, and its own God-fearing legend which translated a stroke of lightning that demolished spire and font, took a couple of lives, and created hysteria and terror, into the work of the Devil. That he actually put in a personal appearance was proven by finger marks he left at the side of the door as warning to a village that had a reputation for loose living, immune to ordinary church exhortations.

On a pleasant summer's day **Southwold** is an open, smiling resort town with a welcoming green, Georgian and Victorian houses, a rhetorical monument or two, a worthy church, alluring shops, lines of beach cottages facing the sea, and pleasure craft to stand for the once-upon-a-time herring fishing which kept the town busy and eating. On a cold summer's night, when the town is stuffed like a wax museum with discouraged visitors who have watched their vacation time blown away by cloud-sweeping winds, the bathing suit inert in the valise, the shops explored, and nothing now to do but sit in the hotel lounge with an array of faces as immobile and sullen as a gallery of imperial Roman marble heads, it can be a dour and inimical demonstration of the sticking-to-the-rules intransigence and the occasional xenophobia that attacks Suffolk.

The enemy are an American and an English lady, the latter the more to be distrusted because she has the accent of sneering London, shrewd, snobbish hellpit to the south. It is 8:30 in the evening and the ladies are hungry. To the nearest hotel and "Sorry, the dining room closes at 8:45." "But it isn't 8:45 yet." "It will very soon be, Madam." The smile stays unchanged through the correction and hint of rebuke. "Might we have sandwiches in the lounge?" (a common enough practice in resort areas, the sandwiches supplied by the bar). "Sorry, Madam, no food is served after 8:45." The smile remains unchanging and, like a mask, passes from the face of one hotel receptionist to another, issuing the same toothy, implacable "No." The pub on the main street, crammed and ringing, denies that it has as much as one slice of bread, palpably untrue. A lean, tasteless, unambitious bed and breakfast place says, "Yes, there is bed and breakfast, but there is nothing— truly sorry—but absolutely nothing at night; all the supplies come in the morning." And they all smile as the ladies' stomachs begin to consume themselves, in their heads echoes of *Akenfield* phrases half-remembered, "They are quite unadventurous in every way," "They are never imaginative," "They have this kind of iron composure." And back to the pub to ask advice of the customers. The best they can offer is the information that a restaurant enjoys its weekly closing on this night but there is fish and chips in a poorer part of town. A lady, watching and listening from a station wagon, breaks her boredom by entering the discussion. In the accent of the north and in its big, generous manner, she invites the women, who have begun to feel like internees in a cruel camp, to come home to her for bacon and eggs, and continues to apologize to the American for English inhospitality. Things are not that serious yet, and they make for the fish and chips place. A section of benches and tables is closed off under a sign that says it closes at 10 P.M. It is not yet 10:00. At the counter, the orders for plaice and chips and shrimp and chips and the request, "Could we sit at the table? We've been driving around trying to find dinner for some time and would like not to have to eat in the car." "Sorry, Madam, that section is closed." "But it doesn't close till ten." "Sorry, Madam," pushing forward the big smile, "it's closed."

Even were they better, the fish would taste like the shrimp, both like the chips, and everything like the paper that soaks up their assembled grease. Welcome to Southwold.

Back to the bed and breakfast house. The host greets his guests with "You had better move the car around the back, it might be blown out to sea otherwise." The sea is dull and calm but he has fed on personal and legendary disaster.

"Is there a telephone I may use, please?" "Yes, we have a phone but it's in the bedroom and my wife is asleep." "In the bedroom? When you have guests who may need it? Strange. Well, where is the police station or is there a phone box nearer here? I must phone London, it's urgent." The proprietor goes into the bedroom, brings out a phone on a jack, plugs it in near the hall desk, an act which absorbs twenty seconds and a corner of his smile.

The next morning, an abundant breakfast with offers of more toast, more coffee. But all that is within the immutable rules, and rules are to be cherished because they mark out the squares of safety.

From the seaside hotels, fishing port, and the distinction of being the easternmost point of England that is **Lowestoft**, on to **Oulton** and its pleasure boats, and neat, boat-loving **Beccles**, a haven for Broads trips but more distinguished for its unique parish church, whose yard looks down on a great fan of marsh-land. And on toward a lyric called **Fritton.** Its touchingly mis-shapen thatched church—a collection of Roman, Norman, and Saxon stone, dim, reclusive—sits near a glittering openness of lake and mirrored trees. The lake is still called the "Decoy" because in years gone, tame ducks, assisted by a seductive sprinkling of grain, led wild ducks into capturing meshes and sent them on to market. **Belton** has a round tower considerably older than its church, the form much more common in East Anglia than elsewhere in England and characteristic of areas where the sort of stone that could be cut for square towers was not available. A similar tower and its medieval church, sustained by Roman brick and tile, came from a Roman fort now called Burgh Castle and claimed as "the best Roman building in Suffolk." Imperial Rome in Suffolk is now a raw core of turret and a long rough-stoned wall that cuts out an impressive area. The imagination must supply filler of houses, soldiers, Roman enterprise and organization, and the fortress position—before the seacoast changed—that dominated sea and a confluence of rivers. A younger wreck is **Great Yarmouth** of the ringing name, so badly bombed in World War II that little is left of its famous "rows," narrow streets that ran up from the flanks of ships in the port. A few of the seventeenth-century merchants' houses have been restored but you will have to search them out, and the medieval Tollhouse, among the newer council housing of the rebuilt city.

The westward road from Great Yarmouth, or Beccles, if you prefer, slips into a gaiety of flowers, shimmer of river, and a sign that welcomes to **Norwich**.

The sign adds: A FINE CITY. It is, and an intelligent city, its enterprise controlled with reason and sophistication. Not much to do about the elderly red brick shafts that share the horizon with innumerable church towers, but new building is so planned that it sets off rather than obscures or reduces to incongruously quaint the medieval, the Tudor, the Georgian. Coiled in dipping, rising medieval paths, the inner city is alluring, revealing, and intimate to walk, yet not difficult to drive in except for a shopping core of modernity laced with ancient alleys to the castle, now given over entirely to the pedestrian and, when the winds stay at sea, sidewalk cafés. Norwich malleability and planning kept the city from shrinking as others had done when the one egg in its basket rotted and broke. The medieval city bought mountains of wool, saw to its weaving, and acted as major market place for imports and exports in trade with the continent. At the same time it managed to diversify in over a hundred other trades and crafts. Like many ecclesiastically dominated communities, the townspeople had violent quarrels with the Benedictine Cathedral Priory (this the most powerful of several orders established in Norwich); they were subject to the decimations of medieval scourges and the beggary of economic collapse. When the weaving of worsteds declined in the sixteenth century, they brought in thousands of Dutch and Belgian weavers, mainly Lutherans, eager to escape the Spanish and more highly skilled than themselves, to bolster up the industry, which stayed high and prosperous until the Industrial Revolution and its machines took the industry northward. Twists, turns, adjustments, and the city returned to an old skill—brewing; it began to make machinery, sweets, mustard (Colman's), and, most important, became a shoe center. At the time of the Domesday evaluations, Norwich—with London, Winchester, Thetford, and York—was among the five leading towns of England; it stayed in the top ranks until the factories and hordes of cheap labor of the new Midlands giants pushed it down the line. Norwich undoubtedly suffered in the debasement, but turned its independent mind to other matters. Early a seething place of Nonconformity, which established a Congregation Society in 1580 (the long and dominating presence of too many Dominicans, Augustinians, Franciscans, Benedictines may easily have spurred the movement) and sent Founding Fathers out on the *Mayflower*, it later turned to the reform of poorhouses and hospitals and still, to judge from markers on various buildings, maintains a lively Puritan social conscience.

The old, old city meanders between and around those medieval bases, the Cathedral and the castle, which looks more acceptably "castle" than it might were it not refaced in the mid-nineteenth century. In the time of the Normans who piled up the high mound and the building, it was fortress soon converted to prisons, and such it stayed until late into the nineteenth century, when it became one of a set of clever museums. One of the facts of Norwich presents itself instantly as you enter the rotunda; signs to a bar and restaurant, a snacks and coffee stand and tables. Norwich enjoys its stomach and permits very few places of amusement or enlightenment to stand bare of refreshment. Among the coffee cups and jar-top ashtrays, a bronze Henry Moore and, to the right, the National History galleries of Norfolk fauna and flora in habitat groups; also (in rearrangement at this writing) Norfolk fossils and pre-

historic skulls, herbs, and medicinal grasses. Opposite, ancient
man in Norfolk as nomadic hunter, as a primitive farmer, as
a miner and maker of flints in the diggings at Grime's Graves.
The galleries not devoted to local beast, bird, and man, extant
and extinct, are given over to art of limited but interesting
variety: a group of small Dutch paintings indispensable to an
English collection, a miscellany of paintings meant to teach
rather than delight, and galleries for the works of painters of
the Norwich School, whose leading members were John Crome
and John Sell Cotman. Both were prolific and highly skilled,
the latter the more adventurous, feeling his way into a tentative Impressionism, hinting at a light-struck Turner sky. The
long central exhibition gallery is always worth slow perusal;
the spring-into-summer show of 1973, for instance, consisted
of a good number of Rembrandt etchings—self-portraits, portraits of his mother and Saskia, and small, incandescent landscapes.

The rotunda balcony holds a large collection of Lowestoft
porcelain, a number commemorative, such as plaques to celebrate the birth of a baby; others are made to be sold as souvenirs of seaside vacations. Silver, some of it made in Norwich in
Tudor and Jacobean times, shapes another collection and still
another is of ancient artifacts, Roman and pre-Roman. From
a reconstruction of the tunnels and votive arrangements of a
flint mine of Grime's Graves, one enters the late Saxon world
and a diorama that gives the viewer the back of Edmund, the
last King of East Anglia, about to be killed by the Danes and
translated into the St. Edmund worshipped at Bury. The keep
is an odd shaping of Norman wall gouged out for a lavatory
channel here, an ancient kitchen fireplace there. The miscellany
here unites crossbows with musical instruments, pottery and
a caseful of desirable rings, and souvenirs of Lord Nelson, born
in north Norfolk near the sea and educated for a time in the
Norwich grammar school. Against the south wall, a fancy be-
cherubbed Parliament chair, a lay equivalent of a bishop's
seat, in which successful candidates for seats in Parliament
were carried through the city. The first and last objects to
catch and hold your eye will be two painted dragons, obviously
made to be worn by a pair of strong, lucky young men. Their
formal names are the "Norwich Snapdragons," who once served
in religious and civic pageants and then were retired to appear

infrequently for charity drives or fun which, hanging fanciful
and homely from the ceiling of the keep, they still are. Norwich always liked dressing up, festivities, and display. Celia
Fiennes writes in her *Through England on a Side Saddle*
of May 1, the day of election of the new mayor: "They new washe
and plaister their houses within and without. . . . All ye Streete
in which this mayor Elect's house, is very exact in beautifying
themselves and hainging up flaggs ye Coullers of their Com-
panyes, and dress up pageants and there are plays and all sorts
of show that day. . . ."

Having told you the above, now adding that the castle section of the aggregate of Norwich museums is neither exigent
nor overwhelmingly important (unless you have seen no provincial museums at all), it might be suggested that you have a
brief look around at the arrangements and leave the castle to
the formidable number of girls and boys who shame one with
their patient, informed interest, to their comfortable Mums
complete with sausage roll and tea at a rotunda table. Head
for the market place, via Davey Place, the pedestrian alleys
into London Street and Gentleman's Walk, by way of the Royal
Arcade, if it is open, admiring its sexy Art Nouveau tile blossoms as you go. The Mediterranean strain in the English expresses itself most explosively in markets, lively everywhere,
jaunty, gaudy, and merry in Sudbury and in Bury St. Edmunds,
picturesque in York, and jaunty, gaudy, merry, picturesque, a
knockout, in Norwich. The nine-hundred-year-old beauty has
painted her many long rows of sheds in carnival colors and
flaunts them in front of the tall-towered City Hall (an often
praised contemporary building whose dark lions, columned
balcony, and wide window surrounds suggest Mussolini's edi-
fices to the less enthusiastic, however). The carefully restored
Gothic Guildhall is easier to understand and love, a gem of
polished flint squares like dark mother-of-pearl bound in white
stone, the dark and light alternating as façade checkerboard.
Across the square, the immense church of St. Peter Mancroft,
wearing a peculiar nineteenth-century spirelet on its fifteenth-
century handsomeness, a place of monuments to local dignitaries, one of whom, Sir Thomas Browne, the physician-writer,
also sits in pensive bronze outside the church. All around,
brightly painted shining houses of the seventeenth and eighteenth centuries and beckoning alleys. Off the huge supermarket

near the Guildhall, Dove Street, an alley of trendy clothing, chastely designed household objects of the Scandinavians, eating and drinking under attractive signs; a lane as confident and worldly as Hampstead's streets or the better stretches of New York's Greenwich Village. Similarly engaging, sophisticated alleys lace together Bedford Street and St. Andrew Street. St. Andrew's Hill has a carved fifteenth-century doorway to show; a puffed-up white, smiling swan is the sign that names SWAN ALLEY. Bridewell Alley hangs a metal fish and an old TACKLE sign, and makes room for an exquisite display of mustard and only mustard in the bags, jars, decorative vats of a unique shop. Behind the Church of St. Andrew, windows that shine on antique bicycles, the model of a windmill, old signs and tools. These are from the collection of the Bridewell Museum, that part of the Norwich museum complex given over to crafts and industries housed in a building of several eras and uses. The flint walls near the church are remains of a fourteenth-century building erected by a prosperous merchant and inhabited, in the first years of the fifteenth century, by the first mayor of the city. A prison-workhouse, named Bridewell after the location of the first such institution in London, filled its walls later, and there the vagrants and malefactors stayed, ran away, or died for two and a half centuries, until the building turned to commercial enterprise. The house had, in the meantime, acquired Georgian sections, picked up here and there in the city, now used to introduce the work of eighteenth-century clockmakers, to hold tasteful juxtapositions of reeds, a basket for carrying herring, fleece and a spinning wheel, a flail, a saddle, a fringed bright cloth worn by a cart horse when he pulled in, ceremoniously, the last of the harvest. Tools and boats and whales' teeth are reminders of Norfolk's sea and rivers, and a huge plow, rakes, awners, crushers, scythes, and tall forks remember farm work. Among brushes and besoms and a large sturdy apple press for making cider, a case of stuffed canaries shaded from dun color to bright yellow, their breeding introduced by the Dutch and Flemish, their color deepened by feeding the birds red pepper pods. The textile trade is represented by looms, several types of cloth ranging from silk to horsehair, a press for glazing fabrics, looms and tools, a pattern book, and shawls in deep-colored designs. The leather room gives some place to a small saddler's shop, an old corset which resembles armor, leather buckets, and a historic parade of shoes from soft-pointed embroidered silks (rather gloves for the feet) to sturdier, hardworking shoes. Bikes with huge front wheels, steam engines, a huge wagon, presses, engraving blocks, a plane built in 1915 by a Norfolk citizen, an early newspaper, all serve to exemplify the variety of Norfolk enterprise.

Then there is Pottergate and the narrow medieval Upper Goat Lane to walk. Off Pottergate, the alley of St. John's Maddermarket (madder roots gave weavers their red dye) and under the tower of that church to a beguiling corner of red brick, a carved door which says NORWICH PLAYERS over a chapel converted into a theatre that imitates the Elizabethan, and unobtrusive modern for coffee and conversation. The theatre is highly respected and of a long line that staged mystery plays and made welcome Elizabethan players.

Off Charing Cross the Strangers' Hall, which may refer to refugees from The Netherlands who lived here or to a later group of churchmen who fled the French Revolution. The fifteenth-century structure, on a fourteenth-century undercroft, was mainly a Great Hall, expanded in the sixteenth century and early seventeenth. Although some decorations came later, the sloping floors, the irregular levels and shapes of several rooms, as well as their ornaments, speak an old language. This portion of museum takes one from the working life of Bridewell through the domestic grandeurs of several centuries: the carved beam and fifteenth-century Flemish tapestries and furniture of about the same time; seventeenth-century furnishings and the remarkable contemporaneous stump-work (padded needlework). In a room from an almshouse that gave each lady her own bed-sitter, a baby-walker very much like our own, and on the bed a great hooped structure, a bed-waggon, on whose lower iron plate a pan of hot embers was placed and, on the hoops, the blankets to be warmed. Oak paneling breaks for a collection of dolls' houses and toys of several centuries, and then gathers around a dark room of early portraits and a roughly designed sixteenth-century wardrobe. The light returns in the pale green and simple furnishings of a Georgian room, the musical instruments and objects enjoyed by the Regency and, of the same time, a frothy, early Colette-style morning room bedecked in chinoiserie and papier-mâché around mother-of-pearl. The rest is Victoriana and Edwardian; the best, because the most extreme, the Victorian sitting room, and one wonders for the hundredth time how they moved or breathed among the overstuffing, the encrusting, the embroidery, the stifled birds, flowers, and insects in their bell jars, crammed into airtight little parlors centered on a round table covered with dust-eating heavy cloth.

Princes Street and Elm Hill, the most evocative streets of Norwich, made up of old inns and carefully maintained houses, hold in the wedge of their meeting a church, St. Peter Hungate ("Street of Dogs" of the Danes), now used as a museum of Church art. It is a rather particular taste and, since the collection is more earnest than significantly rare, you might content yourself with the freshly gilded angels in the ceiling, examples of English alabaster, a book of tracts by the early Church reformer, John Wycliffe, examples of wood carvings, and a group of headless figures (lopped off in the sixteenth century) which must once have made an effective Annunciation group.

At its crest, Elm Street is a triangle of yellow-green and pink irregularities—houses, a spurt of tree, and a low dark brick gallery in the center of the triangle. The street slips and turns, carrying a thatched inn, a combination of diagonal brick and timber of the sixteenth century, a house of a hundred years later and, with another break for tree, rows of art works, antiques, clothing, and choice crafts in shops that spell elegance, compounded of high style and old-fashioned charm. Tombland, a dour name among the many pleasing others, was the Saxon market before it moved closer to the castle and in medieval times a fair ground whose take was contested by the Cathedral and the townspeople. During a riot in the late thirteenth century, the citizenry destroyed a number of the monks' buildings and in penance were forced to undertake the building of St. Ethelbert's Gate, the more elaborate of the two entrances to the Cathedral grounds.

If you've done your duty by Ely, Salisbury, Winchester, Lincoln, York, Wells, and Durham, the sight of yet another cathedral may make your heart sink and your tired feet recoil. But while Norwich Cathedral is good, it is not one of the "greats" and doesn't require the hushed, sometimes uncomprehending attention one feels it necessary to give the others. First, take your opera glasses; next, buy the Cathedral booklet in the Pitkin series of the well-stocked shop in the Cathedral, an informative work that explains terms, practices, the organization of a monastic community, and architecture as related to the Cathedral with easy erudition, another characteristic of Norwich enlightenment.

The tall long nave of two orders of Norman arches ending in massively clustered columns, some diagonally marked; the vaulted ceiling studded with myriad bosses; the misericords in the choir (very few visible); Gothic elaborations; highly colored tombs; the light through colored glass streaking the pavement with color; and the extraordinary dignity of high long aisles of light stone may all be quite familiar though always impressive. What is singularly Norwich is a badly damaged and restored bishop's throne behind the high altar, an echo of a judge's seat in a Roman basilica and the oldest in use in England. Another unique carryover from the Romanesque is a walk behind the altar, here very simply marked with low arches and swelling into petal-like chapels, a graceful device. Norwich of the many churches was heavily punished for them and lost a great many of its treasures through persecutions, through the contempt or indifference of its large Nonconformist population, and the normal preoccupations that pushed aside the care of dozens of churches. (About thirty are derelict at this time and there are societies trying to revive them in resistance to a 1968 edict that called for the demolition of unused churches.) Therefore, the Cathedral has little great art to show—a few mural forms covered with glass and, in two of the apsidal chapels, several panels. Those in St. Luke's Chapel are austere representations of the culminating events of Christ's life, stylized in the Flemish manner against a background of dull gold, the suffering figures ascetic and drawn, the whole intensely and effectively religious. Their source, incidentally, was a church nearby from which they were taken by grateful nobles to present to a fourteenth-century bishop who had quelled, by executing its leader, a peasant revolt. Near the font, an effigy of several centuries before, claimed to be one of the oldest effigies in England, and in its tall thin austerity not unrelated to the later panels.

More intimate folk art peers out of the bosses of the very extensive cloisters, the largest in England. Leaving an orderly

review of lessons from the New Testament and the Old to the
bosses far above the nave, the lower cloister ceilings enjoy a
profligacy of holy figures in and out of glories, sagging in
martyrdom or penance. The jaws of Hell suck in the wicked,
a trumpeting Judgment angel carries off the blessed in the billows of his cloak; the pelican dredges its breast, the Lamb
stands to be adored. The conceptions are amusing and informative if, as has been suggested, the personae in their groupings
resemble the wagon scenes of medieval mystery plays, and the
skillful use—in one example, Herod at table, and the head of
St. John borne on a salver like the next course—of restricted,
awkward space is always admirable and diverting.

To counter the monuments of faith, hope, charity, and the
fulsome praise found on church walls, look for a crudely
etched skeleton on the tomb of Thomas Gooding in the south
aisle. No turning to Heaven and a golden world there, no list
of good deeds, no loving mourners. Thomas Gooding is angry
and points a warning skeletal finger at every passer-by: "All
you that do this place pass bye/Remember death for you must
dye; As you are now then so was I/And as I am so that you
be."

Out now to the Cathedral close, that catches, holds, and releases the strongest winds, to look at the ruins (eerily illuminated at night) of monastic buildings and those still alive, remade
as-pretty houses touched by half-timbering and later Georgian.
The return to Tombland finds, perhaps, a soprano trilling
of Regency balconies, earlier Georgian sobriety and, in Tombland Alley, the wavy, permanently tottering house of a sixteenth-century mayor. Tombland becomes Wensum and across
the river, Magdalen, whose first spur is Colgate, not quite as
fresh as the streets you've seen before. It is heavily be-
churched, at least one church put to civic uses, and a bit musty
of the steams and odors of earlier industry, which has moved
to other quarters. Among an interesting group of merchants'
houses (at least one influenced by the Dutch), a setback leads
to the dignified late-seventeenth-century Old Meeting Hall and,
a short distance beyond, the buoyant Octagon Chapel, much
too aristocratic, one feels, for a "plain" Nonconformist religion.
Crossing the long avenue to Fishergate in an assault of spring
rain, one is grateful to the many churches for quick sanctuary
and, selecting the nearest, darts into stacks and walls of shoe-

boxes and, in hundreds of cartons stamped NEW ZEALAND BUT-TER, bundles of innersoles. Antiquarians may not like it, but practical Norwich turns its unused churches, where it can, into offices, museums, and shoe-factory warehouses, actually a method of maintaining walls and façades that might other-wise be heaps of useless stone. At the end of Bishopgate the oldest bridge in Norwich, of the fourteenth century, near the site where medieval heretics were burned at the stake. In the bend of the river, a short distance northward and set in a no-man's-land of rubble and waste, Cow Tower, once a guardian of river and city, now an impotent curio. Southward on the river, Pull's Ferry, a colorful spot whose arches cover a path that was once a canal for carrying Norman stone to the rising Cathedral and, beyond the river, a view of the flower of apsidal curves and the high, thin spire of the Cathedral rising from stone doily cutouts of the tower.

Tombland southward becomes King Street, which holds the oldest house in Norwich, the steep-gabled section of the Music House. A family of very rich Jews lived here in the twelfth century when, next to London, Oxford, and Cambridge, Nor-wich had the largest Jewish settlement. It is interesting that it is the JEW'S HOUSE in Lincoln and Bury and here in Nor-wich which is the oldest survivor of domestic building, possibly because rich Jews built of stone for protection against assault and arson.

Either on the walk back from King Street or deepening your earlier acquaintance with Magdalen Street, look in at Gurney Court to the right and behind the shops—where antiques have descended to wholesome junk, where plain-faced lumpy ladies have replaced the romantic hair and gypsy skirts of the young of Norwich University—for imaginative housing crescents, bold arcaded shopping precincts, and beyond the plump flint of a pub called the Artichoke, the strong, trim color that enlivens red brick houses.

There is much more to know and see and you may want to spend a night or two in Norwich. The historic hotel, the Maid's Head, has well concealed an antiquity which goes back to the fifteenth century and possibly earlier. Although the court holds a few bygones, including a bar with that dark, warm-womb quality of good pubs, and you are reminded that the first reg-ular stage-coach service to London took off from here in the mid-eighteenth century, the rooms do not suffer from antiquity, a good number being equipped with both baths and television. Bed and breakfast for two, with bath, will probably reach the high category soon. The modern Nelson Hotel, on the river at the end of Prince of Wales Road, is always full of businessmen during the week, serves no breakfast, and asks about the same prices. The Royal, if you can get by its dour face, will be cheaper, and cheaper still the row of small hotels on and off Riverside Road, the converted houses of Unthank Road, and the strange warren supervised by absent-minded but polite ancients on Thorpe Road, about £2. For the same price, the rooms in the minute Copper Lodge Hotel on Lower Goat Lane give close proximity to Guildhall and market.

NOTES

RESTAURANTS: Eating, to repeat, is good and generous. Time your visit to the eighteenth-century Assembly Rooms for the excellent, inexpensive cafeteria lunch, or make it tea and continue on to a film in the small theatre named for a Victorian dancing master, Noverre. The thatched Briton's Arms also spreads a good table and so do, undoubtedly, many untried others. Chinese restaurants line Prince of Wales Road; the London House on London Street stays open quite late; a big comfortable place at St. Ethelbert's Gate on Tombland uses, and fills, family-size plates for individual portions. Among the several Italians is a place that calls itself La Tudor Rosa and, among the architectural blandishments of Princes Street, the Anglian, entered by way of Plumbers Arms Court. The tables are well spaced, the music very soft, if at all, the service and lighting kindly, and the cook, at this time of writing, talented at French peasant dishes—Bourguignon, chicken with mushrooms and onions in wine—served with a lavish hand, the vegetables retaining their identity and integrity. The bill for a full dinner comes (came) to about £2 a head, gladly served.

REMINDER: The Information Centre for maps, entertainments, etc., is across from the Cathedral on Tombland;

more information in the Cathedral bookshop (and souvenir cups, towels, matches, notebooks, postcards) and from the several good bookshops in town.

About 15 miles to the northeast, the watery town of **Wroxham**, almost entirely given over to waterside hotels, the marketing of fishing tackle, a few stations for food and drink and, most importantly for the visitor, boats for riding The Broads, a meshwork of river and canals that widen to lakelike basins. Yacht and sailboat fanciers visit from house to house along broad avenues and alleys of water. For one- or two-hour visitors, Wroxham supplies small boats to navigate by oneself and larger excursion boats which look at the fanciful little houses that hang over the river, at the more stately that maintain lawns and small herds of cows screened by trees. One stretch is a jungly mesh of wildlife preserve, another is rustling reeds, another a shelter for swooping, gliding sailboats, and all the waters are dotted with confident, wily ducks who frighten you more than you frighten them. On a weekend when the sun is kind, the going may be as slow and tight as the back canals of Venice in August. In a high wind, the cover of the engine may fly off and, with luck, be fished out by two nervous sailboats, and the canvas rain cover may lose a pin and flap frantically in the wind, small excitements that enhance an inexpensive, exotic hour or two.

Glowing little gardens and blond thatch, new cottages trying to look like the old, and tiny duck ponds thin out to disappear into scrub-and-pine emptiness, pierced by a whirr of gilded scarlet pheasant and calls of birds. These Brecklands may once have been arable, but overwhelming thousands of medieval sheep cropped them dry to the point where they were referred to as "desert," a land smothered in shifting sand dunes. **Thetford**, a once-great city and religious center, for a time fed by and then consumed by its sheep, keeps a few flinty scraps of churchly power, a few beamed and timbered houses, and has revived simple pleasures—walking, fishing, swan watching on its river. The present, indifferent to churches and their years, gives grudging room to several gravestones stuck in a wall adjoining the liquor department of a brash, big supermarket. An entirely other symbol of American influence stands in front of the King's House—a statue of Tom Paine. He was born in Thetford, attended its free school, and in his late thirties went to the colonies in America. The rest is American history except his burial, or rather re-burial, by the English writer and reformer William Cobbett, who felt Paine belonged to England and brought the remains of the atheistic revolutionary back to the homeland ten years after his death.

Bleakness, brownish bracken, a sign pointing out that no sleeping is allowed in the thin, reforested woods shivering with pheasants, a straight road with few travelers (except at the peak of the summer season), halt at **Grime's Graves,** in an eerie desolation that matches the name. Actual graves figure only tangentially here, evidenced by human bones which were found in these pits—the Anglo-Saxon meaning of "graves"—flung about, scholars say, by Neolithic cannibals. The hollows were noted and sporadically investigated by antiquarians, archeologists, and curious amateurs for three hundred years, possibly earlier. At first the hollows were considered old fortifications attributed to the Danes, then later moved back in time to become Iron Age settlements. In 1868 an archeologist who was also a cleric—a uniquely English combination, to which England owes considerable knowledge of her past—dug deeply into one pit to find evidence of a Neolithic flint mine. Subsequent diggings and finds attempted to extend their existence to the Paleolithic but, as of now, after heated scholastic battles, Neolithic they remain. The shallowest diggings in this chalk earth for the best flint, called floorstone, were probably the oldest, over four thousand years old. The surface veins exhausted, the miners dug deeper to supply what must have been a busy factory of flints for combat and agricultural and hunting tools used by tribes in the area. During the excavations of pits, several chalk phalluses were found and near one, on her own pedestal, a pregnant woman of chalk. Before her, a chalk lamp that illuminated the digging, slabs of mined flint and, on top of these, seven antlers of red deer used as picks and levers by the miners. The presence of the fertility symbols, here combined with offerings of flint and digging instruments, meant that the pits were also ceremonial centers, possibly impromptu, to cajole the goddess into producing good veins of flint, not too dangerous or difficult to dig out, and to have a care for the crops growing above.

Only one pit in this honeycombed primeval landscape is open to the public. One descends on a straight ladder with widely spaced treads into a unevenly domed opening in which a man can comfortably stand. The chalk and the flint clearly show their differences in the layers of stone of the main gallery and in the low radiating galleries, worked by men who had to crawl as they chipped with stone and flint but mainly with the deer antlers of a larger species than we now know. Nothing is left of the worked flints, the fertility symbols, and the hundreds of antlers found when the pits were opened; these have gone to several museums. It is a strange experience to stand in the pit, to wonder how far the shafts go, whether they connect with other shafts, whether the goddess prevented suffocating falls of chalk, what words these men made, what primitive engineer decided the proper place for lateral digging. Was the rough flint chipped, shaped, and polished in the large chamber or sent up to be handled by a crew of craftsmen? And how large —it must have been quite large to judge from the amount of digging—was their joint output and what the value of the ax heads and crude knives in barter? So evocative and absorbing is the short time in the cave that one climbs out bemused, shocked for a moment by the anachronistic sight of a car, the twentieth-century artifact one left fifteen minutes ago.

The westward way to the hidden gold of Castle Acre stops at **Swaffham,** whose distant view tops its church spire with crossed keys or crossed swords. The church maintains a chorus of twittering wooden angels under its hammerbeam ceiling and, near the altar, an Elizabethan lady in prophetic prayer for the soul of her iconoclastic grandson, Oliver Cromwell. As the church exemplifies the styles and taste of the fifteenth century, a number of houses display the building styles wrapped around discreet high life of the eighteenth and early nineteenth centuries, the apogee a tempietto as market cross and, if the church couldn't properly take care of agriculture, a Ceres at its summit to help out. Swaffham's miracle legend centers not on sudden cures or heroic martyrdoms, but on money. The grand north aisle of the church was built by the Pedlar of Swaffham, who had wandered onto London Bridge, maybe to throw his disconsolate self into the Thames.

Among the shops and houses on the bridge he met a stranger who told him to return to his home town, where he would find a great treasure. He found it and rewarded God with a stately row of fine arches and windows.

Through the rise and fall of smoothly breathing fields and signs gathered like primitive weathervanes to little **South Acre,** isolated with its almost forgotten church in a quiet valley. Although it has undergone repairs, they were not extensive and one is left with the purities of medieval centuries: the frail, lacy remains of a screen of the fourteenth century; a doorway of the same time; an old dower chest; thirteenth-century pieces of glass; and a small population of tombs, brasses, and effigies, some marred by time (such as a Crusader)—one or two quite alive: a knight dressed in his robe as Lord Mayor of London and a fourteenth-century couple still holding hands.

Church, big graveyard, the stillness of hamlet are cocooned in a separateness of time and space even more keenly felt in **Castle Acre.** The fields flow up to a mound and a gateway which has stood here almost a thousand years. Inside the gate, a narrow main street of taciturn flint houses whose predecessors once clustered inside the protective walls of the castle bailey, occupied with the business of the castle-fort and the priory next door. The Acres were not, centuries ago, as alone as they now appear to be. On the way to South Acre you may have noticed an overgrown narrow path signaled by a sign that says PEDDAR'S WAY, a commonly used road that predated the Romans who, of course, improved it. At the side of this thoroughfare, near an already existing village of post-Roman settlers, a noble in William the Conqueror's forces, the Earl of Warrenne, built his fortified castle. The Normans lost no time in building a church, but only the remaining shadow of a window and a rounded doorway may be theirs and, above the priest's door, a tall bricked-up archway which may have served for mounted knights who came to the church to be blessed before taking off for the Crusades, rather as riders now take their horses into the churches of Siena before the Palio. The tower, which repeats the theme of battlements, is a work of the fifteenth century, as are the font with the extraordinary cover and the painted panels of the Gothic pulpit, while the thirteenth century made the priest's door and the quatrefoiled piers. One of the twelve Apostles in the fifteenth-century screen was shot in the face by one of Cromwell's apostles. St. Andrew, says the cordial, enthusiastic priest who, like any good host, has an infinity of time and energy for you (admittedly, a rare visitor) and enjoys pointing out the high quality of the painted panels in the chancel and a squint—a peephole, common in old churches—in which there is a death's head. He likes to think it is the skull of a Catholic priest who hid from the Protestants in some forgotten half-buried corner of the church. And why not? No one has a better explanation for the skull. He will make sure, too warmly, politely urging that you see South Acre if you've missed it, and certainly the Cluniac Priory of Castle Acre.

Down a path toward the river, a stand of trees and a flow of endless green from a relic of singular beauty. Although there was, as often, dissension between the Cluniac houses in England and that ruled by St. Benedict in Cluny, the architectural skills and imagination of the French monks were not abjured, and here in the shattered priory (somewhat disturbed by the interference of later "English" styles) are their queenly orders of interlaced arcades, the dignity of tall, slender rounded arches balanced by broad doorways edged in strong diagonal patterns. The former shape of the Priory—what was church and towers and sleeping quarters—can be traced and the large-windowed, large-hearthed Tudor home for a prior who just beat out Henry's decrees can sometimes be seen. But the glory of the Priory is the cadenced elegance of proportions and ornamentation carried from Romanesque France to glamorize the church in East Anglia.

Gayton slows one with its tall round brick tower snipped in warlike crenellations, then releases one to the heady sprinkling of poppies in the fields and equally heady **King's Lynn**, which has so adroitly compromised with time and change as to be a thriving market and port town and yet remain a storehouse of very much alive antiquity.

Your road to town may plunge you into the spacious Tuesday Market, "new" as of the late 1400's, when merchants and shippers moved their solid dwellings northward, leaving the Saturday Market near the big Church of St. Margarets, both as old as the twelfth century. A long loop that encloses the markets, their lanes, the streets on and off the riverfront, vestiges of old wall to the south, gives the essential flavor of the town, neither reticent nor pushy; just easily, healthily there. Do it once over lightly at first, in and out of alleys marked "staith," "quay," "ferry," "water," with their secretive dock warehouses, to see what ships' flags wave over the port, and then to the great medieval merchants' houses once attached to the warehouses on and off King, Queen, and Nelson Streets and their tangents. As you go, try to restore the port's vivacity as one of the most important in England, with close shipping ties in a broad miscellany of imports and exports to Iceland, the Scandinavians, and ports of the Continent, easy to reach by way of the River Ouse and the swell of sea called The Wash. Try to bring back the wealthy guilds and their feasts, their furred, velveted, and gold-plated ceremonials, and King John dining on peacock with the leading burgesses and churchmen of Lynn. It was probably the last festive meal he had, since he lost his baggage shortly thereafter—and his treasures and money—in The Wash while he was pursuing his insurgent barons. (Dispirited by the loss, tired of conflict in a game of changing partners—the Pope was against him, the Pope was with him; the barons were warm, the barons were icy steel— the king soon caught dysentery and died, one suspects not so much of intestinal as emotional anguish and the exhaustion that lets the reins slip.)

A shallow overhang and thin beams to hold old brick peer out of Nelson Street. The low windows were shops in the fifteenth century, added to a fourteenth-century merchant's dwelling and expanded, in later centuries, to become the complex known as Hampton Court, an irregular square defined at the riverside with a long warehouse held in brick piers and cut by arches under which goods were unloaded. The merchant who owned the house and convenient place of business was a member of a family whose mark can be seen carved in a corner over a door on Nelson Street. Hampton Court was continuously in trade and in eating and cooking, sleeping and feasting, until the falling away of business in the eighteenth and nineteenth centuries (now revived, though not of the importance it had when the town supplied 20 per cent of the king's exchequer). At that time the mercantile stronghold was converted to primitive flats and cottages. The alert Preservation Trust thinks this was a sound idea and since housing is scarce, as almost anywhere in England, the Court will be faced with flats and small gardens soon again. A companion restoration, by the same group, goes on at Thoresby College, on Queen Street, whose origins were ecclesiastical, immediately signaled by an important carved door set into churchly recessed bands. The rest of the Queen Street side is of eighteenth-century brick with Dutch gables, a common borrowing from a close business associate. In the course of changes, shops were let into the Queen Street side and, toward the river, a warehouse and household spaces of various sorts. But the quadrangle arrangement stayed, echoing its original shape and use, like the beginnings of, let us say, Christ College in Oxford—a large, gated square ranged by cells. Thomas Thoresby, who died in 1510, was a very rich man who left money and property for a building to house a number of chantry priests to intone Mass for him. Their Great Hall, its space later cut for commercial storage, still carries a roof of indomitable beams and supports in the medieval manner of "Here I am, here I'll stay," compounded of the strengths of prosperous guilds and unquestioned Church. Again, Lynn returns to parallels of old uses by planning the refurbished college as small flats for the aged and a youth hostel.

Old buildings cleaned, shored up, and put to intelligent use help create the characteristic wholeness and optimism that is the town's atmosphere. Peering into gardens, at slits of river, admiring doorways and pediments, gables and brick, find your way to the nearby Church of St. Margarets, a compendium of all known styles in church improvement and furnishings since its beginning in 1100, when it was founded by the first Bishop of Norwich, Herbert de Lozinga, who also built the Cathedral in that city and another church in Great Yarmouth. It was said of him, and still is, that it was not so much pure piety that kept him at church building as guilt and acts of penance for the sin of simony; he had bought his bishopric from Rufus, the irreligious—except when he was very sick—son of the Conqueror. Friends of Lozinga say that was not true, that it was his lay canons (whom he displaced with Benedictine monks) who spread such slanders, still rumbling through the centuries. True or false, his Lynn Cathedral is imposingly big, not so showy an act of penance as standing for three days in thin clothing torn by the winds of Canossa as the emperor Henry

IV did, but sufficiently convincing. Unfortunately, there isn't much but its cold size to wonder at now, except for two sets of fourteenth-century brasses, said to be Flemish and, for brasses, monumental. Both brass gentlemen were mayors of Lynn and one is etched with a full cast of guests at a dinner that featured peacock, the unpalatable gorgeousness this time cooked up in honor of Edward III.

Trinity Guildhall almost jostles the church off the Saturday Market. It is a tall-windowed checkerboard of stone and flint of the fifteenth century attached to a merry Elizabethan show-off bedecked with a great gaud of shields and heraldic animals that match, as show of past splendor, the plate and ceremonial objects inside. And then there is Clifton House (on Queen Street), a dwelling, warehouses, cellars of several centuries going back to the fourteenth, surprising passers-by with fanciful twists of columns and inner Georgian doorway. And the Customs House, a gay, cupola'd box hung with many windows and classical entranceways, built in the late seventeenth century to be a Merchants' Exchange. And St. George's Guildhall where, Lynn's informants tell you, there was a theatre in which Shakespeare acted. After its long years as warehouse, Lynn has again revived the theatre and added an art gallery, both used—as are the market place, the churches, the town hall—in a late July festival of arts, music, film, plays, and ox-roast feasting and dancing in the ample Tuesday Market, supervised by the overdressed Falstaff of a Victorian Corn Exchange.

The gibbets for public hangings and stone that supported pyres for well-attended public burnings have been covered by merchants' houses and hotels, among them the late-seventeenth-century Duke's Head, erected to accommodate visiting merchants with business in Lynn. North of the market place, St. Nicholas Place leads to the chapel of its name, a good-sized church with an attractive ceiling and appealing sections of medieval decoration. To the southeast, new playing fields in green walks, the indispensable library, and Red Mount Chapel, whose contribution to the basket of Lynn charms is graceful fans of fifteenth-century vaulting.

To the north, the evocative melancholy of marsh and unyielding coast and—if your time coincides with the rare hours of the house—the Palladian size and loneliness, in its strange

place, of **Holkham Hall**. To the south, villages that have
dwindled from the size of their churches, where the gravestone
of Mary defines her as the "relict" of her husband John, where
there are too many monuments to doctors and surgeons, as if
parts of East Anglia lived in a gloom of permanent ill-health.
Church spires stand on the backs of old crowned lions, gargoyles spit lead pipes, and the diagonal slates of steeples shine
reticently in the rain. By way of a hundred "Fen" communities,
down to **Ely** and the horse-breeding country of **Newmarket**, of
immense smooth lawns and white stiles and signs that say
LORDSHIP STUD and BEWARE OF RACEHORSES, and maybe at this
point into **Cambridge**.

NOTES

HOTELS: In King's Lynn, the Duke's Head is moderate,
with breakfast extra. Town halls, borough halls, information desks almost invariably have listings of cheaper accommodations. And wherever you stay or eat in East Anglia,
watch your tendency to overtip. Unless he was brought
up on less proud soil, the Suffolk or Norfolk waiter will
turn back a tip—or he did, these things change in uncertain times—above the percentage for service added to the
bill.

Lincolnshire

"The most brute and beastly of my realm" was Henry VIII's view of Lincolnshire. He had reasons, including the fact that during the Dissolution of the Monasteries 20,000 men of Lincolnshire rose in vigorous, if ultimately futile, protest. Lincolnshire remains vigorous, straightforward and, Henry notwithstanding, good-humored. **Grantham**, for instance, hangs a huge red dustpan on the façade of a bright blue building to call attention to the nails, pails, and screwdrivers of a hardware shop that likes the playful title of LITTLE DUSTPAN. On another side of the market square, a similarly inventive mind names its shoe shop EASIEPHIT, and there is a lusty swing to the town's gestures of modern glass and older red brick, and ancient zest in street names like Swine Gate and flavorful coaching inns. The necessary touch of spirituality rests in the slender spire of the church, the reticent, gentle manners of the young verger who shows visitors its slightly boudoiry charms and chained library kept attached to the cases against forgetful borrowers and marauders. (Where age and accident have caused damage, the Great Guardian of books, the British Museum, undertakes repairs at what Latins call "a friend's price.")

Belton House near Grantham is one of the less polite of the stately homes. The visitor is not permitted the wrought-iron gates but must approach, like hoi polloi though not unpleasantly, past twittering bird cages, through a field of indifferent cows, under the bland stare of ponies and the suspicious eyes of black sheep, to meet a sign stating that guard dogs are loosed after closing at 6:30. (Actually, successive doors are firmly shut behind and before you at 6:00 sharp, maybe to save you from the descendants of Cerberus.) Nonetheless, it is an attractive house set in an extensive park of sculptured shrubbery under full trees, ringed by well-balanced outbuildings of yellow-gray stone, attractive enough for Edith Wharton to have had copied for her country mansion. A greyhound at the entrance speaks a frequently repeated leitmotif especially conspicuous in the floridly engraved key plates of several doors and in at least one floor. The late-seventeenth-century house—with some alterations of a century later—has the grace of its contemporaries, the interesting angles of an H shape, large light-gathering windows with

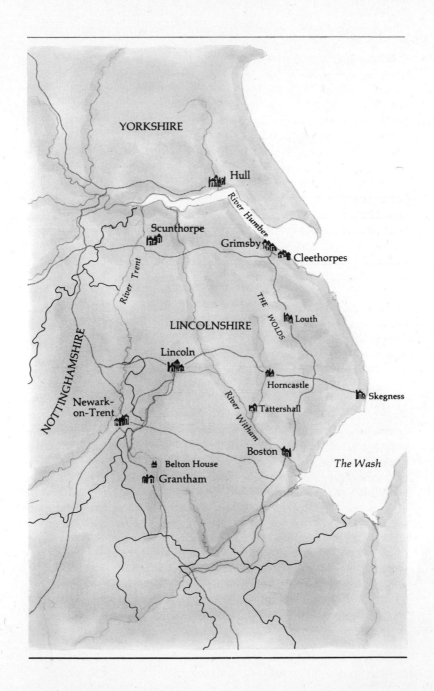

latticework crossbars, and the sense to contain itself in considerate size.

The estate has had an unusually cautious history characterized by a founder, Richard Brownlowe, a lawyer who sank three-quarters of his considerable income, year after year, into property which yielded a sizable fortune and produced the present house, and of descendants who married prudently and became prominent. Reynolds painted a portrait of an eighteenth-century member of the family in the rich cloak of the Speaker of the House of Commons; a sedan chair used by one of the ladies is hung with the medallions and ribbons earned by a gentleman of the family who was an equerry to King George V.

From France, Sèvres china, elaborate fireplace fittings that once adorned the life of Marie Antoinette, feminine pieces of furniture, and an unusually large Aubusson carpet. Pieces of porcelain from China and Germany, small paintings from the northern countries and larger from Italy. And the best from England of its time: the house, though not specifically designed by Wren, owes to his influence its satisfying balance, while the fireplaces in the saloon, weighty with family portraits and heavy silver, were actually designed by Wren. The stupendous bed in the Blue Room, its large combination of bureau and desk fitted with finely smoothed little drawers, and the seventeenth-century needlework bed cover exemplify English strengths, as do the miniatures and the collections of English china. The essential English portraits by Lely, Kneller, the more accomplished Reynolds, and the inevitable lavish royal painting by Van Dyck appear with a small but distinguished group of outlanders, a "Presentation of the Virgin" and a "St. Catherine" by Titian, one of Rembrandt's incandescent studies of an old Jew, a fresh "Entombment" by Tintoretto, a dashing Rubens portrait, an oddly chill little painting of the frail Edward VI and, odder still, a copy of the Mona Lisa, her eyes just a wee bit too close together, found by Sir Joshua Reynolds in Austria and purchased by the family after his death.

Frequently the paintings are divided by or doubly framed by wood carvings, as swelling fruits about to drop, breeze-tossed leaves, fat-bellied, wet-shining little fish, a fin this moment stopped in motion—the wizardry of Grinling Gibbons, the master wood carver to the Crown. On the library tables, family mementos, books, and photographs, one group devoted to King Edward VIII, later the Duke of Windsor, who, it is said, used the chirping chinoiserie bedroom. On some of the ceilings, skilled plasterwork that repeats subjects and patterns of the woodwork below. It is a careful house, richly but not overwhelmingly furnished, of itself pleasing and a telling example of high eighteenth-century hubris and no fear of showing it.

Out of Belton, toward **Lincoln**, the flattish terrain becomes hilly, serious little villages sitting in clouds of tree pierced with church spires. Twenty-four miles later, Lincoln, as truly a hill town as any in Italy, climbing up to its Cathedral and plunging down to amalgams of Norman, medieval, Georgian, Victorian, and later styles.

It can be disconcerting to approach a city of golden auras through industrial plants and raw housing estates or, worse still, survivors of Victorian slums. Better if one does it by wharf-and-ship-laced Bradford Pool, whose imperturbable swans float in insolent rows, turning, gliding, posturing. The pool was expanded from a canal linking the River Trent with the River Witham, one of the engineering feats of the Romans, who took the settlement in A.D. 47. They built defenses and expanded it as headquarters from which their conquest was pushed to York and Chester. Of major importance as one of the four *"colonia"* of Roman Britain—the others were Colchester, Gloucester, and York—*"Lindum"* grew into a sybaritic town with the usual amenities of good houses well supplied with water and sewage systems, sound roads like the extant Ermine Street that led to country villas and farms reclaimed from the marshes, the waters held in a canal system that expanded trade, especially of grains. The center of the Roman city was, roughly, the area now marked by the castle and the Cathedral.

History followed its English course: the colony semi-abandoned at the collapse of the Empire, the Saxons living in ruined Roman stone, a return to importance under the organized Danes who revived the commerce and finance which the city had lost, and lost again with the collapse of its wool trade in the late fourteenth century. Fortune's wheel showed Lincoln only its tenebrous faces; in spite of official release from taxation because things were so desperate, the city could not support its population, which began to drift elsewhere in search of work or alms. The city authorities, with only two thousand citizens to see to in the time of Henry VIII, despoiled the churches of their treasures to please the king and add a few bits of gold to the Guildhall coffers. Plague followed and the devastations of the Civil War. By the eighteenth century Lincoln was a ghost town. The vibrant nineteenth century again reclaimed agriculture and grazing from the fens, cleared the canals once so useful to Romans and medieval wool merchants and, final triumph, brought in the railroad.

Lincoln has recovered from its dismal centuries; it is relaxed, voluble, shouts when it wants to, laughs a lot, its pink-cheeked children fly up and down the streets twittering like starlings, the slender men examine women with an appreciative Mediterranean gleam. The women, Mediterranean, too, in their well-packed girth, respond in kind and when there is no neighbor to talk with flirtatiously, pick up a pair of travelers with whom to pass the time of day. No preamble seems to be necessary, "Steep bloody hill, this. D'you mind it? I do it four times a week. I have a little boy in that place there, that hospital, something's not right with his brain, poor thing, but he does like me to bring him sweets and toys." She takes a Jack-in-the-box out of a basket, laughs as it jumps. The smile still on her face, she says, "I don't think it will frighten him, do you? Naagh, I don't think so. Well, goodbye, I was glad to talk with you," and disappears into the yard of the hospital, a lady of Lincoln who, like her ancestors, knows something of the vicissitudes of the human condition and meets them sturdily and good-naturedly.

At the top of the Steep Hill you've climbed with the Lincoln lady, you approach a forest of buttresses, stone scallops, ribbons, tatting, and scrollwork in the yellow Cathedral stone winging above the stepped overhangs and half-timbering that house a branch of a national bank (you will notice on your travels that the most careful, gleaming restorations are often, and understandably, the work of banks), and, as neighbor, St. Mary Magdalen with St. Paul in the Bail, one of Lincoln's several pre-Conquest church remnants. Up on the hill sits the double-mounded castle enclosure and, close to, the jollities of circlets, quatrefoils, and baby spires in the Gothic Exchequer Gate, built in the fourteenth century to close off the accounting offices of the Cathedral. Apart from the twelfth-century many-

angled shape of an inner keep and the fourteenth-century gateway from Castle Hill, the one medieval survivor is Cobbs Hill,
an ancient prison now well locked and uncommunicative except
for the message chalked on a board that "Valerie loves John."
The other buildings are of the eighteenth and nineteenth centuries, used as courts and archives. A sign marked CHAPEL leads
into a grim area clogged with brown, up-ended coffins that
were the locked pews, one man to a breathless box and a
locked door at the end of each row, for prisoners. The pulpit
is built very high so that the prisoners might see their spiritual
guide and, even higher, benches for guards to supervise the
service. Above the chapel, the courts; and below, beyond a
barred gate, the cells, a neatly economical arrangement. As if
to compensate for these dark buildings and the silenced Cobbs
Hill, the authorities have let loose flamboyant gardening, ivy
spraying like green fountains, big red vases in squares of earth
for bombardments of flower fireworks.

Shortly before Steep Hill snakes into the Strait, also justly
named, there is a metal bar to hold off traffic or to catch a tum-
bler tripped by the icy walk. It was originally placed to prevent the repetition of a wild ride by a local worthy, a Member
of Parliament and a gaming man, who won a bet that he could
drive a four-horsed carriage down the snaking, slithering street.
It hasn't been done since. Good antiques, as opposed to souvenirs, are the business of Steep Hill, and so is the preservation of old houses and the very old. A piece of Roman gate
leaves its presence on the hill, as does a sixteenth-century inn,
loosely bound in wooden bars and arches. Nearby, the stone
and timber of the Harding House, recently restored and probably once a merchant's house, now used by Lincoln's College of
Art. Among the most cherished architectural gems in Lincoln,
and England, are "Aaron the Jew's House" of the late twelfth
century and a "Jew's Court," possibly a synagogue of the same
time, although the word "court" could have been literal since
in that halcyon time Jews could be judged by their co-religion-
ists. Jews were early financiers because of the interdict of the
Church against usury and because Jews were admitted to very
few other professions; in all the vast mercantile history of the
guilds there is only one Jewish name recorded. Aaron of
Lincoln (whose actual house was probably closer to the
Cathedral) was the Rothschild of his day and, like other rich

Jews, high churchmen, and nobles, built one of the first stone
houses for stronger protection of person and property. Aaron's
financial network was sufficiently extensive to employ as agents
Jews in other parts of England and to leave, when he died in
1186, a substantial fortune. On his death, the king, who claimed
the properties of defunct usurers, was forced to establish an
auxiliary to his exchequer which worked exclusively on settling
Aaron's estate, and found that debts due him added up to half
or more of the king's total income.

Not only the richest Jew but one of the most flagrant and last
of the Blood Accusations that recurred in medieval England
belongs to Lincoln. Every few years—and these were usually
troubled years for Christians as well as Jews—someone could
positively prove that a Christian boy was kidnapped, tortured
in a mockery of the sufferings of Jesus, and his blood used in
the Passover ritual. The most celebrated of these young martyrs
was Little St. Hugh of Lincoln, his story treated by Chaucer in
the *Canterbury Tales*. Hugh, eight years old, was supposedly
stolen in 1255, sequestered, and, like any proper sacrifice, well
fed. Selected Jews from the other sixteen Jewry towns, including London, Oxford, and Cambridge, were invited to attend the
sacrificial rite. A Lincoln Jew was appointed Pilate and the boy
subjected to the scourging, the crown of thorns, and the Crucifixion of Christ, accompanied by curses. The body was then
dropped into the well of a Jewish house where the distraught
mother found it. The owner of the house was arrested and, in
response to extreme threats, confessed that such crucifixions
were an annual practice. Furthermore, when the Jews tried to
bury little Hugh, the grave would not have him but placed him
back on the surface of the earth, a potential saint due high
ceremony and burial in the Cathedral. The actual facts that
the boy died several months after Passover, that the Jews
from other towns came to attend a wedding in Lincoln, that
boys occasionally did, and do, fall into wells and drown, that
the confessing Jew, according to a few Gentile judges, was at
least half-mad, counted for nothing. The hysteric was hanged;
ninety-one of the leading Jews of Lincoln were taken to London
for imprisonment and eighteen quickly executed for insisting
on a trial by their peers, Christian and Jew. The rest went to
the Tower and were condemned to execution by a body of
knights and merchants. Because evidence was so circumstantial

and based on an untrustworthy confession, and because wiping out the banking Jewry of Lincoln would cause difficulties for Church and king—Jewish monies, for one thing, helped to build glorious cathedrals—the leaders of a powerful religious order (possibly Franciscan, possibly Dominican) asked the king for their pardon. It was granted, and that was the end of the English version of the legend which still crops up in benighted corners of the world. It faded in England not as recoil from so heinous a miscarriage of justice but because of the fact that by the end of the thirteenth century there were no Jews left. The 16,000 had been expelled by Edward I and their function taken by Italians, who invented pragmatic devices to screen usury.

A cut off Steep Street toward Lindum and the neo-classic Art Gallery is called Danes Gate, a neighbor holds Danes Cottages, and a garage alley at the side of the gallery rise is called Danes Courtyard: living memories of the Norsemen. Northward, Newport Gate, stockier than Roman portals are wont to be since its base is hidden along with the earth-covered stones of a Roman Road. Between Danish and Roman vestiges—looping and turning on Silver Street, Mint Street, Drury Lane, St. Martin's Lane, the waterside markets and wharfs and the many "Gates"—one comes upon a poolside inn, once a wool merchant's mansion of the fourteenth century, whose outer beams make a pattern of archers' bows; several of its drooping contemporaries; and a Norman Guildhall. A sixteenth-century Guildhall with a splendor of churchlike roof and interesting mementos that include ancient documents straddles Stonebow, a gateway on an earlier medieval gateway over a similar Roman structure. Where the Strait meets the High Street, restored fifteenth-century houses, one called the Cardinal's Hat to honor as a sixteenth-century inn the powerful Cardinal Wolsey, once Bishop of Lincoln.

The City and County Museum, which encloses souvenirs of Lincoln's past and county fauna, lives and shows in ecclesiastical stone on Saltergate. The Greyfriars of the early thirteenth century were given this land for a church by local burgesses. At some point in its history, the building was divided and the church limited to the upper story. Thus it functioned until the suppression of the monasteries to become, in time, a poor boys' school and then museum and still the oldest Franciscan church in England. The clarity and coolness of the Georgian sits on Castle Square. A stylistic extravaganza that bubbles up curlicues, griffons, and toothy chalet fringes spreads its optimistic blue and white on Corporation Street above a "noted banana shop." Equally cheery but with less bravura and more charm, the black-and-white patterns of small rectangles, the pinpoints of light in sentinel dormer windows of a sixteenth-century house on the Norman High Bridge at the bottom of the High Street.

While its towers, like great elaborate brooches, fix the Cathedral and the core of the city to the sky, the rest dips and whirls in its medieval hilltown dance, perhaps dropping you in front of the Usher Gallery, several halls of several different strengths not always sharply separated, and it doesn't always matter. Since there are frequent shows of English artists rearranged from the permanent collection, and exhibitions of modern prints, jewelry, and glassware, the old standbys like exquisite Elizabethan caps and gloves may not be on view and some of the fine English porcelain may be hidden by turn-of-this-century painting. Whether the paintings of Lincoln by several artists (one by Turner and several by Peter de Wint) or the lusterware and jugs shaped like cows will be in one room or another is not always certain. But the building is not too large and at least two rooms stay anchored.

The Usher Room, named for a jeweler who was sheriff and donor of part of the building, may be introduced by a case of dolls, another of Victorian dresses, of Chinese silks or fans. Its main purpose is to display a collection of rare watches, some with thick enameled carapaces like jeweled beetles, some transparent to expose their frail beating hearts; some are bound in gems, others are themselves, in the delicacy of their making and exquisite settings, gems. Of a related skill among the minutely precise, a group of French and English historical miniatures and, still in the area of the exquisite, many flirtatious porcelains from Germany, France, China, and several famous potteries of England.

The other room of set tenure is that for Tennyson, born in the rectory at **Somersby,** no great distance from the city. He owned, as a child, a book of nursery rhymes and, as a student, the poems of Milton. He smoked a pipe, wrote and received letters, used quill pens, corrected manuscript pages, was sketched and photographed, and saved the programs from performances of his own plays. There is nothing here to explain the uneven talent, nor how it felt to be a Poet Laureate in Queen Victoria's time, but it is always entertaining to snoop among a famous man's memorabilia, searching for the personal, revealing item that once in a while calls out from these collections.

High above, the clarion of the Cathedral, the quintessence of the city. Before you settle among its large beauties and small charms, walk around the buttresses, the self-contained almost circular Chapter House, the tracery in windows, the crude, moving, literal Bible depictions of the blessed and damned carved into the entrance arch, and the many-centuried stand of houses that circle the Mother House, among them a set of stone doll houses where priests in training lived. Place yourself in the shadow of the tower that reaches toward the Eastgate Hotel, modern gray and glass with a taint of antique crenellations, and find, at Priory Gate, a monumental figure of an old man holding a big, floppy hat, an adoring dog at his feet; Tennyson, as seen by Watts. At the entrance to the hotel, a box of dark brick encloses relics of Roman tower and medieval gateway.

It is not unusual for cathedrals in England to take up some of the functions of art and community centers; Lincoln is especially active in this respect. At one point, soaring space may be devoted to a show of the works of John Piper, including a replica of his superb stained glass in the new Cathedral at Coventry, a justifiably large price attached to it. Another vault hangs high over a well-lit modern exhibition area to show the attractive matter of the Museum of Lincolnshire Life, with examples of straw work, carving of stone, tile-making, and tailoring. Rather than disturb, these displays re-create the strong medieval flavor of Church as the center of popular life, when the great nave was a place for meeting and ceremonials and services held in the chapels.

The history of the Cathedral repeats, in the main, that of its similar contemporaries: decayed Roman stones in a primitive Saxon church on the crest of a hill, rebuilt by the later Normans; destruction by earthquake and fire; and through the thirteenth century rebuilding to magnificence, with changes in English Gothic followed by later mannerisms of church building into modern times. (For those who enjoy following differences in style, the bookstall sells a pamphlet with a back cover depicting the Cathedral in colors that mark different periods.)

Having been absorbed in the amplitude, the successive arches of the nave, and the palm-frond ribs in the varied rhythms on the ceiling, examine the stocky black twelfth-century font, carved with grotesque griffons and chimeras following the fashion of medieval Belgium. The rather plain and fairly modern pulpit, brought from an English church in Holland, hides a vibrant ghost. One of the minor reforms of the Reformation was the introduction of a Bible, set up so that anyone might read. A young woman named Anne Askew not only read out loud but called the canons to task for the corruption of their church. Ultimately, her proselytizing led to her burning, to join an impressive number of martyrs of her time. An earlier notable was Robert Grosseteste, Bishop of Lincoln from 1235 to 1253 and, like his contemporary, Frederick II of the Two Sicilies, a prophecy of Renaissance man—enlightened and independent in his dealings with the Church, a man versed in the sciences and mathematics, music and literature, a prime mover in the introduction of Arabic and Greek thought to the Continent.

The tracery around the north window and its glass of the early 1200's takes on the dancing complexity of the fourteenth century, the glass light-struck bits gathered up and added to after the destructions of the Civil War. Another disaster of the same time had less lovely but more amusing results. The heads of small saints in the lacy screen were especially vulnerable to Cromwell's soldiers, who managed to bash in a considerable number. A mason, charged with creating new heads in the late eighteenth century, gave beards and mitres to all the saints, men and women alike. On entering the choir, one notices again stylistic differences: the upper side at the left is quite simple while the right is more elaborate, both areas touched, however, with fine angels in the arches. As suits the core of the Cathedral, this section is a deftly and deeply incised crowded holiness inspired by the Continent, with charming floral designs, little owls and dragons, and an untypical St. George. The misericords under the seat supports, many survivors of the thirteenth century, open glimpses to a carefree, permissive world which gave equal skill to a rampant centaur, angels and griffons, Christ, a wounded knight, a mermaid.

The high altar, the target of major seventeenth-century destruction, was redone by several hands and doesn't have much to hold one except the proximity of several ornate tombs, among them that of Katherine Swynford. She was the sister-in-law of Chaucer and the mistress of John of Gaunt, the tremulous old man who makes the famous speech in *Richard II* in praise of his "scepter'd isle" and not quite the benign patriarch he appears to be in that immortal scene. She became his third wife and the mother of four of his children, the Beauforts, from whom the uncertain claim of the Tudors stemmed. It is not precisely a holy or even respectable tomb, but her sons were men of great power, the legitimized grandsons of one king and nephews of another, Edwards II and III. Sharing terrain with Katherine of the Beauforts is the tomb of Little St. Hugh, whose story you already know. The legend on the shrine is an apology to "innocent Jews" and a prayer, "Remember not Lord our offences, nor the offences of our forefathers." The resplendent Angel Choir was built in the thirteenth century to accommodate the shrine and the pilgrims who came to draw strength from the boy-martyr. Many more visit the shrine to peer up at the low-browed, bat-eared Lincoln Imp, a vindictive fellow who grimaces out of every souvenir shop window.

If your time in the Cathedral is any summer afternoon, you will find the treasury open and, for a small charge, can see rarities of plate and the greater rarities of William the Conqueror's charter to the Church, and one of the four existent originals of the Magna Carta, issued in 1215. If your time happens to be Tuesday or Thursday, you should be admitted to the library designed in the late seventeenth century by Christopher Wren, on the north end of the cloisters; a library open to all, the collection dating back to Caxton. There was a medieval library here ruined by a fifteenth-century dean who, country squire at heart, loved horses more than he did books and converted the bookish room to stables. The shambles he created were further gutted by fire at a later time and rebuilt on order of a dean who *was* a book lover and collector. The Wren side of the cloisters discards trefoils and quatrefoils and roundels for clear arches with smooth columns to support the balanced proportions of the many-paned windows in fine frames, in just space. Its architectural peer, five hundred years older, reached via a scattering of staring medieval eyes, the aborted medieval gesture of a broken hand, and decorative Gothic lettering, is the superb polygonal Chapter House, spreading its fronds with fruits of bosses from one central trunk, a style adapted for assemblies of Church and lay governors. Since the business of the Church was also often that of the king, it is believed that the throne with a broad, curved overhang and a tapestry bearing a crowned figure and two lions was built for a king of the Middle Ages to use during a session of Parliament here convened.

NOTES

There may be a lecture going on in the Chapter House, a lunchtime concert on the green, a performance of Gilbert and Sullivan later in the day or yet another concert, not necessarily sacred music.

HOTELS: And then to bed at the modern Eastgate for £7 or £8 (recent prices, no breakfast) for two; the more flavorful White Hart for a bit more, or the modest Queen or Grand.

While the Cathedral was chipping away at its last mid-thirteenth-century angel, a Robert de Tateshales was building a stone castle near a stream that met the River Witham on its southward course, a wedge of land well protected by waters. He was the fifth Robert de Tateshales, descended of a knight who fought with William the Conqueror and was rewarded with the estate. The first recorded edifice was the fortress-castle, almost entirely demolished and replaced in the fifteenth century by a fortified house built by the treasurer to Henry VI, Lord Cromwell. There may have been additions by later owners but for over two centuries it was a ruin, to be revived and its moats again filled with water by Lord Curzon early in this century and willed to the National Trust. In 1910, the castle belonged to an American company which may have hoped to sell it to a Morgan or Hearst. The fireplaces were already on their way to London to be picked up by German dealers who had purchased them for transshipment to the States when Lord Curzon stepped in, recovered castle and fireplaces, and embarked on restoration. Although the English manor house was losing its belligerence by the fifteenth century, Lord Cromwell built his double-moated palace with its limited points of access in the old fortified style, with a massive tower that imitates earlier military enclaves. As a key functionary who was not too well loved in a threatening time that was gathering up for the Wars of the Roses, he must have felt the need of protective walls, guarded by space and waters.

Even for its kind, **Tattershall Castle** is extraordinarily massive and formidable, a shocking explosion of brick as one comes upon it glowering above a little guardhouse and frail church. Over the first moat, across the jousting field, and over the second moat filled with colorful reeds and wild flowers, past butts of thirteenth-century turrets and wall, one reaches the great tower. The basement is a series of storeroom cellars, low and vaulted. On the floor above, an anteroom that was used as cloakroom and toilet, served by a shaft that extended to pits deep below, and a large guardroom with an ample fireplace and stained-glass windows bearing heraldic shields. A short climb again to the Great Hall, again supplied with a broad fireplace, colored shields, and on the walls, two tapestries. And that room paralleled on an upper floor by the stately chamber that might have been the bed-sitting-room of Lord Cromwell himself. It is equipped with a "garde-robe" (the dressing room/toilet), abundant light for its time and style, and a section that is canopied by a complex of brick vaults whose joints are carefully worked escutcheons of the Tattershall families. The ladies' chamber—or so it is guessed to be—above repeats proportions, vaulting, and bosses in a less exalted mood and, near the windows, traces of Gothic decoration. Tapestries, shields on a bountiful fireplace sculptured like the others yet in subtly different repetitions of patterns (notice the purse, a reference to Cromwell's position, and the plant called gromwell, that plays with the name) reappear in another large room. From the covered gallery there is a close view of the turrets and spaces in the tower from which invaders could be assaulted by boiling oil, rocks, or whatever were the weapons of the day. For a feeling of "monarch of all I survey," a parapet walk along the roof.

The surrounding landscape is not inspired but the short progress up and down in the tower, undisturbed by furnishings

except for the grand fireplaces, is a singularly pure experience
of medieval fortress might, particularly effective in contrast
with the light, harmoniously spaced church, its surprises of
height and brightness enhanced by the very low entrance door,
a bending to humbleness.

Certainly not indispensable viewing, **Horncastle** has nevertheless a robust personality, with a bull ring (for selling, not goring)
at the end of the High Street, partner of the horse and cattle
market. The Fighting Cocks pub long ago covered its flurried
pit with cement and the church feels too neglected to stay open
all day. Tall, tight, multicolored houses girdle the market square
or search their pastel reflections in the shallow river which
meanders through the town, slipping out of sight, returning
shyly. And Horncastle leads to or from **Louth** (pronounced
Lowth, if you must ask for directions and hopefully they may
include the archaic "yon" still in use here). The parish church of
St. James was severely manhandled by the Reformation and
later by the frenzies of the Victorians. What they couldn't touch
were the handsome rectangles high on the surface whose
flowers, viewed through opera glasses, are gargoyles—big-
jawed, jawless, crouching, leaping, all teeth or tongue—nor the
graceful sixteenth-century tower and its slender spire clasped
in fragile buttresses. Inside, the tower presents an impressive
massiveness, the succeeding arches gathering to a vigorously
designed roof centered on a golden sunburst.

Much of the rest of the town retains a red-brick Victorianism
that reflects its unabashed appetite for food and show. Two
wings of market-square building, prettified with chipped-brick
and white-stone cutouts, flank the tower of the market hall,
which, in the omnivorous greed of its time, takes the Gothic for
windows, a hint of Renaissance Italy for its frames, a clock
cased in Swiss cuckoo style, and spears the sky with a gar-
goyled weathervaned pagoda. The market stalls, heaped high on
Wednesdays, Fridays, and Saturdays with the usual gathering
of produce, flowers, inexpensive clothing, and ornaments, are
redolent of onions and bathed in mellow light from a great
rounded window held in bands of ornamental iron, derived
from railroad-station architecture and effectively used. Opposite this exit to the market one confronts a huge neo-Renaissance
building surrounding a noncommittal Lady Justice and telling
signs that indicate the confusion in which such proud monu-

ments now live. Some of the building is licensed for music and dancing, some of it cares for city treasury business, some of it seems unused. Grandeur calms to the seemly in the small houses, in the main Georgian, on Eastgate, Chequergate and, especially, Westgate. For the rest, just look around, following the streets from the market square, at the signs and symptoms of a robust life. The big butcher shops glisten with links of fat sausage, stack turrets of meat pie, hang curtains of sides of beef; and the lady customers, who leave slimming to the silly young, suit well the plump shine of their surroundings.

The King's Head makes itself unmistakable with a large, rough, regal head and in big blue lettering: FAMILY HOTEL, COMMERCIAL INN AND POSTING HOUSE. At the end of Mercer's Row, Hanson's Caterers and Bakers gives its Art Nouveau ornaments a final flourish of fancy shading. Invitations to buy fishing, riding, and hunting equipment make their purpose boldly known and a horse's head lunges—you can hear it neigh—out of Saddler's Wall.

It says something about Louth that although recently enough it had Woolworth's, a Boots, and Oxfam, there was no branch of the ubiquitous book and magazine store, Smith's. The town has, on the other hand, the rarity of several restaurants that stay open late. One place on Mercer Row fancifully calls itself POP IN, sports on its menu a "With It" list which means curry sauce or beans or chips as a side dish, and lists "Fantasia" as a description of earthbound kidney pie. Lung Chu, a Chinese restaurant on Eastgate, really creates fantasies, or at least oddities. "Prawns with Chinese vegetables" becomes three tiny shrimps in soft English-boiled cauliflower; fine mustard and cress dresses every dish as if it were dainty teashop sandwiches; and, if you like—many locals do—you may have chips instead of rice. There is solid country eating, heavy in eggs and meat, in the hotels mentioned, and adequate accommodations with a big breakfast for modest to moderate amounts. The best travel bargain here is the pleasure of the company of the nosybodies who enrich any trip. Place yourself, for instance, with your binoculars outside the church. One lady, leaning on her cane, stares companionably with you. You offer her the glasses, she looks, not seeing much since she is too polite to adjust them and so lose your focus. She says, "My, I'd never thought there was them there." The next passer-by stops for only a moment to comment, "Cold job, that, for a windy day." A third accepts the glasses, adjusts them, examines, and says, "Pretty, innit?" Give and take a few more words and you're launched into as much conversation as you want; everyone moves briskly but no one is truly in a hurry and always ready for an exchange in the Lincolnshire blending of good manners, openness, and curiosity.

South from Lincoln

If Lincolnshire is your northernmost port of call, and if you have the time, it might be instructive—if it isn't a weekend or foggy—to take a section of the M1 that comes from Leeds to Chesterfield, in Derbyshire, and eastward to **Nottingham** in its shire. The road drives through Midlands industrial development, cutting through huge fuming stacks, slag, collieries, one or two stiff skyscrapers vulnerably alone and disconsolate. (When will builders in Europe learn that skyscrapers are collective entities; they are incomplete and sullen alone, coming to full splendor only when they are glitteringly massed?) In the distance, gray villages; above, a grayed, polluted sky, and seeping through the window, a gray metallic stench. Ploddingly immortal and immune to change, a herd of cattle or sheep ambles along the side of the thundering highway.

D. H. Lawrence was born near Nottingham and there is a Lawrentian passion about the city. It seethes and strives, it is contentious and uneasy, a town of driven appetites, of pride and self-contempt. When Nottingham's antique castle was still new it gathered, as castles and cathedrals did, a community, a market. The market place, still the biggest in England, was the site of the famous Goose Fair. In more recent times, Nottingham was renowned for its lace, which found itself in several unexpected parts of the world, including market stalls in rural Mexico. Other light industries now rule and lace is left to a few misty establishments on Goose Gate, no longer a busy street. The Old Market Square is still the town center, a mélange of heroic buildings, the mouths of ancient alleys, slots into traffic lines that drive cars around and around like squirrels on wheels, then dash them into sudden brick walls. A map marked with stately, elderly names like High Pavement, Low Pavement, The Ropewalk, Angel Row, street names for Shakespeare, Chaucer, and Goldsmith, hardly prepares one for the man who stumbles by in an underground passageway and grumbles belligerently, "Okay, I'm drunk. I'm very drunk and going to get drunker. What's it to you?" You have hardly glanced at him.

On a Friday or Saturday night, at about 9:30, the shops and their frontage are the stage for couples fighting or necking fervidly, often both in agitated alternation. A fat elderly man totters down the street and small packs of young black boys mimic

and dance around him, then tear down the street roaring. A drunken middle-aged woman, emerging from a pub, glass in hand, strolls into the street oblivious of the cursing, brake-shrieking traffic. On the Square, at the sides of large blocks of new housing, insulting the ambition of new hotels, pools of vomit. Nottingham has a highly regarded theatre, libraries, colleges, and imaginative town planning, and the above Night-town view is palpably unfair, sketched here because it presents an intensification of a weekend mood not uncommon to industrial towns. Drunks weave their way out of pubs elsewhere in England, boys shout in the streets, and couples embrace publicly, but not in the numbers and not quite with the ferocity of Nottingham.

Coventry (southwestward) is a name with many echoes. "Going to Coventry" still means going into exile or disgrace. It was Lady Godiva's town and that of Peeping Tom, and busy with enough crafts to have a large number of guild performances of the famous Coventry Cycle of mystery plays from the Middle Ages into Elizabethan times. There is a tendency to blame the demolition of the medieval city altogether on the Germans who, on the night of November 14, 1940, fire-bombed the city in the longest raid suffered in England. The truth of the matter is that the old city had been long-before razed in order to make way for industry; the Germans devastated, mercilessly and thoroughly, a newer city. Houses, shops, and factories have been rebuilt, but the shards of the old Church of St. Michael's speak eloquently of injury and rebirth. Of the body of the old Cathedral almost nothing is left. Two burned beams that fell from the roof, now held by a twist of wire, make the well-known "Charred Cross" at the altar; behind the altar the freshly carved words "Father Forgive," and nearby a modern figure of Christ. That is all except walls, window frames, and stumps of pillar, all open to the sky. Thoroughly ruined and yet alive, the open nave was used for services (and still is at Whitsun and Easter) until the new Cathedral was consecrated in the spring of 1962.

To some, the adjoining new Cathedral, designed by Sir Basil Spence, is too "modern" at first glance; the clusters of triads that fly above the choir stall too much like a flock of birds rather than the crown of thorns they were meant to represent, the lettering on the tablets in the nave too primitively irregular to be dignified, the stained glass not sufficiently explicit, the immense tapestry of Christ and the symbols of the Evangelists too harsh in color and drawing, the pillars that taper downward too disturbingly unconventional. Few stay critical for long, however, in the exalted harmonies of glass colored and etched, the quiet shrine of polished woods and metals, the tints and shapes of stone, and unstressed, gentle reminders of the past and hopes for the future. The high altar cross that holds the cross made of nails which once pinned the beams of the old Cathedral is now used as a symbol for Christian unity in many places. In a book in the Chapel of Unity a prayer: "Let there be peace and let it begin with me."

The busy city, an important center of automobile manufacture, was lucky enough to hold onto its old Guildhall near the Cathedral precincts and wise enough to rebuild well in some central streets, using shattered space for traffic-free shopping malls, placing an open, roomy café across from the Cathedral ruins and, beyond a sunken area of rough stones that were part of Lady Godiva's church, a more formal restaurant. The large glass boxes, not quite skyscrapers, that have begun to line central streets are less certainly successful. It hardly matters. Coventry is, for the visitor, two Cathedrals, ruined old and remarkable new, the combination an indelible memory.

The lures of Stratford-upon-Avon beckon from the south but one should resist rushing toward them too quickly; well-kept dignified old **Warwick** deserves a bit of attention. The castle that looks down on the Avon was a stronghold of the Kingmaker, the Earl of Warwick. He lies entombed in Warwick's Church of St. Mary, in the company of another keystone in English history, Robert Dudley, Earl of Leicester, assigned the role, in chattier versions of history and historical romances, of the Virgin Queen's lover.

Whatever his love life and the gaieties and intrigues of Elizabeth's court, Dudley took time out to found, in 1571, an almshouse in a attractive shambles of buildings—leaning in, leaning out, held by long beams, controlled by wooden patterns; sharp, tiny roofs high and low, broader roofs exploding chimneys. These buildings at the side of an old gateway with a church sitting over its arches predate Robert Dudley and were actually the rooms of an earlier, dissolved group of guilds. Lord Leyces-

ter Hospital is still in use by a number of elderly gentlemen
who like to show the antique hall and the courtyard, which
repeats the half-timbering of the street façades. The combinations of timber and brick, timber and plaster in bold black and
white, meticulously maintained, stand with Georgian houses
and a few of other periods on the High and tangent streets. One
particularly good stretch of medieval housing lives between the
castle and St. Mary's Church, a portion enclosing a Doll Museum. Near the Market Hall, the seventeenth-century building
used as the County Museum; and across the market place, a
well-proportioned eighteenth-century house, now incorporated
in the Shire Hall. For *very* old houses, Mill Street, which considerately ends near the Information Centre and the entrance
to the castle. To frame its charms, Warwick weaves a pretty
fabric of parks and river.

Long pause for **Stratford-upon-Avon**, a shorter pause for
Kineton's amber-toned stone cottages, and, a few miles out of
the village, **Compton Wynyates**.

For an enclave that enfolds battlemented tower and royal
gateway, the manor is almost playful, a higgledy-piggledy castle
nestled in graceful slopes, bordered with bizarre topiary
shapes, a melding of low roofs and high that waft vari-patterned
chimneys. It didn't always have such a benign look. Vestiges of
the double moat, the aggressive towers, and the history of the
Compton family, which has held the house in a direct male line
since the early thirteenth century (possibly before), indicate the
contrary. The medieval lords of the manor established themselves early as government powers both local and national, if
the word "government" can be applied to a vague fourteenth-
century entity that did, however, gather knights together for
"parlements" in Westminster. Their ladies were clever and
practical also. Eager to maintain the estate in the family,
aware of the vulnerable position of women and unwilling to
end their lives in nunneries, no matter how entertaining and
luxurious, two Compton widows arranged leases with their
sons. Each man was to manage and profit from the estates during the mother's lifetime and in exchange would guarantee her
adequate shelter, a set, detailed allowance of clothing as befit a
lady (including furred cloaks), freedom from taxes, and a small
annual rental to keep her in pocket money.

A young William Compton became a page of Henry VIII when

the future king was two, followed him in later campaigns, and on him were bestowed gifts and honors by the king. Queen Elizabeth effected the reconciliation of a wealthy ex-Lord Mayor of London with his daughter and disapproved-of-son-in-law, a Compton who had eloped with his bride by taking her from her home in a large bread basket. Elizabeth was godmother to the first son of this marriage, the second Earl of Northampton (a title granted the family some years before), a close friend of the prince who became Charles I. Adherence to Charles and his lost cause turned the family into warriors. The earl and his sons did valiant battle in the Civil War, which killed the father and wounded one son, the third earl. A year after the death of the father, the house was besieged by Cromwell's forces, who took prisoners, hundreds of farm animals, and money. They looted the house, killed the deer in the park, and demolished the church. Several months later, the Comptons led a raiding party to regain the house but were vanquished after a few hours of battle. Undaunted, the head of the house pursued quixotic plans to free his imprisoned king, again to no avail. The estate was restored to the family on payment of the immense sum, for the seventeenth century, of £20,000 and the promise that the moat be filled in and the battlements made impotent; that the house, in short, be reduced from fortress to manor. A century later, several kinds of foolishness impoverished the family, the contents of Compton Wynyates were sold and disappeared forever, the windows bricked up, and the house abandoned until the mid-eighteenth century when repairs and restoration were begun. The house was not ready for use until the end of the nineteenth century, when it became a home of the fifth Marquess of Northampton.

An imposing relic of royal favor is the Tudor porch which leads to the inner courtyard. Above the entrance, the royal coat of arms bearing the heraldic animals of the Tudors, and above these, a crown marked DOM REX HENRICUS OCTAV; at the upper sides of the arch, another Tudor emblem and the arrows, fruit, and castle that appeared on the arms of Henry's unfortunate first and only devoutly Catholic wife, Catherine of Aragon. This welcome to the king and queen is repeated in the arms worked into the glass of the bedroom they used during their visits. The plasterwork in the ceiling, made early in the seventeenth century, bears another symbol of Henry, of his daughter Elizabeth, of James I, and Charles I, all of whom may have used the room. But not the bed you see. "King Harry's gilt bed" was confiscated by Cromwell's soldiers, tracked down and brought back after the Restoration, to be lost again when the family went broke in the late eighteenth century and sold the bed for £10. The portrait, incidentally, of Enrique el Gordo is one of numerous copies made within a few years of the original painting by Henry's court painter, Holbein.

The logic of the visit returns us to the Great Hall, one of the oldest (late-fifteenth-century) units, considerably changed with later rebuilding but still, say experts, resting on elements of an earlier house. Among the objects in the wood-vaulted Long Room there is an enormous old plank which was one of the tables for retainers who ate with the lord and his family. Above the timber-patterned minstrels' gallery, a stretch of fifteenth-century ceiling brought from the declining Fulbroke Castle, a gift of Henry VIII to his friend William Compton. The screen below the gallery is of linenfold interspersed with carved panels, one horizontal section of dashing and tumbling knights supposedly a description of Henry's and William Compton's successful battle at Tournai in France. At the far end of the hall, Italian tapestry that repeats a favored Roman theme of putti and grapevines twining around each other. (The design is attributed to Giulio Romano, painter and architect for the Gonzagas of Mantua in the early sixteenth century. It is quite possible that the Gonzagas sold the tapestry to agents of Charles I, who was an enthusiastic collector and known to have made purchases from the court of Mantua.)

The Drawing Room, of big floral patterns on the couches and small Oriental rugs, has an Elizabethan plasterwork ceiling and elaborate wood paneling brought from the Compton house in London. They surround a few unusual pieces of furniture and several works of art—a sixteenth-century Italian Crucifixion, a "Virgin and Child" by Giulio Romano, a painting by Giorgione or possibly Titian, and an Orpheus pacifying the wild beasts done in the high, padded relief and complicated detail of late-sixteenth-century French needlework.

Above the royal bedroom and the paneled council room, a small upper room, at the top of three separate sets of stairs. It is referred to as the "priests' room," because of the staircases which might have been used as escape hatches at the times of

persecution of Catholics and because of the crosses scored into
the windowsill. Two wooden panels seem, by their message and
lively crudity, to be medieval. One is a parade of exalted,
crowned figures, the forces of good threatening the persons of
the second panel who are the damned, driven by fearsome
beasts into the jagged-toothed, yawning mouth of hell.

What is left of the moat buoys up waterlilies and then flows
into attractive fishponds, which once actually supplied the
castle with fish. Where the moat has disappeared the ground is
marked with its former shape. The name? "Compton" derives
from the Saxon that denoted a settlement in a hollow. "Wynyates" is less certain and its spelling over the centuries vari-
able. It might have something to do with winds or vineyards;
the latter strikes a foreign note until one remembers that,
though medieval England imported a good deal of wine from
France and Spain, there *were* English vineyards, now ploughed
under hops and sheep runs.

NOTES

HOURS: April to September, Wednesdays, Saturdays, and
Bank Holidays, 2:00 to 5:30; summer Sundays, 2:00 to 5:30.

HOTELS: The Albany is high; the Victoria, George, and
County are moderate.

NORTHEAST

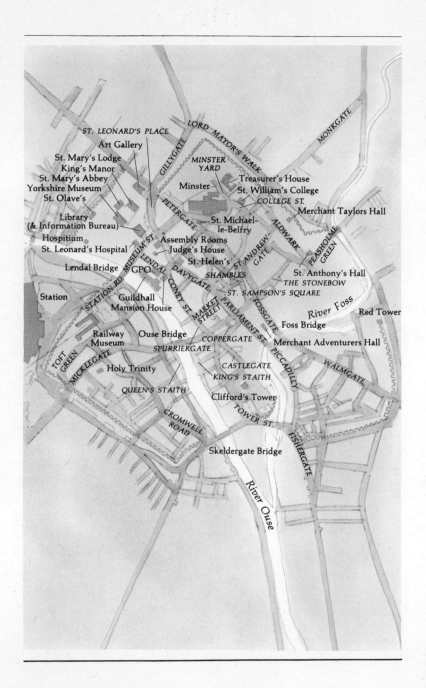

ST. LEONARD'S PLACE
Art Gallery
St. Mary's Lodge
King's Manor
St. Mary's Abbey
Yorkshire Museum
St. Olave's
Library
(& Information Bureau)
Hospitium
St. Leonard's Hospital
Lendal Bridge
Station
Railway
Museum
Holy Trinity

LORD MAYOR'S WALK
GILLYGATE
MINSTER YARD
Minster
Treasurer's House
St. William's College
COLLEGE ST.
Merchant Taylors Hall
PETERGATE
St. Michael-
le-Belfry
Assembly Rooms
Judge's House
St. Helen's
MUSEUM ST.
LENDAL
DAVYGATE
CONEY ST.
GPO
SHAMBLES
ST. SAMPSON'S SQUARE
Guildhall
Mansion House
ST. ANDREW-GATE
ALDWARK
PEASHOLME GREEN
St. Anthony's Hall
THE STONEBOW
MONKGATE
River Foss
Red Tower
Foss Bridge
FOSSGATE
MARKET STREET
PARLIAMENT ST.
Ouse Bridge
SPURRIERGATE
COPPERGATE
Merchant Adventurers Hall
PICCADILLY
WALMGATE
TOFT GREEN
MICKLEGATE
STATION RD.
CASTLEGATE
KING'S STAITH
QUEEN'S STAITH
Clifford's Tower
TOWER ST.
CROMWELL ROAD
Skeldergate Bridge
FISHERGATE
River Ouse

York

Approaching York from the southwest, one comes on domineering monuments of industry: at **Ferrybridge** a clump of enormous cooling towers, hierarchical, wasp-waisted, and mysterious as primitive goddesses, some wrapped in veils of smoke. Among the sky-eating towers, stony Yorkshire villages and, at **Tadcaster**, a Victorian exuberance of brewery, of fancy ironwork and bulging stone, the curlicued firm name repeated and repeated in snug black and white pub offspring. Robust, careful hay houses line the road in early fall, a pub called THE WILD MAN OF YORK sends out its glowering sign, the usual tattoo of brick rows stops for the hotel-villas on York's Mount and there it is, the resplendent Micklegate, the entrance for kings.

The sky of **York** is stone lace touched with amber. The Minster turns slowly to spread her skirts and flash her medallions of golden window, to show the deep cap of her Chapter House. The fine-spun finials of her towers spring from the height of the city walls and into the splinters of light between hooded houses. The Minster—the Cathedral—is in large degree the history of York.

There was, however, an important York before and after the Minster. In order to push their conquest northward, the Romans, on orders from their emperor, Vespasian, marched a legion up from Lincoln in A.D. 71 to embed themselves where the Foss and Ouse met. This fortress they called Eboracum, through which they drove their roads hemmed in for protection by earthworks, and in the third and fourth centuries by stone walls and towers. It was York which had the honor of building the ceremonial pyre and orating the praises of the emperor Septimius Severus, an ambitious African who had come to do personal battle against the Scots and returned to York to die. It was York, too, which arranged the displays and processionals that accompanied the crowning of Constantine as emperor in 306. After the Roman legions left to shore up the doomed Empire on the Continent, the Angles took over (we are now in the latter half of the sixth century) and, having endured battles by contending local kings, left the field clear for the ninth-century invasion of the Danes, who changed the already transmuted name of the city to Yorwik, a short linguistic step from York. Half a century later, Athelstan, King of Wessex, rid the city of the Danes, but shortly before the Conquest the Norwegians invaded, to be driven out by the Harold who had forsworn the English crown in favor of William, and then changed his mind. Some historians say this battle in York may have been a major contributing factor to Harold's defeat at Hastings, where he rushed to try to hold off the Normans with an exhausted, depleted army.

Through invasion and counter-invasion, the city thrived and was several times its Roman size when William the Conqueror built, over a Danish fortress mound, the castle now known as Clifford's Tower. His Domesday Book, a remarkably thorough document of accountancy designed to list taxable property, shows market stalls, sizable houses, and churches already well established in the city, to be expanded in number and size during the reign of the Conqueror's son, William II (Rufus), and on through the centuries when York functioned as the trade and ecclesiastical center of the north. Here Parliament met early in the fourteenth century, here the mayor was dubbed "Lord Mayor"—a distinction held only by London at the time—by Richard II. Trade with northern Europe created guilds whose halls and houses are sturdy, half-timbered reminders of their prosperity and that prosperity contributed to the rebuilding, enlarging, and adornment of the Minster.

The ecclesiastical city lost a number of its monastic buildings and their hospices in the reign of Henry VIII and, at about the same time, the business city found its European trade usurped by London with its great dock-lined, sea-linked river. The Civil War inflicted further damage on York, and in the eighteenth century, reduced in commercial power, it turned to pleasure. Card playing, theatre going, and racing came into high fashion and for these divertissements the proper buildings had to be erected in the fashionable neo-classical style for assembly rooms and the more amiable Georgian for private houses and the mansions of dignitaries. Trade on a modest, regional scale of local products revived in the nineteenth century, and the city's economy was further bolstered by the opening of railroad lines, accompanied by the tall, broad Victorian buildings that now punctuate the vivid mélange of cityscape.

The city, proud of itself for good reason, offers free tours at 10:15 and 2:15 that take off in front of the newish, devoutly

Georgian library on Museum Street. There is no charge; "our reward is your appreciation of the beauty of this ancient and historic city." By all means take it and later do the city on your own, playing now-you-see-it, now-you-don't with the Minster, which soars out of street corners, hides behind narrowed medieval streets, lifts a sudden diaphanous veil of tower.

It doesn't much matter where you start, you will undoubtedly be carried back in an erratic circle of paths of the Middle Ages that gathered like chicks in the shadow of the mother hen Cathedral. Considerately placing you on your inches of ground, advising where you might find PCs (public conveniences), one of several large street maps lures you, let us say, to Davygate and Blake, with its pedimented, columned, porticoed Assembly Rooms, and the show of the Minster from St. Leonard's Place. Here there might be a marching throng of Mums pushing prams, their older children, one grandfather, and one black man. The ten- and twelve-year olds carry signs: CHEAT THE GRAVE WITH JESUS; JESUS IS ALIVE; YOU NEED JESUS; SMILE—GOD LOVES YOU; JESUS IS THE ANSWER TO YOUR PROBLEMS. Football shouts of "Go, go, go!" soar over the tinkle of tambourines and voices lifted in militant hymns. The straggly, buoyant parade is an invitation to join York's Festival for Jesus, a flurry of the revivalist spirit that has old Nonconformist roots in England, spurred on by the lost young who have put aside the ecstasies of drugs for the transcendental joys of Christ's love. You may meet them elsewhere in the city later, still ecstatic and soundful.

One side of St. Leonard's Place is almost completely occupied by glowering Victorian, stopped by an outdoor café with curly tables and, in glass and concrete, a singular modern coffeeshop-bar-restaurant cluster that borrows from several periods. The attached theatre, which presents ballet, plays Shakespearian, Wildean, and Pinterean, is a gem of mossy green afloat with minute, velvet-clad boxes and the languid, underwater flora of Art Nouveau. Small, limited in its uses, the enclave is a good example of the wedding of the older styles with the new, visible in a number of towns but rarely as successful as it is here.

Another map may guide you to the Merchant Adventurers' Hall, off Piccadilly as it trails into anonymity. This was the guild that was the most potent and richest of all and the memorial it left is one of the most splendid of the buildings that ennobled the city in the fourteenth and fifteenth centuries. The merchant marauders, busy giving their due to Caesar—and getting as well, wresting it when necessary from the shipping magnates of the Hanseatic League—ensured themselves heavenly berths by arranging, below their Great Hall, a hospice for the unlucky of their fraternity and a glowing chapel of stained glass and rich altars to gladden tired hearts and rheumy eyes. Now plain and bleak, it stands as recoil from Papish gaud; the black pews and tables, the thin lines of gilt for lists of benefactions and the Ten Commandments enough decoration for the refugee Huguenot weavers who used the chapel in the seventeenth century. Nor was the hall always the haughty restored structure of lavish space and wood hung with banners one now sees. In its early life it bulged with heaped cloth and ledgers, the noise of voices and feet occupied in the varied transactions of this headquarters for cloth export. The Reformation smashed its windows and demolished its religious adornments; the eighteenth century cut the hall in two and the nineteenth found the steep oak ceiling offensive and covered it; the twentieth century, in love with the Middle Ages, brought back black and white patterns and a serenity the hardworking cloth-mart rarely before enjoyed.

Leaving the long, half-timbered building isolated in its strict patches of garden, Piccadilly turns to the shelter, care, and feeding of automobiles, dragging its garages to the Foss River. Fishergate sends out a spunky dart of light stone wall; a mill stands at the river's edge. On a rise, a dark red Victorian pile and the height and swells of Clifford's Tower, segmented and disturbed. The original was a wooden fortress destroyed, along with the Jews who tried to shelter there, late in the twelfth century and rebuilt in stone in the thirteenth, essentially the building one now sees—a rare extant example of its type. It was once undoubtedly a sturdy fortress but the building faults which cracked its curves, the loss of stone pulled away to make lime, diminution by siege and explosion in successive centuries have left it a fragile museum piece. The stern, neo-classic buildings on which the tower looks are now a museum adapted from early uses as a women's prison and a debtors' prison, both of the eighteenth century.

Early in this century a country doctor named Kirk amassed —often in exchange for his services—a staggering collection of plain-to-captivating "bygones" that run an exhaustive gamut from Edwardian hatpins to prettily crowded shops. Remember that exhaustive is often exhausting as you make your hegira, past silverware from the seventeenth century into the twentieth, into the fresh light of a Georgian room and the severe dark of the Jacobean, toward the hardworking accent of a kitchen on the moors and the high-pitched cacophony of a Victorian parlor. Among the many instruments, sixteen brass weights graded from almost invisible to weightlifter size, primitive but workable thermometers and barometers, early telescopes and cameras.

The flutter of dainty fans stiffens to fan screens worked in an extraordinary range of materials—embossed paper, papier-mâché with and without mother-of-pearl; beaded, fringed, petit-pointed, feathered, straw marquetry—to protect the enameled face from melting in fireplace heat. These live near big-knobbed, long hatpins as long, sharp, and threatening as stilettos and, if you have ever wondered how Edwardian ladies kept their skirts out of puddles, a set of skirt suspenders which gripped the hem and pulled it waistward when the need arose. Still among the ladies' adornments, interesting displays of jet, used as ornaments in Roman times and before. The craft of working fine bits of anthracite was revived early in the nineteenth century in the coastal town of Whitby, whence issued innumerable dim-lustered funereal beads and bracelets and buttons. The industry was spurred on by the death of Prince Albert. In her long mourning, Queen Victoria decreed that lady visitors to the court wear only jet jewelry and jet became, inevitably, classy. The less classy turned their jet into crosses to hang on witch-posts as protection of the house from the evil eye.

Stately rows of hundreds of card cases and scent bottles, of cigar and snuffboxes, sewing cases and arabesques of lace-making bobbins, warm-colored Victorian jewelry and the plump, lacy pop-ups of Victorian valentines.

Don't give up, just move a little more quickly through the sea of sewing accoutrements and march toward the domestic objects of wood to look for a torture instrument like a large, flat wooden bra worn by Victorian girls to keep their shoulders square. We then go to the country to sit at farm hearths surrounded by apple scoops made of sheep's bones, knitting sheaths used by the women—and men—who gathered for

knitting parties on the desolate, sheep-strewn moors, witch
stones, linked love-spoons. Tail-dockers, bird-scarers, hoof-
knives, and other implements of a vigorous farm life are
gathered in a big barn. Lighting and heating must have their
detailed exploration and waffle irons and nutcrackers and butter presses and, and, and . . .

The acme of this mind-storming collection? A neatly cobbled,
orderly street of half-timbered houses and bow-windowed displays. Signs gentle and stentorian signal an apothecary and
his tall stained-glass jars, a cuddly general store-post office
which supplied sperm oil and a viscous fluid called rape oil.
A tobacconist, a purveyor of ornaments; shops that provided
sheet music, books, glass, clocks, saddles and boots, confec-
tionery, china, wines, clothing suitable to ladies and gentlemen,
all meticulously arranged. Some of the shops can be entered
for intimate contact with penny candy and nut-brown beer
kegs. For further verisimilitude, the street fills out with a fire
station, a coaching station, and a stone castle to complete the
inviolable perfection of this town composed of authentic bits
of Yorkshire. And the peaceable, untroubled neatness is a balm
of nostalgia that forgets moor storms and lost, frozen sheep,
crop failures, black, crawling tenements, hysterical ladies who
were early vaporous and later mad, the sullen boys who served
homosexual brothels; here all is serenely respectable and prosperous, triumphant and virtuous.

Military displays, ingeniously arranged in the small rooms
of a Debtors' Prison, reluctantly make room for period habitat
groups: panniered ladies in a Georgian room and a stupendous
Edwardian nursery, where Mummy sits, dressed in luscious
white silk and a white boa, and examines her offspring scien-
tifically through a lorgnette. Flight from porcelain Mummy
returns one in the abundance of Dr. Kirk's cornucopia: a toy
collection (no need to say it is immense and varied), a completely equipped schoolroom, and a collection of fine brocaded
vests, buckles, purses, whalebone stays, and a princely christening set used only by the eldest son of a Yorkshire family old
enough to conduct itself on royal lines.

The enchanted, immutable village reappears as a later avatar,
the late Edwardian which was becoming accustomed to signs
that advertised ELECTRICAL SUPPLIES and BEDS FOR CYCLISTS, a
neighboring cheery brown pub and shops that concern them-

selves mainly with late-nineteenth-century crafts. To recall the prison, a lash and thumb screw, instructive scenes of hangings, and the roughly scratched verses and marks of prisoners.

If it is between April and September you may visit the mill and its ponderous necklace of millstones. Otherwise you might stay to share the ghoulish pleasure of the little boys in the prison cells and emerge once again to the uneasy curves of Clifford's Tower.

Back in the center of town, one "gate" slips into another to reach enterprising Coney Street, a Roman street that led from the Praetorian Gate which stood at what is now St. Helen's Square. On its virile, businesslike progress, Coney (from the old Scandinavian for "King") makes an occasional stop at a vestige of its past. A great clock hangs near a bombed church, and shortly beyond, an archway that frames a building like the shallow-eaved, crenellated porches of wool churches. At one side of the building, a slim buttress, and over the entrance a worn angel and wearied prophets, survivors of the 1942 raid that gutted the fifteenth-century Guildhall. (This was not the first damage it suffered. A fourteenth-century building was torn down because it was too small. The subsequent fifteenth-century hall fared better for city business and less well as a theatre for companies of Elizabethan actors who so inflamed their audiences with hot draughts of intrigue, passions amatory and murderous, and the country matters of clowns that they tore apart benches and smashed doors and windows.) Recent rebuilding brought back a churchlike room of well-proportioned windows, one set with modern glass that tells of the important events and personages that affected and were affected by the city. (The building, in toto, is most effective, incidentally, as seen from across the river.)

Out of the modern-medieval into the graces of the Georgian as the Mansion House (the home of the Lord Mayors), uncertainly attributed to Lord Burlington, connoisseur and amateur architect of the early eighteenth century who designed the engaging, impractical Palladian villa at Chiswick outside London. The York house is less Italian fantasy, a usable house with generous windows and doors held in pilasters and hung with flower baskets. The Judge's House, a few paces away and built somewhat earlier, enjoys a lighter spirit lent it by a

double flight of steps, mask and swag on the door, and white
keystones above the windows. Across the square sits St.
Helen's, in medieval years the guild church of the makers of
stained glass. Another low and smaller church, cowering in the
shadow of an almost life-sized golden ram suspended from the
Golden Fleece pub at the meeting of the Shambles and the
Pavement, lives on the shortest street in York, with the longest
name. It had been Whitnourwhatnour Gate, changed in the
sixteenth century to Whipmawhopgate to suit its function as
whipping place for minor criminals.

Rather apart from the vivacious center, Peasholme Green,
whose Black Swan was the station inn for coaches to and from
London. Nearby, the opening of a forgotten street called Aldwark and St. Anthony's Hall, founded in the fifteenth century
as a Guildhall and recently restored to serve as headquarters
for the local Institute of Historical Research. Aldwark Street
drags its blanks and shards toward a lawn edged with attractive houses in several styles. Major space is allowed the Merchant Taylors' Hall, supervised by an enthusiastic man eager
to show off his charge. It looks like a roomy brick barn comfortably settled into the city wall, its top made festive by the
finials of the Minster. By way of a couple of venerable doors
one enters the vast hall with its ample fireplace, a handsome
medieval ceiling, and a minstrels' gallery. Your host points out
particulars: the great crest of Charles II much in favor with
the Taylors and Drapers and Hosiers who prospered when lavish
dress returned with the Restoration; the wood paneling supplied by an association of New Yorkers; the curious amalgam
of heraldic symbols led off by two camels that adorned the shield
of the Drapers; a glass window which portrays Queen Anne
as a saint among angels.

Chapter House Street, under picturesque clouds of overhang,
introduces the long black and white of St. William's College
and its similar neighbors. This building is a vestige of a covered
way built, with permission of Richard II, to provide protection
for churchmen housed in the area to reach the Minster without molestation from irreverent townspeople. Once attached
to the Minster, the college lost its function with the Reformation and turned to various uses; for a half year in 1642 Charles
I kept a printing press here, apparently for the dissemination
of fruitless propaganda. Like numerous historic halls, St. Wil-

liam's College can be hired for dinner parties, meetings, weddings, and thus it is not always possible to see the interior, except for the small, cobbled courtyard and its hundred blinking window panes. On then, possibly, by way of the attractive rows on College Street and Minster Yard, to the Treasurer's House, as near a stately home as York can show in its immediate environs. Changed and changed again and again since it was the house of the properties and monies functionary under the first Norman archbishop, it is now a museum whose strength is an extensive collection of eighteenth-century glass, much of it lovely.

Less stately pleasures sing through the air around the big riverside pubs and small warehouses of King's Staith, under the Ouse Bridge, where the revivalists are now clapping and singing and shaking their tambourines as punctuation to the breathy exhortation of their leader to "Come with Me to That Land." From the bridge, about to enter the long S-curve of Micklegate, one is still aware of the banners of the Minster flying above, but more sharply aware of the modernity of the Viking Hotel on the river and an art center housed in a defunct church. The Micklegate route stops shortly at a street named for George Hudson, a nineteenth-century tycoon who was three times Lord Mayor of York and a major power in the frenetic development of railroads. When his over-extended empire collapsed in 1849, the street name was changed to "Railway" to obliterate his memory. All was forgiven in 1971, one hundred years after his death, when the street again became his. Nearby, another reminder of railroad might, the railroad station. As seen from the stretch of city wall at Station Road, it is a marvel of late-nineteenth-century industrial style—truly a style —both indomitable and fanciful: a ballooning of iron curves, shallow, deeper, and deeper still, to make three immense multi-stranded arches superbly held in yellow wall. In the same area, led off by Victorian tenements and an old roundhouse, sits the Railway Museum, a lustrous display of bygones brought to life by the awe of visiting boys and the enthusiasm of their railroad-buff fathers.

It promised so much and accomplished so much for English industry and finance that the railroad became an object of veneration and every detail a carefully wrought votive offering. The signs for WORKS and OFFICES of nobly lettered bronze com-

memorated rather than simply indicated. And surely the shining giants of steam-driven cylinders and pistons used in repair
yards early in the nineteenth century were shaped for worship,
as were the wonderful wheels and great cogs—the bolts like
royal heads, the valves like scepters—which pulled wagons
of limestone up a steep incline in 1833. The Titan inventors
and innovators look down on an early railroad carriage, still
a coach, whose comfortable middle section was reserved for
first-class passengers while the vulnerable ends bounced the
less affluent. Among the models of parts, a warrior line of
signal rods, trumpeting ironwork on struts, supports, and rails,
and broadsides of rules—ALL COALS TO BE PAID FOR ON DELIVERY—
surrounded by emblems, medallions, and Jubilee china stamped
with the dark seaweed of full-bearded heads. The apogee, the
culminating triumph of science and decoration, of meticulous
workmanship, high polish, and celebration, were the splendidly
garbed historic locomotives with resounding names, their bi-
ographies as public and closely followed as that of music-hall
stars. The famous "Gladstone" of warm buff and red with decorative flourishes wraps up antique glamour and nostalgia.
It was presented to the museum by the Stephenson Locomotive Society, one group of a growing number who spend their
weekends refurbishing old steam beauties, buying a few miles
of abandoned track on which to run them. To these men, the
men and their sons in the museum, and maybe to you, the
steam engine reappears as the most romantic of man-made
animals, promising, threatening, unconquerably wreathed in
swirling white vapor—dragon, horse, and St. George in one.

Like most cities laced through by a river, York divides into
two communities. This side of the Ouse, toward and beyond
Micklegate Bar (Gate), is more passive, softer-toned than the
city that surrounds the Minster. Set back deeply from Micklegate, across from a Georgian row that serves as part of the
university, the Church of the Holy Trinity Micklegate, the remains of a Benedictine Priory and host (if they haven't been
whipped off to the omnivorous Castle Museum) to a set of
stocks; five for two pair of legs and a single—no explanation
offered. Nearby, crusty St. Martin's Micklegate crouches like
an old gray beast under its cover of trees and, soon, the full
stop at Micklegate Bar itself. Gemmed with brilliant shields,
gargoyles, and figures, it is more imposing than the other gate-

ways, more majestic and more forbidding when one considers that high on its white stone, the architectural details were often the heads of political losers. Shakespeare mentions the head of Richard, Duke of York, hanging in 1460 on "York's gates," specifically Micklegate. One result of the Battle of Culloden in 1746 was a garland of Jacobite heads, two of the dessicated ornaments remaining for seven years and then removed by theft.

Off the Bar and toward the station, Toft Green, once covered with Roman mosaic floors, and, in the last century, host to Dickens, who stayed in a local hotel when he came to read for the people of York. Midway between the Romans and the Victorians, in medieval times, the Green was a storage place for pageant wagons (hence the alternate name "Pageant Green") where the guild actors gathered, argued, worried, swore, mumbled their lines, greased their wagon wheels, and finally got the show of mystery plays on the road. As you may know, "mystery" derives from an old form of the French "métier," and refers to the fact that the plays were performed by members of trades. They were based mainly on biblical themes and re-enacted on Corpus Christi Day in June. They are still occasionally given, in abbreviated form and stationary manner, at the evocative ruins of St. Mary's Abbey. In the mid-fourteenth century the cycle incorporated forty-eight plays, a larger number than those of Coventry and almost twice as many as those played in Chester, the two close rivals for vivacity and splendor of presentation. The York plays were performed in twelve places, beginning at dawn at the entrance to Holy Trinity Micklegate, where visiting royalty had seats of honor. On to the doorways of great merchants, then to the Minster gates, to market place and crowded popular corners, finishing at night at the Pavement. Like the Palio in Siena, they were a year's cooperate occupation which melded the interdependent members of guilds more closely. Although props and costumes were casual and haphazard at times, certain traditional personae took on strictly traditional garb and these had to be especially made and refurbished. The women, who didn't perform, contributed their services as cleaners, cooks, bakers, porters of great dishes of food, and decorators of the street, unfurling the gaudiest cloths to hang from their windows. Their husbands, the master bakers, might become portly, resplendent

Magi while their apprentices played astonished shepherds. To the cordwainers, possibly, went the distinction of entering into Jerusalem, and the merriest, most extrovert of the bucklers might play the lead role of Herod, a comic gnasher of teeth, a roarer and sometimes wit, the ancestor of Shakespeare's jesters, gravediggers, gatekeepers, Andrew Aguecheeks and Toby Belches, orating in the alliterations and caesuras left by Anglo-Saxon verse.

One of the stops might easily have been at the chunks of medievalism that adjoin the library, which doubles as tourist information center. At its side, edged by the ruin, a park-museum-ancient abbey compendium approachable in several ways. Try it by way of the river, glancing as you go at the lion of a Victorian fountain placed there by a private citizen in the hope that it might be "of advantage to working men, promote their morality and be the means of perhaps keeping them out of public houses in the summer season." (There is no record of a notable diminution in the number of pubs.) You go on, following signs that offer short river cruises, and turn into the treed river walk, lined with benches, backed by gardens, and inhabited by dogs and fishermen. Iron gates invite to a good-looking, half-timbered house resting on creamy blocks, one branch of the Yorkshire Museum. It is the Hospitium, the guest house of St. Mary's Abbey, whose brittle ruins stand on the slope above. Relic of the leading Benedictine abbey in northern England, the villa for princely ecclesiasts, the Hospitium, given back its fifteenth-century guise, now devotes white, white walls and sturdy black beams to local Roman finds. These are extraordinarily varied, indicating a diversely populated Roman city and lending enthusiastic purpose to the excavations going on at the Minster, near Gillygate, and almost anywhere archeologists choose to scratch in the treasure-laden York earth.

Vestiges of perfume vials, vases, amphorae, altars, ribs of a parasol, bits of casket, surgical instruments, keys, game counters, jewelry and combs, pottery as ornament and vessels (many found under the railroad yards in 1874), female ogres who glowered from building façades, in the Etruscan style. The villas of governors and merchants left mosaic floor tiles worked in the Roman conventions of geometric and floral patterns interlacing urns, masks, and the faces of gods. And since even the indomitable Romans could not conquer death, a good number of funerary objects: the cast of a woman buried with her ornaments, another who took with her only her child; tombs covered with brick, tombs covered with stamped tiles like those still used on Tuscan roofs. From the hand of a master stonemason a stele of a woman and child. Cruder hands produced family groups looking out of balconies into the world of the dead, or companionable couples—again in the Etruscan style—seated on couches, and all similarly ornamented. The group makes an interesting example of the rough quality of the work of artisans very far from the source of models and inspiration, themselves not necessarily Roman—shipped with legions of Gauls and Teutons—and working from copies of copies.

The showy Romans flash some of their goods, too much for the Hospitium, in the main section of the Yorkshire Museum, an enterprising place with an eventful miscellany housed in a neo-classical building that climaxes a slope of tall, spreading trees. It opens with a wide range of booklets and books that deal with aspects of the local history and the reproductions of seals, coins, and jewelry found under local streets. The glories of medieval years are quoted as discolored, scratched, mutilated yet superb alabaster carvings found in recent years under Peasholme Green. Moving back in time, a 1200's chess set (a number of the pieces found as late as 1972), English jewelry, and the sophisticated Ormside bowl of the eighth century.

The irrepressible Middle Ages shoves aside the fossils—one of an icthysaurus who dragged his monumental bulk across Yorkshire moors—stuffed birds, and habitat groups of "Natural History" to give prominence to its gargoyles, and a tympanum from an old version of the Minster that depicts one team of devils holding a corpse while another team pulls out his soul, a miniature body—one of the numerous delectable and educational medieval renderings of the torments of Hell. Soon, amid the mélange (an energetic committee will undoubtedly be driven, one time or another, to setting it all chronologically straight, which would be too bad), the ubiquitous Romans reappear to revive imperial life in their documentary manner: a stele for a bearded armorer bearing into immortality his hammer and tongs, and another for a soldier

and his family. Closer to common life, bits of well-woven stock-
ing, brooches, beguiling animal toys, and firmly laced sandals
that were found, appropriately, in Tanner Row. A goldsmith's
sign with a prayer for good luck added to the identifying
inscription, a segment of painted wall and, inevitably, a relief
of Mithras (found at Micklegate) in his Phrygian cap, grasping
his twisting, sacrificial bull.

The multi-aged, multi-branched museum continues on clearly
marked park paths to a many-angled tower whose base was
part of a Roman fortress. Below the rough semicircle of
wall, crude hog-backed coffins; off to a side, a square Anglian
tower of the seventh century; and toward the library, the
cryptlike ruins of what was, in the Middle Ages, the extensive
St. Leonard's Hospital, a portmanteau word that encompassed
a place for medical treatment, aspects of almshouse, and shelter for ordinary pilgrims. Probably time for a rest now. For
that, a return to the combination of abbey ruins, classical museum columns, and green domes of tree to observe York's boys
using the grounds as little boys do—tottering along ridges of
ancient stone, shooting each other from the ditches and fur-
rows of ruins, making of decrepit St. Mary's Abbey the perilous
cliffs and shot-torn mesas of American westerns. Their dogs
grow frenzied, dash into the line of fire, and have to be raced
on the green, their lolling tongues and the boys' red cheeks
spraying color on the gray autumnal air.

The headless abbey enfolds a perfect house, St. Mary's Lodge,
the eleventh-century gargoyles of St. Olave's Church, and continues as the buttressed wall and turret that are Marygate.
Turning right at a gardened patch below the wall—many cities
have the pleasant habit of filling time's vacuums with flowers—
one reaches Bootham Gate and the Art Gallery. Like a good
number of regional art galleries, it is a teaching institution
presenting examples of important art periods and styles ranging from Oriental porcelain and jade to early Italian, Renaissance and Mannerist, and the Dutch, pausing for concentration
on English painting, with particular emphasis on the works
of a native son, William Etty, whom you have met at the fountain below. He worked here early in the nineteenth century,
creating within the confines of his time allegorical giants and
tragic portraits with pearly tears trembling on alabaster cheeks,

but also breaking loose in fruity still lifes and, as ripe and succulent, several unexpected female nudes.

The gallery can also be reached by a walk from the museum park by way of an extensive Tudor unit that is now part of the University of York. Not all of it is viewable, but one can, at least, wander through the meshwork of courts to examine the carved doorways surmounted by shields and observe again the reasoned manipulation of the old to serve the new. This King's Manor, expanded several times into the seventeenth century and its Baroque mannerisms, originally housed the abbot of St. Mary's and later the head of the King's Council in the north. It was in their time that staggering doorways were carved (as, for instance, to show off two lions, two busty ladies, and mammary fruits) and hung with the noblest shields, one bearing the arms of Charles I, who stayed for a few weeks while the Civil War that ended him was brewing.

In several ways Bootham Bar gives you quintessential York. The turreted gateway surmounted by guardian figures spills an open medieval stairway; its horizon is a filigree of Minster spires and tower arches. At the top of the stairs the crisscross bite of a raised portcullis, and below, a base of Roman wall supporting the reconstructed medieval path you will soon walk. First, a nod at the ghost of a Scotsman who cannot make the walk with you. Dressed in sixteenth-century woolens, he must ask permission to enter the city and once admitted, is prevented by the townspeople, as his ancestors were, from holding office or sitting on councils. Why Scotsman? Probably it had something to do with the suspicion that three Scotsmen might proliferate overnight into a marauding army. Dispel the ghost and take off on one of the most delightful city walks in all England.

One looks down through battlements on houses and gardens neat and wild, on red brick derelicts and the waste that grows in their yards, on tattoos of chimneys, on long lawns and clouds of trees, and—now a glimpse, now standing in full display—the unfolding faces of Minster and Chapter House. As you angle into the Lord Mayor's Walk toward Monkgate, you may hear a flute and soon the voices of French (or German or Italian) students carried away, like you, by the urban lyricism, especially moving on an autumn afternoon when shadows cut fantasy shapes and the yellowing leaves are pulled and blown from the trees by the brisk Yorkshire wind.

Watch out on the dark, eroded stairs of Monkgate. And now where? Old houses in the vicinity? Down Goodramgate and into the glittering medieval and Georgian Streets? Or, surely, it is time for the Minster, the rival in ecclesiastical power to Canterbury and of its own a compendium of English cathedral architecture, encompassing Norman, thirteenth- , fourteenth- , and fifteenth-century changes of style. Not every part of the Minster can be examined closely; screens of scaffolding hide areas in revival. Supporting, replacing, painting, and cleaning have been going on since 1967 at an impressive cost shared by Yorkshiremen and art and cathedral lovers of the world. It is difficult to follow, nor should one insist on, strict chronology in such an amalgam of periods and styles; but the absolute beginning might be the Roman column outside that pins down the plastic covers of excavation ditches and marks a central point of the Roman fortress on which the Minster rose. (The word "minster" means, as you probably know, a convocation of priests, primarily interested in sending missions to the Anglo-Saxons, and the name stayed although York is a cathedral, the place of the bishop's seat—cathedra—the place for major church ceremonials and meetings and now the primary representative of the Church of England in the north.)

There is no record of the first church, which may have been a chapel in a private house, and it may have been from that place that a bishop left to attend Constantine's Council of Arles in 314 which established Christianity as the official religion of his Empire. Three centuries later Edwin, King of Northumbria, an unconvinced far place, built a small church after persuasion by his wife, a princess from the enlightened lands to the south. Made of wood, the church soon decayed, was rebuilt, and then succumbed to the Normans. Their bishop built another minster in the twelfth century; that was rebuilt and the church continued to follow the history of important cathedrals which managed to grow in spite of halts, disasters, and struggles for supremacy, York entangled and wrestling especially with powerful Canterbury.

The latest important change, a product of York's attachment to her past and of her present healthy pride, was the creation

of a stimulating passage through the history of the city and
the Minster in the Undercroft. Through low, well-shaped, and
studded walls bearing informative legends, stopping for concrete testaments of the past, one is moved into Roman times—
heads of the clever, troubled, aristocratic Hadrian and of the
bullet stubbornness of Septimius Severus, and a strange, doughy
head of Constantine, which stares blankly at the section of fortress below the Minster; a stretch of painted wall, an unbeauti-
ful local goddess, Brigantia, added to the permissive Roman
pantheon. The adroit gallery leads up, down, to make tight
angles and coils of space appear roomy enough for a leisured
review of centuries. It hesitates at the ebb and flow of ninth-
century Danish invasion, which left as a mark the many "gates"
of street names, then shortly takes us to an early configuration
of the Minster and the arts it inspired in stone and ivory and
wood. A reproduction of the semi-destroyed and still effective
famous York "Virgin with Child" sits in the stiff, strong folds
of Byzantine holiness, and we are introduced to the learned
Alcuin and the Venerable Bede, whose *History of the English
Church and People* is considered the first English book.

The douceurs of saintliness and the monkish scholarly are
shattered in a *mea culpa* review of York's treatment of its large
medieval colony of Jews. The early years were easy. William
the Conqueror, a practical man in need of people who had a
long, international experience of finance (other fields closed to
them) and free of the Christian interdict against moneylending,
welcomed a group of Jews from Rouen to England. The financial dependence of early kings on the Jews gave them legal
rights in exchange for substantial percentages of their negotia-
tions. The anti-Church William Rufus so cherished his helpful
Jews that he forced a few converts to return to Judaism and,
grabbing Church property wherever he could, turned it over
to the Jews so that they might increase its value for him. The
climate changed during the Crusades, when Christian fervor
was whipped up against the Infidel, a term which included
the Jew, now burdened with the charge, originally leveled at
Mohammedans, that the blood of Christians was used in their
obscene, pagan rituals. Norwich was the first to make the
Blood Accusation: the little boy kidnapped, tortured, and killed,
his blood used for the Passover celebration, his place assured
among the saints. The fact that high churchmen were skep-

tical, that local officials, as officers of the king, tried to protect
the Jews, quenched no anti-Semitic flames. It happened at Winchester, at Gloucester, at Lincoln, and most brutally in York,
in 1189–90, while Richard was off on the Crusades and no royal
threat held back lawless hands. The massacre began with the
murder of the widow, children, and friends of a prominent Jew
who had died of a beating received during an anti-Jewish uprising that accompanied Richard's coronation in London. His
house was sacked and burned and then another, and many
Jews soon left their houses to the mob for shelter in the castle.
Those who were slow were murdered in their homes. The governor in charge of the castle left it for a day and the frightened
refugees, suspicious of his purpose, would not readmit him.
The governor called for the sheriff and with him came an
army sharpened for the kill. The sheriff, worried about the
forces he had unleashed, tried to hold back the mob, but it
continued the attack, spurred on by Church zealots. Without
arms, without food, and with no hope for aid, the Jews decided to repeat the act of their ancestors at Masada under
Roman siege. With a few exceptions, the heads of families
killed their wives and children, then each other, and the last
himself. The survivors, who were promised their lives if they
submitted to baptism, were slaughtered as they emerged. Now
to the core of the matter: money. Led by barons from York
and other areas in the north, the crowd dashed to the Minster
where it destroyed the records of large debts owed the Jews
by Church, barons, and princes. However, the canny accountants of the king had kept duplicate records and the vanished
debts reappeared in ensuing years to be collected by the king,
by decree and custom the sole inheritor of the properties and
debts owed to dead usurers. The massacre is remembered in
the Hebrew liturgy. As an elegy for the Martyrs of York, it calls
down malediction on "the King of the Isles (under) whose garments is found the lifeblood of innocent souls," and on England, "Let there be no dew or rain on the land of the Isle..."

Having made its apologies, the Undercroft Gallery turns to
the enchanted world of medieval illumination inhabited by
busy plóughmen, vintners, and butchers, and then propels us
toward a brightly lit box that encloses the treasury, depleted
by a nineteenth-century fire which spared the enormous carved
ivory Horn of Ulf presented by a relative of King Canute to

the Minster at the opening of the eleventh century and an early-fifteenth-century bowl of silver set into maple that bears the arms of the Cordwainers Guild. A row of masterly medieval figures welcomes one back to the stream of York events and simultaneous happenings on the Continent. Finally, a set of photographs deals with recent repairs and renovation, stimulated by the cracking and shifting of walls. Unrepaired age and weather had done some of the damage, greatly abetted by the traffic that bounds and thumps too close, now, to a number of these vulnerable giants.

Like all immense old cathedrals, the Minster is overwhelming and confusing. Give it time, and if your approach to such matters is orderly, follow one of the booklets in ample supply at the bookshops in and around the church. A reasonable beginning may be to find a verger or a gray-clad, fresh-faced young sister, unexpectedly stationed near a central pillar, either of whom holds the keys to the crypt. Under low arches, among strongly scored columns, you will find the original of the eleventh-century "Virgin with Child," both beheaded by the Reformation, and a swarm of shrieking, naked little ogres cupped in a design of three monstrous faces on the Gates of Hell. This Doom Stone probably stood outside the Norman church, balanced by a Gates of Paradise stone, altogether gone. Whether you do the rest of your exploring methodically or not, try not to miss a group of earthy wall carvings that stand in the light of stained glass of several centuries from the twelfth onward. Become acquainted with imagined portraits of early English kings, sworded, sceptered, and enriched in the late-fifteenth-century choir screen. See if you can detect changes in architectural style and pick out the monuments actually designed by Grinling Gibbons. The Chapter House, as usual, is the most admirable single unit, a drapery of finely carved stone supporting long lancets and roundels of glass. The house lacks the common central support and how this great hive of stone and glass was designed is demonstrated by a model that is a fascinating example of fourteenth-century engineering genius, that word not excessive for the audacious inventiveness of Gothic builders.

The Petergates, Low and High, clasp the hand of Stonegate on one side, that of Goodramgate on the other, and that in turn holds onto Coney and the Shambles, a pleasurable ring-

around-the-rosy for souvenirs, antiques, silver, rare books, and
pottery, and Georgian and medieval houses. Low Petergate
likes glistening, fatty butcher shops, which seem to have moved
from the "flesh stalls" of the Shambles. Where it is High, at its
meeting with Minster Gates, it marks its ancestry as a central
Roman street with a Minerva in a gold helmet, a white owl
cowering in a fold of her ample blue skirt. Her chunky arms
rest on a pile of books to prove that centuries later she
supervised the wisdom flowing from the Bookbinders' Alley,
which once poured books and the scents of glue and leather
into the street. Minster Gates—once literally that—has barred
traffic and so has Stonegate, the Roman via Praetoria, where,
in the early nineteenth century, the curious head of Constantine was found, buried among huddled, bowing building. A
sign on Stonegate points to a Norman shard of house in an
alley; another advertises, in a sign that joins both sides of the
street, YE OLDE STARRE INN; a couple of distinguished bookshops
are reminders of a press that functioned here as early as 1500
and of the well-stocked bookstalls of Elizabethan times.

The Shambles (once Fleshhammels) and its tangent market
still look pretty much as they must have in the fifteenth century, except for the present freshness—the walks free of run-
nels of blood and the thick, sweet, and rusty smell of abbattoir
aired out of the houses that sway toward each other, almost
meeting overhead. Neither dirty or rowdy enough to be authentically medieval, the Shambles is still one of the best examples of market in the Middle Ages and, as such, proudly
painted, polished, and hung with shining shops and festooned
with flowers. Saturday is the best day for jostling and being
jostled, for bumping among bundles, inhaling the scent of
onions and apples, being pounded by hearty Yorkshire voices
in the market tied to the Shambles. But try to go back at a
non-market hour to walk among the furled stall covers and
trace the lines of roofs—steep, shallow, timbered, and brick—
that close harmoniously on the long rectangle to make a distinguished outdoor room.

Intimacy with York's gems, formal and informal, major and
minor, should include a survey of rose-cheeked babies sleeping outside Mum's friendly neighborhood pub; standing in a
supermarket queue with bouncy, joking, robust, "luv"-cooing
working-class women; tea among their more refeened lower-

middle-class aunts in stiff, chimneypiece hats. One York day should culminate in the assault of dramatized history of the Minster's "Son et Lumière" and a walk in a diadem of illuminations from the Minster through the Shambles, washing over the Georgian mansions near St. Helen's, caught in the lantern of a central church. Then return to your hotel television lounge and notice, as your group dwindles toward bedtime, the Yorkshire generosity and impromptu hospitality proffered as a box of sweets: "Coom on, please, luv; they're good, luv." Or insistence that you share a pack of cigarettes, which come high in England, or take a better viewing spot, eagerly offered, not to be gainsaid, and interlarded with "luv" and again "luv," a sound as automatic as breathing. No one with a balanced mind and psyche would mistake the repetition as adoration from the lady at the supermarket checkout counter, from the apple vendor in the market, the policeman giving directions, a taxi driver, a ticket-seller at the railway station, or the transplanted Italian who sells ice cream, but myriad blossoms of "luv" make a cordial field in a warm climate, no matter how the wind may blow and the needles of rain pierce.

NOTES

Merchant Adventurers' Hall: weekdays, 10:00 to 12:30 and 2:00 to 5:30 (winter closing 4:00).
Yorkshire Museum: 10:00 to 5:00; Sundays, 1:00 to 5:00.
Castle Museum (includes the Kirk Collection): 9:30 to 7:30; Sundays, 10:00 to 7:30 (winter closing 4:30).
York Art Gallery: 10:00 to 5:00; Sundays, 2:30 to 5:00.
Treasurer's House: 11:00 to 7:00; closed November to March.
Guildhall: weekdays only, May to October, 9:00 to 5:00.
Railway Museum: 10:00 to 5:00; Sundays, March to September only.
Merchant Taylors' Hall: weekdays only, 10:00 to 5:00.

HOTELS:
High-moderate to expensive—the large, modern, and airy Viking, on the river; the Post House, more "American," a short distance out of town, adjoining the race track.

Moderate—several converted villas on the Mount (outside Micklegate), among them Abbey Park, Mount Royale, and Elm Park, the last once the home of a prosperous miller who caused his house to be emblazoned with Pre-Raphaelite glass panels and touches of Art Nouveau, still (one hopes) to be seen. In the center of town, at approximately the same rates, the White Swan on Piccadilly; and, for a bit more, the Dean Court Hotel near the Minster, and the Royal Station.

Modest to moderate—the small Galtries Lodge on Low Petergate, the Halfmoon on Blake, and "Bed and Breakfasts" near Bootham Bar.

RESTAURANTS: Eating is highish at the leading hotels, a bit less at Le Girondin on High Petergate; less expensive at Terry's on St. Helen's Square, and in the bars named for Dickens characters in the Tavern on the Town on Church Lane; a similar enclave outside Micklegate Bar. Ask the young at hotel desks for recommended Chinese and Indian restaurants. For salads, omelettes, sandwiches, try the polite Trianon on Micklegate. Hamburger and snack shops all over, some of them rather dim-spirited and few of them open on Sunday. You might prepare for Sunday by Saturday shopping in the delicatessen attached to Terry's and at a bakery buy a chunk of parkin, a grainy oat and ginger cake, very toothsome and filling. All else failing, remember that the Chinese and the sweetshops near Bootham Bar and Monkgate work on Sundays.

If you're running out of reading matter, go to Ken Spelman on Micklegate, near the Bar, where you can buy—or could —four used paperbacks for 15 pence. For antiques, the streets near the Minster—Petergates, Stonegate, Shambles, et al.—and the plainer shops approaching the Mount and, again, Bootham Bar, almost as useful and busy now as it was in Georgian times, when it was inhabited by the noisiest, toughest cockpit in town.

Yorkshire Rides

The departure northward toward **Slingsby** is a hilly, wooded road into distant swells of moor above rolling country that takes kindly to farming on large estates, riding, and the hunt. Slingsby unfolds to **Hovingham,** of yellowish, plump, coarse bricks; then into undulating fields and copses that slip into **Helmsley,** a large market town that swells on Fridays, around its market cross, in and out of the Black Swan Hotel and the doors of its stone houses, as sturdy as Yorkshire girls and ponies. At this point the map will indicate that you have come out of the East Riding into the North Riding. There is a West Riding but no South, except as the title of a memorable old film. The explanation is simple: "riding" means "third," a convenient means to divide so large a county.

A short distance out on the Stokesley road, the ruined grandeur of **Rievaulx** (pronounced Reevo) **Abbey,** its tall arches filled with sky, ornaments clinging to unused entrances, vestiges of church, cloisters, dormitories, kitchens, and meeting halls sketched in crumbled stone. The abbey, now rather like a pierced, folded Gothic screen, was the first Cistercian abbey in England, founded early in the twelfth century. The Cistercians were enthusiastic builders and by the late twelfth century had erected the vast abbey in their French style, large enough to house over six hundred men. Shortly after additions to the church were erected in the thirteenth century, the fortunes of the abbey collapsed. Some of the service buildings were demolished and by the time of the Dissolution there was only a handful of monks to dissolve. Enough stands against dense dark trees to suggest what once must have been remarkable might and beauty, in no way diminished by use of the grounds and stones as an adventure playground by visiting children. For those too small or bored with scrambling over and around piles of big churchly bricks there is a swing and the protection of a KEEP OUT sign which, incorporated with the abbey in your camera, makes a stimulating photo and gives you another chance to notice how untroubled and open the faces of English children are, and how vulnerable.

Rievaulx has among its distinctions a lack of tea, a less serious fault to you than it is to many fellow visitors. You may hear disconsolate complaints, breathy with politeness and

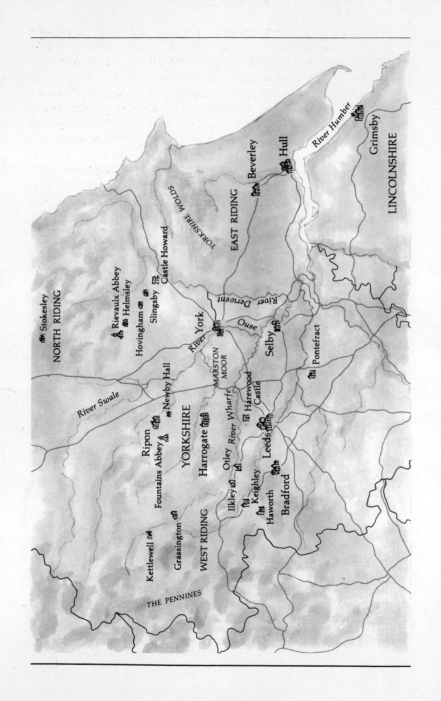

desperation, in the local vowels, elisions, and lilt; variations of "I was wantin' a coop o' tea. There ain't noothin'. 'E was foolin' us was our Graham," and in spite of the indignation, a hopeful lift on the last syllable of the name.

Below Rievaulx, the Yorkshire moors (or dales, as they are also termed) spread their endless fields and coarse shrubbery into the misty mounds on the horizon. Toward **Stokesley**, the road hugs long, low walls, skirts stone villages burrowed into their earth, silken fields held in clumps of trees, thousands on thousands of sheep, signposts to places like **Fangdale Beck**, which has a sound of Beowulf, names that end in "kirk," suggesting a continuity with Scotland not very far to the north. On a clear day the viewing point five or six miles below Stokesley fans out on a quiet, motionless world dotted by confetti of grazing sheep. Should it be raining, the landscape turns to Oriental paintings of clouded hills fading into the distance.

Due east of York, **Beverley** Minster. It shares, roughly, the history of other such churches—dedication to a seventh-century bishop-saint, royal support from the tenth-century King Athelstan, expansion through medieval centuries, and ceaseless restoration thereafter. Not everything you see will be authentically of its time, but most of it has been redone carefully to suit the fifteenth-century gaiety embroidered into sober walls and arches of the thirteenth. It is a light and joyous place, a gold mine of giggling, engaging detail: the run of stairs sheltered by playful arches and slender columns, the side of the choir and the stone figures and misericords that are full of grace, skill, and laughter. One stonemason may have been a musician as well, or simply a lover of music and its instruments. He made it his task to parade a row of musicians pounding on small drums, blowing on bagpipes, pulling bows across fiddles, tootling into pipes, along a section of north aisle low enough to be examined and his technique admired. Across the nave from the orchestra saintly old men and sly old men, gentle old ladies and sisters of Reynard, very foxy. It all shapes a jammed, noisy, medieval fair of characters from *fabliaux*, from biblical stories, from mystery plays, from neighbors and relatives observed with sharp, amused eyes.

The folk fair marches toward the misericords. Turn them up for a mocking fox in friar's clothes preaching at a group of geese. Two roundels under another seat show scenes of hardworking domestic life and an explosion of domestic temper as a woman pulls at her husband's hair, swinging her free arm out to belt him one, too absorbed to notice that the dog is eating their dinner. These and vivid hunting scenes, snapshots of medieval work and amusement, and yet again musicians (here as pig harpists and pig bagpipe players) are not only ornamental but informative documents of medieval costume, implements, and musical instruments and the matter that made folk stories and jokes.

Wherever there are arches that support, or meet, or frame, look for bosses of a steady quality of excellence. Notice how cleverly a buck-toothed ogre turns into a plant, and a luxuriance of humans, animals, and leaves shapes a fine filigree ball to grace an angular joining of ribs.

Even older than the Norman font is the crude chair used by the authorities who investigated claims to sanctuary. Sanctuary rights were granted the Minster in the tenth century and hundreds of malefactors sought its safety until Henry and his Reformation put a stop to a privilege that cast shadows on the power of his courts. The chair is an imposing, grim old entity, sagging with history. For quintessential matter of Beverley, though—the dancing lines, the restless flow and billow of small spaces exuberantly filled with flamboyance—one turns to the Percy tomb of angels, leaves and fruits, bearded heads, crowns, grotesques, and the innumerable shields appropriate to the contentious great Northumberlands, the family of that northern Mercutio, Hotspur.

Depending on time and inclination, one can search out on the detailed map rugged moors and a region that glories in the name of Blubberhouses and proceed northward along country roads, riding with big, well-kept Mobile Library trucks. They may stop at Stump Cross Caverns, which hangs out varicolored sheepskins for sale, or a decaying farm community, or the Miners' Arms which looks on a quarry and its scatter of company cottages. At **Sawley,** a sign to Fountains Abbey, though you may not be ready for monumental ruins just yet. Head for **Ilkley,** a zesty town with a wide winding High Street, whose honest food shops, filled with wheels of meat pie and mounds of cheese, sweat a little, like a fat man who has eaten too much, under their low ceilings.

Ilkley's Manor House Museum and All Saints' parish church sits above the River Wharfe, on a Roman fort established by Agricola. The much-handled church is largely nineteenth-century reconstruction of fifteenth-century use of Roman stones. Other than the building material, which includes Roman altars at the base of the tower and sections of medieval wall, the significances of the church are the three Anglo-Saxon crosses (with a touch of Viking, some authorities say) that stand in the churchyard. They were carved and placed between the end of the eighth and ninth centuries. One theory has it that they were teaching crosses to bring the Gospel to Angles and the invading pagan Vikings; another has it that they were memorials, brightly painted and adorned with glittering stones, to act as tombstones for important personages. Whatever, they are rare examples of the patterns and symbols, badly worn yet showing considerable craftsmanship, that frightened or moved to devotion the Englishman of a thousand years ago.

The Manor House, revived Elizabethan on medieval on Roman foundations, is the town museum and cultural center for exhibitions of local arts and crafts and concerts. As museum, it is modest, concentrating on several periods in its history. Of the prehistoric Yorkshireman, many flints produced by the earliest factories and examples of the mysterious circle and cup marks etched into stones found on the surrounding moors. The Romans left bits of sharply worked bronze, pottery shards, and carved altar stones, a rather sparse gathering considering that the fortress and surrounding settlement were fairly large and densely populated. There were many more artifacts but the ambitious nineteenth century, determined to make a spa of Ilkley, took away treasures it had exhumed and filled the holes with crushed altar stones. A roomful of Elizabethan furniture, a seventeenth-century fireback, and cut-out fireplace figures of a later time fill out the collection. To these one must add the informative booklet that describes governmental organization under the Angles, and quotes from old records which include the sentencing of two Longfellow ladies, ancestors of the poet, who were ducked in the river for being common scolds or just plain garrulous.

Friday spurs on neighboring **Otley's** waning energies by
gathering its bits and pieces into a flavorful market in a tight
circle of shops and pubs. Parking is always difficult on market
day; you could be trapped between an itinerant truck of
shampoos, detergents, and transistor batteries and a stall of
hard, colorful, slightly musty sweets, but not for too long;
lorry drivers will direct or pull you out. It is the poor market
of a poor town. Consequently, the calls of vendors of apples
and sprouts and tomatoes are urgent, raucous, the shoppers
more restless and wary, as they search among stalls pressed
into darkened, basic houses and butcher shops in carved
wooden frames enclosing shining meat pies of many sizes from
street snack to big family size. After offering the glitter of
heaped junk—a chipped porcelain figurine, a scarred paper-
weight, an orphaned earring—sometimes worth picking
through, as in the junk-antique shops of other towns in the
area, Otley releases you to slag hills and isolated small collieries on the way to **Harrogate.** The mood brightens in sight of
the green-flowered expanses and orderly terraces and crescents
of that city. A skyful of large crowns and cupolas, immense
Victorian eccentricities of hotels, neo-classic Royal Baths, a
large population of carefully dressed elderly ladies, and numerous patches of flowers give the city a contained, old-fashioned,
courtly quality undisturbed by its music and arts festivals or
the fishing and race courses on its outskirts. Take its loops and
turns, shops and houses, stately and fringed feminine, in a
couple of walking hours. Equipped with a map offered by the
Information Centre at the Royal Baths on Parliament Street,
fortified by a cup of coffee from the snack bar in the coffering
and pink-red columns of an assembly hall in the Baths, make
your way along Parliament and its eastward tangents for a
measure of the prosperous shopping under slender arcades,
delicate eaves of Victorian glass, iron tatting, and flower
baskets, reaching an apogee of girlish adornments on James
Street. Cutting into the solid spreads of imported and domestic
foodstuffs and lots of creamy cakes are alleys that bespeak an
older city. At the bottom of the shopping area, a broadening
to Market Hall and the flower-hung Station, signaled by a big
market cross with plump Queen Victoria surrounded by votive
patches of discreet, formal blooms (no roses or dahlias or
anything capable of the gorgeous excesses that strut in plebeian

gardens). Cambridge and James Streets meet at the war memorial cenotaph that leads on to the attractive Montpelier Parade and its old-fashioned elegances of tea shops, a museum-piece sweetshop, and good collections of antiques, prints, and rare books that also flow into the Ginnel, suitably and handsomely housed behind fine shopfronts. The walk might continue out toward streets of well-spaced villas, some now guest-residences, or stop at the art gallery or the small museum that shows local crafts and archeology and, as part of its history, the things Napoleonic prisoners wove of straws and carved of bits of bone to erase the dreary length of their trapped days. Try, also, to visit with the renowned Valley Gardens.

NOTES

HOTELS: The city has a good number of them, several of the most imposing and expensive above the Ripon Road and to the side of Parliament Street. The scale is high for provincial hotels, including the rates of tattered splendors that sit away from the center of town. For more modest accommodations check with the Information Bureau or, if you haven't arranged to take a tour from Harrogate to Castle Howard or picturesque places in the dales or to Fountains Abbey, go on to the undemanding shelters of Ripon—the Unicorn or Spa, perhaps—or bed and breakfast in a guest house.

Depending on the time of day, one visits with **Ripon Cathedral** and then takes off for Fountains Abbey or vice versa; it hardly matters since the distance is negligible and they share a common style.

Ripon Cathedral encloses under its truncated, spireless towers a past replete with medieval grandeurs and corruptions. It owned immense stretches of property, its hierarchs lived like kings in palaces whose parks offered rich hunting. They ruled over rulers, withholding or offering help in disputes with rival Church leaders, as the Archbishop Roger Pont l'Evêque of the twelfth century went to the aid of Henry II in his dispute with that dangerous rival at Canterbury, Thomas Becket. When money was needed for restoration or enhancement of the Church, they could induce the Pope to voice a proclamation granting indulgences and daily Masses for living and departed souls to donors. In the train of these ecclesiastical powers, lesser churchmen who were careless, irreligious, pettily corrupt, those whom Chaucer immortalized as "shiten" shepherds of clean sheep.

As architecture, Ripon Cathedral began its life in the seventh century, shortly thereafter made superb by the powerful Wilfred, head of the Church in Northumbria. One can almost recite the litany: Danish destruction, a Norman church that improved and expanded, towers and spires and a regal west front added in the thirteenth century along with a remade choir; damage by Scottish invaders early in the fourteenth century and that damage repaired and sections added some decades later. Time and indifference pulled down the central tower in 1450 and with it some of the fabric of the church below, the tower never raised to its former height but extensive repairs and changes made later in the fifteenth century. Then came Henry VIII, then Cromwell and repairs to their damage, and so on.

Ripon shows its several styles in telling juxtapositions readily. Looking down the nave toward the choir, one sees twelfth-century round arches of the tower giving on pointed arches of the fifteenth and a cluster of columns raised for an arch that never happened. The ceiling vaults in doughty, unpretentious Norman loom over the fancy-cut work of thirteenth-century Decorated, the style of the large window that showers sudden light into the rather dark church. The Chapter House moves back to the simplicities of immediately post-Conquest times and the crypt to the crudities of St. Wilfred's seventh-century Saxon church. Having admired the general ensemble, one might retrace the passage through the centuries with details that evoke a time more graphically than towers and Gothic frills. The first might be a hole in the wall of the crypt, St. Wilfred's Needle which, legend has it, permitted passage only to the chaste. One can imagine all the women of Ripon, virgin and non, dieting as desperately as movie queens in case they were accused of slipping and brought to the judgment of the inelastic stone.

Alabaster carving, a distinguished English craft, lent itself well to the solemn slenderness, the asceticism of holy figures. For these one should visit the library and look, too, at several fine examples of early illuminated manuscripts and rare examples of early printing. The rhetoric of the eighteenth century —mourning ladies, a well-fed gentleman in a curly wig, breeze-tossed draperies—stands near a lost and lovely piece of abandoned pulpit. Nearer our own day, a hand, meant to beat time and still capable of moving if it must, above the choir.

With a stop for prayer at Ripon, a body of ecclesiasts from York proceeded southward in the sharp Yorkshire autumn of 1132 to establish **Fountains Abbey,** primarily to sever themselves from the rot of easy living that had invaded the former monastery. They were Cistercians, whose head was the powerful reformer Bernard of Clairvaux, the thunderer of anathema on the luxury-loving princes of the Church, the adversary of Abelard. The twelfth-century brothers built simply, in accordance with their vows of poverty, interpreted architecturally as an avoidance of conspicuous ornament—no stained glass, no tower and, because even a little knowledge was a dangerous thing, no college. They were, however, members of a widespread, leading order which had to proclaim itself with austere size and might. They were an industrious group of tillers of the soil and keepers of herds and flocks—the founders, it is said, of the local woolen industry—and, in time, attracted large numbers of lay brothers who complied with the rules of the order but not quite as strictly as the monks. In spite of the shadow of St. Bernard and the vows designed for meekness, there was trouble in the hierarchy and in the ranks: in 1147 much of the abbey and church was severely damaged in a fire set off by monks who wanted an Abbot William as head rather than the opposing Abbot Murdac. Murdac stayed while William was demoted, but the latter was returned to his high office in 1153, to be again demoted, this time permanently, by a dose of poison.

The church was rebuilt almost immediately after the fire and the buildings for sleeping, eating, sickening, dying, storing, buying, selling, and praying were rebuilt shortly after. The massive, extensive ruins sitting at the edge of parklands made neo-classic in the eighteenth century still cast shadows of the arrangement and style of the latter half of the twelfth century, with changes made in the thirteenth to accommodate refugees from those monasteries closed by King John. There are traces of tile of about the same time and, disregarding the founding rules, an ornate window and a tower incorporating the tracery and buttresses of the early sixteenth century.

The roofless great church (startling and mysterious in summer night illumination) still tells its shape and purpose in monumental columns that free semicircular arches and, at the other side of the nave, pointed arches which are among the oldest of their type in England. The choir of the church relaxes to the restrained decoration of a set of narrow windows edged with frames held in clusters of stone buttons and wriggles of scallops. The most aesthetically satisfying area of the abbey is the thirteenth-century Chapel of the Nine Altars, a delicacy of slender pillars, rings and rows of stone buttons to limit subtly pointed arches, and a friendliness of horizontal scribbles. Handsome, continuous arcs; low, solid, receding semicircles; troughs for hand washing, and the remains of seating ledge, still clearly describe cloisters. It is other bulks of stone that require some support from the imagination. The peaked piles near the twelfth-century bridge over the River Skell housed pilgrims and guests. Across the bridge, the infirmary, a sketchy thing, and attached to that a meager wall with low, small openings, the rere-dorter which supplied basic sanitation, and beyond that, the extraordinary many-vaulted long cellarium. If this was storage space, as it is generally considered to be, the impressive length tells something of the size of the community and the yield of its lands. Near the Chapter House, where harsh judgment was meted out to monks who deviated from the strict rules of the house, and via a passage to the east, the great hall of the monks' infirmary; adjoining that, a large kitchen with a pit at one side for refuse and broad cooking fireplaces. Those beyond cooking and eating were laid at the other side of the infirmary. That room was the Misericord, where the dying were placed on an arrangement of sackcloth and ashes and prayed over. When they died they were put into a coffin near the church and lowered into a grave which was not covered. When the flesh was gone, the bones were taken to a charnel house and the coffin and grave readied for the next temporary occupant. (One wonders what arrange-

ments were made in times of plague or simply the simultaneous decease of two or three old monks.)

The stone taken from the already decaying abbey in the first
years of the seventeenth century reshaped itself attractively in
Fountains Hall, whose façade of Jacobean probity is relieved
by a turret-like oriel window, an Italianate entrance, and
statued balustrade. Because it sits on a steep hill the house is
tall, wide, and shallow, rather like a monumental stage set,
and a comfort to the sightseer because there are not layers on
layers of rooms and because effulgent light (whatever the
Yorkshire weather feels it can afford) warms the spaces and
their varied fittings.

Immediately southeast of Ripon is the stocky garlanded and
porticoed **Newby Hall,** considered one of the "smaller" houses
of Yorkshire, but it will do for anyone with less than Neronian
tastes. Records of the house sitting in an admirable choice of
Yorkshire landscape go back and back but it was William
Weddell, a connoisseur and collector, who brought in Robert
Adam to rearrange and expand the house in the latter half of
the eighteenth century. He added a gallery wing, a balancing
wing, and classical touches to a house in the Wren style. Like
a number of similar mansions, Newby Hall is the product of a
fantasy, a search for the lordliest of lives as enjoyed by the
god-kings of the Roman Empire and translated to English
lawns and clouds of northern tree as gentlemanly miniatures
of the original.

Given carte blanche and lots of money, the inventive Robert
Adam designed for the dining room the chairs (which Chippendale executed), the pedestals for vases, the long side tables and
their candlesticks, the miniature Roman tub that held the wine,
and the leafy plasterwork designs in the moldings and ceiling.
The highly prized fashionable ornaments of other provenances
complete the almost untouchable elegance: a Lawrence family
portrait, Oriental vases, pieces of Meissen ware, and a
children's portrait of Frenchified little adults against a dreamy,
antique landscape.

The entrance hall is pure Adam, classical motifs over the
doors, panels of the accoutrements of ancient wars, the discreet
curlicues borrowed from more exuberant Roman grotesqueries
drawn on the ceiling and repeated as abstraction in the marble

floor, the characteristic garlanded, marble-topped tables executed by the Chippendale workshop, the overall Adam atmosphere of aristocratic remoteness.

From his Grand Tour Mr. Weddell brought back shining
marble columns that lead toward a splendor of Gobelin tapestries designed by François Boucher. The subject is the bouncy,
curly, sweet erotic innocence of the gods in and at love, spiced
with dimple-bottomed voyeur cherubs. Adam accommodated.
The furniture is French in style, to match the flowery tapestries, and the French rug, also designed by Adam, echoes and
binds together the other elements of the room. It may be too
many marshmallows for modern tastes, but don't leave until
you've had a look at a drawing of the third Lord Grantham,
to whom the house passed after the death of William Weddell,
as seen in Rome by Ingres.

The beautifully shaped library leads to the *raison d'être* of
the rebuilding, the gallery to show off the marble statuary collected by Weddell. Then as now, the Italian faking of antiquities
(Michelangelo, as you know, the most famous perpetrator of
such fraud)—Roman, Etruscan, Renaissance, Baroque, you
name it, they do it, and artfully—was a lively trade and the
very wholeness here of frangible arms, legs, and especially
noses, makes one suspicious. One hopes that the Barberini
Venus, standing under a curve that remembers the Pantheon
is, in spite of her intact shape, authentic enough to warrant the
huge sum of money (spread over annual payments) that Mr.
Weddell paid for her, payments which stopped, according to
a history of Newby Hall, when the owner of this magnificence
died in a Roman bath in London.

Goddesses, gods, emperors, and matrons line three extraordinary rooms painted in pastel colors that combine subtly
with the seasoned white and soon one is freed to the Englishness of various types and periods, to wayward or formal gardens, tea under the umbrellas fronting a feminine orangery,
and a very straightforward Adam construction, the stables.

What with pale sandwiches and milk-tea and extensive
gardens, one has moved quite a distance from Never-Never
Adam Land to be taken even farther away by a Victorian billiard room wallpapered by William Morris, and still farther
away to a collection of chamber pots from Germany, France,
the Orient, and the British Isles in a profusion of shapes and

times; queer, entertaining companions to the refinements that
went before.

NOTES

HOURS: Newby Hall—Easter Saturday to October 8, Wednesdays, Thursdays, Saturdays, Sundays, Bank Holiday
Mondays, 2:00 to 6:30. For Fountains Hall, see current
Historic Houses or inquire at Fountains Abbey.

RESTAURANTS: Harrogate offers an extensive choice. The
Box Tree in Ilkley is highly prized; phone ahead for reservations.

The pilgrimage to the Brontës' at Haworth to the south can
be efficiently done by way of Ripon and Harrogate. Infinitely
more suitable to the doomed, gifted family and their moor-
invaded lives is to make the journey through the moors, perversely at their best in mist and rains. The opening note out of
Richmond is a placid one in **Wensley** and its neighbors, the
makers of bland Wensleydale cheese. The scenery soon swells
to moors, fold on paling fold of hill ridged by harsh stone walls,
held for a pause at a taciturn stone hamlet like **Carlton,** and
released around **Horsehouse** as vari-colored bands of billowing
field. As if the tiny villages were not isolated enough, one or
two houses move off to utter loneliness at the side of a stream.
Each field is alone. Each rare tree, each windswept hillock, a
man in the distance sharpening his scythe, is completely alone;
only the wildflowers at the side of the road are members of a
community. Though countless sheep pick at the stubborn
grasses and rough shrubs in pairs and clots, each seems solitary, apart, brooding as the moors brood.

A brocaded brown-green-gold tapestry field hanging over a
gray-green wilderness is edged by a black arrow of wall that
shoots down its hill to be lost among rills and rocks. Below,
steeply below, the ground softens and yields trees and, around
Kettlewell, field flowers return and the bucolic lolling of cows
in sweeter greens near a leisured river. Across the river, wilderness holds in a sheer, rugged cliff of palisades. The River

Wharfe flows along with the road into **Grassington,** meticulously charming and a worldly relief from the stupendous,
voiceless moors. It scrambles up and down fetchingly, always
in its best dress. The shops show the international gifts of
Chelsea in London, a boutique describes itself as classy pro-
vider FOR THE DISCRIMINATING LADY, a small whitewashed fruit
shop covers itself in extravagant flower baskets that make of
its plain virtues a Carmen Miranda. (You might consider staying the night at either the Grassington House or the Devonshire
Hotel, both pleasant and neither immoderately hard on the
traveler's check folder.)

Brontë country begins in **Keighley** (pronounced Keethley),
and its hooded nineteenth-century rows and a few timid newer
shops uncertain whether they have a right to stay. For some
distance one of the Brontë sisters has appeared and reappeared
as a label on a liquor bottle. The home village, **Haworth,** a dark
snail climbing a cobbled hill, features a Heathcliff Café, a
Brontë Bookshop, a Brontë Hairdressing Salon, Brontë Crafts
and, for parking, Brontë Street, posthumous publicity that
casts, for the Brontë devotee, gross shadows on the gifted
fragile family. Maintained by an active Brontë Society, the
parsonage in which they lived is now a museum, neat and
calm, and, except for a few details, belies the lives. Such seems
often to be the function and limitation of these orderly collections of tangible, inert bits that spin off from life's chaos.
The monumental collection of polished objects that describe
Victorian and Edwardian life in the museum in York, for instance, erases any trace of the many children who worked in
the mines and died of it; a collection of Coleridge's books and
inkpot allows no room for the dissolution of a brilliant, devious
mind rotted with opium. At Haworth, too, one must supply the
clouds that stain the nice, clear rooms. Brother Branwell's
inept paintings, lifted by a singular intensity in the portraits of
his sisters (now in the National Portrait Gallery in London),
should be viewed through a miasma of drink, drugs, and in-
adequacy. The uncommunicative, modest dining room is another world from the room in which Emily, refusing medical
help, met her death in stubborn dignity, rid of what has been
termed one of the most erotic novels in literature. The lace
cuffs, slender shoes, and pieces of clothing Charlotte probably
wore say nothing of her brief glow of fame and love, snuffed

out after nine months of marriage. The toys in the nursery
stand as symbols for any children, not this family of febrile
imaginations and extraordinary gifts and the discipline for
expressing them.

The charts that indicate where, on the local moors, Wuther-
ing Heights stood, the collection of manuscripts, the memorabilia to be carried off as postcards are, of course, interesting.
What may tell you more about the Brontës are the bleak,
melancholy churchyard that peers in through the windows and,
beyond the fields, the empty wilderness of moor and, in a glass
museum case, the roster of Brontë deaths—tuberculosis,
tuberculosis, tuberculosis, tenacious, unrelenting.

The A57 that crosses high Peak country begins with the high
tragedy of erosion, bitter rocks, scored, sterile earth, and poles
as snow-markers. The anger shortly relents to admit sheep
and trees, hills that yield to the urgency of a river, and the
open freshness of **Bakewell.** Its hospitality is as generous as
the rich tart that bears its name and the glorious vistas of
woods, fields, and river and long bowers of green-shaded road.
A few miles to the south is **Haddon Hall** of medieval-manor
style and roses that witnessed scenes of romantic history or
historical romance. Northeastward, **Chatsworth,** a major house
in a major park of the late seventeenth into eighteenth centuries built to surround the distinguished collection of books,
paintings, furniture, and decorations of the first Duke of
Devonshire.

NOTES

For the collector of English place names—the villages of
Whatstandwell, Toadmoor, Belper, Openwoodgate.

Durham

The old-fashioned train out of York is equipped with tables for each set of seats occupied by stocky bundles of nursery pink and blue cardigans for the ladies, workmanlike gray and brown for gentlemen, and everyone in hard overcoats built for endurance, totally rejecting style and flattery as suspect frippery. After the shouted farewells and joking admonitions, desultory, low conversation, a sinking of spirits, a fatalistic bleakness to match the encrusted tunnels of industrial towns to the north. The send-off, however, is a shout of triumph, the station itself a temple of white, flowery capitals, a grand bracket clock, white lights, and curlicues of wrought iron under a tremendous canopy of wrought iron and glass winging a vast, dynamic curve. Under that bold clarion call, a sign that whispers THOU SHALT NOT COMMIT ADULTERY, apparently a local concern and proof that God's all-seeing Wesleyan eye never blinks, even in such splendor.

The tracks etch their way along allotment gardens, a darts board above a pram in a narrow backyard, industrial buildings, cows in a landscape of fields mounted by slag heaps. The station at **Darlington** is a copy of York's, with sheep as spandrel decorations to honor one founder of the local economy, but lacking the sweep of York's curve, lacks dash and fervor.

As the train approaches **Durham**, the slag piles crouching in their scored and pitted skins are brightened by a suggestion of pale Gothic spire on pale church which turns into a white-dust cement factory, its stack and feather of smoke. The station of Durham wears a white iron bonbon box cover of loosely angled glass and punched fringe like old-fashioned eyelet lace, a charming Victorian lady who may have been sacrificed to rebuilding in progress in 1973. The high position of the station looks down at the sloping, turning terraces of brick cottage and skittering chimney. To the side is an immense railroad bridge as high and as mighty as a Roman aqueduct; in the distance, the pile of castle and cathedral heaped like an impenetrable fortress.

Durham was a fortress town, dominated by a prince-bishop until Queen Victoria erased the disconcertingly Papish position and practice. The Cathedral clasped by the craggy castle led armies, fought infidels, thundered anathema at kings, and excommunicated emperors. Here, in the Middle Ages, the king

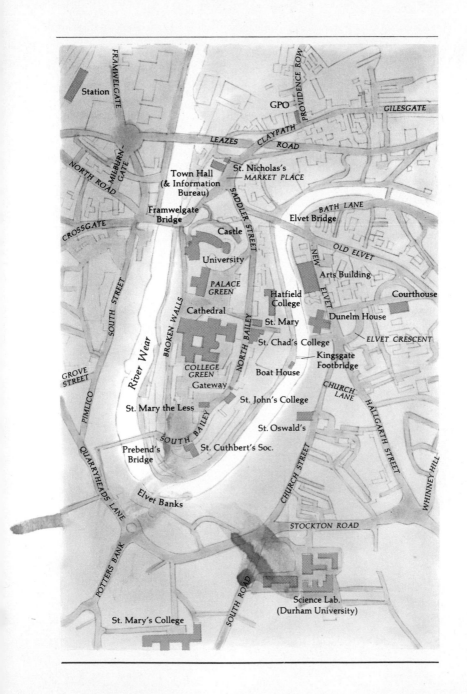

was counted as less than the bishop, who was also the Earl of Northumberland and the supreme power whose army served to hold off the Scots swooping down from the north. Let it come to you, suddenly, from one of the curves of street, or let it loom above you from the River Wear and its low, old bridge, or face its forthright bulk standing beside the massive pillars, deeply scored with virile geometric designs. This is the Church Militant, still, and no enlightened museum or concert program or present uplift can ease its tremendous, stern, and beautiful terribleness. Its story goes back very far, to the end of the seventh century, when the dying Bishop Cuthbert, prior of an abbey on Holy Island, Lindisfarne, off the coast of Northumberland, enjoined his brothers to take his bones, in case of invasion, to a place that was safe and holy. Two centuries later, when the Vikings came, the brothers gathered the remains of Cuthbert, now saint, the head of St. Oswald, a devout Northumbrian king, and some of their manuscripts, to begin a period of wandering until they settled on a high place almost entirely circled by a protective river.

As the momentous year 1000 came into view, bringing Doomsday or the Second Coming, the order built a church for their saints' bones and as enclosure for the cathedral of future bishops. A Norman bishop cleared out the Saxon brethren, though, and replaced them with a Benedictine priory and an entirely new church. The Norman planned so well and lavished so much money on the building that it was finished in forty years, startlingly fast as compared to the centuries-long growth of other medieval cathedrals, and the reason for the unusual unity of style, maintained in restorations. Durham is an encyclopedia of innovations in English architecture—the earliest pointed arches, the first use of the flying buttress, the first interlaced blind arches that adorn many walls of major churches, the oldest ribbed vaults still extant. Another singularity is the absence of a Lady Chapel, omitted in deference to St. Cuthbert, who was an ardent follower of the most vehemently anti-feminist Apostles; he would not bend, nor would the Benedictines, for any woman, including the Virgin Mary. In any case fervent Mariolatry came later, but even at that time no Lady Chapel was added. A mark made in the early-twelfth-century nave limited women to space very far from the altar.

You will observe that there are comparatively few early monuments, the result of a decision, later disregarded, that only St. Cuthbert was to be so honored in Durham. A second luminary lies in the low, many-arched Galilee Chapel that still seems wreathed in incense and the sound of chanting. The chapel was so named, it is thought, because it was the last station of the Sunday processional, led off by the most important dignitary as Christ led his disciples to Galilee. Bits of painted figures, one of them of St. Peter, crucified head downward, lead in the rich dark to the bones of the Venerable Bede, whose life, from early childhood, was spent in the Jarrow monastery, where he wrote his *History* and translations of Bible stories that brought to the Anglo-Saxon mind Abraham as a "Hebrew earl" and his field hands as "churls." The posthumous dignity of lying in Durham Cathedral was offered the writer's remains in 1022, after they had waited for almost three hundred years in his monastery. The first layman to be entombed in the Cathedral was a Neville who defeated the Scots in 1346, and one of the latest monuments is a carved wooden panel: "Remember before God the Durham miners who have given their lives in the pits of this country and those who work in darkness and danger in those pits today." Of the intervening centuries, tombs hacked by Commonwealth soldiers and by defeated Scots of the mid-seventeenth century who, imprisoned in the church, avenged themselves on its dead.

It is often repeated, the statement made by King James that he would wrestle Durham Cathedral against any other in the kingdom. It is not difficult to understand such a response to the dignified vaulted space, the majesty of chastely decorated pillars and arches held in the simplest of bases and capitals. The eye travels up and up into the fifteenth-century tower, to the early twelfth-century crossing of transept and nave, where ribs meet as a gigantic stone blossom, and down to the choir stalls of the seventeenth century, placed to fill the emptiness left by the Commonwealth. A bishop's throne is still "in good heart," as church experts like to say, its fourteenth-century exuberance flying high in bright colors around heraldic shields.

Near the altar, architectural style of the twelfth century changes to the pointed arches and bubbling elaborations of the late thirteenth. The screen, an enchantment presented to the Cathedral by the son of the Scot-defeating Neville, is of the amber-tinted white stone of Caen, shipped to London for carving by a famous master, conveyed up the coast, and trundled inland to be placed before the high altar. The hundred and more small statues that stood in its niches were shattered during Henry VIII's Dissolution and their absence leaves an icy, frail, abandoned thing. Nearby, the thirteenth century spreads its sophisticated beauties into the Chapel of the Nine Altars, whose springs of arches hold a group of fine heads.

Adjoining an alcove in which men seeking sanctuary slept, there is the Monks' Door, a Norman doorway still bearing the ironwork of the twelfth century. This leads to the large cloisters where the monks not only lived but conducted the business of a thriving community. Another remarkable door, etched in geometric patterns of the early twelfth century, opens to the Monks' Dormitory, now the Cathedral museum. From case to case, an easy and interesting meander through details that flesh out the skeleton of the early church. Here again we meet St. Cuthbert and his peripatetic bones. After a long rest in Durham, meant to be his immortal home, they were taken from his shrine when the Reformation threatened, to be returned in the nineteenth century along with a number of significant objects: a double-lidded oak coffin remade of fragments carved in primitive line drawings of holy figures; a comb (found in the coffin) that might have been used in anointing; tenth-century vestments in the distinguished work of Winchester; a rare cross of garnets in gold; and St. Cuthbert's portable altar.

Five wealthy Norman bishops not only expanded and enhanced the Cathedral but left, also, superb relics—brilliantly illuminated Bibles, a remarkably engraved and inlaid crozier, jeweled rings that became, by Papal decree, the traditional bishops' rings, and broad, haughty bishops' seals. A scimitar symbolizes an old custom; such a sword was presented to each new bishop by a feudal family in lieu of rent money, a practice that continued over the centuries until Victoria was a portly widow. The Middle Ages brought in gold leaf on books of Church law and alabaster from Nottingham, the specialist in such work. Another set of distinguished books presented to the Priory evoke an image of a fifteenth-century power, Thomas Langley, appointed bishop for his role in setting Henry IV on a teetery throne. The hubris of man and position, the sense of supremacy—close to that of a king—appear distinctly in the seals Langley used, one very like the king's Great Seal, another like the king's Privy Seal.

The ordered miscellany moves back to Anglo-Roman artifacts and on to a greater strength, four copes in the highly esteemed English needlework, left from those scattered to the winds and by the hands of children of the Reformation. (Many of the best pieces of restored shreds, like discarded alabaster carvings, found their way to collections on the Continent.) Coins, more books, invaluable early documents, examples of early printing, seals both lay and churchly round out a stimulating and not too extensive sampling attractively arranged in an airy hall bound in old stone with an upturned, huge cradle of beams as ceiling.

A taxi from the station, or a bus from the street below, takes one into the grounds of the University of Durham, among whose buildings of basic modern is a set that echoes the uncompromising Cathedral mood. Of them, the Gulbenkian Museum of Oriental Art and Archaeology, sunk into several levels of a hillside. Be prepared for thousands of objects devoted to Indian, Tibetan, Singalese, Balinese, Burmese, Egyptian, and Chinese art. Since this is basically part of a teaching institution, the booklet is a short textbook, the labels fully informative, and the collection too large for the non-expert to linger on piece by piece. If the Tibetan tankas on the top level prove threatening and incomprehensible, go on to the white Chinese porcelain dogs and cows, jolly fat demi-gods and tri-corned European gentlemen being entertained by geishas. Or, stand near the tropical languor of an abundant Indian goddess and move on from her fruitfulness to a Tibetan horror of magicians' aprons made of carved human bones. One finds lacquered Indian toys, frail ivory panels, a small and monumentally calm Buddha, an amorous couple all ripeness and warm curves. To close this fertile area, a flat lamp used in a defloration ritual among Bastar Indians and a cocomer, a palm fruit of the Seychelles, worshipped by a Tantra sect as an "emblem of the cosmic generating organ of the goddess." Nothing subtle about this fertility symbol; it is a dark combination of buttocks and vagina, almost adult-size and smooth textured except for an area of wriggly scratches that inevitably means pubic hair; one of those travesties that nature is so eagerly capable of.

On to a numerous miniature populace, and their tools and artifacts, who accompanied Egyptian dead on their journeys. Abutting the calm Egyptians (on the second level downward), shrieking narrative sculpture erupting on Burmese teakwood crammed with mythological warriors and hunters. Back to poise and grace in Chinese ivory carving and, on the level below, an exorbitant collection of Chinese snuff bottles. Jade appears in many ritualistic forms, as adornment and for the sheer triumphant pleasure of taming the stone—a gliding fish, a cowering little beast, a fierce dragon.

The abundance of Chinese art slips down the stairs to fill that level with porcelain and pottery as containers and figures in the glazes and shapes of several centuries. Somewhere on the way long, comely lady attendants of the seventh century, all in red and brown garments, one holding a cloth, one a goose, one a baby. They might be servants or sisters of another group of conversing, winnowing, dancing women of the same time. There is much more to see, but you might be ready to make your farewells with these vivacious T'ang ladies.

NOTES

HOURS: Monday to Friday, 9:30 to 1:00 and 2:15 to 5:00; Saturdays, 9:30 to 12:00 and 2:15 to 5:00; Sundays, 2:15 to 5:00 only.

HOTELS: The Three Tuns and the Royal County are moderate.

Into Northumberland

Not far from Durham is **Raby Castle**, worth considering for a visit. The repertoire of the interior you have met before—the paintings of horses and dogs, the Chinese porcelain, the inlaid Italian cabinets, the family portraits, the beautifully proportioned and airy drawing room covered in silks and gilded ceiling, a gallery of arms and hunting trophies, a tea room in neatened stables. Particular to this castle is its minstrels' gallery, one of the few of stone now in existence, and of significant history, much of it enacted in earlier versions of the Great Hall.

The Nevilles came to the property from King Canute, by way of a descendant of the king's niece, acquiring their towering name from a marriage with Isabella de Neville, a Norman lady of immense wealth. To secure the extensive properties involved, her son dropped the paternal name for his mother's. The family reached an apogee of power with the marriage of Cecily Neville, "the Rose of Raby," to the Plantagenet Richard of York, to whom she bore Edward IV and the infamous (some say no, there are constant efforts to rehabilitate his memory) Richard III. Their cousin, Richard Neville, became "Warwick the King-maker," whose unhappy daughter married "crouch-backed" Richard. The family commanded for generations until it made a fatal mistake in 1569, perpetrated in the Great Hall where the heads of the family convened with the leading powers of the north. They discussed at length their plan to support Mary Queen of Scots and Catholicism and unseat Elizabeth in the process. It is said that they blew hot and cold, growing colder until they were spurred on by the scorn and anger of the lady of the manor, the Countess of Westmorland—a title given a Neville by Richard II—who, like several ladies of her rank and wealth in English history, was a persuasive, belligerent power. The men went on to their "Rising" which, of course, failed and the family went into exile and impoverished obscurity. The castle and its lands remained Crown property for more than forty years and then was sold to the Vane family, who bought it in the early seventeenth century and, subsequently, by marrying Neville women, revived the Earl of Westmorland title. This, too, was an illustrious family, which produced a scion, Sir Harry Vane, who, not yet twenty-five, ruled the colony of

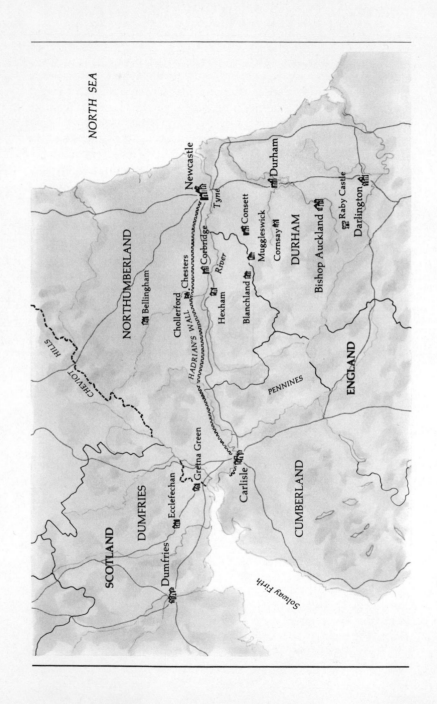

Massachusetts from 1635 to 1637. He later became an effective Treasurer of the Navy and a frightening liberal, a prophet of principles later to be realized by the American Revolution. He was consequently executed by Charles II.

Armed with a scant page of background, walk around outside the castle to mark the curious five-sided tower whose foundations may be as old as the eleventh century, shaped in a style used by the ancient Danes. Notice the narrow windows and the other towers and indomitable towered walls that—in spite of many changes by hands that wore chain mail, steel, Elizabethan rings, Stuart lace, and the woolens of the Victorians— still look as if they were preparing to pour death on imminent besiegers.

NOTES

HOURS: Erratic spring and summer schedule. See current *Historic Houses.*

To the east, the moors and fells, the desolations and wild growths of the Pennines. You will see them only at a vague distance and the map will indicate them by blank spaces, most unusual for a map of England. It is not difficult to imagine, looking across at the sheep-dotted slopes and dark hills, the loneliness of a farm far from a road during the long winter, the snowbound fears of accidents and illness, the struggle to guard and keep sheep in swirling snow storms. It must be a meager life, but not much worse than that in the semi-abandoned towns that served collieries; **Cornsay**, for instance, dismal and lost in a magnificence of valleys. Toward **Muggleswick**, the road drops into fretworks of light trees and bursts of immense fern, rising to golden meadows fringed with slag heaps and the black smoke, the long black boxes and black stacks that are **Consett**. Their backs resolutely turned on the smoky symptoms of coal, summer trippers, responding to a promise of sun, bare their pale chests and shoulders while an elder drags the lunch and thermos out of the boot of the car. As if magicked, they stare into the low hills, wall of hill behind wall, into invisible distances on the moors. Watching the map and signs carefully, skirt the waters of the Derwent Reservoir, to enter the drama of moors and streams around **Blanchland**, a medieval town, some say, while others say it is a Victorian company town built in antique style. It is pale gold and perfect, sitting in a high ring of green silvered with a stream that binds together a small hotel, a house that serves buttery teas, a round, covered marketplace stall, vestiges of abbey and gatehouse, and a winning cluster of cottages that suggests an almshouse.

Shortly, the multiple charms of **Hexham**, with its Fore Street and its Back Street, its Moot Hall, a sixteenth-century grammar school, and an abbey that pokes its nose into the vivid covered market. To complete the picture, a castle and, as in York and Bath and Norwich, baskets of flowers hanging from every available upright.

The prima donna of this show is the abbey, but before you plunge in, walk among the friendly, unstately houses, see what's going at the market at what prices, look in at the cordial shops and try to decipher the fancy lettering on a chemist's window. Nothing in Hexham Abbey is quite that indecipherable except lettering that goes back to Romans stationed here to guard their Emperor Hadrian's Wall, a vigorous stone's throw away. The abbey has everything (except land), plus Roman artifacts and a very eventful history, even for a breed given to dissension, quarrel, and trouble with its townsfolk. St. Wilfrid, whom you will meet in full regalia later, was granted land by Queen Ethelreda in 673; on it he built a church dedicated to St. Andrew and a monastery, a highly decorated complex of polished pillars, ornamented stone taken from Roman buildings, interconnecting passages, and hidden chapels meant to outshine all church enclaves except those of Mother Rome. Shortly after, Ethelreda died and her king married a lady who hated Wilfrid. She and sycophants forced a synod, headed by the Archbishop of Canterbury, that urged, strongly, a division of Northumbria into a diocese centered in York and another in Hexham, vitiating Wilfrid's control. St. Wilfrid forgot about turning the other cheek. He went to Rome for a favorable ruling, and got it. On presenting his document from the Pope, Wilfrid was put into prison, kept there for the better part of a year, and then released to end his days in another monastery. His successor was St. Acca, who completed and further adorned the church and filled it with relics (a good number from Rome where he had gone with Wilfrid), holy books, and music—taught here for twelve years by an Italian who also taught the choir in great Canterbury. St. Acca, too, was pushed out but returned after eight years to die in Hexham and be buried in the church. He then began to act like a true saint. When his grave, abandoned and lost over the years, was rediscovered, his body was found to be "uncorrupted" as they like to say in hagiography. It decayed ultimately but the bones retained miraculous properties: dipped in water, they made it holy and efficacious for curing instantly sundry ills. A century later the Danes came, destroyed the church and pillaged treasures. It was not until 1180 that it was rebuilt, incorporating a crypt and sections of wall that Wilfrid built. Later, it hardly need be said, the church endured subtractions (caused by border raids) and restoration and additions. Dominating but by no means suppressing the cheerful market, the plainspoken pile is made more massive and compact by the shortness of the tower, not unfinished or broken but kept that way in the naïve hope that thus the large monastery and church would remain unnoticed by potential predators.

Some idea of the extent and quality of the monastery can be derived from walking in the environs of the church, tracing the length of ruined walls, the ornamental details on a lavatory, the size and strength of the Moot Hall and the manor office which conceals, one is told, a late-fourteenth-century prison. The interior appears less spacious than one might expect, primarily because too much decoration is crowded into the limited space of the apse. But one does not come to Hexham Abbey for the loftiness or grandeur of its space; it is important as a landmark of history, lay and ecclesiastical, and as an example of architecture and church furnishing.

First, the crypt and a passageway for pilgrims come to stand near relics seen through a grill, in the style of churches in Rome. Of earlier Roman style are the brickwork, the Roman carvings, and, supporting a roof, a slab commemorating work done under the rule of Septimius Severus and other Caesars. At the foot of a worn set of stairs that led to a slype—a covered gallery to shelter monks from inclement weather on their way from dormitory or refectory to prayers—there stands a memorial stone to a twenty-five-year-old Roman standard bearer, mounted and carrying the sun symbol of his company, in the act of trampling an indigenous warrior. All through the church, sprinklings of Roman mixed with Saxon artifacts: Roman altars, bits of torso, a head, a section of pillar used as the bowl of a font in the Saxon church. The Saxons left hog-back coffins, splinters of a Saxon cross, and a large tomb, which may be that common symbol of eternal life) that issue from two monstrous of a king, incised with a sharp pattern of continuous vines (a heads and finish as a cross of leaves.

The conspicuously centered stone seat, believed to have been the cathedra of Wilfrid, stood originally in the apse of his church, under the present choir. This "frith" (peace) stool was the center of sanctuary, a zone which extended for a mile around the church. While in the choir, look at the misericords, neither as fanciful nor as explicit as misericords elsewhere, but to be regarded with respect as survivors of a Victorian clean-up which sold antique benches by the cheap wagonload. Hexham's claim to unique folk carving are figures doing their various things at the sides of a chantry guarded by a rough, staring St. Christopher. Above a border of stiff leaves, awkward Gothic niches hold flat-faced saints with dwindling bodies; staring out from columns, big, startled, saddened heads, rather like those on totem poles. The heart of the entertaining matter is below. An animal thief (a border raider?) with an African-mask face has his neck almost broken by the ledge of crushing flowers; Vanity combs her coarse hair, a harpist plucks, a piper pipes, a jester plays with a small animal, the ubiquitous fox preaches to geese; lumpish, misproportioned, inartistic, and great fun.

Compare these creations of untutored enthusiasts of the late fifteenth century with the delicacy and precision of the carved wood in the rood screen, the taste and restraint in "The Salutation" painting of the chancel screen, and the late-fifteenth-century choir screen (the remains of an altar triptych) paneled with paintings from a Dance of Death series. Above, seven larger paintings of early bishops, including St. Wilfrid and St. Acca, magnificently brocaded, furred, and jeweled, as luminous as Renaissance courtiers and as fastidiously painted.

No great distance from the aristocratic bishops the shadow of Hadrian, maybe the first "modern" man in his uncertainties, his admiration of worlds outside his Rome, his melancholy skepticism and dignified despair. His wall, as every English schoolboy knows, was built between the Solway and the mouth of the Tyne to guard against forays from the north, and to do him present honor there are Hadrian pubs and at least one Hadrian Hotel. Which may bring thoughts of food and lodging, and one good choice is the George at **Chollerford** on the North Tyne River. Sit with a drink at the side of the water and study the circles drawn by the arches of a lovely bridge as they meet their undisturbed reflections. Drink still in hand, go back to wired pens to visit the Chinese pheasants and the little green cockatoos and on through flower beds to a well-served English-Continental dinner.

NOTES

Reserve early and avoid Room Three, not too accessible to toilet and bath and, unless they have mended it, with blood-curdling shrieks from slats in the floor. The cost is moderate, with breakfast and proximity to the Roman fort—one of a number in the area—at **Chesters.**

Northumberland

Toward **Wark** the landscape becomes a high ridge etched with a black and white frieze of cows. The hills tighten and roads corkscrew under awnings of tree, the friezes of cow elaborate to include sheep wearing stains of red or blue on their shaggy sides and hikers with courageous packs making for the Cheviot Hills, on the border with Scotland. The stone houses and highly embellished old shops of **Bellingham** front a boundless horizon of grasses and rough stone walls widely spaced to make room for the slow, stubborn restlessness of sheep. **Elsdon** returns to mining waste, dislocated black machinery, a sample of defunct border castle, and then disappears. Tall fans of fern shield brooks and a vista of long, flat brown-green hills as mighty and uncompromising as Durham Cathedral. Signs informing that you are in Northumberland National Park and surrounded by earthworks, camps, priories, and castles of several venerable times lead to **Otterburn**, which has a tweed mill that sells its wares to visitors; to the poor hamlets of **Thropton** and **Snitter** (which means simply "snow"); and into **Rothbury**, a large gray-stone village favored by English vacationers. Here they take the salubrious air, walk, fish, and picnic in a theatrical bleakness of tall thistle and big rocks, or ride spirals of road that dip into unexpected long tranquil valleys to meet rose-covered settlements and some dressed in sorrow. One vacation day they make the pilgrimage to **Alnwick** (pronounced Anneck) **Castle**, a seat of the Duke of Northumberland.

The Northumberlands have always, it seems, existed although they are not mentioned in the Domesday Book because that monument of bookkeeping did not reach as far as this northern corner of the country, or maybe the recorders would not venture into a territory where, as in the Greek myth, fields shot up fully armed warriors. The first recorded earl set off on the family career shortly after the Conquest by cutting down the King of Scotland, his son, and followers in one of the immortal border raids. History mentions briefly a rebellion by Northumberland against William with the help of a Norman baron who had been given the estate, later taken from him. A more favored Frenchman kept the property and it was he who, early in the twelfth century, built the first heavily fortified castle, expanded and further strengthened—in the size and design it still follows

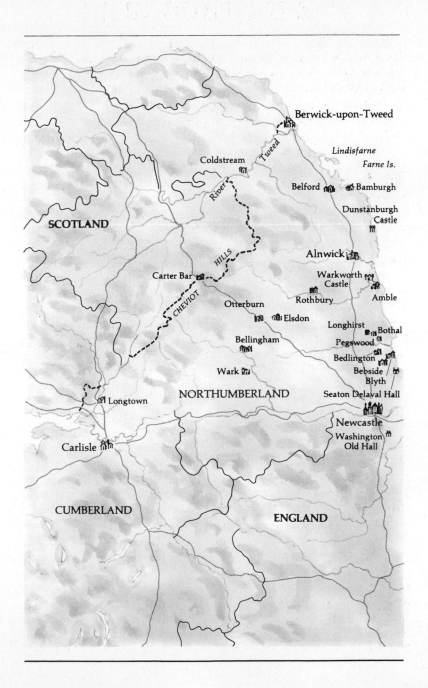

Berwick-upon-Tweed

Lindisfarne
Farne Is.

Coldstream

Belford   Bamburgh

River Tweed

Dunstanburgh
Castle

SCOTLAND

HILLS

Alnwick

Carter Bar

Warkworth
Castle

Rothbury

Amble

CHEVIOT

Otterburn

Elsdon

Longhirst   Bothal

Bellingham

Pegswood

Bedlington

Wark

Bebside

Blyth

NORTHUMBERLAND

Seaton Delaval Hall

Longtown

Newcastle

Washington
Old Hall

Carlisle

CUMBERLAND

ENGLAND

—by his son-in-law, the Baron of Alnwick. The family stayed central to practically all the battles and about-faces of the confused history of early England, and early Scotland and, to some degree, France. (So busy fighting they hardly had time to marry, they appointed bastards their heirs.) During the troubles of King John the lords of the castle joined the northern barons who, in 1212, revolted against the king. The alignment then turned to friendship with Scotland, enmity toward the king; John therefore burned Alnwick. Never much for reigning kings, the family soon produced a son, John, who fought Henry III at the side of Simon de Montfort in the civil war which gave Montfort the rule of the country for a year. The estate was taken, the estate was restored, and finally lost when a young illegitimate heir was put in the care of a bishop of Durham. The bishop has come down in the Alnwick story—justly or unjustly—as the man who sold title and lands to the Percys.

They continued the pattern: war against Scots and English kings (particularly Edward II, whose foul-tongued favorite, Piers Gaveston, they helped murder) and, in pauses, reshaping sections of the castle. On they fought, in France and in Scotland, burning and being burned, and, never far from court plots, helped depose Richard II, to set the "heavy weight" of crown on the head of Henry IV. Having helped make him, they decided to undo him and fomented the "Rising of the Percys," which ended in defeat and the death of Hotspur at Shrewsbury. Back to sacking and burning dealt by Alnwick and Scotland and the mid-fifteenth-century variations in war terrain provided by the Wars of the Roses. As autocratic with serfs as with kings, the Northumberlands pressed their peasantry with levies so unendurable that, in 1489, the fourth earl was killed by "the Mob."

Softer days came in the early sixteenth century, with an earl called the "Magnificent" for his lavish spending and the comportment of a North Country Medici. His son, "the Unthrifty" (the soubriquets begin to echo those of royal lines—"the Bald," "the Unready," etc.)—could have had no love for the crowned head of his time, Henry VIII, who took Anne Boleyn away from him and assigned him a seat on the committee that was to condemn her. He was able to avoid the job but not the imprisonment in the Tower of one brother and the execution of another because they were anti-Henry. Family and house were dissolved, to be restored by the Catholic Mary, and back into the shade again with the rule of Elizabeth. Northumberland left his court job, joined the doomed rising for Mary Queen of Scots, and was beheaded. A succeeding brother, the eighth earl, was also accused of fostering the cause of Mary, imprisoned in the Tower, and there shot by an unidentified hand. The next move for the revival of Catholicism was Guy Fawkes's mismanaged Gunpowder Plot, which resulted in the Tower imprisonment of the earl for fifteen years. You may know him as the learned, irascible "Wizard Earl" of Petworth in Sussex.

The family that collected the paintings at Petworth and had Robert Adam illuminate with delicate gaud its house in Syon near London also shows some of its art and objects at Alnwick. Much of the mid-eighteenth-century "Gothic" with which Adam tried to ornament the castle is gone. Of his work only some furniture is left; the rest is more massive, resplendent "Italian." The ceilings are flamboyantly coffered, marble caryatids heave up marble mantelpieces, niches hold formidable goddesses. And ormulu and marquetry, classical subjects and objects, wall silks and samples of Gobelins; in short, the opulent house accoutrements gathered by English wealth and French and Italian, and America's Morgans and Fricks.

In the multitudinous dazzle, plainer spots of the personal. The Percys acquired the coronation gloves of Edward VI, a pincushion and spoon that belonged to Mary Queen of Scots, and a lace cap made of the hair of the foolish, tragic queen. One Percy liked Persian cups and spoons, another preferred African skins and artifacts, and another found himself in possession of human bones bound together as girdle, bracelet, necklace.

The balconied library repeats the general effulgence. A few fine old books are placed for closer examination, as well as interesting prints and broadsides, a page from a Gutenberg Bible, an edition of Shakespeare dated 1632, a letter from Elizabeth I to her High Admiral concerning the Armada, hung with her ponderous seal.

The pride of the house, as at Petworth, might be the paintings, a not extensive but highly respectable gathering which had to include Kneller, Gainsborough, and Reynolds, and Canaletto, the Venetian who lived in England for a while and, through an enterprising agent, maintained his ties with English buyers. Van Dyck contributes a rather listless—for him—portrait of Queen Henrietta Maria and a dashing tenth Earl of Northumberland. Most of the honors go to the Italians, beginning with a golden primitive in the style of Siena and going on to a moving "Ecce Homo" by Tintoretto and a vigorous red-bearded portrait and section of fresco by Sebastiano del Piombo, now chalky but remarkably accomplished. Titian is represented by a triple portrait centered on an ineffably beautiful young man and another of a not quite so beautiful young man. Remaining honors go to ivory panels and, especially, to six plaques, almost hidden in a corner off a hallway, of Limoges enamel. On subjects out of Virgil, these enamels—once the property of Catherine de' Medici—are quite wonderful, deserving of better-lit, more appropriate space.

After eighteenth-century frills were taken down, the castle reverted to a fair facsimile of complete medieval fortress, now based on stone from the twelfth to the nineteenth centuries. From the slope below it is a rangy, formidable city for watchfulness and boiling pitch at the ready. The barbican and the gatehouse, a set of turrets surmounted with figures that have lost their windy gestures, were built by Hotspur's son in the fifteenth century and designed as a small fortress to protect the big fort; a last stronghold if the rest went. The inner spaces also protect each other in a system of walls and towers within walls and towers, the vast outer bailey separated by a gateway from the middle bailey and that guarded by *its* towers. From this sizable expanse and its eighteenth-century terrace armed with old cannons, one can view the extensive green domains that adhere to the castle. Then, flanked by two mighty octagonal towers studded with worn Percy shields, the entrance to a stone funnel of inner fourteenth-century courtyard, and a round arch cut in Norman "dog-tooth" pattern that gives access to the inner ward.

NOTES

HOURS: April 30 to September 28, daily except Fridays, 1:00 to 5:00.

The Percys echo in the town of **Alnwick** as the name of an estate agent, an accountant, a shopkeeper. Hotspur names a hotel and because it is a town that lives with dignitaries and the arts, a shop of working-class non-exotica adopts Hadrian's name; a LOUVRE sign is all that is left of a restaurant which didn't make it. As you walk through the plain, agreeable town, listen to the warm voices that lilt and lift their statements like gentle questions. A woman asks her little boy, whose face and legs are twisted in an unmistakable need, "Is it a toilet you want? Tells oos, mon." Keep listening. The honeyed speech will give you "down" as "doon," "back" as "bock," "straight" as "stret," and a few words you won't understand at all; but not to worry, the courtliness of the north will translate and explain. On the main street of Bingo, shops, and small hotels, a black St. Michael stands over a shallow, square fountain, St. Michael's Pant (pronounced "pont"), in which two skinny boys are lowering sticks attached to can tops bent as rough shovels, hoping to scoop out a coin or two and not very successful because their eyes and hands are nervous with fear of the police. The fancy market cross and town hall speak neither splendor nor eccentricity, but walk down to the railroad station, now used as a fertilizer plant, and observe a column that stands at its side, four lions at the base and one, stiff-tailed, at the top. Some unhurried elderly gentleman or other will tell you it is called "The Farmers' Folly" and why. Years ago—"bad years," your informant says—the grateful farmers of the country around Alnwick whose rents were quite low decided to reward the lord of the manor with the noble monument. He acknowledged it, thanked them, and rethought the situation. If they could afford this sort of gesture they could easily carry rent rises. The rents rose, hence the name of the monument.

The elderly gentleman expands the courtesies of welcome. Phase one is an apology for the weather and consolation by way of wet, unhappy reports from relatives on holiday in Spain and Italy. Phase two: "Have you been to our pub, the Old Cross?" He tells its distinction, one window full of old bottles which must never be touched. He who touches one dies. Soon? Later? Young? Old? Well, it's hard to say, actually, but his brother-in-law knew a man whose uncle, on a tiddly dare, touched one of the fateful bottles and died.

The forbidding bottles sprawled on each other behind the

dim window have no effect on the hearty noise and crowding inside; tight space given to a short bar, a bench against the wall where the old boys gather, a few small tables, and the darts corner. Every inch burbles with laughing insults, punching, back-slapping, pints of beer in constant motion between bar and table, shouts and cries of triumph from the darts department. The American accent and London raincoat are quickly spotted, and space is cleared for the visitors, drinks offered and brought to the table. A ruddy, merry-faced young man says he was in America two years ago. A pale man at a nearby table says, "Seen the world and still happy to be a farm slave?" "Farm slave, hell, it's the best life, a healthy, interesting life, better than yours, grubbing around in that grimy shop." "That grimy shop is mine and I'm not dependent on the whims of his Lordship." "Oh, come off his Lordship, the rents haven't gone up since his father's day." "Where did you get *that* rubbish?" By now they are shouting at each other with vigor, without rancor. The town man continues, "You Northumberland farmers and your pulling-the-forelock and bowing to the Little Father like Russian serfs!" "And you revolutionists, when your shop's blown up and you under it, I'll be sitting on my tractor whistling and the family back in the castle." They are interrupted by a man bearing a pad and pencil who asks for everyone's choice of a number and 5 pence in the nightly lottery for a pound win.

The door opens and a southern townie swings in, approaches the bar, extends a Savile Row arm to the publican, and greets him as "Gov'nor." A second's bewilderment, a handshake, and the instant courteous poise. "It's some time since I've seen you. How are you? What'll it be?" The Londoner mentions a drink with an unfamiliar name and the barman looks blank. "Well, isn't that what you people call whiskey here?" and he speaks the word again but "you people" refuse to recognize it, embedded as it is in over-affable condescension. He takes his whiskey to the argumentative table and asks if he may sit. A stool is pushed in for him and he proceeds to make mistake number two, a large gesture for repeat drinks all around, his treat, before the group is easy with him. Some accept, some refuse. He picks up the drinks at the bar and returning to the table makes mistake number three by announcing that he drove the distance from Oxford Circus in a little more than

five hours. The effrontery of suit, accent, and rapid chummi-
ness is intensified by the clumsy hint at the ownership of a
powerful, expensive car. No one questions him, no one expresses admiration over his feat. The atmosphere at this table
becomes a becalmed eye in the good-natured typhoon of noise
that whirls around the bar and the darts board.

The Mayfair accent, in an attempt to restore bonhomie, "You
people have a good landlord here. I know, I do business with
the castle." Rumble from pale man, "Yes, he's Big Daddy who
loves us. When the town put down paving stones at the top of
the street, he had them pulled up because they didn't suit the
approach to the castle. And when his people run the June fair
he takes off for Syon." "Come now, Tom, what about the low
rents?" again from the farmer. Before there is time for an
answer, London interjects with "I know he does a lot for the
town and I happen to know he's losing money." Even the merry
farmer guffaws a little and by tacit consent the company turns
the conversation to a shouting discussion of football.

Pondering vestiges of feudalism and wondering whether the
mead in a window display is worth drinking (or should one
leave untouched a legend of strengthening liquid gold drunk
by tall, burly Saxon heroes cloaked in wolf skins?), one comes
again on the boys fishing for coins in the Pant. Pickings are
nothing, the shovel loses its scooping end, the fishing is soon
over. To prolong the encounter you ask the boys to show you
the town. The older is a conscientious guide in his limited terrain, slowed by the younger who insists on entering every
dwelling to feel for coins in letter boxes. You ask if it is usual
for people to leave coins there. "Do you find much?" "No, but
I like to do it," pulling one scarred arm out of its short sleeve
to hide it in the body of the torn shirt.

The sparse conversation thickens in time. The younger says
he doesn't like school and he doesn't go much. No, no, he's not
cold and, suddenly, in the hoarse, desperate whisper of a much
older man, the keen, soiled ivory face and rust-gold eyes screw
up to spit "I want to get oot o' this doomp." His friend, hands
always hidden in trouser pockets, says admiringly, "He's an
adventurer. Me, I don't mind it so much here. I've got a job.
We've got a lot of kids and I have to help." He works as a
gardener's apprentice at 50 pence a day. Doesn't he have to go
to school? "Oh, no, I'm sixteen." He might just make a pale,

skinny fourteen. You offer the smaller, demonic spirit a few coins. He accepts. The working man refuses money, pulling 50 pence, his day's earnings, out of his pocket, betraying torn, raw hands, as achingly ugly and battered as the hands of child weavers in the East.

Neither the Artful Dodger nor his plodding friend is likely to live in radiance. The younger will probably leave the "doomp" only when he is sent to Borstal for theft, the older will probably never leave, going from one unskilled job to another as his hands grow leathery sheaths. Both seem mired in a class system upheld by last night's Londoner ("If we educate them all, my dear, who will be the dustman?"), discouraging to find in a generally advanced society.

In several ways Alnwick may remind you of poorish southern towns on the Continent, if you substitute for the cordial pint of beer a glass of wine offered by a thin pocket, the workman's cap molded to a characteristic, individual slant by long use, the mellifluous tunes on dialect words and, above all, the argumentative, laughing gusto. An appealing place and a reasonable stopping point, whether the next leg of a journey is Scotland or back across the alluring, frightening moors to the Lake District or for the turn southward.

NOTES

HOTELS: The modernized Hotspur and the White Swan, both in the moderate category. Simpler, cheaper, and wreathed in smiles and solicitude is the Plough, across the street from the Hotspur.

Running toward the sea, the road springs up, suddenly, to the semi-ruined pile of **Warkworth Castle**, another keep of the Northumberlands built in the fourteenth century on eleventh-century beginnings. Nowhere near as prepossessing or large as Alnwick Castle, it still merits a half hour for its vaulted halls, an ancient wine cellar, depths that were probably dungeons, the chapel, the Great Hall, an expansive view of the countryside and, looking down on the river, if the light agrees and the grass and trees, the components of an Impressionist landscape.

The moor hills turn to hills of slag, verdant slopes draw back from stacks and cranes and dark heaps. You are back in colliery country, trailing hamlets with rural memories of a time when there was reason to be called Longehorsely or Sheepwash. Not too far off, the sea laps at black sands painted by coal, but inland, the village of **Longhirst** washes off the slag and dust, drapes itself in flowers and sturdy children with clear, high, altar-boy voices. Out of **Pegswood**, yet another castle, that of **Bothal**, and in Bothal itself St. Andrew's Church, which contains a swaying alabaster tomb with crooked arches and strange symbols. The most significant thing about the chipped monument, though, is the attached sign, THIS WAS ONCE A THING OF BEAUTY, a reflection of the vandalism beginning to invade a civil, orderly country. Notice the shambles of immense slag hill, stacks, sheds, tanks, row houses, and sprawling town center being unconvincingly developed that is **Bedlington**, the grim rows of **Bebside,** and the huge colliery site at **Blyth,** and consider the possible reaction of *your* young to such an environment.

Past the bath houses on low dunes, a marker points to a leading stately home, **Seaton Delaval Hall**, a large Frenchified and Italianate palazzo built in 1718–29 by the dramatist-turned-architect Sir John Vanbrugh, a man with a taste for the sententious. Visiting time reveals the furniture and china, the paintings and objects, the gardens, as before and elsewhere, here displayed among considerable glories. (The Hall, incidentally, was one of the first of the stately homes to turn its Great Hall over to entrepreneurs who stage "medieval" dinners. Inquire locally for times and prices.)

Should you have saved the gray beauty of Durham for a southward journey from Northumberland, try to make a stop at the very first ancestral home of the family of George Washington, the **Washington Old Hall**, a sensible, gratifying restoration performed by Anglo-American money. The first recorded ancestor came here as owner of the hamlet—with the exception of Church lands—late in the twelfth century. He dropped his former name and took on the name of the estate, Wessyngton, a combination of Anglo-Saxon words that adds up to "Hwaes family estate." Not necessarily in a direct line, but close enough, the family lived here almost 450 years, after which, early in the seventeenth century, it sold house and lands to the Bishop of Durham, who built the unassuming stone house one now sees. The Washingtons left for Lancashire (one of the twigs off this branch was Winston Churchill), for Westmorland and Northamptonshire. Two brothers emigrated and settled in Virginia in 1656, one of them to make his mark in history as the great-grandfather of George, who was born in the Virginia county of Westmoreland, a reminder of the old country.

The house near Durham decayed to tenements, in 1936, declared too derelict for people to live in. The rehabilitation committee chipped away, rebuilt, brought in sections of house furnishings from other parts of the country, and restored portions of the medieval manor house. In spite of the massive Jacobean furniture and paneling and the formality of orderly rows of pewter, it is a livable house, with great spits in the broad kitchen fireplace, copper and pewter all around, a pleasing carved stairway taken from an old inn of Guildford in Surrey, and the Washington mementos kept to scale in size and number. An old cloth print tells the story of the child George and the destruction of the famous cherry tree, a copy of the Declaration of Independence indispensably appears as does the impressive Washington family tree, and a fan presented to Martha Washington by Lafayette. The rooms upstairs have been converted for meetings and receptions in the community and you may be caught in a bustle of chair-placing which will, with the unfailing north country courtesy, step outside to continue its discussions while you view the house undisturbed.

The village is a long street of dark brick and self-effacing shops bewildered by a complex of highway and a modern glass box of hotel called the Washington Post House set among a few frail trees and lamp posts waiting for WASHINGTON, NEW TOWN. You take your own bags to the lifts in supermarket carts, and trundle them into rooms which are arranged as studios in sunny, well-coordinated colors. The cost of a stay is high, though not inordinately, and if you've opted for one of the homelier inns of Alnwick, you might consider a meal here, unusually good for a region that never heard of Lucullus. The steak au poivre, for instance, is thoroughly authentic and the Salade Niçoise almost. A full dinner with wine is fairly expensive but there is no tipping and at dinner, gratis, a dramatic horizon of lights and flares from distant industrial plants.

NORTHWEST

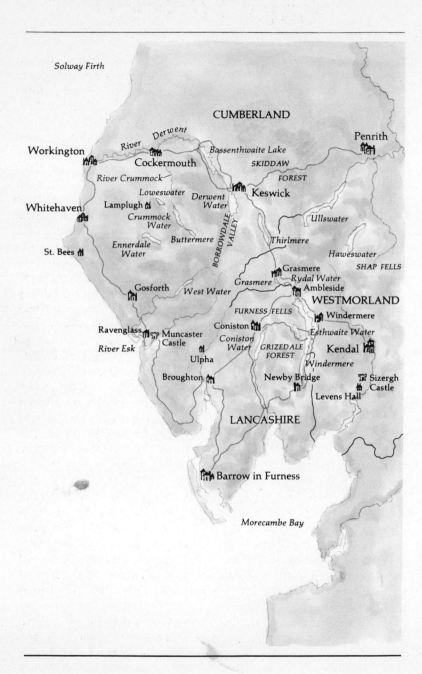

Solway Firth

CUMBERLAND

River *Derwent*

Penrith

Workington

Cockermouth

Bassenthwaite Lake

SKIDDAW
FOREST

River Crummock

Loweswater   Derwent
Water   Keswick

Whitehaven

Lamplugh

Crummock
Water

Ullswater

St. Bees

Ennerdale
Water

Buttermere

BORROWDALE VALLEY

Thirlmere

Haweswater

SHAP FELLS

Grasmere
Rydal Water

Gosforth   West Water   Grasmere   Ambleside

WESTMORLAND

FURNESS FELLS   Windermere

Ravenglass   Muncaster   Coniston   Esthwaite Water
River Esk   Castle   Coniston
Water   GRIZEDALE
FOREST   Kendal

Ulpha   Windermere

Broughton   Newby Bridge   Sizergh
Castle

Levens Hall

LANCASHIRE

Barrow in Furness

Morecambe Bay

Lake District

The partnership of Westmorland, Cumberland, and northern Lancashire, much of it National Park, which forms the Lake District, represents multiple satisfactions—except for easy summer access when the roads to the famous lakes and hills (fells) are as jammed with traffic as central London on the rainy afternoon when commuter trains refuse to run. The slow-moving line holds out to A and his family boating and fishing, ultimately; to B, climbing the snakelike paths of fells; to C, the primitive joys of living in a tent, or a trailer, under a hill that slips into a tree-bound lake. D, E, and F might be searching the paths Wordsworth and his sister Dorothy walked, the fields Coleridge crossed, before laudanum swallowed his brain, to visit them; the place where De Quincey observed his own contests with opium; the cottage in which Shelley spent his honeymoon with poor inadequate Harriet; the countryside through which frail Keats walked and possibly should not have; taking the children to the house where Beatrix Potter nurtured the animal families of her children's stories. For still others, the Lake District substitutes for the expensive, too-distant mountains of the Continent—altogether a superb, sometimes frightening, large area that fills a roster of needs and proclivities. For this reason no rigid route can be offered. You might do the journey on a series of zigzags to or from Scotland, in one large loop or a series of loops through unfolding immense views of lavender and russet-scored ocher peaks, of sloping fields, of vast carpets of wild flowers, of great trees and lakes—some of them blue dimples under misted cones of hill.

If it makes travel logic you might head up the M6 and by way of the southern road that goes through **Newby Bridge** and **Broughton** into the narrow, challenging roads that run past beautiful, desolate **Ulpha** and to **Ravenglass,** a clutter of basic shops and houses, small boats tumbled on its sands, large wet stones that represent a Roman port, a miniature railroad and intimacy with the cold Irish Sea—if the army has suspended firing practice.

At short distance away one finds **Muncaster Castle,** which must have been a lost, wild place when it was part of a network that protected the Roman road to the port and still wild when it was established in the thirteenth century by the Pennington family (still a Pennington holding). The approach to the castle is by way of a longish walk through a zoo, water-fowl of several exotic types, and a garden center that sells plants and offers gardening advice. Its strength is varieties of rhododendron, a reflection of Muncaster's famous billowing clouds, and walls of the flowering bush. On a rise near the building, a view of the narrow-winding Esk River slipping through dense green spotted with the deep tone of copper beeches. Two isolated farm houses touch a hill whose rising green spills rusty, tawny shrub. Over the top of a nearby tree, on its own hill, a small Roman lookout tower.

The exterior of the castle, redone to someone's notion of what a castle should look like on medieval remains, is not especially attractive, but the interior houses a stimulating mix-ture of objects that found their way to this far coast from several countries and periods. A handsome Burgundian knight jostles a few ancestral portraits; a piece of Elizabethan tap-estry, mugs of pewter, rounds of copper, medieval Flemish carving, Cromwellian armor and a gigantic pair of boots, a flat fifteenth-century portrait of Henry VI—the Unfortunate. The dining room with its red cut-velvet chairs in dark carved wood and heavy silver, the library and its stolid furniture, lightened by miniature models of chairs, keep more or less to one period and mood. An octagonal Victorian room resumes the roaming and comes up with Sèvres porcelain and Italian bronzes, one hopefully a Cellini. Led by a commentary piped through the major rooms, one comes to a unique hanging of Bokhara embroidery, a fine piece of Jacobean needlework, and the king's bedroom that wanders in quality from a thick Jacobean bed to the charms of a lovely Queen Anne spread, from inept painting to skillful seventeenth-century carving around the door and fireplace. The Elizabethan takes over for a while and ranges among furniture, remarkable fireplaces, tapestries both English and Flemish, and a portrait of a man in a gown of bright checked material of the gaudy patterns and colors that belong to a clown. He was a clown, Tom Skel-ton, the last fool employed in Muncaster Castle and, sup-posedly, a friend of Shakespeare. A miscellany of chests and family portraits is surrounded by Italian and English cabinets, a fine Italian table, and a froufroued later French table and, among the objects, the odd combination of an aged icon and a silver ring in which potatoes were served in the Irish homes that could afford silver rings.

The attached church affords an opportunity to see one of the antique crosses that dot the area. It is a worn plinth whose interwoven bands are just about discernible and whose circled cross has lost its place and lies at the base of the column. It was an Anglo-Norse preaching cross, used before there was a building for prayers and ceremonies.

Passing the considerable number of guest houses, farms that offer meals, souvenir shops (and, more rewarding, the many rich shades of red and reddish-blond hair framing now florid, now alabaster faces with golden-brown eyes and significant brows and noses), one reaches the famous late-tenth-century Saxon cross of **Gosforth**, conspicuously tall in the yard of its Victorianed church. It seems to be a curious combination of Christian and pagan. Among the knots and pitted bumpy bands of pattern there appears a man with outstretched arms who might represent the Crucifixion. What to make of a horseman riding upside down among other unchurchly human figures and animals consuming each other? Such ornaments, purportedly Scandinavian, may also have come from the East by way of Romanesque churches where heathen symbols became Christianized. From the Mediterranean to the distant north seems a long way for aesthetic influence to travel in the "immobile" Dark Ages, but such a witness as the Gosforth Cross may revise the common conception of that time to include the mobility of pilgrims and friars among far-flung churches and abbeys.

The hills lose their drama and flatten as they approach the coastal town of **Whitehaven**, decaying and rebuilding with little grace. The town and its attached communities are endless terraces of repeated fundamental design, the new houses in pale colors, the older wrapped in brown stucco. A pause allows for an occasional patch of modest Georgian houses and a few pleasant villas, for a modern church, a huge new hospital, a ramble of glassy, low school buildings, and back to the iron rigidity of utilitarian houses whose views are mirror images. In the near-distance, smokestacks rising among coal and chutes, and locks and barges that thread their way to the sea.

Walking in the heart of Whitehaven you may pass a pub named for Distressed Sailors, a cluster of Victorian churches—one defrocked, one ruined—a Church Street which is rebuilding (Georgian houses, whose integrity of design should be easy to follow) with startling innovations. You may notice that, in deference to neighbors and to maintain impartiality, one street has been divided as "Scotch Street" at one end and "Irish" at the other. Not far from the locks, a fancy old market wearing a large clock and a dunce cap of lead, a barred building that was once a jail and all around decay and demolition which, an American assumes, means bomb damage. Not so; this is an old quarter of town permitted to decay and to be rebuilt at some future time. One stubborn stayer is a cobbler whose low window is lit with the gleam of metal tips on red, green, blue, brown "Lancashire clogs" of all sizes. They are extolled as the BEST TYPE OF PROTECTIVE INDUSTRIAL FOOTWEAR FOR THE QUARRIES AND MINES, IN THE MILLS AND FACTORIES, ON THE ROADS AND THE LAND. Your professional life may not match this list and the sturdy clog be too stiff and heavy for your tastes but, unless you can steal a thatched roof, this is one of the few pieces of authentic rural craft you can bring back from England.

The kindly GENTLEMEN and LADIES sit at the foot of the green slope above the harbor, and with them a LITTER TUB that was once a mine cart. The monument at the crest of the hill tells a good deal about Whitehaven and its black beach. The tall tower was the shaft of the Wellington Mine which tunneled into the sea and in which fifty men were killed. Under a set of cliffs across the town there is another abandoned seaside mine in which one hundred men lost their lives. Only one mine still burrows in this pitted, uncertain moist earth. Low tide stretches a sprawl of boats like discarded toys and restless clumps of gulls and, beyond these, gas works, shafts, turrets of lights, a crawling train dwarfed by dark palisade and, farther away, the gray steelyard of Workington and the coast of Scotland holding Solway Firth. It isn't pretty, but a severe contrast to the lyrical, southward and inland, and the scene of a strange (and probably psychologically important) even in the life of Swift. A sickly child, he was brought to Whitehaven by a nursemaid, who kept him there for three years. He returned to his home a stronger, sturdier child.

The town of the deceptively dreamy name opens a road—

A595—to the town with the flat-footed name of Cockermouth, paramount in the Wordsworth story. Or, choosing to leave Whitehaven to its reduced destinies (it was a major port for many of its past centuries), go from Gosforth by way of secretive moors and huge industrial stacks circled by cows in fields studded with red, red stone to **St. Bees,** whose sheep live in the folds of swelling hills falling to the sea. An infinity of low hills open and close on each other wearing the scrub of moorland cropped by sheep, space lightly held in hedge and wall and stopped here and there in its flow by pine forests. A stone circle on a high plateau promises prehistoric mystery and turns out to be a nineteenth-century circle that once marked fair grounds. Past Lamplugh and its pub called the Pack of Hounds, the hills become smooth farmland and reveal a sign that indicates the HOME OF WILLIAM AND DOROTHY WORDSWORTH.

Cockermouth is a village stopped in time and old-fashioned country habits. The shops are sparse of light and space, reflecting a crowded coziness that economized on light and heat. The signs on pubs and hotel are touchingly literal: a beauty parlor expresses itself in the staring portrait of a Thirties vamp; FLETCHER'S FEARLESS CLOTHING hangs above a display of rural conservatism; in the window of the chemist's, a bowl of Hoof and Mouth meal.

Cockermouth's reasons for cherishing or not are mysterious. Dark stone plaques with blackened lettering commemorate the fact that Robert Louis Stevenson was a guest of the Globe Hotel in 1871 and that a native son, John Dalton (1766–1844), the "discoverer of the atomic theory," stayed here often. Andrew Carnegie merits a mention as the donor of a Free Library in 1903; toilets on the High Street are vigorously marked, yet the city is demolishing, if it has not already destroyed, a medieval hall which once sheltered Mary Queen of Scots in one of her flights and has closed the path from the market place that led to it. Nor is much of the house in which Dorothy and William Wordsworth lived, until she was twelve and he thirteen (when their father died), open to the public. The garden, edged by the River Derwent, in which the children played can be seen; besides that, only two rooms of a substantial house. In one room, Wordsworth's desk, portraits of his literary friends Scott, De Quincey, Southey, Coleridge, and Leigh Hunt, a few pieces of old china, and books that bear William's signature. More books appear in the drawing room and contemporary newspapers, one turned to a page that advertises the decamping of an apprentice and the warning that anyone who hires him away from his master will be prosecuted. The major distinctions of the drawing room are an early painting by Turner and a graceful, gilt-ornamented piano. Across the street, in a parklet of its own, the heroic head and strong throat of William, thrusting out of a poetic open-collared shirt. Wordsworth comes to one's notice again in the Church of All Saints, on a rise from the town. Under one of the broad gravestones lies his father, John, who died at forty-two, and beyond the stones a small building that served as schoolhouse for William and a schoolmate, Fletcher Christian, who grew up to be the famous *Bounty* mutineer. If it is not yet demolished, one can look down into the medieval warren that included the "Old Hall." Then, descending to the bridge that crosses the Derwent, up to the ruined thirteenth- and fourteenth-century Cockermouth Castle.

Noting the northern flavor of a street called "Kirkgate" and the masses of Wordsworthian daffodils that trim the road, you might take the southward roads toward Loweswater and Buttermere, in the occasional company of large, round fell ponies. The irregularities of misty hill that slope from Loweswater sharpen to a tall peak whose scabrous texture of gray rock, fouled green, and harsh rust scrub is one of the dramas of the Lake Country. Crummock Water is sprinkled with commas and semicolons of islands and framed in smoother, easier hills at whose feet spray densities of fern. A steep hill pauses for a minute hamlet busy with a rivulet that leaps among its rocks, and joins again with heights closely superimposed on each other like pieces of off-register printing. Guest houses nestle in the clefts of the hills and the lakeside and lower slopes soon grow clumps of summer people who seem prepared to settle in and stay forever, their fortresses built of large picnic hampers, beach chairs, folding tables, and piles of newspapers and books. You are in one of the most popular areas, at the side of Lake Buttermere, whose waters cut out tiny scallops of beach in sloped lawns that feed trees and sheep.

On the way to lovely **Borrowdale** and the ripple and shine of narrow rills, the landscape turns angry; the hills are scored and gouged with the precipitous black of landslides; a huge rock stands up-ended, a stone creature of omen; a sign explicitly warns against falling boulders; a great pile of slate looms above its eviscerated quarry; falling roads carry warnings and then, again, in red, admonish, YOU HAVE BEEN WARNED. The mood changes from the threat of Honister Pass as one turns northward to Derwent Water and Keswick. The slate quarries appear sporadically, a few fells are bare and a few wear scratchy beards, but most of the terrain is softly shaded green, a sparkling meshwork of rivers and brooks, teetery fences, the tops of crags dressed in plumes of wind-swept tree and, below, the clear gem of water.

Trippers in sportive sweaters and hiking boots, attached to ice-cream cones, announce the advent of **Keswick** (pronounced Kezzick), a center for walks, sports, and entertainment information, and a place to meet again with the Wordsworths, the Southeys, and Coleridge—the last held in contempt by locals because he was so irresponsible. Southey, by comparison with Coleridge's faults, takes on heroic size in Keswick. But more of that in its proper place. Walk, first, along the edge of the lake, past St. John's Church which rises handsomely between Derwent Water and hills. Rowboats and motorboats circle piles of green island that answer the shapes of hills above. Beyond the National Park Information office at the lakeside the trees gather in thick screens to stop at Friar's Crag where, to its roster of the famous, the town adds a head of Ruskin, who came here as a child, probably stepping carefully, as you must, on a heavy web of oak roots.

In an important sense the Lake District is the creation of writers: of the intrepid, cool Celia Fiennes, of Defoe who found the area "barren and frightful," of Thomas Gray who inspired Lakes touring, of Dorothy Wordsworth's astute and sensitive journals, of William's *Guide to the Lakes* and his translation of the landscape into poetry, of Ruskin's glowing childhood memories and his reflections on his surroundings at **Brentwood,** near **Coniston,** whenever clarity shone through the confusions of his aging, disturbed mind.

Hotels, souvenir and sweetshops, lawns and playing fields sitting contentedly among the cadenced fells, Keswick takes a sharp dart upward along Station Road to show its ancient monument, the prehistoric ring called Castlerigg, and ambles down among tennis courts, playgrounds, bowling greens, and other active salubrious greens to feed its mind and curiosity at the museum. Like most of the breed this is a hodgepodge; one of the better hodgepodges, however. Inescapably, eels and local trout coiled in glass jars glare accusingly. As inevitable, stuffed dead birds and Roman odds and ends. No sentimental bygones except one demonstration of local ingenuity: a case devoted to an early pencil-making works shows how it grew from a piece of graphite clapped between two pieces of wood by a farmer to the "biggest pencil in the world." Other than a large model of the Lake Country, the rest is musical, artistic, and literary. A complex xylophone of amorphous stones, iron keys, and bells gives off the sounds of faded woe. Among the books, documents, and engravings that deal with the Lake poets, an early Turner, a wall of Brangwyns and, from the well-informed curator, conversation about any of the objects in his charge and, one suspects, the art lessons advertised at the door. It might make a well-rounded vacation—water sports, hiking, painting, and talk about the poets: Shelley's harried honeymoon with the sixteen-year-old Harriet, Keats's awe at the sight of Castlerigg Ring, Coleridge's brief flight in and out of Keswick, Southey's dogged persistence with forgotten epics and his much-admired fidelity to stern duty.

On the search for a glimpse of what is left of Southey's Greta Hall, one might, on leaving the museum, take the path along the river at the side of Fitz Park and, passing an old riverside factory, a bright youth hostel, a set of attractive houses and playing fields, come on to the Carlisle road whose modest "villas" bear romantic foreign names—Padua, for one. But no Greta Hall, except for a distant corner embedded in a remade edifice, and no traces of the Coleridge-Southey ménage. As the story is told in Keswick, Coleridge found the house, invited his brother-in-law to share it with him, hoping Southey would pay the rent. Coleridge soon left, Southey stayed and so did the Coleridge family, without Papa and often without Hartley Coleridge, who lived for long periods with the Wordsworths. They were joined by another sister of Mrs. Southey and her brood and Southey kept grinding out for decades whatever he could to support his expanded family.

Grasmere rests in lower, sweeter fells and is a twisting village that first signals its importance as a tourist center with worldly shops that sell boots from Austria, Italy, and Czechoslovakia, socks from Norway, woollen caps from Switzerland, and trustworthy raincoats from the mother country. It is, primarily, the site of the Wordsworths' Dove Cottage, a former inn to which William and Dorothy came late in 1799, the place to which he brought his bride. (The relationship between brother and sister was obviously complex and one is not surprised to read in Dorothy's fascinating journals that she was very sick the day he brought his bride to the cottage.) Here his children were born, here he wrote some of his best poetry with the untiring, dedicated help of Dorothy who, by her suggestions and collaboration in revisions, may have had a greater part in the making of the poems than is generally conceded her. A description of daffodils by Dorothy is closely echoed in William's poem, for one example.

It is a small basic house still alive with Wordsworths and the modest objects they owned: a cuckoo clock, a tinder box unique in the area, a washstand, a kitchen table, the poet's bed and his passport, the bedroom that Dorothy papered with newspapers, chair seats worked in wool by Dorothy, a Coleridge daughter, a Southey daughter, and a Wordsworth daughter. These are part of the furnishings of the sitting room, now hung with portraits of Wordsworth and in its time the room in which Sir Walter Scott was entertained and, for endless hours and days, Coleridge. This was the room, too, in which Wordsworth and Dorothy worked, she constantly astonished at his capacity to compose here in bad weather surrounded by family, visitors, and playing children. The good-weather writing place was a hut built in the garden lovingly reflected in the poems and Dorothy's journals and, maintained almost as it was at the opening of the nineteenth century, still a beguiling place.

The attached museum was shaped of a barn where once lived Molly Fisher, the Wordsworth servant. It serves to combine Wordsworth memorabilia with artifacts of his time. In a typical Westmorland farm kitchen, for instance, one finds the cape, a wide, fine old straw hat, and walking stick that Wordsworth used in his old age. On an upper floor, portraits, letters,

and manuscripts, Dora Wordsworth's book of poems and
sketches by her father's renowned friends and acquaintances,
books owned by the poet, and an engraving of Milton which,
according to De Quincey who moved into Dove Cottage when
the family left it in 1808, looked just like his friend Wordsworth. More personal objects appear also: a pair of skates, a
snuffbox, an eye shade, an embroidered waistcoat of his late,
prosperous days of government grants and positions. Most
pleasing and intimate of all is a moving sketch of two backs, the
tall accomplished poet and the short lost poet, Hartley Coleridge, his wild hair pouring out of the brim of his hard schoolboy hat. In a few lines the drawing reveals the excitable alert-
ness of the boy and the affectionate interest—often profound
concern—of the older man who was substitute father for his
errant, decaying friend. Wordsworth's concern for the boy
continued throughout his short, erratic life. He lies buried outside the Grasmere parish church in a plot chosen by Wordsworth, surrounded by William and his wife, Wordsworth
children and Dorothy, a member in death as in life of his
adopted family.

To the south, a later, more spacious Wordsworth house,
Rydal Mount, partially shrine, partially guest house, supervised
by a Wordsworth descendant. On the highway close by, Nab
Cottage, bearing the date 1732. Here De Quincey lived with the
local farmer's daughter he had married and here Hartley Coleridge ended his blighted days. Southward still, **Ambleside**, an
affable village of old streets and endless rows marked BED
AND BREAKFAST. These signify the holiday busyness of the Lake
Windermere area, undoubtedly quite lovely when the vacation
atmosphere is erased from the scene and Ambleside returns
to something of the quiet it enjoyed as Lakes literary center
in the mid-nineteenth century, when the redoubtable Dr. Arnold, Master of Rugby School and father of Matthew, built a
house here and Harriet Martineau, a fiery writer for social reform, settled in and entertained the literary lights of her day.

Soon, the dignified pleasures of two unusual houses, **Sizergh
Castle** and Levens Hall, both near **Kendal** and a nexus of major
roads. The name "Sizergh" goes back to Scandinavian times,
and is recorded as part of a land grant given to a Gervase
Deincourt by Henry II in the twelfth century. In the thirteenth

century a Deincourt heiress married Sir William Strickland and assigned her estate over to her husband. The Stricklands had a long, convoluted history too elaborate to tell here, but one might pause at a few significant places in their progress through the centuries. In the fourteenth century the sister of a Strickland married a de Wessington, the line which produced George Washington. In the mid-fifteenth century a Walter Strickland put on the multi-colored robe of rich indentured servant, marauder, and warrior worn by medieval knights. He entered the service of the Earl of Salisbury, vowing fealty to him on an arrangement which required that he turn over important prisoners and booty to his boss for just financial rewards. Later in that century a Strickland married a Parr, the family of the Catherine who was Henry VIII's last wife. Later Stricklands, passionate royalists and close to the Stuarts, followed James II into exile in France. Their fortunes decayed but were restored with marriage, to collapse again in the late nineteenth century. The family turned the house and lands over to the National Trust in 1950.

Though there are documents to prove that Deincourts and Stricklands lived there earlier, the oldest extant part of the castle is the tower of the fourteenth century, one of a system established by border lords to hold off invaders from Scotland. The rest is an accretion of additions and changes, an appealingly confused entity, free of the strictness of other stately homes. That which gives the predominantly Elizabethan house its warm feeling is the wooden paneling in a number of rooms, some of it classical linenfold, some simpler and some more ornately patterned, and the ebulliently, masterfully carved overmantels to fireplaces. One such fireplace in the Queen's Room is topped by the royal symbols of England and France, a Tudor rose, and the legend VIVAT REGINA, flanked by the repeated dates 1569. Neither the name of the room nor the legend means that Elizabeth I actually slept here; it was the fashion of prosperous builders of new houses to carve such mention of the queen in their stylish oak panels. It was never certain that she might not descend for one of her imperious, impoverishing visits and the flattery of finding herself immortalized in the wood could not come amiss. The shine on wooden panel plays an echo game with the shine of distinguished furniture

from the sturdy dark bulges of the Jacobean, to the easy and
sensible of Queen Anne's day, to the attenuated elegancies of the
eighteenth century and, in addition, an oak bed (in the Bind-
loss Room) made from a pre-Reformation family church pew.
The rest of the furnishings are good and modest in number: a set of Chinese hangings, a Flemish rug, a reasonable
collection of china and glass, mainly English, and an early-
eighteenth-century spinet. What remains of wall space, always
allowing for the bravura show of intricacies in the paneling,
yields to countless portraits of Stricklands and the worshipped
Stuarts, interspersed with an Italian primitive, an early Dutch
religious painting, and a still life or two. Portraits and mementos of the Stuarts continue on in the tower museum, along
with pieces of old furniture and eighteenth-century clothing.
Here, too, the gloves of an Elizabethan gentleman; the special
insignia of Sir Thomas Strickland as keeper of the Privy Purse
to the wife of Charles II, Catherine of Braganza; and the records kept by Robert Strickland, treasurer and receiver-gen-
eral for the exiled queen of James II. If it is on display (not
always sure) you may find the thirteenth-century deed of land
given by Sir Walter Strickland to his sister, Joan, on her marriage to Robert de Wessington. As suggested, Sizergh is not the
noblest of houses, nor does it contain staggering art objects,
but the total ensemble—nothing too emphatic (except the
extraordinary Elizabethan fireplaces), of comfortable size, the
objects of several types of good workmanship, a touch of eccentricity here and there and, again, the glow of fine wood—
adds up to a contented hour or so.

Levens Hall is even more personal and, if that might be said
of a stranger's house, an affectionate place. The descriptive
booklet, written by a member of the Bagot family which owns
the house, opens with graceful hospitality, dedicating the
booklet to the visitor and opening its arms with "The old
house was accustomed to great parties in the past and there
is no reason why it should not continue to have them now."
The booklet, having explored family and house, finishes with
a list of gardeners who designed and maintained the grounds,
and a grateful mention of their longevity. Also, a short descriptive list of house ghosts in animal and human shape and a

welcome to that list extended to Mr. Bagot, who was heard to play one of the harpsichords he made and keeps in Levens while he was actually in Keswick.

These good-natured, mildly eccentric introductory notes sounded by a member of the family waft the visitor toward the house in an unusually expectant mood and he is not disappointed. Gardens and gardens, clipped and strict, blowsily abundant, make room for a wilderness of topiary fancies—chickens, hats, cups, rings, bowls, an Elizabethan lady, concentric green circles, low pyramids on squares topped with dashing hats. At one side of the fantasies, an Elizabethan coach house, now converted into flats with glittering windows, and beyond, *allées* of ancient oaks and beeches in a park that shelters deer as well as old steam engines.

There may have been a house, or rather fortress, here as early as the twelfth century, although there is no trace of building earlier than medieval times. In the sixteenth century, Sir Alan Bellingham who, according to the chatty pamphlet, "had done spectacularly well out of the Dissolution of the Monasteries," bought the estate from a lady who lingered and lingered to bury two husbands as well as the new owner, who could not take over the estate until her death. But the stubbornest must ultimately die and the property was taken over by Alan's son, James Bellingham, responsible for major changes in the house. After a century of Bellinghams, Levens was lost to gambling debts and became the property of Colonel James Graham who, with his gardener, Beaumont, planned the gardens begun in the late seventeenth century and since maintained (except for one wild, overgrown period) as originally designed.

The hall sets the Elizabethan tone with a plasterwork ceiling in intersecting circlets of floral motifs and repetitions of something that looks like an oil lamp but is said to be the bugle that was the Bellingham crest. The wall paneling is interrupted by a few pieces of armor over the fireplace and, above these, the motto, shield, and heraldic animals that belong to Elizabeth Regina. Considerably smaller and stiller than the honors to Elizabeth, a moving fifteenth-century Florentine painting in honor of the Virgin and Child. The personalities of the present owners intrude attractively in the shape of two harpsichords made by Mr. Robin Bagot. The interest in keyboard instruments is manifested as another harpsichord and a modern clavichord in the large drawing room, mounted with a tremendous Elizabethan overmantel and an eye-catching, puzzling painting of a lady. It is clearly the work of a master but who, or is it of several hands? The fingers have the unnatural length and gesture of early Dutch painting, the glowing gems at her throat and dangling from her broad, black hat seem to come from Renaissance painting, the face is plump, contented, yet very much alive, and exquisitely painted. The lady is Anne of Hungary, as copied by Rubens and undoubtedly improved on —from a German painting—to create a curious, luminous canvas.

Paneling and colossal carved Elizabethan overmantels (made a few years later than those at Sizergh, the style already somewhat overblown, the workmanship not always as meticulous) give way to stamped Cordova leather on the walls, which lends warmth to bedrooms and dining room and the well-made furniture they contain; especially attractive, the chairs and chest made by a famous Lancaster craftsman, Gillow, of the eighteenth and the beginning of the nineteenth centuries. On one of the beds, possibly the earliest existing patchwork coverlet of delicate matched bits and microscopic stitching (about 1700). As often, the small objects are of large interest: for instance, a beautifully boxed and landscape-painted Sèvres coffee service that was to be sent to Napoleon's mother at the time of Waterloo but was waylaid and redirected by the Duke of Wellington to become a gift for his niece—an ancestor of Mr. Bagot. Among the cabinets in the small drawing room, a watch presented by the duke to another Bagot ancestor who was one of Wellington's couriers, an imperial initial from Napoleon's carriage and an imperial blotter, minor spoils of Waterloo. Elsewhere, a few pieces of fine silver. The house is light, you will notice, in ancestral portraits, substituted for by excellent Brueghel drawings, an unusual small Gainsborough, and a delightful Bonington. These, the harpsichords, an imaginative piece of art work by one of the youngsters of the household, and glasses used during the Radish Feast early in May (when great hordes of people gathered under the trees to eat slabs of bread and butter and piles of radishes and washed them down with home brew) convey a fun-loving, music-loving, art-loving cultivated atmosphere past and present.

NOTES

HOTELS: The most popular centers—Keswick, Grasmere, Windermere, Borrowdale—are laden with them and the rest of the district is generously sprinkled with various types of accommodations. Too many to report on accurately, it is suggested you choose from a travel agent's list for one resting place and make your own selections (except in the height of the season) thereafter, in the course of your Lakes exploration.

Inquiries and arrangements for a variety of water and land sports, including pony trekking and adventure trips for youngsters: Lake District Leisure Pursuits, 3 Crescent Road, Windermere, Westmorland; 'phone, Windermere 4421. Hotel desks and local information kiosks of the National Park Information Service offer numerous pamphlets on walks—some very specific about distance, heights of hills, and what paths to take where—and athletic and non-athletic entertainments in the area.

A small theatre, Rosehill, in Whitehaven, maintains a program of theatre and concerts of high quality through most of the months between September and June. For details, write Rosehill Society, Whitehaven, Cumberland.

SOUTH

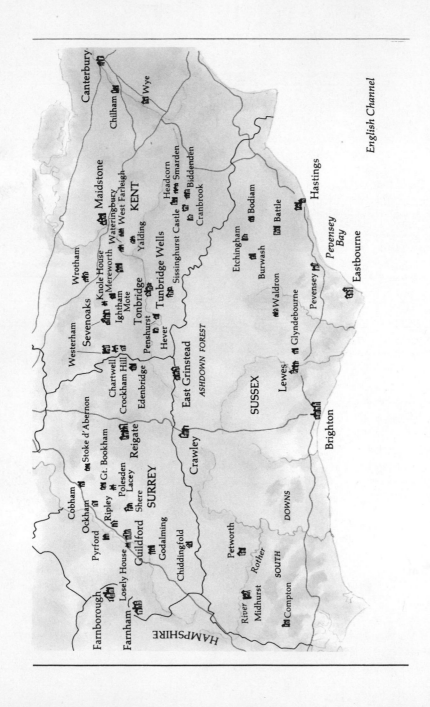

Surrey, Kent, and Sussex

A car can do it on open roads a few miles from comely **Guildford**, the more adventuresome will leave the auto in a car park there, find Sandy Lane off the Guildford Road (practically in town), and walk through bowered trees at the side of picturesque small houses and a minute church toward spacious outbuildings, flower-bordered walks, a viscous moat good enough, though, for a duck or two and the dulled reflection of a brown cow strayed from the large herd. On a vast table of very green green, cosseted by generations of gardeners, one of the handsomest and most affable of Elizabethan houses, tan-gold in color, its units balanced in a satisfying rhythm and within that balance, sufficient difference—arrangement of window, off-center door, and irregularity of chimney—to sharpen the eye's interest and pleasure.

Losely House was built by Sir Christopher More, an adviser to Queen Elizabeth I, who, like many of his contemporaries, helped himself to the stone of an unemployed abbey for his manor; thus the walls are considerably older than the house and may account for its gentled color. The family, now More-Molyneux, lives and works in the house, runs its farm and the production of dairy products and naturally grown vegetables. Since the aim is to keep the look of house and diminish the museum atmosphere, there is a lack of prohibiting ropes. The Great Hall is all a Great Hall should be—spacious, comfortably littered with furniture, china, old chest, little boxes, a Coronation Chair used by William IV set apart, and plasterwork animals held in circlets and squares on the ceiling. The paintings are entertaining, particularly a sullen set of James I, the "wisest fool in Christendom," and his wife, Anne of Denmark, presented to the family to mark a royal visit. The big, big painting that dominates the room is of early-eighteenth-century More-Molyneux and eight of their eleven children, three either too young or too old or too much for the size of the canvas. A more modest and interesting work is a portrait of Edward VI, wearing as king the collar in which his father was painted. There is no mention of his visit—too sick, perhaps, and dead too young to make the sort of overbearing visits his half-sister later enjoyed. (Never a woman to curb her tongue or demands, she wrote, before one of her three visits to Losely, that she expected, this time, that straw soften the progress of her carriage along the road and that the house be cleaned more thoroughly than it had been before.) By searching among the panels you may find the initials "K P" for Katherine Parr, the last, kindly wife of Henry VIII whose Nonsuch Palace yielded the smoothly worked wood when it was torn down. The heavy fruit bosses and grotesques in the wood of the minstrels' balcony were the work of Grinling Gibbons.

Queen Elizabeth apparently left a section of a traveling box which hangs, dated 1570 and carved with her initials, in the intimate library. Above the bookcases and a Venetian painting that might be a Canaletto, a tribute to the pleasures of reading, in Latin. Since all royal visits required flattering preparations, we find in the drawing room a gilded ceiling placed in honor of James I when he came to stay. It is a field of flowers and small birds real and mythical, almost obscured by the swarming chimneypiece designed by Holbein and marked by the presence of agitated, slant-eyed, chalk-white Polynesians. The cushions of the low-backed, wide Maid of Honour chairs are said to have been made by Elizabeth I. Other reminders of Elizabeth are a graceful flower painting on glass of blooms symbolic of the queen and, along with other flat, Tudor paintings, a portrait of her mother, Anne Boleyn.

Broad tapestries, thick Jacobean carving, and regal four-posters comprise the rooms of Queen Elizabeth, of James I, and Sir Christopher More, interspersed with silver and china in cabinets, winsome children's portraits. Lacing the spaces together, friezes of birds and mulberry tree, the tree a symbol of the sturdy lastingness of the family, the birds a representation of the shorter, individual More-Molyneux lives, a gentler view of life and death than the black sixteenth-century allegory on a landing near the bedrooms. The virtuous, as in Doomsday paintings generally, are separated from those swollen with sin, the sinners crushed under vehicles, crippled, distorted; should the lesson not be clear enough, the disorders—epilepsy, scabies, paralysis—are labeled.

After that, a life-giving encounter with a sociable cow and at a long picnic table ice cream or yoghurt or soft cheese, highly respected Losely products, from the adjoining shop. Another long look at the façade and its lawn, shadowed by a few big trees, as it sweeps up to a distant dark green fringe. A short distance away, **Compton,** whose distinctions are an attractive pub with an excellent restaurant, fine cottages in close fields and trees, the Watts Gallery devoted to the works of one of the most favored late-nineteenth-century English painters, and an obsessed, mesmerizing curio—a supreme folly, if you like—the chapel built by his wife and village people to his memory.

Herself an artist, Mrs. Watts went to the Romanesque, to Celtic illumination, and the stylish Art Nouveau, and mixed them to cover a meeting of four Romanesque apsidal bulges in red brick. Romantic, mystico-Christian symbols caught in endless knots and coils of Celtic–Art Nouveau seaweed, non-stop convoluted runs and turns and meshes, symbolize unbreakable bands of immortality or the inviolable line of the divine coursing through mortal life. There is no inch over, under, between the tight loftiness of arches that is not covered in plasterwork and every inch means something. In bright colors washed with a blue green-silvery glaze, studs of Romanesque capitals name the virtues; medallions speak balance, fortitude, wisdom, and love; ledges proclaim that "their hope is full of immortality but the souls of the righteous are in the hand of God." Silvery roots and greeny-pink branches are the tree of life, angels show alternate front and back views of their flat sexlessness to mean the light and the dark, life and death. Baby heads in heart-shaped roses must mean innocence and/or resurrection. Some people enjoy the chapel very much, admire the swirls and springs of bands as exquisite Art Nouveau jewelry and the dark luster as that of old enamel. The chapel makes others uncomfortable, pulls them into a swirling claustrophobia lashed by whipping reeds. You have been invited and warned.

A short walk on the road below will take you to George Watts, in his gallery. While not built by Mrs. Watts, it was improved and supervised by her for many years after his death. Theirs appears to have been a marriage on the "young, worshipful woman dedicates her life to the elderly genius" design. She was in her thirties and he almost seventy when they were married, Watts repeating an earlier act, a figure in a complex psychic pattern that propelled him at forty-seven into marriage with the sixteen-year-old Ellen Terry. (She, not over-inclined to devoted submission, released herself from the unconsummated marriage in a very short time.) Mainly self-taught, Watts drew excited attention by two paintings (a self-portrait and "The Wounded Heron," both in the gallery) worked when he was barely out of his teens. From then on, under the patronage of influential ladies, it was—with intervals of illness and black thoughts—fairly steady sailing until his death at eighty-seven in 1904.

It is an interesting gallery for a number of reasons. Primarily as a study of tastes, yours and theirs, only a century ago and less. How could a big chiaroscuro head turned away from a harshly lit, grotesque shoulder have been so highly praised by Ruskin as "Michelangelesque"? (In justice to Ruskin it must be said that he changed his mind shortly after his first enthusiastic whoop.) Could people really have admired and paid well for the chalky allegories, for the swollen, cute babies, the sticky "Ophelia" for which Ellen Terry posed? Yet "The Irish Famine" may remind you of the starved figures of Picasso's blue period and you may find the drooping head above furs and silks and rings of "For He Had Great Possessions" emotionally convincing. Consistently best of the Watts paintings are the portraits, a number of the women long-lidded, pale, seething types inspired by the Pre-Raphaelites. The men are treated more factually, the collection in this area incomplete since the most famous of distinguished contemporaries are in other places, the National Portrait Gallery in London, mainly.

There may still be a young man in attendance who, while he has a less than prayerful attitude toward Watts, is knowledgeable about him and painting in general. Ask him for a look at the storeroom where you will find Watts's illustrations for a book on cricket that became a series as popular as "September Morn." There, too, one finds sculpture studies for the large bronze of Tennyson at Lincoln and a huge nude on a horse. To finish, photos of the keen portraits of luminaries of his time: Lord Cecil, Browning, Carlyle, Lord Leighton, Millais, George Meredith, William Morris, Swinburne, Tennyson, Matthew Arnold, Rhodes, and a roster of lords and earls.

With a little foresight you may have booked a table for lunch at The Withies in Compton, highly prized by many locals and not-so-locals, and followed that by wandering in nearby Surrey to see the shapely, timbered alleys of **Godalming** tumbling to its unused canal wharf; a medieval bridge, a thatched roof on a gas station; steep, pinched, shingled roofs that give houses a sly, shy look; swans and protective trees; crooked house beams that explode in all directions; a crude old chapel and a careless mill, all on the way to **Chiddingfold.** The green there is a large, loose gesture that stops for a church which might be bizarre and naïve elsewhere but seems to suit the village. And so does a black and white house of squares and diagonals. And so does the big Crown Inn, with its vast fireplaces, beams, and homey plush chairs, which serves a good cosmopolitan (not cheap) lunch near a fireplace dated 1615. On, past well-kept, prosperous greens and houses to colorful, active **Midhurst** and its ugly, jaunty new church, its sooty, old flint church, streets called Duck Lane and Knockhundred Row, and next to the polo grounds at the edge of town, the double turreted gateway and sky-filled Tudor windows of an unreal, dreamy ruined castle.

Except on "Connoisseur's Day," when the visitor is admitted to an extra room or two that betray signs of living—piles of magazines on a table, a tangle of papers on a desk, seats that have borne recent human weight—**Petworth House** is primarily museum, interested in several periods of art, with emphasis on Turner.

In spite of the cool, timeless museum atmosphere, the house is full of colorful, impassioned ghosts. The family tree is ancient, fascinatingly gnarled, and huge enough to spread over much of England. It must suffice to say, though, that it belonged to the Percys who controlled Northumberland, a tribe avid for trouble and power. The central line dwindled in time, and the female inheritors married into powerful families, accruing wider-flung lands and titles which, in the mid-eighteenth century, were divided between a son-in-law who changed his name to Percy and was given the Northumberland estates, and a nephew, Charles Wyndham, who inherited Petworth and estates in Cumberland. A member of the Cumberland branch was the third Earl of Egremont, Turner's friend and patron.

Two of the family greet one from the stairs of the hall. The plump, elderly gentleman sitting against a dark sea was the seventh earl of Northumberland, a supporter of Mary Queen of Scots and beheaded for it. The ninth earl earned himself the title of the "Wizard Earl," a man of culture, the collector of an impressive library for whom the quiet life of learning was not enough. He was implicated in Guy Fawkes's Gunpowder Plot and consequently spent fifteen years (some of that time a neighbor of Sir Walter Raleigh) in the Tower. The payment of a colossal sum of money released him and he used his remaining years in scientific investigations. Since he was a savant of the early seventeenth century, the lines of inquiry led often to alchemy and thus he became the "Wizard."

The tenth earl and his father gathered a distinguished collection, too extensive for more than appetite-whetting here. Early in the show, an amusing Teniers painting of the Archduke Leopold's collection. Teniers supervised the assemblage of paintings and although his tastes and considerable skills ran to sweet small gardens and appealing old men fondling pipes, it was obviously a necessary flourish—and a fashionable subject at the time—to immortalize his breathless crowding of classical subjects among putti, columns, and goddesses, all under examination by aristocratic connoisseurs.

The next room continues with mainly Dutch painting, and a large, soft biblical landscape full of Roman classicism by Claude Lorrain. The star, though, is a glass case that holds a rare illuminated vellum *Canterbury Tales*, made not too many years after Chaucer's death for one of the early earls of Northumberland. Don't charge on yet. Stay with the contented Genoese Lady painted by Van Dyck, the placid "View of a River Town" by Cuyp, and "An Allegory of the Martyrdom of Charles I" that borrows from Bosch to show Hell breaking loose and London burning as retribution for the death of a saintly king. A return now to Dutch genre and landscape paintings, among them two small, singular studies by the prolific Teniers. At some point, the show turns British; among the native laces and satins of the seventeenth and eighteenth centuries sits the mother of Sir Philip Sidney, as painted in the sixteenth century, a large black and gold composition that shows off well her red hair and clear, open face.

Before you give yourself the flood of Van Dycks in the dining room, look at the artful carving on the wooden curtain swags, the work of Jonathan Ritson, a Cumberland craftsman who came close to the skill of Gibbons. The portraits—some by Lely —give you Percys and Wyndhams in full, gleaming regalia, but here and there a hand probes more deeply, as in the pensive, posthumous portrait, strongly suggested by the earlier painting, of the Wizard Earl. Roman statuary encourages the cool stateliness of the big Marble Hall, a curious setting for the warmth of Reynolds paintings, particularly the immediacy of a portrait of James Macpherson.

A forceful painting by Titian of a plume-hatted, blond-haired young man holding a skull, a curiously modern (notice the portrait of one isolated child) painting of a peasant family by Le Nain, the sly, humorous face of a Teniers lady, and good pieces of china lead toward the Beauty Room. The theme is set by a head of Aphrodite (if she is still there) claimed to be by Praxiteles, or one of his peers. The Beauties are the vedettes of the Court of Queen Anne, friends and rivals of a Percy lady who married a Duke of Somerset. Michael Dahl and Sir Godfrey Kneller shared the honor of painting them and shared, too, the need to make them all sullen and disdainful, the required mien of the high-born Helen.

Petworth's Grand Staircase is painted in grisaille, trompe l'oeil, and fatty color as gatherings of gods and muses whipped about by Olympic breezes. The central goddess is the Duchess of Somerset, her allegorical apotheosis dressed in the sweet simple garb of a millionaire milkmaid, waiting to be crowned by the gods with a modest chaplet of English flowers; in attendance, a bevy of recognizably English ladies standing about uncomfortably in the neo-classical rejoicings.

Out of the colorful storms, one takes refuge in the early, mainly Dutch, paintings among the mirrors and china in the Little Dining Room. These include masterful panels by Van der Weyden, a fine, delicate "Adoration" which may have been painted by Bosch, a couple of French paintings that have the sureness of Clouet, the best of these small works well arranged on one wall.

The windows here give on a great smooth lawn, a long-cherished heirloom that slopes to water and is punctuated by copses of trees as laid out in the eighteenth century by (who else?) Capability Brown. Turn, then, to the wood carving of Grinling Gibbons, a joyous profligacy of wood in high relief shaped as restless birds, as squirming cupids, and flowers and leaves, all tremulant, fresh, laden with invisible dew, bending to an invisible breeze. Somewhere in the Gibbons Paradise one of the ubiquitous portraits of Henry VIII after Holbein and a low-keyed Reynolds of Kitty Fisher, Courtesan, hardly seductive but nicely arranged as a triangular composition of pleasant head and wide lace sleeves.

The next goal is the Turner Room, hung with over a dozen paintings of several periods. There is nothing one needs to say about the mesmeric sunset view of a stag drinking at the lake at Petworth, a fairly late work, or the sunset scene of fighting bucks of the same time, streaming red and gold and yellow sky above a muted, dazzled landscape. Though the later paintings hold one in astonishment, the early ones are interesting for the passages of prophecy in their conventional presentations: a banner of dense, Turner yellow in a conventional sky, a heaving, twisting Turner wave in a traditional sea painting, the honey of "Chichester Canal."

"The finest surviving expression of early nineteenth-century taste"; the booklet quotes an expert on the gallery built and filled, partially by agents in Rome, in the late eighteenth century. The modern eye recoils for a moment, distracted by the airless arrangement, the Roman emperors and matrons, and the frozen Greek figures as copied by the Romans. Much more rewarding are a misty "Hulks in the Tamar" by Turner and of a later time (1830) his "Jessica" from *The Merchant of Venice*, an advanced painting of a girl whose Mediterranean face peers out of a sun-struck balcony. Were you told it was touched up by Bonnard you might be only mildly surprised. Madhouse faces peer out of Reynolds and William Blake paintings and studies of witches by Fuseli. Then back to the reasonable Englishness of Gainsborough loving the silken coat of a setter and Reynolds wandering from his portraits to paint a "Charity" which owes much to the Italians, who were better at this sort of thing.

The above and a glimpse of a much-changed medieval chapel is about all that is available to the 30-pence visitor. For the 40-pence special dayers there are the Stone Hall, whose main entrance is furnished with an early-nineteenth-century foot scraper, a surveyor's measure of about the same time, a few pieces of sixteenth-, seventeenth-, and eighteenth-century furniture, and a group of decorative iron firebacks. The art here shouldn't delay you except for a glance at Sir Robert Walpole surrounded by a hunting pack of which he appears to be thoroughly frightened.

The effect of the Stone Hall, obviously stripped of splendors, is relieved by the pretty, lacy rococo White and Gold Room, thought to be Turner's "Drawing Room at Petworth." The room breathes a perfumed feminine air that serves well as background for four Van Dyck ladies, pampered, velvety camelias, who might be more fun than sour Isaac Newton hanging in the library or the splendid, arrogant Florentine "Youth" of Bronzino. The Dutch return briefly and so does Turner, in two water colors painted for the lady on whose dress he spilt a jug of cream while staying at the house. As you casually examine French furniture and old bindings, watch for one section of bookshelf to open and close swiftly on some inhabitant or servitor. The room looks lived in and a fleeting form is witness to the fact—unless it was a ghost, the metaphysical Wizard, one hopes.

NOTES

Hours: Open April to October, Wednesdays, Thursdays, Saturdays, and Bank Holiday Mondays, 2:00 to 6:00. Connoisseurs' Days, April to October, first and third Tuesdays, 2:00 to 6:00.

The unemphatic slopes rise politely to distant woods, roll slowly, affectionately, enfolding cosseted villages shining with fresh paint and perfect little duck ponds, on their way northward to **Farnham**. It is a place of wide streets with self-respecting, lively houses and a castle or parts of a castle—long lancet window, pointed and rounded arches, old and older walls and the shadows of a yet older, timbered house, all of it protected, beguiling, and altogether of a lost world.

Half-noticing the self-conscious names on pubs, you might mount the road over the Neolithic Hog's Back toward Guildford, stay, or skirt it for **Shere**, a prototype of a "picturesque" village unkindly over-picturesqued. The needle-sharp dented steeple of the church pierces the sky above a fragrant churchyard, drunken old houses fall on each other companionably, ducks waddle at the sides of a winsome stream under a winsome bridge, a gaunt manor house peers through a screen of trees. Came the builders to fill in gaps of green with their presentations of "Surrey cottages," haphazard shapes in striving colors, distressing strips that muddle the smooth design of the village.

A few miles to the north, through country busy with riding, an almost contiguous trio of National Trust Houses, **Clandon Park** a rather harsh house, **Hatchlands** less harsh, both with furnishings, plasterwork, classical elements, and paintings in the groupings common to these houses; and one wonders why so many? They are expensive to restore and refurnish, where refurnishing is needed; maintenance costs and so does gardening. The Empire collapsed, the Commonwealth threatening to dissolve, industrial unrest blowing a strong, ceaseless wind, it is understandable that old securities, symbols of a steadier age where everyone knew his place and accepted its limitations and privileges, should be clasped to Britannia's bosom. But need there be *quite* so many reminders of halcyon days?

Polesden Lacey shines radiantly through the repetitions. Late in the eighteenth century, Richard Brinsley Sheridan became the owner of the estate and the wreck of a seventeenth-century house as part of the dower of his second wife. His decline into poverty kept him from making the improvements he planned, and after his death, his son sold it at auction. The old house was demolished and replaced with a bewitching Regency country house that sits happily with its earth. From the pillared porch, the land decorously dips and rises in a courtly bow. Around the side, softly rounded sections, a flirtatious cupola for a weathervane, and windows, windows, windows for smiling at the world outside. Even where the paneling is dark and heavily carved and the tapestries sententious, the light freshens them. Only the lower floor is open to the public and that is essentially a museum of paintings, objects, and furniture once owned by the Honourable Mrs. Ronald Greville, who bequeathed her house to the Trust. French furniture and English, a few pieces built around Chinese lacquer, and some Italian stand in the corridors and in the drawing room. The smallish tea room better suits its French paneling, little French tables, and eighteenth-century French canvas-murals. English portraits appear in a small, token number, several of them brisk, airy portraits of children by Raeburn. The rest is collector's pleasure: a distinguished, varied show of Chinese porcelain as dishes, vases, and figures, interspersed with Meissen, Sèvres, and English pieces of high quality, heavy in shepherdesses, cupids, and boy with dog. A category that interested Mrs. Greville's father, from whom she inherited the house and its contents, was Italian majolica, much of it made in the sixteenth-century workshops of Urbino. The champagne of the matter here is in sections of corridor, small galleries for small paintings: two masterly portraits by Quintin Matsys; fine royal portraits by the court painter of Henri II of France, Corneille de Lyon; a group of Tuscan primitives. Of the Dutch, landscapes by Cuyp; misty rivers and shores by Ruisdael; the non-stop gaming of Teniers the Younger; and by Terborch a dancing couple whose lady wears a white satin dress worthy of Vermeer.

Back of the houses, chestnuts that bloom abundantly in late spring, rose gardens under bowers of rambling roses, neatly placed shrubs and borders, and the serene view. One is told that the Queen Mother came to Polesden Lacey with her new husband, the Duke of York (later George VI), for a few days of their honeymoon. One can understand the choice after strolling for a while around comely Polesden Lacey.

Ripley is a center for reputable food—the Clock House, the Talbot Hotel, and the Toby Cottage equally esteemed. From here, if you like, a perambulation through telling characteristics of "broker's" Surrey. **Great Bookham**, a dart off the main road, with an engaging post office-cum-stationery-cum-sweets-cum-groceries-cum-toy shop, and a church of colossal, explicit monuments. The scrupulously kept church, yard, and surrounding lanes of **Stoke d'Abernon**, famous for its brasses; **Cobham**, with its well-proportioned new and old houses that trail a slow stream and swans; the tight houses of **Ockham** and the sudden depth of wood and deep glade, covered in last year's fallen leaves, that shelter a not-much-used church. Round out your day in **Pyrford**'s Anchor pub which sits on the edge of a river and you may, too, drink in hand, watching the small craft put-put up to moor and drink.

Springtime in Kent is a dappling of cherry and apple blossoms and screens of barren hop poles. If late summer and autumn is the time, the apple trees will groan with fruit and the hop poles unfurl and flaunt their green flags. A regional map (essential as a raincoat, sturdy shoes, and an elementary knowledge of English history) will indicate the Pilgrim's Way to **Canterbury**, living in its nimbus of martyrdom, Chaucerian tabards and wimples, and the gaiety of its youth gathered on the platform of open café in the city's center. The splendor of its historic ages shows as pilgrims' houses and those of Huguenot and Flemish weavers and in the awe and mystery of the entrance to its powerful Cathedral.

East of **Dorking** and its West Street row of antique shops, bright, ample pub-inns on the highway, and the rise of Box Hill, gashed with yellow-white quarries. Toward Sevenoaks and the A25, the traffic rides over suddenly widening vistas of field orchard, narrows to neat village greens, and diverts you to the Churchill house, **Chartwell**, immediately south of Westerham.

In 1922, Winston Churchill bought himself an elderly house, Chartwell, on a vast slope of weald and oast houses with jaunty white sleeves, and remodeled it extensively to his needs. The house is an autobiography, pulled into the present by the guardians of the National Trust, which now owns the house, with arrangements of fresh flowers, cakes on the tea table, this morning's newspaper in the drawing room. A Lalique cock presented by General de Gaulle, a jeweled saber from Saudi Arabia, a head of Franklin D. Roosevelt, portraits and busts of Sir Winston, medals, wartime orders, political cartoons, letters and photographs of wartime associates and, of course, the famous Churchill paintings evoke the man. He wasn't a good painter but was enthusiastic and devoted to the Impressionists and Postimpressionists: from Gauguin a stretch of pinkish beach, from Monet a glow of light, from Van Gogh a swirl of tree, brushed in with verve and pleasure.

The most hospitable room in the house is Lady Churchill's bedroom. Although it too makes room for display pieces, like medallions and white and gold china that once belonged to Napoleon III, rescued from destruction by Mrs. Jerome, Sir Winston's American grandmother, there is still a feeling of flower-and-chintz comfort and through the small windows a mellow slope of lawn framed by heavy firs and rhododendrons. If one had to choose a perfect bed-sitter, this might be it.

The next group of rooms has a more public-life character, set apart to show uniforms, ceremonial objects, and enlarged photographs both stately and informal. Search for one of a French worker in a cap, cigarette dangling from his mouth, amusement and some malice in his eye, offering to light the immortal cigar. The study, pretty much as Churchill left it in the autumn of 1964, combines the statesman and personal history—photographs of friends and family, a portrait of his mother, Lady Churchill, by Sargent, one of his father, Sir Randolph Churchill, flags and banners of personal and historic significance. Here, too, a painting of immense Blenheim palace, where he was born, the desk that was a gift from his children, as was the immense book in the dining room, illuminated with flower paintings and made to commemorate the rose walk they presented to their parents on their Golden Wedding anniversary.

Like the house, the gardens are generous but do not stretch to exaggerated, lordly distances. Near the house a lush, flamboyant nook where Sir Winston sat and fed his goldfish, the rest reasonable garden and orchard, limited by brick laid by the great man himself and, at the end of a row of cottages, his studio complete with easel, worn leather chair, unfinished paintings, plaster busts in niches; homely, workmanlike space in judicious proximity to sources of food and company.

It has its eccentricities, its uglinesses—especially an outer section crisscrossed with bare beams that plead for an ivy blanket—but the numerous amiabilities add up to an evocative, personable house.

If your mood is for more historic houses, there is, within easy reach, **Knole**, near Sevenoaks to the east, a palace begun by an Archbishop of Canterbury in the mid-fifteenth century, enlarged by a courtier and functionary of Queen Elizabeth I, who gave him the house and lands, now a formidable collection of unique furniture and furnishings of the seventeenth and eighteenth centuries. By way of the green, lacy canopies of **Crockham Hill** to the south and the new houses of **Edenbridge** strictly modeled on its distinguished old, you will find **Penshurst**, of carefully preserved authentic and inauthentic Gothic and notable gar-

dens. The house belonged to a Sidney in Elizabethan times and
it was here that Sir Philip Sidney was born. The Great Hall is
of the fourteenth century, the crypt earlier, the rest added on
through the centuries, filled with objects and portraits and, to
make it less formal, a toy museum and teas in the old kitchen.

Scenic arrangements of green continue on to nearby **Hever
Castle**, a moated Tudor house built into a medieval enclave and
surrounded with riotous English gardens and the strict Italian.
The house and grounds are alluring (and therefore to be avoided
on summer Sundays and Bank Holidays) of themselves and
especially for the colorful ghosts that pass each other in the
timbered courtyard. The first echoing name is of a Bullen (or
Boleyn as it was later spelled), the father of Mary, mistress to
Henry VIII before her more illustrious sister took over, therefore the grandfather of Elizabeth I. Later in the sixteenth century, the house belonged to Anne of Cleves, lucky enough to be
set aside by Henry, who gave her the house he had taken from
the Boleyns. In the late seventeenth century its mistress was the
illegitimate daughter of James II born to Arabella Churchill,
the daughter of the first Sir Winston. In the early twentieth century, William Waldorf Astor, who chose to become an Englishman, bought the estate and expanded it with cottages in har-
monizing Tudor style, adorned the house with the rare furnishings of several provenances and periods and, above all, hung an
extraordinary collection of portraits, mainly royal, by Holbein,
Cranach, Titian, and Clouet.

From Sevenoaks ask and stumble your way toward **Ivy Hatch**
directly eastward along a secluded path through tall hedgerows
and come on—if you stay alert for signs—**Ightham Mote**, open
only Fridays, 2:00 to 5:00, and closed earlier during the short
winter days. At those times, reputedly, one can see the Great
Hall with an enormous fireplace, a chapel with a painted ceiling, the big primitive kitchen, and an ancient crypt. Any day,
however, gives you the best of the old manor house, the total
ensemble hidden from the world and time: a broad gateway,
low bridges, a long stretch of timbered, small-windowed wall
sitting over the moat in so profound a silence that the ducks
and big swan plucking and preening in the narrow waters seem
painted on clouded glass. Experts will tell you this part is fourteenth century, that fifteenth, that other portion later. Time

and isolation have created a blending subtly integrated; the result is a consummate portrait of a gentle, venerable place.

The road to Ightham runs into tunnels of trees that break for a herd of cows, an amble of drowsy horses and riders, stubby pencils of oast houses and their off-angle cones of white. From the scramble of black and white beamed houses that are the tiny village of Ightham it is no great distance to the distinctions of **Wrotham**, in a sampler of Kent villages.

Wrotham's St. George's Church has an imposing fifteenth-century tower that plunges straight into the middle of the main street. It is hollowed through by a passage probably cut to afford pilgrims and priests holy ground under their feet rather than the unconsecrated town road below. Inside the low archway there are crude marks which, some say, were crosses scratched by pilgrims on stones brought from Canterbury. Or they may have been hex marks to protect the church and its faithful from the demonic beings that filled the medieval air. Opposite is a broken stone whose legend says it once bore a ring which assured sanctuary for those who grasped it—except, of course, those unfaithful to King or Church. The clock as church clocks go is quite old, dating from the first decades of the seventeenth century. For the truly antique, one must go into the church to observe the worn stone of the font, the empty niches once used for holy water, the fourteenth-century screen, the blank, arched space on the north wall—the oldest—which may once have held an effigy of the church founder, Richard de Wrotham. Near his empty space, a bulge in the wall that, in the early church of no pews or seats, was the support for elderly parishioners. Again we come to a hamlet of brasses edged with minute but numerous families of children. The most lively is that of Elizabeth Crispe, who died a year before Shakespeare. Her engraver bedecked her in a large, ornate hat, a stiff bodice, and puffed skirt ornamented with a line of fine bows, a gallant court-appearance costume that defies death.

On to **Mereworth**. The astonished eye runs up to a steeple that stops for neo-classic echoes of Baroque Italy, a faint memory of Borromini tamed by English conservatism. Down again to a rounded, pillared porch that remembers the church of Santa Maria della Pace in Rome and covers it with a shallow projecting roof in the "Tuscan" style. Inside, the reverence for Italy forces a hand to paint marbled lines on Doric columns

and to try painted ceiling coffering, à la Pantheon. The restrained painting, boxed into architectural units of pagan temple to repeat Christian and Hebrew symbols, lets go at the
trompe l'oeil that stands for an organ. The booklet that describes the Church of St. Lawrence of Mereworth candidly says,
"The combination of plasterwork and painted decoration is
well calculated to provide a dignified appearance without re-
sorting to the expense of mouldings and ornament in relief."

A short distance along the road to **Wateringbury,** off to the
right, there is a broad wooden gate that closes an avenue cut
into a treed lawn and, like a mirage at the end, a pink villa with
a columned portico, classical swags, and a large dome: **Mereworth Castle.** The house is not open to visitors, but if the trees
are not in- full leaf and you position yourself skillfully at one
end of the gate or other, you may see a fragment of white statuary and the edge of an identical portico on another side of the
house. It doesn't require a connoisseur's judgment to link
Mereworth Castle with the church. Built in 1723 by the seventh
Earl of Westmorland, it is not only Palladian, it is Palladio, a
fair copy of the Villa Capra that adorns a hill above Vicenza.
Neither Mereworth and its English counterpart, the Chiswick
Villa in London, nor the original, with its limited, four-
porticoed sides and commanding dome, were houses built for
living. Rather, they were meant as gathering places for the
élite in intellect and art, temples of taste and exclusivity and,
in a sense, the most appealing of English "follies." The earl,
some twenty years after the villa was built, needed space for
expansion. An old church which inhibited his plans was torn
down and the present church, Palladian wedded to Mannerism,
was put up at his behest and expense.

Hops and fruit carry the country road over a modest old
bridge into **West Farleigh** and on into a Kentish combination
that doesn't readily say its name. There is the big thatched
house, the huge, venerable brick-and-timber barn, a nice curve,
a bit of lively hill, a church properly set among its sad yews, a
very long bridge, a few cozy old houses, and yet it doesn't work;
the ingredients are there for a "charming Kent village" but the
proper melding is absent, or wrong, and one isn't surprised,
inquiring of a trendy young woman pushing a pram, "Is this
Yalding?" to hear her say, "Unfortunately, yes."

Brenchley (southward) helps restore the Kent image, fully restored in **Cranbrook**, a vivacious tumble of pretty wooden houses flopping on each other, sloping to and climbing a pin-wheel of effective streets. On one rise, a mirage of immense windmill that, as suddenly as it rose, disappears in the drop of a street. Cranbrook's economy has suffered several declines and recoveries through the centuries, but its high point was the time of the rebuilding of the church by prosperous Flemish weavers and merchants of the fifteenth century. Legend says that Queen Elizabeth walked here on a path of broadcloth something under a mile long and during her visit was given a fine goblet. Earlier, medieval royalty stayed at a now wobbly inn. To further spice up a lively history, add sixteenth-century Catholic martyrs held for a while above the porch of the church and a later witch hunt that yielded a satisfactory num-ber of victims to the public moral safety.

Cranbrook is still present as one turns into the famous gar-dens of **Sissinghurst.** It was among these lands that an early works relief program was successfully established. The unem-ployed who suffered in the depression following the Napole-onic wars were sent from Cranbrook to establish and work a farm which flourished for decades beyond the time of crisis.

Sissinghurst Castle isn't, really. All that is left of a large Tudor complex is a long, warm-brick entrance, an inner gate-tower, bits of house, a run of moat, and in the ruins, outstanding gardens. In a country of ruins picturesque, sullen, stimulat-ing, incomprehensible, this may be one of the most attractive groups though its history is as dark as any. It began as a thirteenth-century moated manor of considerable splendor, too old-fashioned for new owners of the late fifteenth century who supplanted the manor with a Tudor palace. The owner and builder was an interesting gentleman, Sir John Baker, "Bloody Baker" for his reputation for black deeds. A son destroyed his father's house in the late sixteenth century, leaving only the entrance stretch, then built the tower and behind it a new great house, honored by Elizabeth in one of her royal progresses. Later generations added sections, among them the still-existent Priest's House, and then, in the seventeenth century, the house hit a series of misfortunes and fell like the House of Usher. One Baker backed the wrong side during the Civil War, the male line died out, the females produced no children, and by the mid-eighteenth century the unused mansion was deep in decay. It found a function when the government used it as a prison for French sailors, one of the most brutal of prisons, whose inhabitants avenged themselves on the remaining shards. The rest was dismantled by an owner who left only the portions of the buildings now extant. Decades of farm hands lived in the ruins, using empty spaces as a convenient garbage dump. As such the writer Vita Sackville-West, a Baker descendant and the wife of Sir Harold Nicolson, found it and envisioned its potentials as living space and gardens, in 1930. Husband and wife planned well and carefully so that, no matter what time of the growing season, you will share with other ardent gardener-visitors singular explosions of colors and shapes. A conspicuous central low maze of hedge is given over to the rose—flat and delicate, multifoliate and cabbagy, rampant or timid—in numerous varieties, while another section, the White Garden, limits itself to the pristine and very faintly tinted of many species in beds of cloudy, silvered whites. The herb garden offers no overt beauties but the subtlety of infinite shades and forms of green and old-fashioned, occasionally repellent names. Nut trees and an orchard border banners of common flowers flying vigorously around frail exotica.

The lived-in rooms, a few still used by a Nicolson, shape an eccentric house, of which the library—a long, low room hung with a good, old family portrait, brightened with pieces of antique Persian pottery and furniture of several venerable provenances—can be visited. Also available for viewing are a couple of tower rooms, one the snug, pleasantly disordered study of Vita Sackville-West, where you will notice a worn, intimate chaise, a copy of the Brontë sisters' portrait that hangs in the National Portrait Gallery, many books and mementos. Another floor displays notes and letters that refer to the remaking of the house, especially the planning of the garden, and documentation of the house as it was in various stages of its life. The very top places you in a center of broad views of the Kentish Weald, as far as Canterbury, they say, on a day when the fog doesn't roll in from the sea.

One of the quiet joys of the visit not mentioned in the explicit booklet is the conversation of fellow visitors, often elderly couples, still friendly and polite after many years of marriage, who discuss quietly, reasonably, the advantages of trying this rose, that silvery bed, those spikes of delphinium, dreaming themselves out of their front yard patch into a large, aristocratic garden, the fantasy of many middle-class English gardeners who dream of long, brilliant avenues of flowers as other men dream of money and golf championships.

Biddenden's town sign shows two queenly girls whose broad skirts touch, indicative of the fact that they were Siamese twins, the locally famous Biddenden Maids who lasted a fair time and left, according to legend, a legacy which afforded the village the wherewithal to make and distribute little cookies printed with their inseparable images. Biddenden's church is of the broad, self-confident style favored by the wool merchants of the Middle Ages and later. Some of the glass and the roof go back to the fourteenth century and there is good wood carving of several eras, but the *pièce* here is the collection of brasses, unusual even for Kentish churches which abound in these mementi mori.

Smarden continues the tumbles of old black and white houses that trail toward **Headcorn**, its houses introduced by a confusion of brick and timber that has the size and hoary look of a tithe barn. Although the church is not quite as well proportioned as its neighbors, the churchyard has all the rueful, funereal lyricism one expects, and rarely gets, in the too-well-kept church grounds of many villages. This is deep and shadowy, the gravestones like old snaggle teeth, and, to complete the picture, a huge, cracked, gutted oak which may have, five hundred years ago, witnessed the coming and going of the masons, carpenters, stone and wood carvers who made the original church.

Curly little nested villages unfold to dignified good looks on the open streets of **Wye** and its harmonious houses. Approaching the church, after a leisured look at dwellings of different periods living decoratively with each other, one passes the college built in the fifteenth century, still possessed of its ancient size and architectural echoes. The church, erected at about the same time, has suffered the usual changes and one unusual: it appears cut in half, a row of good columns, a simple, sparsely timbered roof pointed up with several colorful bosses stopping at a peculiarly shaped canopy of dark blue ceiling. Concentrate, instead, on one of the elaborate tombs of weeping angels, twisted columns, shields, and fulsome prose setting down for the ages the benefactions and virtues of the entombed, and several bits of brass mounted on wood, one the burial souvenir of Alice Palmer, her two husbands, and a bubble of eleven lightly etched children. Outside, standing at tombs like mummy cases, look for the faces carved on the turret near the porch and then walk around to the north for an expanse of countryside and a row of grotesque lions, goats, and monkeys which served the multiple purpose of embellishment, of entertaining stone carvers, and recalling to the general populace the beasts of Hell.

Everything that is prettily manicured cosiness in Kentish village gathers to shape **Chilham**'s square—the huddle of bright-eyed houses with darts and dashes of black timber on white, well-shaped, highly polished doors, antique shops, and luminous pubs; the gates to a fine Jacobean castle, some of it claimed, uncertainly, to be the work of Inigo Jones, and a street sign that says PILGRIM'S WAY. Below, the old village hall of deep red tiles, timber-held brick, overlapping rough slats, tiny windows, and low, long wings. Above, the impressive rise of church tower, and not too far from the square, one of England's many Neolithic earthworks used as a Roman tomb. Ergo, the undocumented conclusion that Julius Caesar trod and conquered here. All of this is so complete and perfect that in spite of many summer tourists the village feels like stage scenery, flat and unpeopled, returned to its Anglo-Saxon name, "Chill Home."

In Sussex, if you have limited time in cordial **Lewes**, it might be a good idea to go directly from its castle and museum to the Anne of Cleves House Museum on Southover High Street, a short and interesting walk from the main High Street. The house itself is an engaging naïveté of small windows under precipitate eaves, cookie-cutter hung tiles, checkerboard flint on the outside and a colossal web of beams on the inside. It was given to Anne as part of the divorce settlement that dissolved her marriage with Henry VIII. (He transferred the house to her from a dissolved priory.) Built in the first years of the sixteenth century, amended and freshened, it is now the Folk Museum of the Sussex Archaeological Society. The displays are changed from time to time but you should be able to see the fancies in decor and dress of the Victorians, models of ships—one made by French prisoners of the Napoleonic Wars—

and of a sixteenth-century house. On a sixteenth-century four-poster bed, a "bed wagon" devised for bed warming. And needlework, furniture, toys, costumes, English tapestries, jugs, pottery, and shepherds' smocks, a huge Victorian coil that was a hearing aid which may not have amplified sound much but effectively warned. It is an entertaining miscellany that emphasizes Sussex iron punched as figures and ornaments for the famous firebacks, hammered and polished to make graceful fire tongs.

NOTES

HOTELS: Sussex has many pleasant country inns. Should you prefer to stay in Lewes as a center for country excursions, consider the venerable White Hart Hotel, moderate in price.

RESTAURANTS: For a diversity of sandwiches and snacks and robust coffee, look for a small cafeteria set between a large greengrocer's and a wine shop near the Castle Gate on the High Street.

For the mild eccentricity of opera-going at **Glyndebourne**, the best method is to take a train in mid-afternoon, dressed in full evening costume, for a curtain that straddles the normal matinee and evening performance times. This usually means dinner during the long interval, reserved at the Glyndebourne restaurants (one called Nether Wallop), or a slim packet of sandwiches. Traveling by car means the pleasures of unloading dinner from the trunk and eating it on a bench or a patch of grass. Or on a raincoat spread near the pool, on a blanket under a tree, joining velvet-clad gentlemen dragging a large plastic cooler, two ladies who have borrowed their children's sand pails for portage of wine bottles, parties lugging crates as large as coffins, the awkward corners scraping jet buttons, hooking pearl necklaces. The fun really begins when the weather chooses not to cooperate with picnickers. Then crates, pails, baskets, valises, attaché cases, and string bags lose their dinner-jacket cool, jockeying for position on the tables of the tea room. The experienced make an arrangement with a tea lady for an assigned table bound in their blankets and baskets to mark out territorial rights. This doesn't always work. While your eye and ear were held in enchantment by Monteverdi, a great clothing box superbly draped in plastic has appeared on your own private, dearly beloved table. Your best copper pan closed on one fried chicken looks poorly beside the plastic-domed basket showing off a linen tablecloth, candlesticks, choice wines, a high-chested turkey, and a club of French bread to go with a collection of Harrod's cheeses. A refined, infinitely refined, argument ensues amid shining swift eyes that hope to witness a terrible altercation, both parties carried off by the constabulary, so that one of the witnessing, eager-eyed with stretched-forth neck, may succeed to the table. Instead, one of the ladies of the tea is called to stand in judgment. Frozen in the dignity of her role as working-class judge between two of the feeble and not quite honest gentry, she restates her prior commitment and sails off muttering "Fair's fair."

Glyndebourne, as everyone knows, is a place of imaginative management, inventive directors, and fine artists. Too bad some of them, resting backstage, have to miss part of the fun: the contrast between Janet Baker's ineffable Penelope and the opera lovers in the rain-bashed tea room, transformed—for the moment by their box-laden dashing, by their anxious glances, and nervous arms extended for grabbing—to market hustlers.

NOTES

Performances begin, usually, between 4:30 and 5:30. Check for precise times. The present cost of tickets ranges from £3.50 to £8.

Waldron puts together a little church and its gate, a big lopsided barn, an oast house or two, a white, steep-roofed, hooded-windowed "Weaver's Cottage" to compose an ideal village and then, holding onto the rural picturesque, points you to other village neighbors with names like **Cross in Hand, Muddle Green,** and **Black Boys.** The road to **Burwash,** a wholesome village of Georgian houses and fresh brick cottages and a church with a pinched tower roof, directs you to Bateman's, the house where Kipling lived for over thirty years. Rather grand, though not very large, set among gardens and classic figures at a pool, it is warmed by a bower of espaliered apple trees, an old mill and dovecote, and the homely heads of donkeys cropping in an adjoining field. The light walls hold few treasures except the rooms where Kipling conducted some of his life and the study left for the visitor as he left it.

NOTES

HOURS: March 1 to October 31, Mondays, Tuesdays, Wednesdays, and Thursdays, 11:00 to 12:30 and 2:30 to 5:30; Saturdays and Sundays, 2:30 to 5:30 only.

Etchingham paints vistas of hedged fields enfolding sheep and lazy companies of cows. Its major art work is the church, whose tower is braced with metal bands and studs. Around the side, a worn pretty portico. Inside, a well-carved bishop's seat, a number of good brasses and misericords, and a curved roof in good shape despite the invasion of death-watch beetles, which you are asked to help fight with a contribution. (There is practically no church, you will have noticed, that does not need, want, and implore you to H-E-L-P!)

Toward **Bodiam,** expanses of field and feathery trees, hop lands cross-hatched with poles and string and, on a slow-rising height, the romantic approach to a moated castle. The ports of Rye and Winchelsea were frequently under French attack, often retaliatory, in the late fourteenth century. Among the defenses devised was the fortification of a manor house to guard the River Rother that flowed to Winchelsea. It never had to show its strength against the French and when challenged, a century later, during the Wars of the Roses, gave itself up without a struggle to continue an obscure life until it melted into ruin. The Marquess of Curzon bought the pile in 1917, revived its antique forms and color, and left it for the National Trust to control and care for. The rooms of ladies, lords, and retainers, kitchens and chapel, Gothic details that suggest fine windows, slots for portcullises, slits for mayhem, have been traced out and reshaped. Best, though, is the total of towers round and square, cut in tiny windows that look down on a screen of waterlilies in the moat. From the top of a tower reached by a spiral staircase, the lively movement of water where lilies don't impede it, triplets of oast houses, pens of sheep, the faint bleat of lambs, and gashes of red earth among the hops. Below, in part of the caretaker's cottage, there is a small museum that tries to flesh out the castle with photos of excavations, a copy of a medieval document concerning disposition of the property, and an alabaster torso of a knight bearing the arms of the first inhabitant of the unproven fortress.

The Momentous Coast

Many roads in this tight island lead to **Rye**. One could do it
meandering through the tawny fields, the stretches of intense
agriculture south of **Hawkhurst**, the sloped and thatched
houses held in brackets of hedge toward **Great Dixter**, the sun-
flecked roads under ferny bowers that open to seas of sheep
at **Peasemarsh**, around the low thatched houses of **Udimore**;
fruit and hops swallowed by patches of marsh as one enters
Rye. Or more quickly from Bodiam.

Above the Rye of sagging inns, antiques, pottery, and souvenirs, there is a quieter, secluded town, the town appropriate
to Henry James, who lived and worked here. Having admired
the decorative buttresses of the church and its gargoyles, at
the top of town, and been threatened by its long clock pen-
dulum taken from a Poe story, peered into the tea and cakes
shop which was an ancient vicarage and the house of John
Fletcher in the sixteenth century (this near the church entrance), look into the nearby cobbled streets and bright, toylike houses draped in vines and roses. Where the buttresses
swing out, an elliptical Georgian (1735) water tower of warm
brick topped like a bonbonnière, the neighboring ancient
Flushing Inn, and on to Ypres Tower.

At this end of the church square an attractive white brick
house heads a minute street that leads down to Lamb Street,
a tiny church, and a row of Georgian plaster and timber houses
that seem now to be studios. Watchbell Street, to the right,
slips toward rounded green hills, carrying with it a stretch of
hung tiles, the remains of a large-windowed, noble house, a
viewing balcony that might have been a widow's walk, and
returning toward the churchyard, houses with myriad windows
and roof tiles painted by green moss. Then down on rivers of
fudge and marzipan to Market Street and the town hall to two
potteries at the end of Cinque Ports Street. Also in this lower
part of town, near Fish Market Road, a tower and gateway
no longer effective as it was in the centuries of might and, off
the London road, steep, small streets of strange, gaunt wooden
houses which may have been warehouses or hangers for nets,
and now appear abandoned.

Winchelsea is impeccable, a small town of seclusive charm

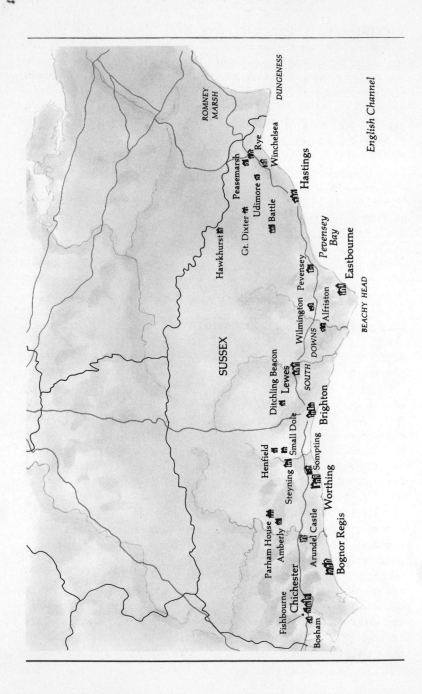

ROMNEY
MARSH

DUNGENESS

Peasemarsh

Udimore 🏚 Rye

🏚 Winchelsea

Gt. Dixter 🏚

🏚 Battle

Hastings

Hawkhurst 🏚

Pevensey
Bay

Wilmington Pevensey

Eastbourne

Alfriston

SUSSEX

Ditchling Beacon

🏚 Lewes

SOUTH DOWNS

BEACHY HEAD

Henfield

Small Dole

Brighton

Steyning 🏚

Sompting

Parham House 🏚

Worthing

Amberly 🏚

Arundel Castle

Bognor Regis

Fishbourne

Chichester

Bosham

English Channel

with little overt interest in selling itself. The gates, the church, and the museum are tokens of a tempestuous history calmed to the present quiet of careful repair and fair roses. It was not one of the original Cinque Ports—Hastings, Romney, Hythe, Dover, Sandwich—organized for mutual protection and expansion of commerce. The confederation was already a seasoned one, linked with obligations to the Crown and privileges established by the Crown, when, in the twelfth century, Winchelsea and Rye were added to the thriving shipping and naval community. By mid-thirteenth century Winchelsea, then on a spit of land into the sea, was important enough to demand rescue by the Crown from the erosion which was consuming it. A new, walled town on a hill was laid out—an example of early town planning—late in the thirteenth century.

This re-beginning is marked by the Court Hall, site of the prison, residence of the bailiff, and the oldest building in Winchelsea. Of itself interesting, it is also the seat of a small museum and the place where, on Easter Monday, the town mayor is elected in the ceremonies and phrases of the fourteenth century. The church speaks eloquently of medieval splendor and destruction. In the planning, the broad cap of the hill was selected as church site for the early elaborations and graces of Decorated Gothic. The merchants had money and so did the Church and, in any case, it was preferable to use the money locally rather than send it to the exigent Papacy. No expense was spared—native marble quarried, the pale stone of Caen imported; great Sussex oaks cut down and planed; superior craftsmen brought from the Continent to work with English stonemasons and carpenters. It was to be a blazing show, worthy of a town that was doing well fishing and importing wines, worthy of royal visitors making their route between English and French domains.

Not a century had passed when the French invaded to burn the town and the church and kill a large number of the population, already depleted by the plague. It happened again and again until the mid-fifteenth century, when the last invasion against Rye and Winchelsea took place. While the French were sacking and burning, the Rother, Winchelsea's arm to the Channel, began to choke on silt. The double-pronged attack of the French and nature finished the town and the possibilities of extensive restorations to the battered church, although some repairs were made. There is no longer a tower, the end arches of the extraordinary west front frame nothing but space, the interior is disorganized and patchy. Nonetheless, the magnificence is not altogether dispelled—as witness a window frame, the light carving on the stone seats in the St. Nicholas Chapel, the flight of arches and, especially, the beautiful tombs of the Alards, a family of naval leaders of the Cinque Ports fleet. To prove that the dead live longest, a group of very old tombs, probably transferred from the old, lower church, is a knight in armor, a lady, and a youth whose worn marble display details of dress fashionable seven hundred or more years ago. The parts, although not quite so great as the distraught whole, combine as one of the most suggestive of England's semi-ruins; not to be missed if you are in the area.

NOTES

HOTELS: One of the best-known inns is the Mermaid of Rye, a genuine antique graced with Tudor carvings; high to moderate. The George and the Hope Anchor are both less historic, thoroughly usable, and somewhat cheaper. The New Inn of Winchelsea guarantees a more sedate, calmer visit at a moderate rate.

Turning westward along the coast, **Hastings**, and a short distance inland, the village of **Battle** and the bastions, gated tower, and white doves of its abbey, built by William the Conqueror to commemorate his victory, to send up prayers for the dead in battle, and to assuage the uneasiness of guilt in the immortal equation of riches for blood. Although the Pope supported William's right to England and, it was alleged, Edward the Confessor had promised him the succession—and the contending Harold had sworn William fealty earlier in Normandy— Edward, it appears, had also promised Harold the crown. As in many struggles for power among high prelates and kings, William's claim was not quite clear, but he made it.

Once, according to the map in the attached museum, the

abbey had properties that stretched into Wales and northward
to Norwich and, "because of the very great dignity of the
place," the men were classed as "Burgesses" and the village
as town. The abbey is reduced now to sharing its truncated
walls and gardens and mini-maze hedges with a girls' school
and an occasional invasion of local yeomen, fortified by spirits,
who re-enact the battle of "brave Harold le Saxon" against
the Normans on high, open Senlac Ridge nearby. It must share
its precincts, too, with English trippers, who carefully examine
the Gothic details on the gateway, the deeply vaulted monks'
common room, remains of Norman stone, and the towers of
a Tudor house in which Elizabeth I, the ward of a post-Dis-
solution owner, Sir Anthony Browne, was meant to live but
didn't because he died before its completion. (The monks he
displaced put a curse on the family, promising that fire and
water would destroy it. The curse was slow to act but two
centuries later another property, Cowdray, originally given the
family by Henry VIII, burned down and a few days later the
owner was drowned. His sister, who inherited the Cowdray
estate, lost two sons by drowning. For Henry, also, a miserable,
disgusting death was prophesied and it happened.)

The museum shows one lead coins used as token payment
for hop gatherers, coins of the Romans and the Saxons and the
Normans before and after 1066, worked Sussex iron of many
centuries, and a copy of the renowned Bayeux tapestries that
depict the Conquest landing and battle, made on the order of
Bishop Odo, William's brother. The village itself is also museum in a valid sense, a demonstration of changing house
styles that stemmed from the thirteenth-century houses of
craftsmen and laborers hired when the abbey buildings grew
to luxuriance. To fill out the medieval portrait, one must place
on the present parking lot a weekly market and an autumn fair
whose stallkeepers paid part of the proceeds and booth-space
rental to the abbey. On the town green, the stimulations of
bull-baiting, and at the gateway of the abbey, stocks for malefactors. The earliest extant house is the restored Pilgrim's
Restaurant, actually a shelter of the fifteenth century built on
the site of an earlier hospice. Other buildings were remade
after the collapse of the abbey, to accommodate the families
of iron merchants, those of the late seventeenth century often
incorporating the stone of the abbey kitchen. It was pulled

down by the owner, Lord Montague, in 1676, the stone and
roof lead sold for substantial sums.

If you care to pursue the Battle of Hastings to its absolute
beginnings with the landing of the Normans, go seaward to
Pevensey, a funnel of old houses and fallen stone now visually
unrelated to its history of Roman soldiers, followed by medieval knights who manned the fortress-castle which taught the
boy Thomas Becket courtly ways.

Momentous memories give way to the winsome in the villages
west of Pevensey. Orchards and the gaiety of oast houses
tipped with musicians' reeds run toward **Wilmington**, pausing
for a lift of downs scored with a "Long Man," an obvious
rival to the Cerne Giant in Dorset and obviously not as primitive. Some say he is a great scarecrow, made gigantic to
frighten off predators; some that he was a joke perpetrated
two centuries ago. Whatever you decide about the "Long Man,"
you will find the hamlet of Wilmington a jewel of brick and
timbered lanes smothered in flowers and greenery.

On to **Alfriston** among the slow sweep of downs, an out-
cropping of chalk, a trail of hedge, billows of yellow-green,
gray-green, emerald green. Alfriston might be—like Lavenham
in East Anglia—the trippers' village of the area, a fastidious
line-up of souvenirs, twinkling shops, half-timbered houses,
one of the oldest inns with a history of smuggling, and a church
with a good roof and a complex of frame and red and blue
cords for bell-pulling. Beside the church, a prized antiquity
and unique, the Old Clergy House, of heavy beams and deep,
dark thatch that shelters minute windows. One large whitewashed room of this house for priests is open to the public,
and so that no one is tempted to immortalize himself on the
walls, there is a book provided for signatures.

Ditchling Road runs westward to **Ditchling Beacon**, a high
point used by prehistoric man as a hill fort and by the Elizabethans for a beacon to signal the approach of the Armada.
Now it is an eyrie for looking over to **Brighton** as it grows
inward from the sea and over the cow-covered downs stippled
with the broken light of wind-whipped clouds; a top-of-the-
world emptiness of stiff breeze, dark shrub, and gorse scratched
with walkers' paths. Down along the slopes then, to mullioned,
beamed **Ditchling** village, toward **Henfield** (the introduction to

West Sussex), to pine forest and waves of down, and a village
with the melancholy name of **Small Dole**. In the distance, a
high clump of two-hundred-year-old beeches that shape the
Chanctonbury Ring which appears again as a huge, dark mush-
room above **Steyning**, and again and again from the outskirts
of villages that turn smilingly, lazily, like dolphins, in the
shadow of the dark dome.

Dunes painted mustard-green, earth-red, tawny yellow, and the
scraggly village of **Sompting** near the coast are bound together
by an oddly shaped ancient church with a unique Saxon tower.
An intriguing confusion of styles has, fortunately, left untouched not only the tower wrapped in its pearly flint but also
Saxon ornaments as bits of frieze, carvings in the belfry windows, and stones used to support and decorate later elements.
Small, retiring, the church is perked up by the helm roof of
the tower which might, in another context, be a paper cut-out
punched and folded as a party hat.

Northwestward again to **Parham House**, near Amberley, a
delightful, richly gardened Tudor house that holds extraordinary needlework, some of it stitched by Mary Queen of Scots
and her ladies in the long years of captivity—it is said. **Amberley**, embraced by river and cliff, leads southward to the not
very old **Arundel Castle**, best experienced from a photogenic
distance (the approach to the village, for instance) and westward to **Chichester** and its neighbor, **Fishbourne**, an important
Roman site.

Early in the nineteenth century, builders struck their picks
into a flat, resistant area that turned out to be a floor of Roman
mosaic. In another place, shovels stumbled against shards of
Roman baths. These finds were lost, but remainders of the
Romans kept reappearing in the watercress beds south of the
village. About fifteen years ago, workmen digging to place a
water main came on a rich find centered on a Roman harbor.
The major testament is sections of a once-stupendous palace,
possibly that of a governor or a native king of a tribe that gave
the Romans no trouble.

A well-planned museum shows, among its ornaments, coins,
and objects, layers of building material from many parts of the
Empire used in the slow growth of the palace, and a model
of the luxurious buildings and gardens as they probably were

in Roman times. Armed with these images and those of models of Roman ships and a photo-montage of excavation in progress, one enters a classical portal to the reconstructed section.

Detailed booklets explain what you see and what you might be seeing were there fuller reconstruction; even without their aid it is an imposing experience to walk through the area and its formal garden and hedge plantings. Most impressive are the floor mosaics, those in black and white quite modern in feeling; others in colors arranged in the floral, paisley-leafed elaborations of the East, and one of earth colors for medallions of playful sea monsters surrounding a boy on a dolphin, as fine as those of villas in Rome. If your experience of things and places Roman is extensive this may not be worth a detour to you, and yet worth some time if only for the care and scholarship that went into the study and reconstruction of the palace scheme and the orderly, helpful museum displays.

Bosham, nearby, is heavy with history: reputed to be the oldest Christian community in Sussex; stones of a Roman basilica incorporated in the church tower; its Saxon church, attributed to Harold, shown in the Bayeux tapestries; King Canute's daughter buried here and a nineteenth-century exhumation of a stone coffin that did not quite prove it. Unimpressed, dozing Bosham now sits dangling its feet in its estuary, playing with small boats, trailing a baby canal.

NOTES

As you may know, Chichester runs a renowned theatre and, attached to the theatre, an imaginative self-service restaurant with sophisticated standards.

SOUTHWEST

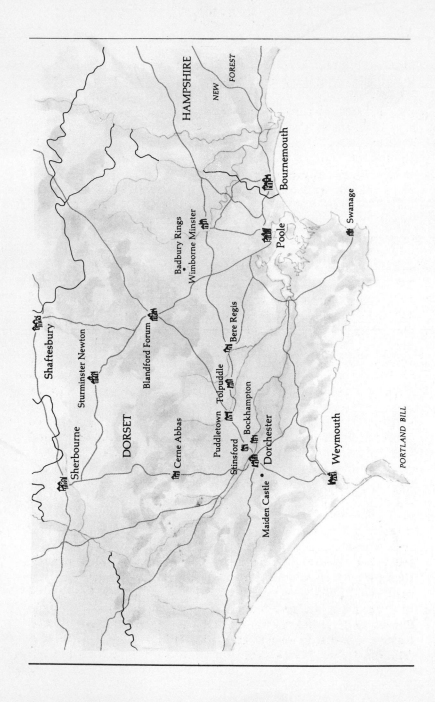

HAMPSHIRE

NEW FOREST

Bournemouth

Swanage

Poole

Badbury Rings
Wimborne Minster

Bere Regis

Blandford Forum

Shaftesbury

Sturminster Newton

Tolpuddle

Puddletown

Bockhampton

DORSET

Cerne Abbas

Stinsford

Dorchester

Sherbourne

Maiden Castle

Weymouth

PORTLAND BILL

Dorset

Moderate, sweet Dorset, whose tactful hills rise to neat plateaus and drop to nestlike valleys, is haunted by dramatic ghosts: martyrs of an early attempt at unionization of starving agricultural workers, raw chalky circles in scratchy bush that were the settlements of prehistoric Englishmen, a priapic Roman giant and, most pervasive of all, the monumental shadow of Thomas Hardy, a native son. There is no piece of Dorset tourist literature that does not identify Dorchester as his Casterbridge, indicate where the Turbervilles (D'Urbervilles) were entombed, where Tess spent her grotesque honeymoon, the villages of *Far from the Madding Crowd*, the heath on which Eustacia Vye pulled doom around her.

A hub of Hardyism, a comfortable place from which to visit the rest, is **Dorchester**, free of imposing monuments, contented to be a thriving market center noted for its durable sheep and cattle. Defoe said of it, stressing the civilized amiability, "Dorchester is indeed a pleasant agreeable town to live in—the people are not all of one mind, either as to religion or politicks . . . yet they did not seem to separate with so much animosity as in other places . . . there is good company and a good deal of it; and a man that coveted a retreat in this world might as agreeably spend his time, and as well in Dorchester as in any town I know in England." That quality can be quickly sensed as one threads one's way through the High Streets East and West and South Street, "agreeable" streets dedicated to selling, with subtle differences in atmosphere. High West is "county," with a refinement of boutiques of sensible, conservative clothing, and an old-fashioned sweetshop pleased to tell passers-by of the amount of good country butter in the chocolate "couvertures" around myriad delectable fillings. The bins on bins of sweets are gorgeous, sincere, and outrageously tempting. On the other side of the street, another sort of wholesomeness, the rational design of Georgian houses, balanced by the sadistic spirit—still said to be stomping and shrieking with rage—of the "hanging" Judge Jeffreys who lodged and held court in the Antelope Hotel, which bears as its sign a long-wigged portrait of its distinguished guest of 1685. In that year of the "Bloody Assizes," following the Monmouth Rebellion against

James II, 300 prisoners were tried for treason, over 290 of them
condemned to death and, of that number, 74 hanged in Dorchester and a score of heads impaled as rotting ornaments
on the railings of St. Peter's Church in the center of town.
Those heads and sections of body not accommodated by Dorchester were sent out to adorn other Dorset communities. An
easier memory of the site is its use as the Hiring Fair, where
men wore symbols of their trade—strands of straw for a
thatcher for example—as described in *The Mayor of Casterbridge*.

South Street, with its curious juxtapositions, is the most stimulating of the central streets. It billows and ebbs with the
movement in and out of famous chain stores, the indispensable
Boots, Marks & Spencer, Wimpy's, for instance, all well dressed
in modern glass. Their older companions are less formal and
more picturesque. A timeless small vegetable shop, which arranges its artichokes and tomatoes as if they were crown
jewels, looks across to a breathless jumble of sheepskin coats,
fishing tackle, cord, creels, shopping baskets that curtain and
overhang the door. A shamefaced old HOVIS bread sign and a
café that serves both "light" meals and "filling" meals blink
in the glare of Frisby's shoe shop, plastered with big signs,
lettered tall, lettered wide, lettered in sonorous rotund gold
to repeat that one must wear *their* shoes and that they spe-
cialize in repairs, the repetitions an Edwardian version of the
later reiterations of TV. A neighboring Georgian house bears
a plaque that identifies it as the probable dwelling of the
MAYOR OF CASTERBRIDGE before his fall, and nearby a restored
building that sports a good black clock above low stone scallops which conceal the courtyard of a set of almshouses, Napper's Mite, founded by a Robert Napier early in the seventeenth
century to house ten poor men. Now it shelters shops and a
café with a fireplace stamped 1636.

A distinction you may note as you stroll in the heart of town
is the unusual number of rare book and print shops, which
speaks of extra money to spend and, possibly, an intellectual
bent, also suggested by a local news poster which placed important football news below the fact that "Famous Poet Dies,"
referring to the foreigner, Ezra Pound.

The paucity of very old buildings, although Dorchester was
an important town in the Middle Ages, as it was in Roman

times, is explained by a succession of fires fed by the attractive, dangerous thatch on roofs. Of the few survivors there is St. Peter's Church, not as interesting as it might be except for a Norman doorway, a monument to a Hardy ancestor and, of particular interest to Americans, a brass commemorating the Rev. John White. "A man of great godliness, good scholarship and wonderful ability and kindness. He had a very strong sway in this town. He greatly set forward the emigration to the Massachusetts Bay colony, where his name lives in remembrance." He accompanied the Pilgrims as far as Plymouth and there exhorted them to build a church immediately on their arrival in the new land. This they did, in the town of Dorchester, Massachusetts, at about the same time that the settlement at Cape Ann was being organized under its first governor, a Captain Endicott, also a man from Dorchester.

Between the church and the museum, the next Dorchester port of call, there stands an elderly gentleman in old-fashioned dress, the city's second favorite son (though neither was actually born in Dorchester), William Barnes, born about forty years before Hardy. He was that not uncommon phenomenon of a poor brilliant boy deprived of much formal education who spent most of his life filling in the gaps and educating others. He mastered the essential Latin and Greek, the major European languages and a few more foreign, and went on to become adept at several musical instruments and the principles of composition. But his fame rests primarily in his fine dialect poems, almost forgotten except for a few angry enthusiasts: "Indeed, the Scots over-rate Burns as perversely as the English neglect and underestimate Barnes" (says John Hyams in his *Dorset*).

The museum is part Hardy, part Dorset bygones, part history, part archeology, part zoology, part modern art, sprinkled with a bit of local this and that and the total an engaging place. The entrance opens on a miscellany of reproductions of local Roman mosaic and of a sizable brass rubbing across from a water color executed by Hardy. Thomas Hardy was a gifted draughtsman and prize-winning architect before he turned to writing and it is no surprise that he had some painting skill. The bookstall is, not surprisingly, heavy in Hardy material: maps of Wessex marked with Hardy towns, booklets exploring many aspects of his work and his life. Opposite the bookstall is the most eye-catching entity of the collection, a wall design of old wheels, gears, bars, machine-tool patterns, of themselves good-looking and dynamically juxtaposed. Wandering through space of scattered hog-back coffins and past a couch covered in William Morris cloth, one comes to Hardy and family and souvenirs arranged under a curving, high-colored Victorian canopy of fine ironwork. A movable set of wall boards, like a large, stiff book, tells the salient facts of Hardy's life from forebears to death; cases bear photographs and some memorabilia of Napoleon, in whom Hardy was greatly interested. The hall makes room for attractive paintings and etchings of the area, for illustrations to the novels and drawings suggested by scenes in the novels, their quality high in the emotional narrative power that the novels provoked. Somewhere in the assemblage there is a painting from a photograph of Hardy's first wife, a girl with elaborately dressed blond hair and a full earth-goddess face, both wise and innocent, with a teasing resemblance to someone—the young Simone Signoret in *Casque d'Or*.

Adjoining space takes you through stuffed birds and fossils, Stone Age pottery and flints, and, from the Romans, a mosaic floor and a cache of over 20,000 coins found in the city and imaginatively caught in plaster as they spill from a pitcher at the moment of discovery. A back section reproduces agricultural instruments, the tools and household goods of a century and more ago, and then releases one to a broad area with a modern ceiling and lighting, and a minute garden for a few white doves and a Silenus. It is an airy, well-lit gallery, with seats provided for pondering on a painting or two in a local show, an indication of Dorchester's regard for itself and its painters.

Weymouth Avenue takes one past a stubby accretion of Victoriana, a COUNTY CONSTABULARY that recalls rural Gilbert and Sullivan, and shortly to the not altogether comprehensible earthworks, Maumbury Rings, a rise of 20 to 30 feet around an irregular low ellipse. Since it was used as execution grounds in the eighteenth century, as military practice grounds by anti-Royalist forces in the seventeenth, for cock fighting in the Middle Ages and, centuries before, by the Romans as an amphitheatre, and subjected to millennia of weathers, the structure now bears only a vague resemblance to its original circular "henge" shape. According to archeologists, this particularly English Neolithic structure was a ceremonial place, to judge from the phallic fertility symbols found there, where ritual offerings were made to the earth that produced crops or could withhold them.

One of the colonies that used this sacred ring quite possibly lived in the vast hill-fortress of **Maiden Castle**, two miles south- west of the city. At some point the primitive settlement became a burial center that witnessed human sacrifice and probably the cannibalism that transferred one's victim's strength to oneself. Later, the enclave was surrounded by additional ditches and walls as warfare became more sophisticated, par- ticularly with the introduction of the sling. After that, the Romans, in a lightning assault, and after them, scholars who found a rich load of military and domestic objects that spoke of layers of settlement back to four thousand years ago.

The shadowy ancient mysteries of these places evoke Hardy and the next reasonable step is north of Dorchester, for the church in **Stinsford** (Hardy's "Mellstock"). One says it reluc- tantly, but the church is low, damp, smelly, like a burrowing unclean little animal. Out, quickly, to search among the large blocks of stone marked HARDY and the complex that holds Thomas Hardy's heart, which remained in Dorset when his body was buried in Westminster Abbey.

The next pilgrimage stop is **Higher Bockhampton**, where Hardy was born. It can be approached through light woods, particularly lovely in their tawny gold-yellow and orange au- tumn foliage, accompanied by an hospitable black dog who has appointed himself guardian and guide, or on a direct road that stops at a rough leaf-clouded obelisk monument presented by American devotees. At the side of the road the deeply thatched cottage and dense garden curtained by trees. One should tele- phone for an appointment to visit the house, but the inhabit- ants entrusted the house by the National Trust are kind and hospitable. The viewable rooms are few and the visit short. Beyond the entrance, the expected pamphlets of Hardy interest and copies of his books on sale. The rest of the rooms are soft with layers of whitewash and quite small, although the house itself, with little windows twinkling out of two or three tons of thatch, is substantial. The family were relatively prosperous master masons (thence the natural step to architecture for Thomas) and the Hardy furniture may have been more elab-

orate than that supplied by the National Trust. A broad fireplace, since then boarded up, once held an inglenook whose
depth can be judged by the thick wall behind the fireplace. All
the rooms one sees are limited and cozy, probably built for
maximum warmth, and one wonders how two grown women,
Hardy's schoolteacher sisters, could have lived in such tight
bedroom space—no tighter, though, than that shared by
Thomas, who wrote his first book here, with his brother. A
miniature hallway was the accounts room and its tiny window
used for handing out the pay of workmen. From the bedrooms
furnished by the Trust with a good chest of drawers and a
quilted coverlet about 150 years old, one descends a steep toy
ladder and, with a look at Hardy novels translated into Korean,
Japanese, Serbo-Croatian (among the forty languages in which
his work appears), one leaves, inspired to reread, immediately,
at least a few of the paperbacks on display in the sales room.

A robust age called the stream that runs merrily along the side
of streets in local villages the Piddle. Some communities kept
their names built around "piddle," others, burdened by later
refinement, changed theirs to incorporate "puddle." Hence
names like **Puddletown** and **Tolpuddle**, northeast of Dorchester.
The former shows its domestic charms in an area called the
"Square" adjoining a church of the fifteenth century on earlier
sections that incorporates a remarkable collection of medieval
tombs. **Tolpuddle** hasn't much to show except a few reminders
of the Tolpuddle Martyrs, heroes of the beginnings of the trade-
union movement led by a Wesleyan preacher, George Loveless,
who, with five other men, formed a "secret" group called the
"Friendly Society of Agricultural Workers." They had asked
that their inadequate wages be raised to the 10 shillings a
week paid elsewhere. This was in 1834, a time of starvation and
unrest, workers subject to a cynical Establishment and an indifferent Crown. After it was agreed that the poverty-stricken
workers get their increase, wages were again reduced, and to
destitution level. At this point the society was organized and
shortly thereafter the members were arrested on the technical-
ity of having sworn "secret" oaths (although there existed
other unmolested, non-working-class secret confraternities) and
sentenced to seven years' "transportation" (exile to Australia),
leaving helpless, hungry and, it was alleged, maltreated de-

pendents. Members of other growing Trade Societies, many of the clergy, and Members of Parliament organized protests and sent a petition, signed by 250,000 citizens, to the heads of government who, now mindful of rising industrial storms, brought the men back after two years.

A sad little village, hooded in thatch, staring over a long slope, was Hardy's "Kingsbere-sub-Green Hill," the **Bere Regis** that was the burial place of Turbervilles whose founding ancestor came with William the Conqueror. The village bears its regal name for the fact that King John built a castle there and in it frequently held court. Two centuries before, Queen Elfrida came from the Dorset coast to take refuge here, fearful and contrite after she had murdered her stepson, King Edward the Martyr, so that her son, Ethelred the Unready, might take the throne. Long before her, the Romans in a hill-fortress and, after John, the most powerful of the barons, Simon de Montfort, who was reluctantly granted the manor by Henry III. Henry VIII gave it to a Turberville. It is the church one comes to see, introduced by imperfectly shaved, lopsided yew trees and memorial rose bushes. It is an imposing church for its size, still revealing, through several rebuildings, Norman sections incorporated in the late-fifteenth-century improvements by Cardinal Morton, a native son who became Archbishop of Canterbury and Lord Chancellor to Henry VII. One enters under a pair of long hooks held by heavy chains, early-seventeenth-century implements for ripping down the thatch of burning cottages. Inside, a twelfth-century font and Turberville tombs obscured by nineteenth-century glass. Craftsmen's versatility and humor show on the carvings of pew ends, no two alike, and in the figures and heads carved into the capitals of the pillars—small animals, a man palpably in the grip of a headache, another's face distorted with toothache, and a grotesque whose small arm reaches down to pull his mouth open painfully, perhaps ready to have a tooth extracted. (Evidently at least one mason had dental problems.) The prize of the church, a brilliantly colored box of crude, big toys, is the roof built by Cardinal Morton in 1475 for the greater glory of the church and himself. The bosses in the centers of bright curlicues depict him as a fat, flat grotesque head, show the arms of Canterbury, the pink rose of the Tudors whom he advised and supported, and a knot to signify the marriage of the Tudor

Henry VII to Elizabeth of York, a troublesome but judicious union that helped resolve the conflicts of the Roses. At the side of the roof, twelve almost lifesize Apostles shoot out like men from a circus cannon, sudden, stiff, primitive, and singular.

The northwestern roads out of Dorchester lead through villages with roadside piddles, clusters of thatch over pale, off-white houses, and winging fields that flow from the attractive village of **Cerne Abbas**. The number of inns, crafts and souvenir shops among distinctive houses more than suggests a busy tourist summer trade, but the village is yours in the fall when the swells of field are shot with gold, the hills topped with dark buttons of shrub, and mists of faintly russet trees rise from the thin October fog. The abbey which gives the village its name has left only a trace of what was once the abbot's hall. On Abbey Street, a group of medieval houses whose overhangs rest on anciently carved wood, a stately house, and across from them the distinguished tower—particularly notable in an area where towers are low, squashed, or nonexistent—of St. Mary's. Built in the early sixteenth century, it is slenderly buttressed and studded with gargoyles, but its special distinction is a lovely Virgin and Child in a high niche. The interior of the church gives one patches of medieval murals, a later screen, and a solid Jacobean pulpit.

In spite of its several lures, the chief reason one comes to Cerne Abbas is to see its giant, cut into the chalk on a rise above the town. He is 180 feet tall, carries a large, heavy club like Hercules, his nudity enhanced by a penis 30 feet high. There are several theories about his origins. One has it that he is prehistoric, another that he was a folk-tale devourer of sheep, or that he is a sixteenth-century rebuke to purportedly corrupt monks of the abbey. The nineteenth century said he was nothing, he didn't exist, and was pleased that his outline and prominences were fading under encroaching grass. Now the giant is plucked regularly and the favored theory is that he is a Hercules scratched out by local Romans late in the second century A.D., possibly in honor of the emperor who, like other Roman rulers, saw himself as a Second Coming of the super-masculine god. But there must be more to it, particularly in an area whose subsoil is littered with fertility figures. We are told that a small earthwork above the giant was the place for that English phallus, the maypole, and that barren couples had intercourse within the outlines of the giant's body, and still "visit" him for relief from sterility. One wonders about his present meaning to a village that catches him at almost every street corner and full and clearly a few yards from the last house. Certainly, he is a useful anatomy lesson to the children, a speedy introduction to sex education.

Sherborne is a visitors' town, pretty and sparkling, with gift and tea shops in quaint shapes, easy open rambles of appealing houses with and without thatch, a large abbey enclave sitting in an abundance of lawn and, thrusting into the town, a fifteenth-century monks' washing place. Tea and cream cakes eaten, a souvenir purchased, a meander of streets (try Long, Cheap, Half-Moon, and their tangents), and houses of several times and styles examined and one can address oneself to the abbey church. Its history is expected: Saxon, later rebuilt by Benedictines who made a good thing of wool and woollens and became rich autocrats resented by the townspeople; partial rebuilding when the church was fired by a flaming arrow in 1437; the Dissolution, the abbey and lands granted a favored gentleman who sold it back to the town. Restoration and brightening in the nineteenth century gives a honeyed, fresh look to the church that has held on to its Saxon west wall and, with irregular fifteenth-century overlays, its Norman shape. The misericords give off their usual bouncy folk humor, the Baroque monuments their usual humorlessness. The best of the show is the elaborate fan vaulting, soaring out of curious paisley-leaf ornaments, ringed by florid bosses in the high style of the fifteenth century.

Part of the abbey buildings remain as sections of Sherborne School, which goes back so far that some authorities date its founding with that of the abbey in the first years of the eighth century, while others take it only to Alfred the Great, who was probably schooled here. In any case it is venerable and since it is still functioning, may be one of the oldest and longest-lived of schools anywhere. Fifteenth-century improvements saw to a set of almshouses, still decorated with substantial portions of their original glass and wooden screen, and a reputedly unique triptych of about the same time, possibly Flemish or Dutch, very much worth seeing if and when the almshouses are open to visitors.

East of the town, signs lead to OLD CASTLE and NEW CASTLE.
The old castle is ruins; the new dark, dun-colored, and misbe-
gotten. Both were pawns in a typical play of favorites, their fall
from favor, the rise of new golden boys under new kings, and
the autocratic erasure of earlier promises and rights. The pivot
here is Sir Walter Raleigh, who had to have Sherborne Castle,
controlled by the bishops of Salisbury from time immemorial.
He nagged Queen Elizabeth, adding to the verbal persuasion the
more persuasive gift of an expensive gem for her to give the
incumbent. Raleigh was granted the lease for a yearly rental
that about equaled the cost of the gem. He had wanted it badly
but, after making a few tentative changes, decided to build a
new castle close by. This was hardly completed when he was
thrown into the Tower (1603) on charges of treason. James I,
on importunate requests from a particular friend, Robert Carr,
found a flaw in the deed to the property and transferred it to
his favorite. A royal friend of Raleigh bought back the estate
at a large sum but he died—under suspicious circumstances—
and Carr was again king of the castle. When Carr, in his turn,
was executed, James handed the estate to another favorite, one
of the earls of Bristol, Sir John Digby. In the meantime, the
last surviving Raleigh son tried and tried fruitlessly to regain
the property that was rightfully his. The death of James did
nothing to change his fortunes. Charles I was offered the then
regal sum of £10,000 to make sure that the Digbys remained in
possession and they did, ultimately throwing the aging Raleigh
a yearly pittance. The old castle was almost totally demolished
during the Civil War and Raleigh's house considerably changed
by Digby revisions to become the bulging oddity one now sees,
set in the clever manipulation of nature to make it more acceptably natural by the gifted Capability Brown.

The green of beeches and the green moss on tiles and stone
that often lends an aqueous atmosphere to roads and hamlets
and long, smooth waves of hill in autumn mists will accompany
you toward **Shaftesbury**, "an Ancient Saxon Hilltop Town," as
the pamphlets say. With all affection for Dorset, one cannot
urge a stop unless it happens to happen on the way elsewhere,
and the dimming of ancient glory and a broad view of the surrounding countryside moves you.

In a place of reticent church towers it comes as a surprise to
see, approaching **Blandford Forum** (there were no Romans here

but the name was chic in a classic-loving time), a small dome on a neo-classical cupola and, coming closer, its supporting church and square in a remarkable integrity of design. A fire in the mid-eighteenth century razed the town almost completely, taking with it the workshops of a company of architect-mason-master craftsmen named anciently and indelibly "Bastard." Between the public and Parliament, money was found for rebuilding, assigned to John and William Bastard, who expressed the taste of their time with extraordinary vigor. There is admirable energy in the white pilasters and pediments and the sturdy keystoned window frames that band a characteristic tweedy mixture of red, gray, lavender, green bricks and stone. For contrast the brothers added feminine wooden porticos on some of their shops and houses and varied the white of surrounds with yellows and greens. Blandford's citizens know a good thing when they have it, so they make improvements cautiously, maintaining the spirited Blandford manner as a yellow door, a fine green wooden box to hold a shop, and broad white lettering among the pilasters. In spite of later changes, the church holds its classical mood and, outside it, a miniature classical portico shelters a pump as memorial to the great fire. Behind the church, a domestic stretch of town house and soft-colored neat cottages with carved overhangs above the doors and, nearby, a survivor of the fire, a heavy-eaved, heavy-doored oddity of seventeenth-century red brick called the "Old House."

Blandford Forum shortly gives way to a superb canopy of century-old beeches crested with autumn flames that march toward **Wimborne Minster**, a town almost crushed by its immense church of stubby towers. Between the towns, a cut-off leads to a vast Iron Age fortress, **Badbury Rings**. The Romans used it as the hub of four roads, an early king re-established it as a fortress against a rebel contender for the Crown, and during the Civil War meetings were held here by citizens pleading with both sides for peace. Now, to judge from the litter surrounding several conspicuous garbage containers, it is a careless picnic ground. The sweets wrappers and drinks cans fade readily, though, when one looks up to the zigzag of chalk paths lost, here and there, in coarse bushes and spiny grasses. There is nothing to see there but irregular rings and their inhospitable growth and yet there is an enigmatic unease that grows as one walks the rough paths held in circles between brambly

trenches, wrapped in a silence that makes distant specters of
walkers 20 feet away. One recalls Hardy's reminder that this
region was Lear's kingdom, and his portrait of Egdon Heath,
centering on an earthwork: "As with some persons who have
long lived apart, solitude seemed to look out of its countenance.
It had a lonely face, suggesting tragical possibilities."

NOTES

HOTEL: The King's Arms, Dorchester, dating from the
eighteenth century, has space gathered here and there to
make a fair size above the deceptively small public rooms.
The rooms are fresh, with decent sitting space and an
alarm-clock tea or coffee maker, equipped with the mak-
ings, to wake one pleasantly. All this, plus a well-served
breakfast, for a moderate sum.

Devon and Cornwall

The temptation to streak from London to the Cornish coast in a matter of six or seven hours (off-season, that is) is understandable, but Cornwall is a place that should be worked up to rather than down from.

Let us assume you've left Dorset at Jane Austen's resort of **Lyme Regis**, not too showy, not too striving, a genteel, smooth cap of houses on the rise from the beach, a narrow walk between houses and stream and, to show that it is a border village, both a Dorset Hotel and one that chooses to call itself Devon. As always, the choices are numerous and not too distant, but since there is a fair amount of coast awaiting, it might be well to head inland to **Honiton** which, like many localities, produces pottery but whose distinction is the making of Honiton lace of weblike delicacy and design. Like all crafts, this slow, demanding work, which necessitated the interweaving of fine cotton thread from hundreds of bobbins, is dying. There is a lace shop on the main street, however, that has modern examples, limited to a leaf, a flower, a butterfly, small enough to be mounted as a brooch, but the items for sale are mainly old— sometimes as much as a century—bought out of local collections and not expensive for what they are. A pair of half-fingered mittens, the front of a christening dress, two or three incredible butterflies are not for sale but quite wonderful to look at, and to wonder at the patience and concentration of the woman who manipulated and tamed the wilderness of bobbins to create a flower one-eighth of an inch in size or the marked body of a minute butterfly.

If the April wind is blowing, it will ruffle the feathers of crows snapping at the fields; they lose their sleek assurance and appear distraught, disoriented. They totter crazily on the red Devon earth, which shows off effectively neighboring spreads of pale early greens, the gray and black of winter-bound trees, and the dark hedgerows that dizzy the fields. Swirling rain clouds gather as curtains at a thin opening of sky to paint a Turner water color, or throw out a shaft of pale sun that splinters on the greens and reds and screens of thin, rigid trees.

Exeter's is one of the queenly cathedrals. Getting to it through a fury of improvements as glass blocks, supermarkets, and octopus roads may diminish returns. It is worth braving,

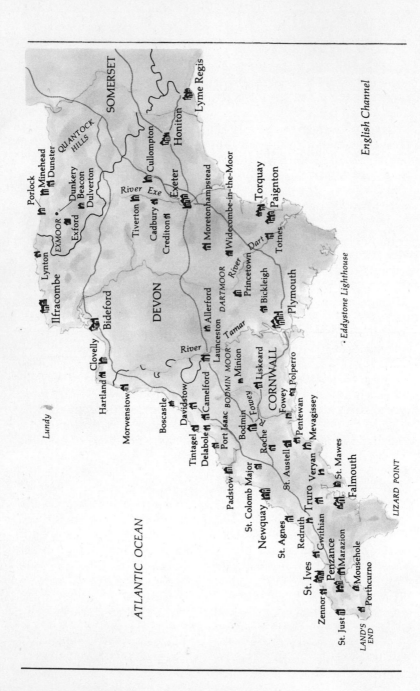

SOMERSET

QUANTOCK HILLS

Lyme Regis

Porlock
Minehead
Dunster
Dunkery Beacon
Dulverton
Cullompton
Honiton
EXMOOR
Exford
River Exe
Tiverton
Cadbury
Crediton
Exeter
Moretonhampstead
Wideombe-in-the-Moor
Torquay
Paignton

Lynton
Ilfracombe
DEVON
Allerford
DARTMOOR
River Dart
Totnes
Bideford

Clovelly
River
Launceston
Tamar
Princetown
Bickleigh
Plymouth

Hartland
Morwenstow
BODMIN MOOR
Minion
Liskeard
Polperro

Boscastle
Davidstow
Camelford
Bodmin
Fowey
CORNWALL
Fowey

Tintagel
Delabole
Port Isaac
Roche
Pentewan
Mevagissey

Padstow
St. Columb Major
St. Austell
Pentewan

Newquay
Truro
Veryan
St. Mawes

St. Agnes
Redruth
Falmouth

St. Ives
Gwithian
Zennor
Penzance
Marazion
Mousehole
St. Just
Porthcurno
LAND'S END

Lundy

ATLANTIC OCEAN

LIZARD POINT

• Eddystone Lighthouse

English Channel

though, if your route includes few other important cathedrals. Then north or south for a circle of Devon, an easy two days or less of tasting its cushiony douceurs, its strong cider, and its acrid Dartmoor. Directly southward lie **Torquay** and its attached neighbor, **Paignton**, the former expensive, with sea-commanding Victorian hotels and formal gardens and a necessary nod at hoi polloi with an amusement parlor or two and rowboats hugging the quay. The latter is rows of small hotels, many tiny cabins on the shore, shops, clots of nearby trailer (caravan) areas, insubstantial arcades to shade cafés and ice-cream parlors. Paignton boasts of two houses at the extreme ends of showiness. Looking up from the main road, the incongruous vision of a high, classical mansion, Oldway, built in 1874 by Isaac Merritt Singer, a white mass of big columns and swags, magniloquent statuary, and an entrance held by two Victorian-classic sphinxes. Putting and tennis playing are permitted on the grounds, maybe among Italian gardens, but the opening hours of the house are irregular (probably more stable in the summertime) and all the information that can be offered at this time is that some of the rooms were shaped and decorated in imitation of Versailles. The other house, off a street in the middle of the town, is Kirkham, a medieval house of bright red stone and gently turned old oak, cleaned up, restored, and quite empty. One yearns to move in, to put settees near the fireplaces, hang ironwork lamps from the high beams, place small choice ornaments in the spaces between the beams of the upper gallery, and establish a studio, from which fine works *must* emerge, in the big whitewashed airy bedroom.

The scored crouching animal backs of Dartmoor's far-off flattened hills begin to shadow the contented smoothness of Devon near **Totnes**, neat, pretty, and prosperous, a village whose dramatic gesture is a high mound surmounted by a low, round castle, as incomplete and simple as a spur of archeological earthworks from a distance. The well-being of Totnes displays itself in a few minutes of walking up the High Street from the bridge on the River Dart, a casual exploration that reveals an unusual number of antique and bookshops, imported kitchen equipment, continental delicacies, and the price of cracked eggs as high as that of unblemished eggs in London. Halfway up, a clock held in an arch breaks the ascent and invites one to climb the ramparts of the old village for a sight of the sixteenth-century Guildhall. Continue on, through an arcaded section lit by flowers and fruits, glimpses of buildings with modified overhangs, and up to the castle, splendidly presented from the dipping street to its entrance. Nothing is left but a thick ring whose ramparts can be circled (carefully) for vistas of the town and the sheep-dotted fields. The best view of the ruin is from the benches on the lawn, a pleasant place to sit, looking up at the rough pile, its arrow slits now harmless eyes in broken scallops. Returning, look for a couple of Georgian buildings and at the grotesques that support the timbers of the Elizabethan museum building, and try to imagine the town when some of its retired settlers and shopkeepers put on Elizabethan garb for local celebrations.

A measure of Totnes's quality is the fact that it maintains two reputable restaurants, Ffoulkes on the High Street and the Elbow Room, an inventive restaurant—Porc Orientale, Chicken Mexicana, Lemon Posset, seaworthy crab soup—in a cottage reached by going back and left of the church. Both are fairly pricy.

The River Dart continues into unusual modern houses (as mentioned, English domestic architecture is very conservative), several crafts shops and studios, and the famous progressive school of Dartington, then plays hide-and-seek as it runs through villages, gathering moor streams on its rush to the sea.

The lofty, leafy hedgerows on narrow lanes run through farmlands and the woods of National Park that open now and then to thatch and stone cottages like illustrations in fairy-tale books. Fields billow toward the coarseness of moor as **Widecombe-in-the-Moor** appears with its souvenir shops and old pub and convenient conveniences and church. It is magnificently placed in a vortex of green field and red rising to moor anger of rocky, tawny earth and black cowls of burned heather brushed on the long, unshapely hills. **Postbridge** sits in a land of streams, one covered by a bridge and a line of slate slabs, not uncommon here and some reputedly very ancient, used to ford the waters. Over charred heather, and the relief of clumps of yellow gorse, one comes to **Princetown**, where the famous Dartmoor Prison sits, big harsh prison blocks surrounded by unrelieved rows of gray cottages, as inhospitable a place as the endlessness of barren moor that surrounds it. It is not difficult to imagine how securely strategic the position of the prison is. Where would a man go to find shelter on the bleakness, how long could he hide in the pine woods a distance off, what roads could he use that might not be easily blocked?

(This peak of moor vastness, you should be warned, does strange things to drivers. Be prepared for sudden stops, for turns into a view or a rare inn without warning. They feel, as you will, alone, isolated, losing awareness of other cars and people.)

Still riding high on the wilderness patched with pine forest, the sheep now accompanied by dark square Highland cattle and, if they are not shy that day, Dartmoor ponies, one begins to see the grateful, comfortable greens and reds of fields and the village of **Moretonhampstead**. It is no larger than its name but obviously a favored vacation spot since it contains two small hotels, offers of bed and breakfast, a stimulating junk-antiques shop run by a merry couple, and Devon cream teas calling from several windows. Before you settle down to scones heaped with jam and thick cream the consistency of whipped butter, walk to the church and, at its right, turn toward tall chimneytops. These belong to a set of almshouses of the early seventeenth century, cut of unfriendly granite and curiously hung with an arcade of small arches derived from a memory of Romanesque arches carried from very early churches.

Crediton is the Devon village that proves not all of the county is plump and rich, in spite of its spunky color, the herds of black-faced, black-footed lambs that tumble in the neighboring grasses, and its finely proportioned church. Its neighbor, **Bickleigh**, seems to fare better, or maybe it is merely the snug look of thatch and the rich combination of dark gold straw against very green fields and very red earth in pillow shapes. Not impassioned by prospects of tourism, Bickleigh leaves its roads rough, narrow, and twisted and a meeting with a tractor or a wagonload of manure may present interesting driving problems. They work out in one polite way or another. Before you try Bickleigh's road and thatch, however, you might want to climb, on foot, the hill of earthworks, signposted as a CASTLE, near **Cadbury**. A placard at the bottom welcomes with the advice to LOOK OUT FOR ROMAN RELICS BUT BEWARE OF THE DRAGON as you approach the Iron Age structure under excavation, dug out in the hope that it will reveal King Arthur's

Camelot. It is one of several places where that valiant, cuck-
olded king might have kept his army of miracle- and adventure-
seeking, amorous, neurotic knights, and this site, in its enchanted hills, seems much more acceptable than Camelford or
(mistakenly) Norman Tintagel in Cornwall as their abode and
stage for deeds and feasts. Cadbury has a slightly leading claim
at present because the archeological hill-fort has been traced
back to Arthur's time, at the end of the fifth century, and
because uncovered shards of pottery from the Mediterranean
of the same period prove the existence of a fairly sophisticated
settlement.

Cullompton or Cullumpton (a parish church pamphlet says
there are thirty acceptable ways of spelling the name) is a
plain, Devon-respectable place deep in country, marked with
wooden weathervane signs and gathered around an extraordinary church, St. Andrew's, a structure of the fifteenth century
and the sixteenth. Its story includes Celtic missionaries, ownership by a son of Alfred the Great, by Benedictine monks under
the aegis of William the Conqueror, and ultimately wool money.
The harmoniously arranged façade decorations of pale elements
on dark stone are, unfortunately, almost gone except for boxes
of openwork tracery near the top. Lane's Aisle, at the south end
of the church, is a delight of fan vaulting, and one of the windows below, clearly Pre-Raphaelite in rhythm and contour, is
attributed to William Morris. The ceiling in the nave turns
from the sophisticated grace of fan vaulting to the high colors
and gilt of boxes and crossed bars and upright folk-loric
angels. As you leave, to the left of the door examine a less
cheery piece of medieval craft, a pair of heavy oak trunks
carved as rocky places full of skulls, bones, and holes that probably held crosses, a memento mori which recalls other such
toothsome representations of death that frightened and
scourged the medieval peasant.

Tiverton is a good place to elude cream teas. It is large
enough to serve coffee in one of several cafés in the shadow of
its endearing vase-shaped Victorian town hall and, besides, it
has a church at the side of the river that is hung with an attractive carved porch which bears, among religious and heraldic
symbols, panels of ships in full sail, probably a reflection of
lucrative wool exports of a lost time.

Following the trail of cream teas that breaks off for well-made, well-kept barns, red cows the color of Devon earth, slopes daisied with sheep, the swift glitter of the River Exe, and a sign that tells you this is SOMERSET, you might taste the pink and thatch, bordered by stream silver, of **Dulverton** and on through rougher country to **Dunster**. It must be blocked to invisibility in holiday seasons but in early April, when winds blow from the seas and the moors and the hotels and shops are occupied with airing unused bedrooms and polishing Toby jugs, the village rests in its undisturbed charms. The High Street that runs down from an ivy-covered inn, now the Luttrell Arms Hotel, carrying sheepskin and souvenir shops and ACCOMMODA-TION signs on pale yellow, pale blue, pale pink houses, trails off to the right as Church Street, a lesser yet equally well-kept repetition. However, the blandishments belong to the High Street, a folly of round tower rising above the trees at one end, Dunster Castle on its leafy mount at the other, and at the swelled top of the street the seventeenth-century yarn market, a gay octagon of deep slate broken by twinkling windows in triangular projections, the slate then fanning out to shelter the timbered supports, a stellar piece among the old market sheds that still brighten many villages. The castle, whose sign says PRIVATE and lists times of visiting during summer months only, cannot be reported; but brochures describe a fairly standard miscellany of antiquity considerably redone, family portraits, plasterwork ceilings, sharply carved woods, fine furniture in-cluding the work of Chippendale and, instead of the more usual tapestries, stamped and painted leather panels that tell the story of Cleopatra, her lovers, her enemies, and her death. If the castle is closed to you, try the church, which is mainly of the fourteenth and fifteenth centuries, with monuments to the Luttrells of the castle and fine carved oak as its screen. Behind the church, carpets of flowers and the attractive jumble of red stone houses on Priory Green.

NOTES

HOTELS: Besides the Luttrell Arms, high-moderate, there are many places to stay, at considerably less, along the High Street and Church Street. A decent bed and breakfast can be had for about £2 at a number of places and, for a reasonable extra sum, a palatable dinner. Toilets and baths will very likely be in hallways, but exceedingly clean and, when things aren't too hectic, you may have the company of a house child or two; or, from the kitchen, the sound of the Grieg Piano Concerto punctuated by the rattle of pans. You may also become acquainted with the lavish country use of baked beans—in a ring of bacon for breakfast, with sausages in inexpensive luncheon cafés—that arrive with and without chips as solid fillers for modest meals.

Exmoor is tamed, orderly moorlands for the simple reason that much of it has been encroached on by farming. And the hunting of Exmoor stags. After looping and twisting in lanes that have become your own, you are shocked into immobility by frenetic activity and traffic blocks in **Exford**, a hunting center. Big horse vans stand every which way, directors direct, weatherbeaten, jowly ladies in small black riding hats march their horses along the road and through the village, booted gentry gather in clumps to follow the hunt on foot, if necessary, or in small, eager cars. This is bloody blood sport, a stag isolated, chased, and torn at by the dogs before it is shot. The societies engaged in the prevention of cruelty to animals—with much higher endowments, incidentally, than those that see to the prevention of cruelty to children—and the private citizen take exquisite care of dogs, lap or hunting; extra horses are brought to the hunt to relieve those that might tire. But ripping open stags doesn't count as cruelty. And besides, they say, if stags weren't hunted they would die of starvation that ensues from overpopulation. Other peoples meet this problem by periodic, decisive shooting, but where is the charm of ritual, of aristocratic tradition, of shows of keen horsemanship and the release of pent-up ferocity in that?

Hopefully, the hunt will not chase you away from the moors toward **Luccombe**, where fields turn to blackness and to coarse gray-green stoniness scored with snaky paths that fall from the highest point of Exmoor, **Dunkery Beacon**. Far below, the coast touching gentle green; close to, the black-brown-green of low thick plants tufted with beards of yellow grass; then again, sea and golden coast. A short ride but eminently worth a castle and a church.

Remember Coleridge's Ancient Mariner? His departure point was supposed to be **Watchet**, a few miles from **Minehead** on the coast, at the edge of Quantock Hills, where Coleridge and the Wordsworths walked together. And remember the man from **Porlock** who dissolved the dream of Xanadu? He came from a seaside village at the end of Porlock Hill, said to be the steepest road in England. It *is* steep, and long and hairpin-curved, its chills and thrills sharpened by signs that advise cyclists to walk and warn of danger from vehicles out of control. Porlock achieved, it turns into clusters of thatch, of brick, of a weir near the sea's edge, and a tumbled round stone building lying in the water. Better than thatch or weir, the stupendous hills rising from the sea and the strange little houses roofed in tile, spiculed with minute dormers, more Alpine than English, of neighboring **Allerford**.

Moor and sea, fat fields and absentminded sheep follow the road that drops and rises to Gothic Revival and guest-house **Lynton**, and twists down to the long, thatched inn and the balconied red brick tower of the harbor at **Lynmouth**. Anyone for coffee? **Bideford** is the place, and the place to see what a couple of coats of paint can do to bulges whose basic plainness is here masked by generous dollops of orange, lemon yellow, pink, lavender, white, and black in combination or, as on the Royal Hotel, three vigorous shades of blue. The town puts its bus stops and major shopping on a riverfront avenue, also busied with ships, to make an alert townscape. It has left a few medieval walls near the quay, encouraged pleasure boats on the estuary of its bay to brighten the lives of cranes and barges, and left a few dunes to give beach atmosphere to modern hotels on the sea. Vivacious and besotted with color, a very nice town.

Names like **Fairy Cross** and **Ford** and long, once-meaningful names like **Woolfardisworthy** (pronounced sensibly as Woolsery), new elegant thatching with overlays like pennants, and suave flows of field point to alluring **Clovelly,** a salubrious challenge to feet and wind. Down from the car park, a 10- or 15-minute walk on sharp cobbles, beside spills of white houses and trees, to rock-strewn shore, souvenir shops, and picturesqueness. And then there is the climb back. There were once donkeys to carry you down and up, and a few still munch the local grasses in happy retirement since it was decided that the work was too difficult and inhumane. No one seems to be concerned with man's humanity to himself, and some of the stalwart stagger up gasping for breath. Have a bash at it, if you like, or save your breath for more exciting coast under less precipitate villages in Cornwall.

Here ends, absolutely, the land of neat, clean villages, puffed and pink with amour propre, of cows that nestle in lushness, of softness, of gentle-voiced peaceability. Two cues to Cornwall—where no hamlet or livestock nestles, where lushness is an inappropriate word, where the coast spits up a fury of crags—come near **Hartland**, still Devon, whose trees are bent and shorn by the winds, keening the bitter tune of Cornish coastal trees, and off Hartland Point, the cliffs sharpened to cruelty.

When one says goodbye, bound for Devon or Dorset, to London friends, they say, "How lovely. It's sweet, pretty country and don't forget to have Devonshire cream." Of East Anglia, "I've never been there, but I hear the people are a bit odd." Cornwall may elicit a spate of fervent responses, largely xenophobic, about "them," more foreign and mysterious than Sicilians. "Don't go with anyone with an English accent; they hate us but are nice, for the tourist money, to Americans. They're steeped in superstition, in magic spells; they're fanatic Methodists; they've been isolated for so long, they're all mad; they're poor and cruel; they used to set beacons on cliffs over the rocks so that ships would be wrecked and they'd get the leavings. They're smugglers. They're like the Welsh, like Bretons and who knows what else—notice how dark some of them are—but they're certainly not English," this the final, direst warning.

The swirling, pounding seas sharpening rocks to great files and wedges are wreckers, assisted or no. The isolated gray stone cottages speak desperate poverty and a separateness that must breed eccentricity. The speech sometimes sounds Irish or Welsh and, surprisingly, like New England Coast at times. (A Celtic tongue, related to Welsh and Breton, was spoken here until the end of the eighteenth century.) Thick, dark caps of hair almost meeting heavy black eyebrows are not especially common or uncommon, about in the numbers one finds in the border counties to the north, where the Romans who guarded the long wall of Hadrian and its fortresses stayed long enough to tint numerous generations. Desolate coastal lands and truculent moors throw off strange scatterings and heaps of worked stone, mystifying witnesses of rites and burials clouded in old time. Directions are given not in distance from the village church, but from the more important chapel, sometimes Baptist, sometimes Unitarian, and usually Methodist. Since the world—and governmental controls—has become almost too much with them, the Cornish have given up their wrecking and smuggling. Their lucrative tin and copper industries were pre-empted by rivals in the Americas, Africa, and Asia, the fishing very much reduced, and there is not enough arable land for agriculture nor grazing for large flocks of sheep and cows. Nothing much left to do for a living but work the china clay pits, take in Easter and summer boarders and regale them with stories of the sea (always boasting of its lashing violence), of ghosts and murders, of bravos like the tin miners when they controlled the county, of madmen who amused or terrified their neighbors.

Rounding the coast from Devon into Cornwall, the road opens a bit for **Morwenstow**, whose churchyard carries the graves of a few drowned sailors, a particular concern of a nineteenth-century vicar, the Rev. Stephen Hawker. He was a recorder of events and people Cornish and a vivid relic of a time when vicars were expected to be especially eccentric. (The eccentric vicar is still indispensable in books and films, as everyone knows.) Every writer on Cornwall has a favorite peculiarity of the Rev. Hawker to quote. One likes the fact that he was always accompanied on long walks by a black sow, another mentions his declamatory poetry, a third pictures him sitting on a rock by the sea, his legs wrapped together, seaweed on his head, mirror in hand and crooning a tune of Lorelei, the ship-destroying siren. One would like to meet him, searches for him, but is given only the pulsing, crashing sea that eludes the most careful man-made protection when possessed by one of its fits. **Boscastle**, for instance, a village of stone houses with sway-backed slate roofs, has erected a complex system of breakwaters to secure its inner harbor where small boats hide. When the sea forces its way through and across the breakwaters as if they were of cardboard, the boats have to be lifted out, and quickly. From a height above the village look down at the sea walls and try to imagine what it meant to thread a ship into the harbor when the seas were high. And if it should happen to be Thursday afternoon and the shops that sell souvenirs and antiques closed, the flocks of tourists not yet arrived, the capricious Cornish sun sulking behind clouds, try to imagine what it must mean to live in such a still, lost hollow.

Tintagel (pronounced Tin*taj*le) has been peopled with King Mark, Tristan (or Tristram) and the two Isoldes, King Arthur, Guinevere, Launcelot, Merlin, and the rest of the court (claimed by several places of the West Country in the local version of "George Washington slept here"). The dramatic mass of ruin that climbs cliffs and runs down to sea is worthy of its legends when the season is off, the heaps of stone empty, wind-swept and desolate, and the local ploys for attention and trade not yet avid. The village post office is a shambling stretch of shored-up medievalness; the rest is King Arthur and Company as hotels, cafés, and shops. Car parked, fee paid, and detailed booklet bought, one descends a path into folds of green, yellow, and rust slopes, small bridges that cover a tuneful stream, and up to escarpments. A fee is asked again and one is admitted to a view of the sea, a deep drop to shattered rock, sharp clefts and paths and steps that climb along battered walls, once the castle of a twelfth-century Earl of Cornwall, the illegitimate son of Henry I. In the thirteenth century it was inhabited by an earl with ambitions for the throne of the Holy Roman Empire, although he got only as far as having himself created "King of the Romans" with no realm other than Cornwall to rule. Centuries earlier there was, it is said, a monastery founded by a Cornish missionary, the sort of hostel that sheltered wandering priests who spread the Gospel. But how did Arthur and Mark get to these crags? The Early Middle Ages was a literary time. Not only were monk-scribes enriching their libraries, but lays, *fabliaux*, legends were warmed up, regilded, reshaped, passed from mouth to mouth and country to country, occasionally written down as story or its twin, history. One of the historians was Geoffrey of Monmouth, who helped himself freely to traditional tales and to his own fancies and in the mid-fifteenth century issued them as a history of the Britons. He pictured the monumental thrust of torn cliffs and placed there a Cornish lord and his wife, seemingly safe from the invasion of a warlord of the Britons, Uther Pendragon. Uther, how-

ever, had his magician Merlin, who wafted him by super-
natural, devious ways, into the castle and the presence of the
lady, whom he seduced. Of this union Arthur was born to
become, according to imperishable legend, lord of the castle.
Here Merlin was given a low cave, trembling in the roar of the
sea, to ponder new spells. And because Tintagel was so perfect
a place for high drama, King Mark was moved from South
Cornwall to this northern coast, which witnessed his suffering
over the perfidy of his nephew and the infidelity of his wife—
again the effect of magic, here the love potion entrusted to
Brangaene, Isolde's handmaiden. Inevitably, the legends were
linked and Tristan appears in the *Morte D'Arthur* of Malory as
a member of Arthur's court, proud of the love and beauty of
Isolde, who was more beautiful than Guinevere. To walk with
the people of these mingled legends acted out on Celtic monastery ruins among Norman castle ruins, it is essential to bring
them with you in the spring (not Easter) or fall to avoid a time
and atmosphere that, to quote an English commentator, turns
"a poem into a bazaar; Isolde into an ashtray." And try not to
see the twentieth-century Tudor hotel that contests the heights
with Tintagel.

Equally antique, at the furthest remove from high romance,
is the slate quarry at **Delabole**, described by locals as the biggest hole in Europe. The village is a mining village anywhere,
here centered on a Shell station across from the chapel. A rough
side road bumps into small diamond-shaped fields, a spill of
gravestones and sheep, sheds and smokestacks, and a huge, long
pile of slate dragged up from the immense depths which, they
say, should be more closely visible to visitors at the time of this
writing. It should be an impressive sight, to judge from photos,
and an encouraging one if it is working fully, in this country
where £20 in take-home pay is considered a good wage. Delabole
men can even now afford to maintain a pub, the Beetle and
Chisel, not a common luxury of Cornish villages prohibited from
pub pleasures by their chapels and their poverty.

Before you swing into the coastal run of what might be
grouped "Winsor and Newton fishing villages," you might turn
inland for what lies in and around Bodmin Moor. Don't look for
Camelot in **Camelford**; there are no hints except a resemblance
in names—enough for a few stubborn insisters. Better to skirt
it for **Davidstow**, the road fenced by piles of stone and slate

wrapped in shrubs and grasses that slip away to glimpses of
sea under gaunt, slate-strewn hills. April, who laughs her girlish
laughter and a moment after weeps her girlish tears, is apt to
be a mature, fascinating hysteric on the moors. She sprinkles
snow on Bodmin, then hurls it as hail, covering the sparse greens,
the yellow gorse, the rusted shrubs, the bleakness of low hills so
that they resemble at times a view of bleached white country
from a plane. A few minutes later, capricious April in capricious Cornwall sends the sun out to silver the droplets on
shivering, shimmering hedgerows. Near the Tamar River (the
border marker between Devon and Cornwall), surrounded by
slate-covered, earth-huddled stone cottages meeting as **Tregadilett, Polyphant, Altarnun, Tredaule**, a sampling of the Cornish
place names that mystify and enchant, neighbored by a roadside house that proclaims itself Daphne du Maurier's JAMAICA
INN, sits the town of **Launceston.**

Launceston's distinctions are a high, round ruin of castle on
a central mound, an arched gateway, and the Church of Mary
Magdalen, every foot of outer wall enthusiastically carved with
plumes, heraldic animals, shields, religious symbols, tomb figures, geometric patterns and flowers and, on the façade, riders.
The tower and blue clock marked with golden hours was once,
it is said, an adjunct of the meat market where the smaller
varieties of livestock were weighed. No more of that irreligious
hanky-panky now; it stays in the market that flows from the
neo-Gothic market cross designed to match the church. A jolly
town, Launceston might be a place to stay, for slower examination of the old houses along Church Street, for sauntering in
the market, for shopping among the innumerable booklets
Cornwall produces about itself—cuisine, shells, legends, tin
mines, smuggling, views, castles, wrecks, saints, bygone times,
and a long strand of etceteras—for bed and breakfast in the
White Hart Inn, the Eagle, or cheaper household lodgings.

Crossing Bodmin Moor toward **Bodmin**, long wavy lines of pine
wood bowing and stretching in the wind, pits of water and one
of lake size, Dozmary Pool, where Arthurians say the sword
Excalibur disappeared; dusty white, oddly shaped china clay
hills spotted on barren space or the heaps pushed together and
wrinkled, a herd of mud-covered elephants.

At Bodmin you ask for directions to prehistoric worked stones. The lady in the sweetshop says she has heard something about ancient tombs off the Liskeard road but you can get terrible lost on the moors. The elderly car park attendant says he saw something like what you want at **Roche**. Roche is not the place but the road is not long and it is wide, free, and a relief after miles of creeping covered lanes. Turn in on the corner with the school (a few yards beyond the Rock Inn) for a riveting scene of excrescences of rock, a heaving sea of rock that spews up a tall pile on which there has obviously been an attempt at building. This, other clamberers among the rocks tell you, was the hideout of a man eluding demonic spirits, with no success. There might easily be ceremonial stones among the Roche heaps but they are not quite those you are searching, so you continue in the other direction from Bodmin, digressing from stones for a while to visit **Lanhydrock House**, southeast of the town and locked in a densely treed area about the River Fowey. Its past is classic for such houses: a priory dissolved in the sixteenth century, the estate given or sold to a leading family and resold to another family who held it until it was turned over to the National Trust. The family tree gave fruit to several members rather singular for their time and class. The first builder of the seventeenth century, Richard Robartes, lacked the usual eagerness for a title and was forced, on the threat of a substantial fine, to accept the role of "baron," a marketable, expensive commodity sold the reluctant purchaser by the king at a cost of £10,000. His son, John, who continued the building, opted for Cromwell, fought with him while the estate—with the Robartes children imprisoned on it—was taken by Royalist forces. Though the line faded, the wealth stayed, and the baronetcy was bestowed again in the latter half of the nineteenth century. This Lord Robartes augmented his considerable wealth with ownership in the then productive mines of Cornwall. A God-fearing man infused with the Victorian combination of guilt and enlightenment, he was a sterling example of the benevolent landlord who found alternate employment for miners when jobs gave out, established a hospital for his miners in the industrial town of **Redruth,** and built unusually livable cottages for his farm workers. For rebuilding sections of his own house he hired George Gilbert Scott, whose work was destroyed by fire in 1881, a catastrophe that took the lives, in a remote sense, of the owners, both advanced in years and both dead within a year of the fire. (The house has since undergone restoration, as many show houses have.)

The seventeenth century still lives in the playful gatehouse wearing a cap of pinched obelisks, in the designs of most of the plasterwork in ceilings, in English tapestries and furniture, and in a few portraits, one of a long-lidded, cherry-ripe-lipped Restoration vamp, another of her father-in-law, all done up in a profligacy of pink ribbons, shoebuckles, garters, fan, a collection of bows as belt. The rest is mainly Victorian and an interesting example of how a large (nine children), wealthy family, fond of comfort and given only to modest forays into conspicuous consumption, lived at the end of the nineteenth century and into the twentieth. Garnished with water colors, heavy silver, the best English china, souvenirs, and small personal collections of Egyptian scarabs and classical statues, the house is an assemblage of bygones: snug little ladies' chambers with cut-velvet tablecloths sweeping to the floor, little padded chairs, lace-covered dressing tables, a staggering Dresden fancy, swinging brass lanterns to accommodate primitive electrical fixtures. The smoking room is warm, commodious, crowded with comfortable deep chairs and souvenirs of no aesthetic importance but informative witnesses of a privileged, secure time and place. The billiard room is a marvel—sporting prints, precisely arranged cues, and clear lights—straight out of an Edwardian drama on BBC television.

The family used a finely made fitted wicker basket for picnic teas, saw to it that maid and men servants were not led into temptation by putting them in separate sections of the house reached by separate stairways. It weighed itself on a dark, heavy scale that might well have served for sacks of grain, bathed in a cast-iron tub whose height and depths could be reached only by a stool, while Papa chose to use a big saucer bath placed with its containers for soap and sponge near the fireplace of his room. That the family was fairly advanced in its tastes is reflected by a number of rooms hung with William Morris wallpaper. Luckily, the disastrous fire spared the mid-seventeenth-century barrel ceiling of the gallery, every one of its many inches paneled with borders of grapes and pods to separate rabbits, dogs, birds, flowers, griffons, sheep, goats,

camels, bears, sphinxes—all grace notes for two dozen Old
Testament scenes. Adam and Eve shame each other and God,
Cain batters down Abel, Abraham lifts his sword to Isaac,
Jacob dreams, the scenes often set in rural landscapes strewn
with cattle and working tribesmen. They are the work of a
family from the good-humored town of Bideford in North
Devon and, like the town, neither naïve nor over-sophisticated,
the figures expressive yet never carried away to the distortions
of passion. William Morris wallpaper, a few intensely Pre-
Raphaelite paintings by his contemporaries, and musical instruments inhabit the Music Room, but they can't compete with
the evocative parade of biblical events, no longer craft, not
quite art, on the concave gallery ceiling.

Now back to the pursuit of prehistoric stones. The A38 runs
toward **Liskeard** to show a Celtic round-headed cross, clearly
younger than others you will see in several places, and a noble
piece of Victoriana in a high railroad bridge soaring above the
treetops. The road will narrow to irregular piles of walls lavish with wild primroses in the spring, as it cuts off to **St. Cleer**.
On the way, two tall shafts, etched in the ribbon webs of Scandinavian and Irish ornamentation, stand for a monument to a
King Doniert. The shafts originally bore two crosses to safe-
guard the soul, it is said, of a King of Cornwall who was
drowned in 875. Some short distance beyond the village of
Minion a path among pale stone moor cottages leads to the
"Hurlers," broken rings of big stones, some still standing, as at
Stonehenge and Avebury, upright. Since they stand in John
Wesley country, such stones were easily translated into the
frozen damned who had spent their holy days at the game of
hurling or, worse still, danced. In moor emptiness, among
shards of tin mines and rusty piles of slag, watch for signs that
point to **Trethevy Quoit**, the word for burial place roof. Behind
a row of cottages extended by sheds of corrugated tin and lines
of wash, an astonishment of broad, slender slabs under a deli-
cately balanced, slanted roof stone. The shapes of the plinths
and the space between them, an eye of blue in a hole worn in
the stone and the skyward thrust of the roof compose a stunning structure, its effect heightened by the dim aura of antique
death rites for priest-kings and the background of bare moor.
There were many more of these formidable, mounded tombs

once, carried off, as were the stones of myriad monuments, by later generations for more mundane uses, often the zigzags of diagonally placed slate in rough walls.

NOTES

HOTEL: If you have chosen to follow the coast from Tintagel to take inner Cornwall later, and are now looking for inexpensive accommodation, consider the Atlantic View Hotel in **Treknow**: affability, information, bed, breakfast, and dinner for modest sums and, when the winds and sea howl, an almost excessive intimacy with life on the Cornish coast.

Port Isaac opens a panorama of green and gray cliffs waving yellow banners of gorse and, down below, black stains of caves resisting the sea which pounds into the harbor. Small hotels and whitewashed houses and shops run down to a quay bundle of bumpy old houses and sheds where meaty, fresh crabs are cooked, cleaned, and sold, by a good-looking young woman and supplied by her young Viking husband (if they are both still there), who tells you sadly, and a bit proudly, that he is allergic to crab. Crab eaten or carried off in a plastic sack, walk through the sloping clusters of Dolphin Street and Rose Hill and stop, when you've left these attractive funnels, to watch the true masters of this coast, the hordes of big screaming seagulls, streaking, swooping to pick up a piece of offal, resting and blinking on a pile for a moment, planning another offensive. Although the pilchard fishing that once fed much of Cornwall is now greatly diminished and enterprise turned to tourism, Port Isaac hasn't yet taken on the dedication of other places: one souvenir and miscellany shop instructs its customers to look for the proprietor, should the door be shut, at the pub down the street, where he can be found in a corner playing chess. On one of the upper streets, a sign points to **Port Quin**, a two-mile walk over cliff and sea, the site of a not uncommon Cornish tragedy. All the men of the small community went out on a fishing trip together and all were lost. The women abandoned the village, until recently derelict and now slowly reviving for use by holi-

day people with the help of the National Trust, which controls
and safeguards large portions of the coast.

Sooner or later you will meet Celtic saints turned specifically
Cornish—St. Mabyn, St. Tudy, St. Merryn, St. Issy, St. Breock,
who is probably Brittany's St. Brieuc. One or another of them
and fishing signs and caravan sites will usher you into **Padstow**,
a center for buying sports clothing, flasks, fishing equipment,
car hire, sweets (you will have noticed the plethora of sweetshops in many vacation villages), cafés, the ubiquitous fish-and-
chips shop, and bakeries featuring Cornish pasties. Look at the
houses on the quay, one still based on crumbling wood almost
old enough to be coal, another identified with Sir Walter
Raleigh, a native of this part of England, and an arty, nice confusion of old, new, and improvisations in between, once part
of a medieval abbey. Though it is April and the moors wear
a crust of hoarfrost, the pre-season season has started in
Padstow, the time when trucks carrying timber and paint
and frozen foods threaten each other and the ladders of painters and repairmen who wake the village up to paint its face
after the winter's sleep. (The traffic gives a sampling of summer car lines that stand mired for hours, and getting in and
out of little Port Isaac may take as long as an hour and a half.)
Despite the cars and trucks, Padstow is a good place to be, to
glance at the villas over the waters off Dennis Road and Station Road, to drink at a pub called London, whose sign is the
swell of St. Paul's dome, to admire the exuberant red and
gold of the firehouse sign, the dignified black trim on the
white Old Ship Inn, the green and flowery spurts that hold
together the vertical slates in the walls leading through
miniature lanes and houses on the way to the church. The
broad yews, those dark English mourners, surround a solid,
low tower, old roof beams and arches, and a painted monument of several men and one woman kneeling in a setting of
skulls and prayer stools, perhaps a reference to the name
of this leading Padstow family, the Prideaux (the name inevitably suggests prie-dieu), who tell a good deal about themselves in a long legend spelled in the relaxed manner of their
be-ruffled time.

Through colonies of trailers below cliffs gouged by the wind
and sea, through shallow woods and unexpected mats of lush

foliage, one comes to the tall aristocratic tower and slender finials of **St. Colomb Major**, a village of small stone houses intimidated by a few big signs painted in an optimistic past. One sign in the middle of the village advertises a HIGH CLASS FAMILY BUTCHER and his traditional straw hat, a second points out AUDREY'S CAFÉ. The stairs below this sign lead to the church, which has a very old cross in its graveyard, broad, strong, well-carved pew ends, the barrel ceiling common to the area and, returning to the stairs, an irregularity of medieval slate-hung houses. Fish and chips, of course, and a big Methodist church, and the grandest building of all, red brick Victorian Gothic— turreted, banded, convoluted—wrapped around a bank.

Roads near the sea are edged with torn, cut trees bent before the wind, roads into and out of towns and villages are burdened with the frantic call of BED AND BREAKFAST from every house, particularly near **Newquay**. Southward, a fury of building among the existing hotels of **Perranporth**, a deep cove in which two semi-submerged masses of rock might be unfortunate churches. The proprietress of the grocery-tobacconist-sweetshop at **Trevellas** will direct you to what she says are the freshest and best hot pasties in the neighborhood, at the Miner's Arms a short distance off the main road. On the slender porch of a shop a slow, sleek cat and another in a doorway near the pub and you realize how few cats and many dogs you have seen elsewhere in England, how many cats there are in Cornwall as opposed to dogs; another proof that the Cornish are not really English. As you wait for the pasties to heat in the snug bar-room, you notice the stuffing beginning to sneak out of one seat bottom, the upholstery braid falling from another, the veneer cracked on an arm, no copper or brass or polished beams—the uniform of "improved" pubs—the only decoration a bouquet of wax flowers in hard colors among leaves of dusty green. A visitor cannot be sure but must suspect that these are the accustomed furniture and ornaments of the local houses, too poor to make repairs or replace the sagging and the fading. The pasties arrive, very hot and fragrant, 12 pence each if you take them out and 15 if you sit at a pub table. A spindle of shortcrust pastry is lined with mashed potatoes and, inside that, meat and onions. Even if the smell and heat don't tempt you and your diet is horrified by the combination of dough and potatoes, have one to experience yet another peasant invention

(Italian minestrone and pasta, German dumplings, Chinese rice dishes, potatoes in many guises)—to fill a stomach and cling. And before you leave, look for the sign that says, THOU SHALT NOT STEAL EVEN FROM THE CORNISH, a reminder of Cornwall's reputation for careless ethics. (Celia Fiennes in *Through England on a Side Saddle* thought the women "comely," with "good black eyes and crafty." There may have been an abundance of pasties in her day, too, but she speaks with respect of Cornish apple pie with clotted cream and sugar on top, though adding that her pleasure is marred by "the Custome of the Country which is a universall smoaking, both men women and children had all their pipes of tobacco in their mouths.")

Unadorned with souvenir shops and the hopeful, white blandness of new hotels (although these may come in the current building activity), **St. Agnes** is an unpretty, moving cemetery of tin mines, an accusing landscape of gutted broken stone, tall and narrow, clinging to taller stacks ready to tumble from the steep hills above the sea. Tin mining was a venerable trade, now ready for revival according to some optimists. It is at least as old as the power of the Carthaginians, who sent their ships to buy the metal essential for the bronze in their weapons. The industry grew through the time of the Romans and continued to flourish after their departure, to be organized, with a system of rights and taxes as a major guild might have been, in the twelfth century. The antiquity of the trade, the clouds of secrecy that surround all borers into the earth, gathered about the tin miners of Cornwall: their deaths in primitive mines gave rise to evil spirits; their protests at times of low employment bloodier, more violent than those of other workers; their hunger not passive but exploding into murderous theft; when wages were coming in, their pleasures more pagan and reckless—and little wonder. (In the late seventeenth century Celia Fiennes tells of the "Great many people at work almost night and day, but Constantly all and every day including the Lord's day on which they are forced to prevent mines being overflowed with water.") It was they and the wreckers and smugglers who put the Cornishman outside the boundaries of civilized society. The Industrial Revolution with its voracious needs and improved machinery swelled the tin as well as the copper industry to become major sources of the world's supply. Toward the end of the nineteenth century, with the discovery and exploitation of such mines in other parts of the world (which could also supply cheaper labor), the teeming mines that had employed many thousands of men went into sharp decline, leaving the country spattered with stone ghosts and abandoned by those who could afford to leave for work in foreign mines.

A small terrace at the side of the path to the sea looks out on ripped hills, a cliff bearded with gorse, a slope of slag heap, lava-like rock pouring into the vast sea. On the other side of the terrace, a small pool that acts as seal sanctuary where sick seals or the injured are brought for curing, only a few of the yearly hundred or more—most of them pups—tormented by the winter sea and then discarded on the shore.

Rock disappears under great creamy dunes and pale dune grasses at **Gwithian** and reappears, somewhat tamed, at **St. Ives,** itself considerably tamed since it was a picturesque haven for painters half a century ago. The road approach lined with hotels prepares one for a big town and it might be, were it ironed out flat rather than tightly creased into narrow paths that climb up from the broad main beach. It is difficult to know on short acquaintance whether a place of well-appointed galleries, the center of a renowned modern pottery, of studios whose totems may be a shaggy copper devil, is actually an art center or simply arty and a lodestone for summer trippers who cram its ribs of path. (English friends will urge you to go off-season, when St. Ives returns to its authentic, engaging art-colony role.) As you stare out to sea, try to visualize the diminutive Irish saint, St. Ia, naturally of high birth, naturally a virgin, who missed the missionary boat to Cornwall. She wept and prayed and wept and prayed some more until she was wafted across the waters on a leaf to land in St. Ives Bay sooner than her fellows, a miracle which made her the patron saint of the town.

Radiant paintings and color-washed cottages standing on each other's heads fade among the scored, tumbled, and burned rocks of the road to **Zennor**. On the crests of slopes, rocks that seem deliberately assembled and may be quoits. The road rises to wide views of the sea, drops to cows and rises again to sea, drops again to a few low stone farm houses threatened by huge rocks. The tiny, silent hamlet of Zennor has a small Folk Museum and a reputation quoted by John Hillaby in his *Journey Through Britain* as "a place so poverty stricken that not so very long ago a cow is said to have eaten the bell-rope of the church." One believes it as the scattered stone cottages pass, too discouraged to paint one streak of whitewash or color on their grayness. **St. Just** stops the rocky desolation of a strange, fascinating ride with its homey little shops and a good central square.

Toward Land's End are a few of the palm trees that make the Cornish claim their climate is softer than that of the rest of England. You are on a road whose fascination has dwindled, its drama vitiated by the time you see a sign at Land's End Airport which advises you of the danger of low-flying planes. The airport safely negotiated, one meets the FIRST AND LAST SUPERMARKET IN ENGLAND, a FIRST AND LAST PUB, a sea of trailers, a stretch of parked cars, a couple of plain hotels, a souvenir shop that sells boxes covered with gleaming little shells like enameled fingernails, a snack bar, and not a hint of momentous sea or cliffs except a hotel sign that says the cliffs are dangerous and that the hotel supplies a tow rope for those who risk the danger. The sign cannot be credited, the heart sinks at these undistinguished facts of ordinary seaside resort, until one walks beyond the cars into a bitter fantasy of rock carrying a lighthouse and, surging out of the sea, immense stands of striated rock that seem cut into big blocks and re-built as towered fortresses by a mad giant. The sea crashes and bursts against them while around the half-submerged rocks nearer shore it churns up swirling, pale, icy green waters, the color of a Poe drowning. Even the seagulls are awed to quiet, finding neat piles of square rocks on which to converse in cooing whispers rather than their usual rusty-hinge shrieks. The snack bar hangs a number of photographs of wrecks as if there were need for proof of what this terror of rock and sea can do to ships.

Mediterranean color and ordered, elegant tameness hide in the cove at **Porthcurno**. Smart cottages luxuriate in full gardens and the discreet plash and burble of a brook that, flowing seaward, covers itself in dune shrub and grasses, the green and rust tassels of a silken cloth of golden-white beach. The cliffs, cut

like those of rougher, darker coves, are here enameled in a
glaze of creamy pale green and seem to embrace rather than
attack the clear blue sea. Summer busyness may change it but
in the spring, dotted with a few dreamlike figures among the
muted colors, it resembles a version of tropical Paradise. High
over the sea, the Minack Theatre, a small amphitheatre cut
into the cliffs, surrounded by toylike balconies and classic portals that look out superbly over endless waters. It comes as no
surprise, in this setting, to hear Italian spoken by a group of
visitors; the neo-classicism, the dramatic site, the extravagance
of such a summer theatre are more Latin than Anglo.

Places with the names of **Treen, St. Buryan**, and **Trewoofe**
lead into **Mousehole** (pronounced something near Muzzle), still
given the courtesy name of fishing village though it spends
most of its thought and energy on being a minor St. Ives, little
stone houses and souvenirs on deep clefts that slip down to the
quay. Yachts and fishing run with the sea road toward truly
fishy **Newlyn**, working hard at selling serious fishing gear, doing
a little canning, filling slippery, damp warehouses. Among its
hotels and palm trees, **Penzance** works as hard in its boats
and freighters and shops. Little *dolce far niente*, in spite of the
suggestive name and the reputation for being a warm strip of
the Riviera of Cornwall. Almost across the bay, the pile of **St.
Michael's Mount**, the local Mont St. Michel, a privately owned
castle which can be visited via causeway when the tide is low
or by ferry from **Marazion** when the tide is in. (Names like
Marazion, according to Hillaby, are conducive to supporting a
theory that the Phoenicians or related Semitic peoples from the
Mediterranean area came for their tin to Cornwall and left their
imprint in the name given to melting pits, "Jews' houses.")

Lizard Point is as harsh in looks and action as Land's End.
Its favorite grim story, among a number of unpretty tales,
explains a singularity of Cornwall. Daphne du Maurier in
Vanishing Cornwall tells of a wreck of two centuries ago that
swept about two hundred corpses in to shore where the people
in the vicinity found them, wedged and crushed against the
rocks, when the tide went out. They dragged the dead men and
the piles of weapons the ship had spilled to a field above and
began to bury the corpses in pits. It took some days and during that time great packs of starving dogs gathered around
the as yet unburied corpses. They were driven off and for

years the local people would have nothing to do with dogs. The tradition may have spread and stayed; as you must have noticed, only where the "outsiders" live and visit does one see dogs with any frequency.

Teasing, ungraspable names—**Praa, Pensanooth, Halvasso, Restronguet**—trail their way through caravan camps, motels, beach huts, driving ranges, abandoned mines, and innumerable invitations to send your friends cream by mail. Then, access to the large port town of **Falmouth** or inland to **Gwennap Pit**, near Redruth, a low arena shaped and smoothed of the abandoned mine where John Wesley, in the mid-eighteenth century, convinced thousands to leave their wild, superstitious ways for the strict morality of their plain chapels. A few miles away, **Truro**, whose Victorian Gothic cathedral spires fail to quench the blazing color—teal blue, lavender, orange, lemon yellow, shocking pink—of its houses and the bouncy air of a contented market town, hardly the place described in the late seventeenth century as "Ruinated, disregarded." Green of slopes and woods, the amber of fields around **Tresillian** and the high walls of shrub and trees of a narrow road (off B3078) wind to **Veryan**, a white and green flowery village whose central paths show a rounded section of thatch on one house and two completely round white houses. According to legend, the shape was dictated by fear of the Devil, who was known to lurk in corners; to make doubly sure, a cross was placed at the top of each house. This safety in roundness is echoed in walls and, on a nearby street, in a group of attached cottages which were undoubtedly almshouses.

You might want to hold off on Veryan's round houses, though, to combine them with Mevagissey. In that case, B3078 will take you into the splendid bay, the yachts, the fine houses and wooded patches of **St. Mawes** and, as you approach, an appealing baby castle, miniature castles in its arms, and a cupola that resembles an ample baby's bottle. The approach to little **Portscatho** is less pleasing, something of a black off-season joke when your car plunges straight down to an unexpected, unobstructed opening to the sea. **Mevagissey** has her "Celtic Crafts," "Antiques," shops of souvenirs and pottery, a sheepskin shop, none of them especially aspiring, the most stimulating a barnlike place whose sentinel is a rhino's head yawning a staggering array of teeth. Among the simple houses of brick and plaster, the expected snack bars and guest houses and, down at the harbor, a small amusement parlor. But a neighboring café offers dishes of pilchards (midway between sardine and herring, and once a major export) and the waterfront smells of fish; there is mild bustle around scales, storage sheds, and vivid fishing boats; again the incessant screeching bombardment of hundreds of gulls and, lingering near the boats, a group of crusty fishermen in dirty work clothes with wind-carved faces and deep-set dark eyes. The compact town climbing high above the sides of the harbor and sea walls, the yellowed-green of roof mosses washing into the color of the cut cliffs, the pastel boxes of house, the angles of roof and cliff, arrange themselves naturally as a well-designed semi-abstract painting screened by a restless veil of gulls.

The cows and fields of **Pentewan** hang miraculously above the sea, and beautifully, until their circus act is interrupted by a beachful of trailers, then by the light dust of clay works in **St. Austell**, and farther on, the houses of **Par**, overwhelmed by their dramatic landscape. The careful signposting of **Fowey** (pronounced Foy) returns one to the yachting, the gleaming shops, the boat-owners' clubs, the solid houses in pretty coves of prosperous retirement-and-resort Cornwall. Not too far inland, the worn crosses that speak of missionary-saint Cornwall and, of the Cornwall of tragic, royal legends, the long shadow of King Mark, whose castle was believed to have stood, looking on the sea, near the Fowey River.

You may be ready now to head for Somerset or, with time and inclination, clamber around **Polperro** and **West** and **East Looe** (pronounced Loo) and make the patriotic gesture of stopping in **Plymouth,** although German bombing destroyed almost all its antiquity.

NOTES

HOTELS: For a night's stay, with a chance of being awakened by sea and wind and seagulls, try the Metropole in Padstow, which rents a big room on the bay, provides electrified coffee or tea service usable at any hour, a shoe-polishing and buffing machine in an alcove, for moderate to high rates. The respectable dinner is not as high as the room rates would lead one to expect. The Dinas is somewhat less expensive and there is the black-and-white Old Ship Inn in the center of town and the many bed and breakfasts.

Near Port Isaac, the reputable Port Graverne Hotel, a seventeenth-century inn made hospitable; moderate. Near Portscatho, the Rosevine House, whose nicely decorated rooms look out to gardens, palm trees, and sea. The agreeable management gives you a double room, a shower, dinner and breakfast, and the company of raucous crows for a high-moderate sum. If you seem a little taken aback at the price, the manageress will suggest other places you might like and at less cost, like the Roseland House, which also sits by the sea. The big, lustrous hotels of St. Mawes, St. Ives, and Fowey will run, of course, higher, but these towns provide, as well, countless smaller places. There are very few stretches of the coast, and inland as well, that do not provide at least shelter and breakfast, and if the amenities of one town or village do not tempt you, there is always another fairly close by.

RESTAURANTS: Cornwall is innocent of the Lucullan, even in fairly expensive hotels where, as in cheaper places, food is sometimes punished in boiling water, as if it were the roots of sin. Take what you can where you can and don't fret; there is an inexhaustible supply of pasties or fish and chips.

Westward

Fresh-faced **Odiham**, in Hampshire, presents crooked timber in black-and-white houses, sparked with purple doors and yellow window frames. The parish church, All Saints', has a number of gifts to give, besides the oddity of its mismatched pillars. The font, chipped and smoothed out of one huge chunk of chalk, is incised with Gothic lettering of the opening of the sixteenth century. The highly carved wooden pulpit was put in place a few years before Cromwell's troops prised the brasses from their stone beds. They are now in the wall, in good shape and include women like Pied Pipers leading lines of minuscule children; one lady pulls along a diminishing trail of nine. In the back of the church the wheels of a flat wagon that carried coffins and a doorless telephone box, the "hudd," which long ago sheltered the clergymen who intoned prayers over rain-swept graves.

Before the church stand the punishing stocks whose wood is now silvery with age and the whipping post with rusty restraining bars. At the end of the graveyard is Odiham's pest house, now an innocent little structure with big yellow roses climbing its chimney. Two of the gravestones here mark the deaths of French officer prisoners of the Napoleonic Wars. They and their co-nationals were held in a cottage near the war memorial and in another at the top of the High Street, where the chimneys trill a gay tune. It was between these two houses that the Frenchmen were granted the un-French perquisite of a walk in the invigorating country air.

Four miles north of **Basingstoke** there is a curious house called **The Vyne**, in memory of a Roman wineshop or vineyard on a Roman road, or, according to the genial National Trust custodian of the house, in honor of an emperor who sent vines to be planted locally by his colonizers. Whatever the source of the name, this was Roman territory, as attested to by nearby finds and, most spectacularly, by a ring worked as a head of Venus, now one of the possessions of the house. The first sure records of the house appear more than a millennium later, with the record of its building by William Sandys, soldier, functionary, and ultimately Lord Chamberlain to Henry VIII. He was a conservative, elderly gentleman, who probably found it difficult to entertain his king and his new queen, Anne,

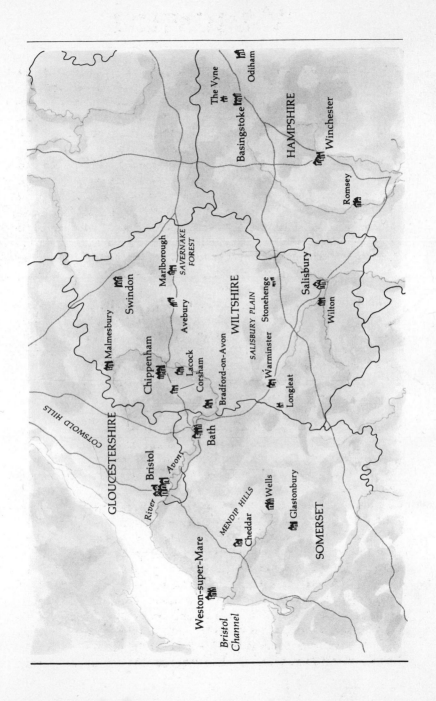

while his fealty stayed with Catherine, and he managed to stay away from the court as much as he judiciously could.

Although the house retains its shape of the early sixteenth century, only the diapered red brick work and the Gothic windows of the south front are original. Later owners, particularly John Chute, cosmopolitan, "man of taste," and amateur of the arts and architecture, designed many changes. The northern façade centers on a portico he ordered of a follower of Inigo Jones, certainly not the first English structure out of Palladio by Jones but the earliest such portico to be attached to a country house.

The interior, too, was changed by John Chute and before him and after, although his is the most effective hand, as witness eighteenth-century chimneypieces, the plasterwork ceilings in rococo arabesques, and most markedly in the hall and stairway done in "Grecian theatric" style to substitute for the Tudor Great Hall.

Look for a number of remarkable sixteenth-century portraits and notice the furniture, in several English, French, and Italian types, of painstaking workmanship and finish. Head for the chapel, built by Sir William Sandys and not too drastically changed from his time, for the richly carved woods in varied patterns, in mischievous putti and, on the ends of the pew stalls, folksy matter such as an old lady supported by three acrobats. The glass in the windows is luminous and authentic, thought to be the best Flemish work of its time and dedicated to the Tudor royal family. Here are Margaret, Queen of Scotland, her brother Henry VIII and his wife Catherine of Aragon, all dressed in ermines, ruby reds, deep blues, and glowing purples, each accompanied by patron saints and royal symbols. Religion is here made subservient to royalty; so that Henry's shield and Catherine's Castilian castle can fit properly, the order of Ascension, Crucifixion, and Calvary has been reversed. Federigo da Montefeltre, whose beaked profile appears on a tile near the altar, would have seen to it that his artist combined religion and royalty with balanced respect, but he was the great Duke of Urbino and had no need to flatter a king. (The portrait tile and its group were ordered from a workshop in The Netherlands established by an Italian of Urbino.)

In the course of your progress, several Roman busts that make no attempt at authenticity, groups of satisfying miniatures, and the Tudor Oak Gallery. Its length of plain paneling is unusually fine and additionally carved in animals and human shapes, crests and insignia of Lord Sandys and his king and queen, including the fateful joining of the Tudor rose with the Spanish pomegranate. One detail, Cardinal Wolsey's hat, helps date the paneling within a few years. The earliest possible year is 1515, when Wolsey became cardinal, and the last possible just before 1528, when Wolsey had powers and treasures taken from him by the king he had so assiduously served. The visit ends on two lively ladies. One is Frances, Duchess of Richmond and Lennox, a mistress of Charles II who became his version, reproduced on numerous medallions, of "Britannia." The other is a warm-skinned lady whose name is Mrs. Penobscot, of the tribe in Maine. The legend on the frame doesn't say so, nor the house booklet, but some local informant may tell you that she was one of four Indian ladies brought back, on a courtier's request, by Sir Walter Raleigh, and became, like her three sisters, a favored courtesan. She has an open, mischievous, childlike charm and one hopes that she had a long, petted, jeweled life but fears more realistically that she was cut down early by "the pox" (syphilis).

NOTES

The Vyne is open April to September, Wednesdays and Bank Holidays, 11:00 to 1:00 and 2:00 to 6:00; Thursdays and Sundays, 2:00 to 6:00 only.

RESTAURANTS: Good lunches are to be had at the buffet-bar of the College Arms, a pub near The Vyne.

Within ten years of the Norman completion of **Winchester** Cathedral, its tower collapsed. Rather than blame the planners and workers, it was bruited about that the destruction was a sign of protest from the committees of Heaven because William Rufus, the Conqueror's son, was entombed beneath the tower and he was blatantly anti-religious. Rufus was allowed to stay and, in time, forgotten in the fourteenth-century rebuilding which produced the largest Gothic nave there is and the less magnificent west front. The Middle Ages also made intricately embellished chapels and chantries, the most elaborate that of the Cardinal Beaufort who helped burn Joan of Arc. The Lady Chapel was remade by Henry VII to celebrate the baptism of his son, Prince Arthur, who might have succeeded to the throne had he lived long enough. Instead, his brother, Henry, moved forward in the succession and took with him Arthur's widow, Catherine of Aragon, that marriage—which he later chose to interpret as illegal by biblical law—the first of the flamboyant marital career. In the chantry of Bishop Wayne-flete, the chair in which the one surviving child of Henry and Catherine, Mary Tudor, sat during the ceremony of her marriage to Philip II of Spain; above the choir screen, casks of ancient bones, among them those of King Canute and his Queen Emma. In the south transept the grave of Isaak Walton and, nearby, a high point of English woodwork in carvings of twisted silk skeins to do honor to a Prior Silkestede. In the Chapel of the Holy Sepulchre and in the Guardian Angels' Chapel, restored wall paintings that must, in their time, have made a world of pity and awe; a twelfth-century font of black marble from Tournai in Belgium, then a center of Church art. And, not to be overlooked, the carved marble stone that speaks of Jane Austen—"The benevolence of her heart, the sweetness of her temper, the extraordinary endowment of her mind"— who was buried here, having "departed this life" at the age of forty-one. Plenty to see and know, but the showpiece of Winchester is the great nave, the bosses in its high ceiling vaults, and the Gothic tracery among the smoothly banded pillars.

One of the brightest tombs is that of a bishop swathed in gold cloth, at his head angels, at his feet tonsured monks in prayer. He was Bishop Wykeham, a rebuilder of the Cathedral and the founder of Winchester College, a monastic school as early as the late fourteenth century, now one of the aristocrats among public schools and a pleasant place of greens, a rambling diversity of low buildings and, if the season is right, boys in longish shorts and peaked jockey-style hats, with rosy knees. Other than the statue of Alfred the Great, prominently placed early in this century, there is a college devoted to the arts; a hospice, St. Cross Hospital, that still serves the traveler bread and ale; a huge painted wheel, the Round Table, that hangs on the wall of the Great Hall of the castle, decorated with the Tudor rose and names of King Arthur's knights to please Henry VIII, who came to visit with the emperor Charles V in 1522. The city betrays few further singularities. The bowed windows and beamed inns, the Victorian Guildhall, a row of seventeenth-century buildings for Church functionaries, venerable house overhangs supported on beams, an arched gate, neat Georgian houses, attractive corners, and a ghetto that left the name "Jewry" on one of the central streets, the Cathedral close and its churchmen's houses might all be the property of almost any small English city. And like its counterparts, an inviting, seasoned place.

On a dip almost equidistant from Winchester and Salisbury sits **Romsey**, an old and new town around a singular abbey. Its development is familiar: Saxon chapels supplanted by Norman might, added to over the centuries into the fifteenth, diminished after the parish paid £100 for the church of the dissolved abbey and pulled superfluous sections down. There is still much, however, to admire. At the south wall, a mutilated, impressive Norman door and beside it, under a number of restored stone heads, a Crucifixion, the Christ rather relaxed and soft-bellied, guarded by the Hand of God that emerges from a cloud. Purportedly Saxon and considerably damaged, it yet appears worldly for a time of harsher, cruder, more emotive carving. Among the monuments, look for the explicit memorial to John St. Barbe and his wife, Grissell, he in full Cromwellian costume, she in a full mop of curls, both life-sized and colored, staring out into their new uncomfortable void. Yet more explicit is one of the "accounts with God" monuments, this of a later time (1817) when a man's worth and charities were displayed in explicit detail:

He directed his Executors to place the sum of £6700, 3 percent Consols in the hands of Trustees to Endow six Tenements which he had built in Romsey and to invest the Rest and Residue of his Estate in the Public Funds in their names. The Interest arising therefrom to be paid by them in equal Moieties in aid of the current Charges and Expenses of the Salisbury Infirmary and the County Hospital

of Winchester. In Conformity with the Will of the deceased
this Tablet is Erected.

The essential matter of the abbey, however, rests in other
objects: in the Chapel of St. Anne, a crude Saxon crucifix of
Christ and Church Triumphant, the upright of the cross in
flower; in a strange, small alabaster Pietà that appears to be
Elizabethan though the provenance may be foreign; in the
scratched roundels of wall painting of the thirteenth century;
in the painted wooden reredos of the Resurrection as witnessed by early-sixteenth-century saints and savants of the
Church. Most satisfying of all are the architectural elements
of the original Norman church, the long windows with interlaced arcading below, and especially the Norman arches repeated, above, as open, double arches joined at slender pillars,
lending the choir, particularly, an airy lightness. On a capital
in the Chapel of St. Anne there is a scroll that says, in Latin,
"Robert made me." With a nod of thanks to Robert and his
co-workers for the splendid design, you may be ready for a
glimpse of Romsey's quite modern post office and an ancient,
tottering neighbor of wattle and pinkish brick, dipping perilously under its weight of pink roses like a wind-swept summer
hat.

The ethereal spire of **Salisbury** Cathedral, misting the sky
at a long distance, meets gratifyingly the expectation of a real-
life facsimile of Constable's painting. Resist the world-famous
Cathedral for a while and lend yourself to the swells of Tudor
stone and glass, the houses of brick, stone, flint, often combined, that ring the Cathedral, and the attractive shops by
Cathedral Gate. On the High Street near the escutcheoned gate,
a bookshop installed under curved timbers that support the
pristine walls. On New Canal a cinema whose name is spoken in heavy gilded Gothic letters and whose dark Jacobean-
style woods surround James Bond and Elizabeth Taylor bursting through livid posters. Very new is a fresh parking field, the
old represented by the workers' cottages (look for Rose Villa,
the establishment of a talented potter) dressed with bright
doors and a picturesque bridglet on Water Lane. Crane Street,
too, is a matter of small bridge and narrow river walks and,
in from Fisherton, beyond the clock tower, a view of the Avon
hung with trees and fishermen and its short bridge. A wedding

of old and new appears in the plywood used to guard reconstruction, painted in vari-colored Gothic arches to repeat Cathedral design.

The enterprising Cathedral lent its immense Close to a show
of Henry Moore sculptures several years ago; it runs tours,
concerts of high quality and, through the summer, a nightly—
except Sundays—display of historical drama as "Son et
Lumière." In the refurbished, pierced stone of the cloisters,
automatic machines, like those in the New York subway, for
hot soup, coffee, and soft drinks. The admirable present-day
animation loses itself, nevertheless, in the imposing and, for
some, uneasy sobriety of the interior. Salisbury has a rather
remarkable unity, almost entirely built in a short period—for so
grand a project—of the thirteenth century, the style Early English into the more elaborate Decorated. The spire and towers
were added less than a century later, creating serious problems.
The tower vault, touched with colored bosses, centers on an
opening which, from its great height, seems quite small until
one learns that it was through this hole that the stone for the
spire was hoisted on a treadwheel manned by a couple of
intrepid medieval workers. But even these extraordinary
masons could not handle the difficulties of securing weighty
spire and tower, afterthoughts of the original planning, so buttresses were erected. Still the spire leaned and the clusters of
black and lighter gold-banded pillars bent with the ponderous weight. Broad arches were erected to hold back some
of the force and inverted arches—less imposing than those at
Wells, yet agreeable surprises and breaks in the regularity—put
in to make absolutely sure.

One picks one's way through skeletal monuments in the
Morning Chapel to examine myriad tiny heads and their buoyant angel companions, quite battered, yet charming on their
thirteenth-century stone screen. Next, look for the vivid jewel
box of color on fan vaulting in the Audley Chantry (for intoning
Masses to protect the soul of an Audley who became Bishop of
Salisbury) in the manner of the sixteenth century, and the bare
entrails of the oldest working clock in England (fourteenth
century). At the extreme eastern end, a stand of unusual monuments. That of Thomas Gorges, who died in 1610, was built with
some of the money granted the family by Elizabeth I, who had
had it from a wrecked vessel of the Spanish Armada. It might

have been lifted bodily from a Baroque church on the Continent:
an open box of twisted columns and scored pilaster topped with
mysterious symbolic ornaments and obelisks devised by a fore-
runner of Piranesi. A towering compilation and repetition of
classical elements makes the multi-tenanted Hertford monument. A key figure was Catherine, the wife of Edward, Earl of
Hertford, also the sister of Lady Jane Grey, she who was on
and off the throne in nine days. Catherine, a likely successor,
was imprisoned along with her husband in the Tower and there
died, having been delivered of two sons inside the prison walls.
In the vicinity of a St. Jerome by Ribera, a much more graceful
Gothic tomb of stone foliage and angels for the thirteenth-
century bishop who officiated at the consecration of the
Cathedral.

We leave the tombs at an ancient memento, the base of a
shrine to St. Osmund, cut with three openings through which
the sick could touch the healing bones of the saint. And on to
the beautiful Spanish cloth made 350 years ago in honor of
St. Theresa and now in the Chapel of St. Margaret. Off the deep
large cloisters, the majestic Chapter House, whose central cluster spreads to meet fine groups of peripheral columns that float
toward the ceiling and cusp the large windows. In the area
above the continuous run of low arches, leading personages and
events of the Old Testament carved well and naturalistically.
Notice the eagerness and admiration of Jacob as he gazes at
Rachel; the older Rachel and Jacob recoiling in horror when
Joseph's brothers show their parents a coat that is proof of
Joseph's death; the stony manner of Potiphar's wife. Imagine
what they must have been in color, flushed in the rich light
from stained-glass windows which no longer exist. Imagine the
incandescent chamber the Chapter House must have been when
its time, the late thirteenth century, was new.

Salisbury not only rejoices in one of the country's most impressive cathedrals but also a Tudor house redesigned by Inigo
Jones and later hands that holds an unusual collection of paintings and objects. **Wilton House** is immediately west of the
town; sitting confidently, in the Tudor manner, on an immensity of lawn under venerable cedars.

William Herbert, a member of an old Welsh family, who had
been hiding out in France after killing a man in a street or

tavern fight, returned to England about 1530 and shortly thereafter married the sister of Catherine Parr, who was to become the last wife of Henry VIII. When Wilton Abbey, already considerably decayed, was abolished, Henry gave the lands to his brother-in-law. The story goes (without documentation) that William Herbert consulted Holbein, the court painter, about designing a house on his new estate; some authorities see traces of Holbein in the Tudor entrance at the eastern façade. With or without Holbein, the house became the stately mansion that suited a gentleman potent enough—adroit enough—to become a guardian to the frail young Edward VI and, on his death, adviser to the Catholic Mary and, when the succession went to Elizabeth, an important figure in her court. Among other high honors he accrued in the course of his career was the title of Earl of Pembroke, which accounts for the tags on many paintings in the house.

His eldest son, Henry, continued in important service to Elizabeth, who visited him and may have been entertained by the literati—Spenser, Sidney, Ben Jonson among them—who were invited and sponsored by his wife, Mary Sidney, the sister of Philip. There is a possibility, not fortified by records, that Shakespeare's company performed two of his comedies here. Testimony to the house as a sanctuary of literature and the arts is the dedication of the first folio edition, published a few years after Shakespeare's death, to the Earl of Pembroke and his brother, the Earl of Montgomery. The arts continued to flourish at Wilton, paintings commissioned and collected, collection and estate held intact during the Civil Wars because the incumbent Pembroke sensed the way the wind was blowing and, unlike many of his fellow peers, chose against Charles I. He was punished by irate Royalist ghosts with a fire that destroyed his house, except for a center portion of the east front. Inigo Jones was commissioned to rebuild Wilton, but he died before the job was finished. The work was carried on by his disciple and nephew, John Webb, on Jones's plans which called for maintaining the Tudor scheme with classical flourishes, the interior centered on a group of large, Palladian rooms.

A later family disaster was a murderous profligate who cost the family many of its acquisitions, sold to clean up the debts he left. Restitution was made by an accomplished brother who held important positions and honors (we are now at the opening of

the eighteenth century) and spent freely for the arts and rare
books on the Continent, one of his acquisitions the famous
Wilton Diptych, now in the National Gallery. It was he, also,
who imported the most artful weavers to establish the atelier
that produced Wilton carpets. Family tastes turned to architecture, here manifested in a Palladian bridge complete with
arcade, tempietti, and regal stairs. A later descendant confined
himself to English portraiture and added to the family roster
of accomplishments pictures of horses and books he himself
wrote about riding. Early in the nineteenth century, an heir
found the house unsatisfactory and made some major changes.
Succeeding generations undid some of these changes, cata-
logued the house treasures, and at least one recent member of
the family kept the traditional family link to the arts as a
trustee of important national collections.

The visit opens with an unusual revelation of personality; in
the low entrance hall, a case surrounds a pair of Fred Astaire's
dancing shoes bought by an admiring contemporary Earl of
Pembroke, the shoes astonished to find themselves with the
wearied Florence Nightingale and documents heavy with the
seals of gone kings. The two "Smoking Rooms" maintain the
Inigo Jones forms and door detail, sport the finest Italian
marble in the fireplace surrounds and singular pieces of late-
seventeenth-century English furniture. Then, horses, horses,
horses. The first group is large paintings by a Swiss, with the
Swiss proclivity for substituting detail for fantasy or drama,
in the green-gray non-colors of his time and background. The
horses set in the larger room, small and hung closely under a
fine ceiling, are not necessarily technical improvements but
infinitely more engaging. There are fifty-five paintings, each of
one horse and one rider of the famous Spanish riding school,
every horse a compilation of voluptuous curves as painted on
order of the tenth Earl of Pembroke (mid-eighteenth century)
by a noted riding master to the Austrian emperor.

A Pembroke's taste for stuffed fish and birds follows displays
of china and glass and leads to Pembroke portraits and a rhetorical Pietro da Cortona "Rape of the Sabine Women." The
next two rooms are a miscellany of Dutch and Italian painting,
most of them of unusual quality. The names appear—Rubens,
Rembrandt, Lorenzo Lotto, Poussin, Van Dyck, Teniers—but
the less resounding are also represented by variously stimulat-

ing paintings. By Van der Goes, of the fifteenth century, a tender, ascetic Nativity; of the sixteenth century, a young prince in northern hat and high lace collar, his expression that of numberless Renaissance bloods who stare scornfully out of their frames. Leda embraces her adoring swan as she gazes down at her *two* sets of twins lying in their *two* hatched eggs, an Italian exaggeration. Painted by Cesare da Sestro, a Leonardo pupil, she wears a Leonardo face. "The Card Players," by Lucas van Leyden, a work of the early sixteenth century, is, at first glance, a naturalistic painting of players and spectators, their garments, cards, and coins meticulously rendered. Their frozen attitudes, eyes staring into a distance or at the spectator, a lonely piece of landscape out of a window, move the painting into Surrealism.

The superbly decorated, pilastered rooms that follow take us to the English painters, mainly Reynolds and Lawrence, occupied with family portraits; then to Van Dyck, seascapes of Van der Velde, two exquisite French royal portraits in the manner of Clouet and, finally, Rembrandt's luminous portrait of his mother, in a brown cloak and headdress, eyeglasses low on her pinched elderly nose.

The Double Cube Room of Inigo Jones, 30 feet high and wide and double those dimensions in length, is the acme of Wilton decoration, all white with golden garlands, bouquets, heads, and shields and monumental figures sharing a broken pediment. This is the room of Van Dycks, all the paintings his except one done by assistants in his studio. Charles I, a familiar subject, sits in brilliantly rendered shining dark armor, a small smile between his pointed beard and long thin nose. His French queen, Henrietta Maria, is all lace and silk and curls and pearls, a subtle warmth in the dignity. Above the fireplace, three of their children, Charles II, James II, and Princess Mary, gorgeously dressed little grownups with round baby cheeks and cherry lips. The rest, more or less, are Pembrokes, singly and as gathered in one immense family group.

The family continues, proud, handsome, and stunningly cocooned in the gold and white of the Single Cube Room, the painting honors here divided between Van Dyck and Lely, who must have had a happy time painting the wife of the seventh earl. She sits in a dusky, romantic glade, her hair wayward, her eyelids lazy, her mouth full and fresh. The dégagé silk she wears gapes and falls, about to slip off the nipples of perfect breasts. This Countess of Pembroke was the sister of the Duchess of Portsmouth who was the mistress of Charles II, and one wonders whether the juicy girl stayed a respectable wife or paced her sister's dance in a gay, permissive court.

One can go on describing many more works of art and objects but it might be best to close by urging that you make this notable house and its collection one of your prime choices among the many stately homes.

NOTES

Hours: Open April to September, weekdays and Bank Holidays, 11:00 to 6:00; Sundays, 2:00 to 6:00 only.

Northwestward, on the way to Bath or Wells, through greens that roll lazily to meet the swans in the Avon, strides—one can't say it sits—Longleat, big and omnivorous, to be taken, if possible, after the variety that lies to the north, west, and south again in Wiltshire and Somerset. Thus, up to world-renowned **Stonehenge** on Salisbury Plain, awesome in the sparse light of early or late day and, like so many places, best without crowds of summer tourists. Through Savernake Forest, reputedly the only forest that is not Crown property, to scatterings of thatch and antiques and the high color and movement of **Marlborough**. It sits on slapdash arcades which stop at one end of the High Street near tower and town hall and one bright blue and one olive house crowding each other out like children pushing for prominence in a photo. At the other end of the High Street, a church trimmed with four pointed ornaments and vanes, a schematic version of a castle.

Through the tawny yellow, green-gold, grass-green, and tree-green of fields like a calm sea, past a dramatic church tower thrusting out of a low plain, one comes to signs pointing to **Avebury**, an ANCIENT MONUMENT, and so it is, about four millennia ancient and the largest Neolithic ceremonial circle yet discovered in Europe. No one would expect stone forma-

tions to stand unharmed for too long; these did not. Many of
the stones—it is estimated that there were more or less one
hundred—were buried in the Middle Ages by a church and its
flock who found the rough, heavy stones, joined in mysterious
circles, uncomfortable and pagan, clearly the Devil's work.
Some centuries later, farmers in the vicinity cleared the land
and chopped up the stones to make walls for houses and fields.
Although arcs of rock were given names—Devil's Chair, Barber's
Stone (for a skeleton accompanied by barber's tools who was,
the theory goes, crushed during a medieval stone burial)—the
site is not comprehensible, though awesome for its secretive
crudeness. Best to buy a booklet or postcard from the museum-
shop and, as you walk on the bank of the outermost ring,
reconstruct with the help of a few stones here and there, plus
the pamphlet sketch, the paths and circles within circles that
were so momentous to Neolithic worshippers, or astrologers,
some say.

To counter German propaganda in World War II that advertised the English as hewers of human flesh and drinkers of
blood, England disseminated the photographed charms of a
"typical" village, serene and chastely picturesque. That was
Lacock, whose brick, stone, wattle and daub banded in timber,
and the abbey with its brickwork chimneys twisted in Tudor
fashion, are wards of the National Trust. It rises, falls, and
turns sweetly, the color of its stone is amber, the tiled eaves
steep and cozy, and its abbey looks on the Avon River. You may
observe that these cottages are wider and have more window
space than many of their contemporaries, an indication that
this was a weaving village and important as such in the Middle
Ages when it stood on the "cloth road" that ran from Bath to
London. With competition from other places, prosperity did not
last forever and Lacock, like many weaving villages, found itself
in hard times. A poorhouse was needed, and then a larger, still
visible from the church. The annals of the village are grim: a
jammed lockup for drunks and weavers and farm workers who
protested against their starvation wages, a miserly bread dole
allowed only for children under seven. Those inhabitants of the
poorhouse capable of movement went to work in the fumes and
damp of the tanning pits. Anyone who could somehow scrape
money together fled to the New World. That is all over now,
the village an elderly idyll with a few old inns, a bow-fronted

shop or two, a dense coat of ivy on one house and another, and everywhere decorum.

The aficionado of Norman architecture and decoration can speed northward to **Malmesbury** Abbey, once a fount of leadership and learning with a library-scriptorium that produced some important volumes of early history, and at a later time a weaving establishment set up by a sixteenth-century manufacturer who bought the property from Henry VIII. It still preserves a few rare antiquities, among them an illuminated Bible. One of the windows remembers someone called Elmer, an English Icarus who put on home-made wings and leaped off the abbey tower. He wasn't killed, simply indignant because he lacked a tail which would have acted as rudder to control his flight. Elmer-Icarus aside, the reason for coming to Malmesbury is the uniquely fine carved doorway, the decorations and figures carved into the porch beyond, and a churchyard tombstone that tells of Hannah Twynnoy, an early victim of empire building, who died at the age of thirty-three in 1793:

> In bloom of Life
> She's snatched from hence,
> She had no room
> To make defence:
> For Tyger fierce
> Took life away
> And here she lies
> In a bed of clay,
> Until the Resurrection Day.

Since Malmesbury, if it is included in your itinerary, can be combined with the Cotswolds you might prefer to go directly to **Corsham,** located between Bath and **Chippenham.**

Originally Elizabethan, **Corsham Court** was partially replanned by Capability Brown to house the extensive collection of art and objects of a later purchaser, Mr. Paul Methuen, the heir of a diplomatic family whose considerable wealth was founded in wool. John Nash, the planner responsible for an extensive area in London, was called in to expand the house about forty years later (1800) so that it might accommodate more of the Methuen collection and to hang a north façade in the style of the buttressed and turreted "Gothic" castle then coming to high fashion. In the mid-nineteenth century, an additional collection was brought into the house by marriage and much of Nash's work was undone, not so much because it was ill-adapted to showing paintings as because it was too insubstantial to keep out the chill damp that corroded flesh and pictures. This sort of change, concentrated on one purpose of the house, involving partial remaking with little attention to the rest, lost the unity of design, and Corsham is hardly an architectural gem. To compensate, it is a gem of early property history. When Ethelred the Unready was King at the end of the tenth century, this was his royal manor. William the Conqueror turned the lands and their proceeds over to a monastery in Caen, but it somehow reverted to Richard the Lion-Hearted who, since he wasn't around much anyway—chasing Saladin, being shipwrecked in the Adriatic and ransomed (with some family reluctance) from the clutches of the Holy Roman Empire —gave the estate to his brother John, possibly to erase the name "Lackland," by which the latter was known. The next inheritor was King John's son Richard, who lost the estate when he went over to the side of the barons then engaged in forcing the Magna Carta on the king. The manor was later restored to Richard, who turned it over, for a sizable consideration, to his tenants under feudal regulations and customs of tenure that lasted into this century.

A century or so thereafter, Corsham became the property of a line of royal ladies: Philippa, the wife of Edward III, then to her daughter, and on *her* death, to Anne of Bohemia, the first wife of Richard II. The manor, referred to as Corsham Reginae, continued to go from queen to princess to queen, from Catherine of Aragon to Catherine Parr, to Elizabeth, who turned the estate over to one of her favorite courtiers, the exquisite Sir Christopher Hatton, but kept control of the manor herself; and so it went to subsequent queens, stopping at Henrietta Maria of France, the wife of Charles I.

Although not necessarily sharing period or place of origin, the paintings and furnishings lend dignity to each other, the quality in a case of miniatures equal to that of the precision and delicacy of Adam filigree on the furniture. The huge Chinese vases and extravagant Indian chests covered with skate skin around mother-of-pearl inlay speak the language of other Mannerist excesses. The china reflects the delicate fauna and flora that tremble on the frames of eighteenth-century mirrors; rich upholstery that repeats damask hangings, plasterwork ceiling patterns echoed in the carpeting, create a harmonious luxury that enhances the collection.

Not unexpectedly, Van Dyck leads all the rest in the long picture gallery with the famous equestrian painting of Charles I framed in a triumphal arch, a large, stormy "Betrayal of Christ," and an expressive portrait of an old man. He is flanked here by many Italians of the sixteenth and seventeenth centuries, among them Caravaggio represented by "Tobias and the Angel," a strange alluring "Tancred and Erminia" by da Cortona, a unique "Baptism of Christ" by Reni, a small intense Tintoretto of the "Adoration of the Shepherds," and two contrasting views of St. Catherine. Il Domenichino sees her big and placid, a Mother-Earth figure, while Bronzino's saint is stern, elegant, and a touch masculine, both a universe apart from the plain, beguiling "Gaddi Children." A respite for examining the Chippendale wall ornaments and furnishings, and the Italians take over again in the Cabinet Room. Here a fair, tender Tuscan "Annunciation" by Fra Filippo Lippi, interesting to compare with the same subject by Granacci, who was born at about the time that Lippi died. Reni contributes a portrait of Pope Paul V, del Piombo "The Scourging of Christ" (on a drawing by Michelangelo and revealing a faint portrait of the Master), and as a grand tutti to the room, a huge cartoon of a curvacious cherub swinging on a ripe classical festoon, the basis of a mosaic in St. Peter's created by an artist with the dashing name of Il Cavaliere d'Arpino.

In the Octagon Room, a fairly balanced mixture of the Italian, Dutch, and English that includes a somber painting of the elderly Queen Elizabeth trying to resign herself to the flight of time in Death's hourglass.

The areas to the Music Room feature English portraits and a mixed bag of statuary and *objets*. The best of these are sets of Chinese porcelain and vases that go back to the tenth century and a rare pair of Persian bottles only a century or two younger. The Music Room gives us the chiaroscuro of Bassano's "Announcement to the Shepherds," a naïve "Rape of Europa," and from Muzio Clementi, one of his well-made trustworthy pianos. The visit ends with English painters, especially as they painted Methuens. You may have noticed Christian Methuen, née Cobb, later Lady Boston, in other rooms. Here Reynolds sees her as a solemn, overdressed baby doll in the shadow of her gleeful brother on a canvas that seems to have darkened markedly since the eighteenth century. Romney's painting takes her into the maturity of velvets and ermine among gilded surroundings. Yet a later Methuen child, of the nineteenth century, worked by a painter designated only as being of the "English School," is fresh and young, a symposium of Reynolds, Gainsborough, Lawrence, and Romney techniques.

Now, encouraged by the informal sight of students (Corsham houses the Bath Academy of Arts) in their trendy beggar costumes charging up on bicycles, one unpacks the lunch of Scotch eggs, local cheese, apples, and chocolate bar picked up at the village grocer's, sits on a bench in the extensive park, and studies the map for Bath and Bradford-on-Avon.

Bradford-on-Avon is a village of old stones in tall steep houses with slate roofs that stand close and yet isolated on changing levels, at sudden angles. A small harsh chapel—some say jail— sits on the bridge over the Avon. Holy Trinity Church is laden with prosy death notices, a few wrecked medieval monuments, and ponderous yew trees. Bradford's Saxon Church of St. Lawrence is unsteady, practically unwindowed, and meagerly decorated with a row of blind arches. It was concealed and incorporated in a dense cluster of houses until 1856. Signs of antiquity appeared during the course of repairs then and archeological scholars became highly enthusiastic about the possible discovery of a church founded by St. Aldhelm, as mentioned by the historian William of Malmesbury. William wasn't sure nor were later scholars, but ascertainable facts point to Saxon and some early Norman building which would make it tenth century, with later touches. It is minute, a rough drawing of a church, with little art to show but the angels whose discovery revealed the church, the arches, the design of the few windows, and vestiges of Saxon cross. Yet it has the power to evoke admiration and affection, as does a companion piece, not quite so old, a short distance from the village. This is an immense barn with a deeply sloping roof and eaved doors that give on a handsome and functional complex of roof beams, doubly functional since it supports nests of swallows which skim freely among the roof bricks held in the timber. Linger with the stone and slate of the houses, some of it the color of

tobacco stains, with the Shambles (old meat market), on Bradford's restless alleys, possibly to discover that while it isn't a
smooth, "pretty" village, it is beautiful.

Unless, or until, most of the city is destroyed in current demolition for modern rebuilding (which may be slowed by fervid
public protest), **Bath** should be a gratifying place to visit. As a
mélange of several essential elements, it might be the complete
English city: conspicuous Roman remains, a stand of medieval
wall, an important event in English history—the coronation in
973 of Edgar, the first King of all England—an old abbey and a
newer that had itself improvidently built very soon before the
Dissolution, a river, a long roster of literary and regal visitors,
incidents which brightened innumerable pages of English history via gossip by column or mouth, under monocle or behind
fan, and distinctive architectural planning. It favored and was
favored by a saint and by attention from the Germans in
World War II, who managed to bomb a few unoffending places
in trying to hit the Admiralty, which had removed itself to Bath.
As Northumberland comes to the literary non-English mind as
a province, not of England, but of Shakespeare, so Bath lives
as the country of Chaucer's bawdy, free-wheeling, gap-toothed
(meaning, in its time, to be endowed with a healthy sexual appetite) Wife of Bath. Bath is the country of Jane Austen's subtle
amatory campaigns among the teacups, of a prosperous society
of free Englishmen bowing for decades to the exigencies of a
dictator of fashion and manners as if they were frightened
Roman senators to his Caligula.

To begin at the beginning, Bath's lush, warmly rolling countryside runs with streams and here they spring in prodigious
thousands of gallons at a steamy temperature. Lovers and connoisseurs of thermal baths and inventors of refinements that
make our bathing habits appear primitive, the Romans built
their clever ducts and pipes to feed a splendid thermal center
and around it a stylish, sybaritic city. The early English contribution to Bath's story is less concrete. It involves the legendary Lear. The father, a prince, was banished from *his* father's
court because he had leprosy and was therefore forced to tend
swine, who liked a heated swamp. The warm swamp cured the
leprosy and the prince returned to court only to kill himself,

as Elmer of Malmesbury almost did, by trying out a do-it-your-self flying machine.

City and baths disappeared, the waters ran loose after the Romans left but were again harnessed under the Normans who, first things first, began a vast cathedral in the ruined city for which they had paid their William Rufus, the Conqueror's son, an impressive pile of silver. The sick and the aged soon made their pilgrimages to the newly established baths and to the hospices for the feeble.

In the Later Middle Ages the baths lost importance to the thriving wool trade and decayed to rancid pits when the abbey began to dissolve of its own corruption. By the time the six-teenth-century Queen Elizabeth visited them, the baths had improved. There followed other famous personages, often tact-fully bribed by city fathers, who spread the fame of life-giving Bath. One visitor of the late seventeenth century was Celia Fiennes, whose detailed account in *Through England on a Side Saddle* relates that "Ye town and all its accommodations is adapted to ye batheing and drinking of the waters and to noth-ing else . . ." She mentions five baths of several degrees of heat and goes on to describe the arrangements of the Cross Bath, the coolest and consequently most used in the summertime:

> The Cross in the middles has seates round it for ye Gentle-men to sitt, and round the walls are Arches with seates for the Ladyes . . . there are Gallery's round ye top that ye Company that does not Bathe that day walkes in and lookes over into ye bath on their acquaintance and com-pany . . . There is a sarjeant belonging to ye baths that all the bathing tyme walkes in galleryes and takes notice order 'is observed and punishes ye rude. The Ladyes goes into the bath with Garments made of a fine yellow canvas, which is stiff and made large with great sleeves like a par-sons gown. . . . The Gentlemen have drawers and wast-coates of the same sort of canvas, this is the best linning, for the bath water will Change any other yellow.

The "sarjeant" who punished the rude and dictated costumes for the bath found a later, more powerful counterpart in Richard "Beau" Nash, who controlled fashionable life, down to the most rigid detail, through half of the eighteenth century.

It seems hardly likely that he seriously affected the lives and habits of such independents as Sheridan, John Gay, whose *Beggar's Opera* was first performed here, Addison, Oliver Goldsmith, Smollett, Fielding, who found characters, settings and, often, satire in Nash's more devoted followers.

It was during the Beau's time that the city took on its distinctive architecture in ample crescents, squares, circuses, and terraces as stately runs and curves of pilasters, pediments, keystones, and acanthus. One of the initiators was the architect John Wood, with important assistance from an inventive and enterprising Bath tycoon, Ralph Allen, who sat for his portrait as Squire Allworthy to Henry Fielding in *Tom Jones*. Queen Square came first, then the Circus with its three classical orders, completed on Wood's death in 1754 by his son, who continued on, in the same regal style, with the Royal Crescent and new Assembly Rooms for meeting, gaming, gossiping, inspecting and being inspected for innovations and extravagances of dress and behavior, and there were plenty of both.

The Georgian city rows (referred to by an eighteenth-century critic as "collections of hospitals") developed northward and one might as well start there, high over the lower city, above Lansdown Terrace. If the trees permit, one observes the lilting feminine tune—the curves and answering curves, the graceful S-turns, the trip of little streets resting at docile greens—that the city sings in a curious androgynous duet with its strong houses. Lansdown Terrace, built by John Palmer at the end of the eighteenth century, is in an S-curve, its length eased by openings near turret-like extrusions and, in the center, a flat pediment on tall pilasters. The classicism of the buildings is mitigated by fine ironwork arches at each doorway and an even parade of chimneys above the shallow eaves. Somerset Place, of the same time, makes a suggestion of classical austerity with a broken pediment, then turns to coquettishness with small iron boxes as balconies.

Down and southward toward the almost awesome majesty of crescents and squares called King's, Queen's, Royal. (One house on the Royal Crescent, Number 11, fell from dignity when Richard Sheridan ran off with Elizabeth Linley, the daughter of a family who had hired and kept the pretty, ambitious Emma [née Lyon] Hamilton as a maid.) Off Brock Street, near the Circus, a pedestrian walk called Margaret's Buildings,

which places a bench across its street and then settles down
with its laundromat, tobacconist, bookshop, grocer, and cobbler in a bubbling of bow windows. On Broad Street, a monument to the bewigged Dr. Oliver, an influence in selling Bath
salubriousness and, it is said, the inventor of a favored companion to Stilton, Bath Oliver biscuits. Milsom Street and its
companion Old Bond, partially closed from traffic, present a
trio of Bath charms: flowers, flowers, flowers; careful round
lettering on shop fronts; rounds of bow windows that continue to beam, also, from shops in the tiny, ancient streets
near Abbey Green. The shopping is famously good, varied, and
especially enticing in Bath, and a partial reason for that is the
proud look of the best shops, all of black and glass fronted
by white pillars, as on Northumberland Street; fine black with
white lettering on Pulteney Bridge, designed by Robert Adam
to give Bath a proper Ponte Vecchio but infinitely neater than
the original. Graceful lamp posts, good doorways with fan-
lights and embedded lanterns, chaste designs around a window and explosions of flowers from sidewalks, from shop
baskets, flying from lamp posts. Notice them splashing around
the arcades of Bath Street and bursting like music from white
organ pipes near New Bond Street.

Much of the town is crusty and blackened—a condition which
may change with the erratic "improvements" in progress. Discolored Victorian tenements would be no loss if they were
destroyed and the huge gas tanks at the edge of town should
be masked. But why the heartless demolition of artisans' cottages? Since you cannot do anything about this, enjoy Abbey
Green, its Lilliput Alley and nearby Church Street, thank the
city fathers for a pedestrian's right to space, have tea in the
swarming plaza, and make your peace with yet another abbey
visit.

This is easy and fast unless you study the lavish flower arrangement and are addicted to tombstones, the very tissue of
the church. It was built rather late (although an abbey, as
mentioned, existed long before) so you needn't look for Saxon
stones hidden in Norman arches and corroded alabaster
knights in faceless helmets. As abbey façades rarely are, Bath's
is amusing, its turrets etched with ladders for angels scrambling up to Heaven and down. Inside there is light and freshness, attributable to the proportions, the size and abundance

of windows, the color of the stone, and constant cleaning and repairs. The few symbols of antiquity are pieces of Saxon cross once mingled with the debris of the Roman Baths, an arch of the Normans, and a capital of that time whose eroded yet virile figures teach the joys of martyrdom, supervised by a swinging Gorgon-headed angel. Several seventeenth-century poor boxes were provided with double locks, which says something of the parishioners and the distrust of their religious mentors. The sixteenth century provided clear, not too elaborate waves of fan vaulting and the fragile tracery of a chantry and, in a case near the entrance, an edition of Chaucer printed in 1561.

The abbey is Elysian Fields for the reader of long tombstone messages to and from the dead. The spread is ubiquitous and democratic: "Beau" Nash and a Founding Father of Pennsylvania; an early Governor of Australia, a Cromwellian notable contemplating his dead wife, both mourned by squat children; a savant of botany in pristine marble, striding out of his boat on the Styx to deliver a bouquet of plants to the underworld gods of a distant temple; a sub-governess to the daughters of George II; a veteran of the war of 1812; a missionary to the "Southern savage islands." And later an entire population of functionaries who found the waters and amenities of Bath good for retirement, after the sedan chairs, the feathers, the jewels, the curls and beautifying face patches, the brocades and fans, the rules of refinement, the popinjays (the Macaronis satirized in "Yankee Doodle") and their musicians, writers, and painters faded from the scene.

Launched on the route of official sightseeing, the next stop is the Roman Baths, rediscovered in the nineteenth century in the shadow of the abbey, a square serenity of warm mist surrounded by reconstructed columns and blocks of Roman marble. The visit includes the shock of gushing water, a round pool believed to have been used by women and children, a view of Roman artifacts, commemorative stones and lead piping, a bronze Minerva head like that of the famous Bocca della Verità in Rome and, of hoi polloi, battered utensils and loaded dice. Above the Roman Baths and Museum complex, the Pump Room, built when the Roman pools were seven yards down and out of sight, where the waters were ceremoniously drunk three times a day to the chatter of voices and the tinkle of

light music. (The tradition is maintained: there is coffee and/
or mineral water with music still available here, plus teas and
lunches.) It is an aristocratic room but not quite of the splendor in the Assembly Rooms built to the north (1770's) for
greater proximity to the lordly houses rising in that area and
designed by John Wood the Younger. They are clearly too pristine to be authentically of their age; a restoration of 1938 was
wiped out four years later by air raids and the job had to be
redone. The results are two octagonal rooms, one in a dress
of yellow laced with white plasterwork, and the Ball Room
in pale gray-green and ocher etched in fine bands of Greek key
and floral motifs, with good fireplaces and gleaming, spidery
chandeliers. The rest of the apartment is absorbed by a costume collection: embroidered men's shirts of Elizabethan
times, gossamer babys' clothes of the sixteenth and seventeenth centuries, including dollsize gloves that appear designed
to thwart thumb sucking, the embroidery, lace, and sequins
of a court dress of the eighteenth century, pointed silken shoes
with pattens to match, an exquisite lawn apron embroidered
with commedia dell'arte figures, and on to Victorian flounces
and the bead-hung shifts of the twenties.

Like the American hamburger—with all the familiar and some
unfamiliar trimmings—the milk shake has come to colonize
England. If stomach nostalgia hits, try a coffeeshop attached
to a grocer's at the corner of Abbey and York Streets that provides a reasonable facsimile. For a slender English sandwich
sprinkled with mustard and cress among flowery, old-fashioned
attractions, search Northumberland Passage, Milsom, Margaret's Buildings, and a dozen similar others. Fortified, on to
the American Museum at **Claverton Manor**, a couple of miles
from the city and situated over a splendid vista of hills, farms
sitting in webs of hedge, toy hamlets struggling up or slipping
down a slope.

The museum, initiated in 1961 by two Americans and housed
in the early-nineteenth-century Claverton Manor, is an unusually well arranged and exhaustive display of furnishings, decorative elements, crafts, necessities, and some luxuries of
American life from the late 1600's to approximately 1850. The
English visitor and his children are offered substantial furniture and Bible box in a Puritan room arranged for family Bible

reading. The basic trundle bed in the "measles" or "borning room," near the kitchen for proximity to maternal attention and hot water, contrasts with a well-dressed parlor of the eighteenth century. The diversity is informative and attractive: furnishings and utensils around the vast fireplace of a late-eighteenth-century tavern; bright Mexican serapes in an adobe room of New Mexico; the integrity of Shaker design; the luxury of high-life New Orleans; the peasant design of Pennsylvania Dutch; Georgian neo-classicism as it appears in Henry James's New York houses. Indian arts have their section, so has American navigation and the opening of the West. A folk gallery shows primitive and not so primitive paintings, sculptures, and carvings. Look especially for a horse, probably the work of an itinerant artist-peddler, which is as solid and satisfying as an ancient Chinese horse.

On the grounds, still more Americana, from a dainty hat shop to a covered wagon, as well kept and displayed as the rest of the impressive collection.

NOTES

OTHER MUSEUMS:
Holbourne of Menstrie Museum, on Great Pulteney Street. Extensive silver, miniatures, porcelain, English painting, Renaissance bronze, and changing exhibitions.
Victoria Art Gallery, on Bridge Street. Collections of glass, watches, prints, and English water colors.
Exhibition Rooms, at 18 Queen Square. Changing exhibits and geology.
1 Royal Crescent, now owned by the city and preserved inside and out as eighteenth-century Georgian for the pleasure of visitors.

HOURS: During July and August the Roman Baths are opened on Tuesday, Thursday, and Friday evenings at 8:00. Nothing like they were in the old, glorious days but there are mineral pools to swim in. (Inquire of your hotel or the Tourist Information Office near the Pump Room.) For less watery entertainment, folk dancing Saturday afternoons in the abbey churchyard, a fairly active theatre, several cinemas, band concerts in the Parade Gardens near the Avon, symphonic concerts, led off by the distinguished musicians who take part in the Bath Music Festival (usually early summer, though the season may have been extended). For a visit at Festival time it is best to book a hotel well in advance; for information about the concerts, Bath Festival Office, Linley House, Pierrepont Place, Bath, Somerset. Between concerts, a ride on a no longer busy canal (Saturday or Sunday afternoons) aboard a boat that leaves, 3 P.M., from Widcombe near its meeting with Pulteney Road, or try other blandishments listed in pamphlets from the City Information Bureau.

A booklet that dashes through a survey of basic English Cathedral architecture carries on the cover a picture of a broad creamy nave with fronds on its grouped pillars, heads soaring from the sides of arches and strong lines of vaulting in the ceiling, imposing height and size and muted, dignified light, but not especially more imposing than Ely, Lincoln, Salisbury, York. The singularity of **Wells** Cathedral, pictured on the cover, is an incomplete figure eight made of a huge arch carrying a section of inverted arch above it, the point of meeting held in two immense stone circles, an extraordinary structure that lends movement and vivacity to the traditional architecture. The set of arches was not part of the original planning of the late twelfth century, near the end of the reign of Henry II— he of the conflicts with Becket, the husband of the indomitable Eleanor of Aquitaine, the father of the vainglorious Richard of the Lion's Heart and the chameleon John. The supports of the central tower were in the convention until it was decided in the early fourteenth century to heighten the tower, which then began to lean and to crush the structure below, causing ominous fissures in the fabric. One, or a team, of the anonymous geniuses of Gothic architecture thought out this stunning surprise as a solution which has worked for over six hundred years.

The Cathedral, whose presence makes Wells a city, the smallest city in England, affords other singularities: the vaulting of the Lady Chapel, slender lines of color on delicate ribs that gather as clusters, and its two windows of fourteenth-century glass. Above one section of the worn cloisters that look burned, as they probably were during the time of the Commonwealth, there is a chained library of seventeenth-century books and earlier, one a famous illuminated psalter. The spacious octagonal Chapter House, hung from one clump of slight pillars, is unique in England because it is double-storied, the upper meeting room—notice the plates for members of the council in the niched stalls—introduced by a worn, curved set of thirteenth-century stairs. (Wells has chosen to place at the bottom of this venerable slope and meeting hall a tomb of painted marble in honor of John Still, who wrote "Little Jack Horner.")

Not far from the stairway to the Chapter House, the Wells clock, not quite but almost contemporary with that of Salisbury, cased in a colorful box surmounted by a turret, on its face a sunburst that tells the hours and a star for the minutes. As any experienced church visitor should, you have been looking up to ceilings for bosses and around the arches for animals, flowers, and medieval allusions; here a strongly arched lizard eating a bunch of grapes, there a keenly observed fisherman. Near the door to the cloisters, animated, naturalistic scenes that show men stealing fruit, being apprehended and beaten for it. In another group, a man scowling over a thorn in his foot and another with a toothache, a common subject and particularly appropriate here since one of the saints frequently sought in Wells was a gifted toothache soother.

Watch the clock, struck at the quarter by soldiers in medieval armor, and for the hour, two knights trying to unhorse each other, dealing alternate blows with each strike. But they are too old to go the full count of ten or eleven, so another clock takes over. Remove yourself a short distance to observe the buttresses, the polygonal Lady Chapel and Chapter House, the lively Gothic scribbling, the sparkling windows and superb doors hugging each other and their tower. Examine the façade, its weathered saints, the play of small double-arches and quatrefoils, toylike spires that punctuate a central panel of long window, and see it become the side of a fine reliquary or, in the style of many churches in Italy—Lucca, Orvieto—a magnificent brocade curtain to lure to the church within.

The outbuildings form a rarely complete ecclesiastical com-

pound, though there never was an abbey, since the founding
monks were missionaries rather than a housebound order.
Past a gate in a wall and across a moat south of the church
sits the Bishop's Palace, part of the palace built in the thirteenth century, and the wall and moat in the fourteenth by a
bishop who was having trouble with the townspeople, serious
trouble one would judge from the protective elaborations. (The
old conflict is remembered now in a boisterous spring boating
meet on the moat, which ends in overturning the bishop's boat
and his inevitable immersion.) The moat is occupied by ducks
and swans who, one is told, pull a bell rope to signal their need
for bread. Either the shortages of World War II untrained
them or tourists are too generous, for they rarely perform any
more and you had better spend your time threading your way
through the Cathedral gates, the Bishop's Eye and the "Pen-
niless Porch" where mendicants held their begging stations,
both of which lead to the market. A curve off the stairs of the
Chapter House connects with the windowed Chain Gate, a
fifteenth-century accommodation to conduct vicars to the
Cathedral from their hall, and the arresting Vicar's Close, facing rows of adjoining houses in gray stone, tan stone, and brick.
Houses and hall were built in the fourteenth century by a
humanitarian bishop who deplored the uncertain living con-
ditions of these lower-echelon churchmen, substitutes for
absent superiors in the long, frequent services. The disconcerting spears of chimney added a century later disturb the Gothic
mood, which returns, however, at the low wooden door and
tight space of the chapel at the end of the close and, especially,
in the queenly rise of medieval complex as one returns toward
the Cathedral, replacing the children in the little gardens with
dark-garbed men tending roses, the cars with high, rough-
wheeled carts, the house dogs and cats translated into their
sly misericord portraits.

Because it is small and so fully packed, Wells is a delight to
explore, straying in almost any direction from the significant
combination of market place, town hall, and Cathedral buildings: the modern canons' houses, loudly deplored, loudly admired, whose strong rectangles are ground base for the trilling
of the Cathedral façade; the modest stateliness of New Street,
so named long centuries ago; the homeliness of St. Thomas
Street, framing a good view of the Cathedral; a noble early-

eighteenth-century house on The Liberty; a pub crawl into the beams and yards of old inns. Behind the parish church of St. Cuthbert's, on Chamberlain Street, a set of fifteenth-century almshouses around a tidy garden, and on the same street good-looking Georgian houses. At 28, an unassuming structure of yellowed plaster whose minimal windows surround the legend,

> Glory be to God, Mr Archibald Harper one of the 8 masters and in the year 1702 Mayor of this city did by his last Will and Testament settle this House and £500 upon Trustees for the perpetual use and maintenance of 5 poor men old decayed Woollcombers of this City of Wells. Mr Harper died: May 11 1713. Blessed be the merciful—Matt: 5.7.

You might want to offer the miniature city the compliment of visiting its unworldly museum, eager to show a drawing that concerns the "Witch of Wookey Hole," whose bones were found in a nearby cave, eighteenth-century hotel bills, coins, samplers, valentines, English pottery, a fossil, a battered tuba-like ophicleide, a dulcimer, a lace-making pillow with its dangling spindles, churchless angel corbels and, for the cosmopolitan touch, a pair of Latin American castanets; in brief, an amiable, provincial grab bag as before and everywhere.

To the west, the rounded, luscious country of cows and cows that supply the Cheddar cheese of the area. To the south, Glastonbury Tor, the highest point on the Island of Avalon (once in marshland), which carries at its crest a Gothic chapel, one of the way stations of pilgrim's progress to the important abbey of **Glastonbury.** As befits a rich, influential monastery, it gathered vivid legends. Christ's disciples themselves founded it; St. Patrick was the Apostle to Ireland out of Glastonbury; Joseph of Arimathea came across continents and seas to preach, heal, and protect this corner of Somerset. Nor was all of Glastonbury's mysticism left in the past. Recently members of a new cult were accused of sacrificing a dog on Glastonbury Tor. They sued, and won the suit, for libel. They had held an annual midnight meeting to celebrate Midsummer Eve, but their ritual was pure and bloodless.

To the religious mythology, new and old, one must add legend, here as the presence of King Arthur, who lies buried with his faithless Guinevere under a marker that says so in the abbey ruins. What is left of the "cradle of Christianity in England" is extensive ruins in a large area encroached on by new housing and the sound of traffic, and stones incorporated in the houses of the decent brick town which used the abbey for building material after the sixteenth-century decrees. The size of the ruins, the richness and fineness of detail, attest to the vanished might and splendor; the spaciousness of the abbot's quarters, and his separate kitchen, to the number and importance of his visitors. More humble visitors left carved lettering near a foot-bridge above the crypt, which calls on Jesus and Maria in the thirteenth-century lettering of northern Italy. On the High Street, the slightly sagging medieval law courts controlled by the abbots and, not far off, a tithe barn where tenants paid their rents to the abbey in grain to be kept there for the use of the monks. Sheep played an important role in the economy of the abbey, whose wealth impressed even the Norman compilers of the Domesday Book, and sheep still make their presence known not only as bundles on surrounding slopes but as a sheepskin shop and, a short distance out of the center of the town, a factory assembled of old brick, tin, and wood that makes sheepskin footwear.

Through jaunty hills and a couple of subdued villages, finally **Longleat**, lying like many Tudor houses in a sheltered park ringed by wooded slopes, no longer hilltop fortresses, preferring to hide when possible from accusations of conspicuous consumption. Present-day Longleat lies low but it cannot possibly be judged inconspicuous in size or furnishings; nor is it, nor has it been for a long time, markedly Tudor. More of that later; the Lion Reserve beckons. For £1 (probably more since prices soar exultantly) for each car and its passengers, one enters the society of rhinos, giraffe, zebras, and pink-bottomed monkeys who like to jump on a car hood, ride awhile on the top or back, jump off to honor another carful of children with faces glued to closed windows. The road winds and winds to give the illusion of long distances traversed and excitement, a sense of danger inspired by the signs: IF IN TROUBLE HONK HORN AND WAIT FOR WHITE HUNTER and REMEMBER LIONS ARE VERY DANGEROUS. A big skull scowls near the gate to the lions, and scattered safari wagons are manned by attendants in safari jackets carrying guns. Pelicans stalk at the side of cars, a snail-paced

pack on Sundays, and secretary birds. Soon, more rhinos and
elephants, a glimpse of the immense house beyond jungle
habitats (where do they keep tropical animals in the winter
time?), and shortly back to a variety of well-posted pleasures—
refreshments, boat rides, meals, postcards, stuffed toy lions,
jigsaw puzzle pictures of the house, and . . . the house itself.

You enter the house, pay a fee of 35 pence or more, find
yourself with a display of the costumes used in the well-known
BBC TV series of Henry VIII and his six wives, and fitting
royal fanfares that seem to come from the minstrels' balcony
in the Great Hall which shares its hammer-beamed height with
dry branches of antlers, broad hunting canvases, and a mighty
fireplace of the seventeenth century. By way of family portraits, Chinese vases, cabinets of Japanese lacquer, and Chippendale chairs, one enters the increasing luxuries of the house,
no longer Elizabethan nor even English. The fourth Marquess
of Bath, whose family owned Longleat and still does, was a
wealthy Victorian gentleman whose models for a reasonable
domestic ambience were the palazzi of Renaissance princes.
His designer and agents bought ceiling paintings in Venice
and imported Italian workmen to paint friezes erupting with
putti and mythological figures, to shape a chimneypiece like
one in the Doge's palace, and imitate the patterns in a room
of Peruzzi's faultless Palazzo Massimo in Rome. To go with
these Italianate glories, Flemish and French tapestries of the
sixteenth century, Sèvres china, silver show pieces, and the
peak of the furniture maker's skill as expressed in several
Italian, French, and English periods. The walls are sheathed
in stamped Cordovan leather, the rugs are choice, the boxes
are of bronze and crystal, of silver and cornelian, and a Sicilian
clock is made of enamel and coral.

The State Drawing Room blazes with gilt and marble that
show well against the cut velvet on the walls and point up the
delicacy of the floral designs of colored marbles in an alabaster
doorway, not quite Taj Mahal quality, yet not too far off. This
is a room of distinguished paintings which, unfortunately, are
cut off from close inspection by a rope. With careful peering
you may be able to make out Titian's "Rest on the Flight to
Egypt," a "Susanna and the Elders" by Bassano, a "Madonna
and Child" by Lorenzo Lotto, and among the less sententious,
gay panels from Italian wedding chests. If you can, compare a

skillful Longhi painting of "The Watercress-Seller" with the less artful and much more entertaining painting of François I of the sly little eyes and the long clever nose, and his mistress who has a candy-box face and protects herself—maybe against rampant VD—with a caduceus.

The glorious show trails off into family dress for ceremonial occasions, red velvet blazed with ermine, coronets and sweeping cloaks. Display cases of English and French china gather round an unbelievable Meissen temple, twisting, coiling, convoluting to a Brunnhilde-Minerva, and then large white birds and animals—an apogee of Meissen craft. The Grand Staircase leads to broad narrative paintings, royal presences, and an appealing family portrait centered on a row of six young children, their ages indicated above their heads, the faces almost identical, all with staring round eyes, all bound in stiff courtly dress and merciless ruffs.

A WAY OUT sign leads through the shop and one is again impressed by the enterprise that devises safaris, boat rides, two pamphlets for the house rather than the usual one, strips of matches featuring Elizabeth I to sell. Understandably, it takes a great deal to maintain a vast house and its furnishings, but the assiduousness is a bit offputting as, come to think of it, is the imitation Italian magniloquence. One leaves (trailed by a white peacock screeching like a banshee) somewhat in sympathy with an eighteenth-century owner who left the overwhelming pile to rot.

NOTES

From *The Times* (London), Friday, May 25, 1973: "Viscount Weymouth this afternoon unveiled the mind-bending paintings and sculpture-paintings with which he has encrusted the walls of his stately home inches deep, acres wide and of fathomless significance. . . . Unlike most professional artists, Lord Weymouth lives not in the red, in an attic, feeding on booze and fish fingers, but in the purple, in Longleat House, near Warminster. . . . The 'paranoia' murals show on a gargantuan scale Lord Weymouth's hangups from inside the womb to 'the persecutions of my upbringing'. . . . The Kama Sutra bedroom, which plays such a conspicuous part in the advertising of the exhibition, depicts forms of congress impracticable for all but determined contortionists. The mural consists of thirty-three aphrodisiac apples, suspended from huge phallic trees, and containing a variety of sexual performances from a multitudinous, multiracial cast. Lord Weymouth expounds: 'To my eyes, this mural is a poetic expression of man's joy in womanhood and vice versa. I sincerely hope that tourists will be able to view it in the same spirit.' "

HOTELS AND RESTAURANTS:

Salisbury—The White Hart Hotel, on St. John Street, is moderate; the King's Arms and Red Lion are somewhat less, still moderate. Snacks, and pub lunches on Market Square and adjoining streets. Haunch of Venison for English dishes, the Grange and the Provençal French for continental food.

Bath—The Francis (breakfast extra), Royal Crescent, Grosvenor, Royal York, and Pratts are moderate to high-moderate. The Hole in the Wall, very popular, closed Sundays and Mondays, has distinguished food and atmosphere; book and prepare to pay reasonably well. Bruno's, French and Italian, at 2 George Street. Da Pietro, at 39 Gay Street, mainly Italian touched with a few harmless English eccentricities and Italian affability. There are, in addition, the Saracen's Head on Broad Street; pizza and Indian places; and ice-cream and tea shops, one on Gay Street owned by a man with the imposing name of Achille Pettemerides.

Wells—The Crown, Star, King's Head, Swan, and White Hart are all moderate, some still possessed of the crooked charms of old inns. Eat in the hotels (moderate), and for smaller meals in simpler places on and off the Market Square and pubs.

For inexpensive accommodations, consult with the local bureaus for suitable guest houses.

NEAR NORTHWEST

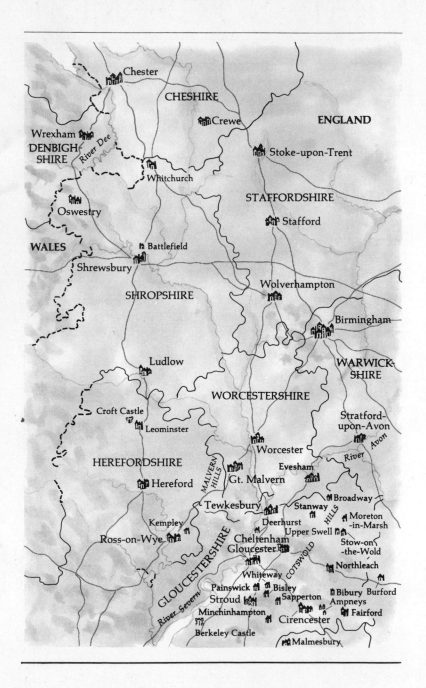

THE OTHER COTSWOLDS AND NORTH TO CHESTER

Let us assume that it is the summertime and that, despite their
manifest charms, you would like to avoid the crowding on
wheels and foot which obscures the pastel houses and rhythms
of hills and valleys in the more frequented Cotswolds towns—
Broadway, the multiple Chippings and their immediate neighbors—and head instead for the villages on the Gloucester–
Wiltshire border and some of those to the north and west, well
planted in Gloucestershire. Your first Cotswold village may
be **Burford** or, slightly to the south, **Fairford**, a good example
of old Cotswold wool prosperity, guarding its solid, creamy
houses, unwilling to appear as if it needed tourist trade, supplying few souvenirs. It does not need to primp or court.
Fairford's Church of St. Mary has a most expressive set of
stained-glass windows, singular for quality and completeness.
The low, broad mass with its sturdy tower and broad windows,
sitting on extensive tombstoned green, is exceedingly well kept
and well fitted. Handsome lozenges commemorate some of the
more distinguished local dead, the misericords are alert vi-
gnettes of domestic life, the flowers are fresh and attractively
arranged, robust angels are ready with armor and shield to
soar down from the arches and roofbeams to protect the congregation, the tower is guarded by grotesques, and the bells loop
down from the tower in a neat, tentlike shape. Fairford has
brasses, also, one rather pertinent to the story of the church.
Surrounded by shields, he in full armor, she in the tight-
bodiced long gown and pointed headcloth of the fifteenth
century, lie John Tame and his wife Alice. He was a successful
wool merchant who caused the old church of Fairford to be
razed and built the present church in 1497. It is said that he
hired the master glass craftsman of Henry VII to design and
put in the windows, but there is no documented proof of this.
Whoever he was, he was an extraordinarily skilled artist (or
artists), not unaware of what was going on in art on the
Continent. With John Tame's financial help, he designed twenty-
eight large windows that deal with the Old and New Test-

aments, prophets and saints, and evil men—Herod, Judas—who persecuted holy men. Observe the tranquility of the Garden of Eden and the fanciful serpent, something snake, something cat, something woman, offering a sample from the fruitful tree. Notice the weight of the body of Christ in the Descent from the Cross and the contrasting movement and spirit of the panel to the right when Christ's spirit speaks out to the people. This display of high skill for rendering figures and landscape, balancing colors, arranging lines of lead to enhance composition and texture, reaches a climax in the gleaming picture of Hell, its imps and victims in harsh blues and dead white, the backgrounds the hellish red of dried blood, and Satan himself a foul, shark-toothed monster with eyes in his belly.

Give Fairford's merchants' houses, which reflect as does the church an economic pinnacle of the community, a half-hour of walking time; then choose from the cornucopia of Gloucestershire zigzags, circles, and loop-the-loops through treed paths, smooth hills, and sudden vistas that lead in and out of **Bibury.** It is an English water color (William Morris thought it the most beautiful village in England) of stream and ducks, miniature stone bridges and miniature stone houses on the reedy river; in the distance, a bundle of lordly chimneys among clouds of treetop.

By way of the somnolent **Colnes** and the corrugated-tin **Ampneys,** one reaches **Northleach**, whose church is, like that of Fairford, unexpectedly large, robust, and accomplished, again a testament to the wealth of God-fearing Cotswold wool merchants. Instead of radiant glass, Northleach has an impressive tall south porch whose inner aspects include the figures one has begun to associate with wood carving under choir seats. Here vague, worn gargoyle types, a just-discernible cat playing the fiddle to three entranced mice, a woman with a badly swollen cheek, and a pair of ladies, one lean and one fat and both furious. Northleach's patron was a fifteenth-century gentleman merchant called John Fortey, who paid for much rebuilding, including the nave and the ample windows that make the church "more lightsome and splendid," as he wished to see it. Gone are the medieval glass and all but pale fragments of wall paintings, but other stimulating details remain: a graceful stone pulpit of the fifteenth century in the perpendicular style, a repaired fourteenth-century font, several sharply carved bosses and heads as corbels, and the marks of workmen who refused to be anonymous. Some left in the church their pleasure in music in the form of fife and bagpipe players, some gave rein to their fancy—particularly at the base of the font—in little demons, while others left their mark more straightforwardly. In the southeast corner of the nave there is a column-base that bears the name of Henrie Winchcombe, believed to have been a master mason because of the symbol near the name. At the other side of the column, "Edmunde" let himself and his work be known and scratched in a little prayer, "God grant us His grace." The church is also rich in brasses that date back to the opening of the fifteenth century, several incorporating wool symbols: feet resting on woolpacks or sheep, a pair of scissors for a clothier.

Northleach doesn't seem to have been quite as successful as Fairford but yet has a few typical houses of its halcyon days to display and broad arches which were entranceways for great heaps of wool to reach the areas behind the houses where it was stored and worked.

By way of shy villages hidden behind a sudden copse or tumbled off a hill skirting along the edge of a high plateau of golden grain fringed in green, the road slips past a row or two of urbane houses and shops and comes to a startled halt at the brouhaha of **Cirencester**'s big market square. The variety of houses in several colors, kept in harmony by a fair uniformity of height, the brisk streets that swell and curve to and away from the most imposing of Gloucester's parish churches, arrange a bustling, cordial welcome, as that of a plump, garrulous, and good-natured food vendor, for example, or her husband who fills the glasses high in the local. Cirencester publishes a number of maps and pamphlets, issued at the tourist center to the side of the market square, that take you by the hand and lead you to Georgian houses and earlier, back to the Tudors and a Weaver's Hall of the Middle Ages converted into an almshouse. As a sampler, follow Gosditch Street, which becomes Dollar and then Gloucester as it strays from the market place, turn into Thomas Street and then Coxwell, back to Park, Black Street, and Silver. For the determined walker, there is Cecily Hill (for St. Cecilia, who once had a shrine here) and its endless avenue of trees that shade a scatter-

ing of folly-like buildings and the park of the Earl of Bathurst, where you may walk on your own legs or those of a
horse but no mechanized vehicles, please, nor dogs. Here, too,
polo is played on frequent summer Sundays to a knowledgeable group of spectators.

Although the most luminous time for Cirencester, as it was
for other Cotswold towns, was the fourteenth and fifteenth
centuries, when England was the greatest wool market in
Europe, busily supplying the weavers of Flanders, it was no
mean city a millennium and more earlier. In the second century it was the Roman city of Corinium, second in size only to
Londinium, and a hub of road spokes that led to other important Roman settlements like Bath, Lincoln, and St. Albans,
just north of London. Only shadows of Roman wall, gates,
and amphitheater exist; the town proper, whose meeting
places—markets, courts, baths, and temples—probably stood
near the present market streets, left its remains (although it
must be assumed that there are still objects buried under
roadways and supermarkets) in the Corinium Museum on Park
Street. As always, the displays are intelligently grouped and
labeled and, as always, the question is whether Roman provincial artifacts interest you, how many you have seen, and
your appetite for more.

Should you go, you will find several large frames of reconstructed floor mosaic that symbolize the high style of living
the Romans introduced to their Empire communities almost
immediately after they sheathed their conquering swords. The
"Orpheus" mosaic was made for a country villa in the immediate environs, while the "Seasons" mosaic came from a town
villa almost directly beneath the Information Centre. In neat
arrangements the instruments of living and dying: work tools,
fine pottery and crude, ornaments and mirrors for ladies, heating tiles, coins, and urns for the ashes of the dead. Among the
votive and funerary objects that comprise much of the sculpture display, a few local adaptations of Roman deities and con-
versely, Roman absorption into its pantheon of conquered cult
figures. Here the conquered peoples were Celtic and they may
have invented the snake-footed divinity displayed, or gathered
together, with the help of the Romans, the female deities as the
Mother Goddesses who did the motherly things of protecting
households. Of the *echt*-Romans, the old familiar faces of dour

Mars, dreamy Mercury, efficient Minerva, and several of their quarrelsome relatives, and of Roman English superstition and magic-making a Latin acrostic scratched into plaster. Straight across, it states a man's name and the fact that he ploughs well; with a bit of manipulating it can say "Pater Noster" vertically and horizontally, and may have been the invocation of a secret Christian. The acrostic returned to pagan use in later centuries, possibly as a magical spell to be muttered during the pin-fixing and melting of a wax effigy.

The bus that runs through the town and into nearby villages stops in front of the great Church of St. John the Baptist, and you should, too, sitting on a bench near the stop, watching English trippers say "Cheese," like a lesson seriously and well studied, into each other's cameras, Dad reluctant, Mum eager. Watch the kaleidoscope movement and colors of the market place for a while. Then try your hand at skittles and have some wine in a monk's cellar off the market place.

Since Corinium lasted into Christian times there might have existed, among the temples dedicated to divers gods, one set aside for Christ, but though a Roman column appears in the chancel of the church, there is no proof that this was its site. A Saxon church existed nearby and was removed for the building of a twelfth-century abbey (a vestigial gateway still stands) and the Norman church which, with many changes, grew into the present edifice. It is a grand Cotswold church in its proportions, in the use of golden white stone, the seven-sectioned window above the chancel arch which helps make it fresh and buoyant and, above all, the presence of the wool tycoons. They rebuilt the entire nave early in the sixteenth century and had placed high on the pillars a company of angels who hold the arms or trade symbols of the sponsors of the rebuilding. They immortalize themselves again among the monuments of the Trinity Chapel and the Lady Chapel. In the former a number of brasses commemorate a merchant of the fifteenth century who had fourteen children and another who had four wives. A fulsome monument in the Lady Chapel presents the family of another merchant named Bridges who flourished in the time of James I and who was proud to show on his tomb his covey of daughters and, to judge from their modest dress, a group of female servants.

The elaborate, highly gilded and colored pulpit is unusual in that it dates from the fifteenth century and managed to escape the pulpit destruction of the Reformation. The Chapel of St. Catherine was given its elegant fan vaulting by an abbot a short time before the abbey was dissolved, when the chapel's frescoes of St. Catherine and St. Christopher were clearer and more complete.

Inside the good-looking Guildhall (now town hall) south porch there is a windowed box that holds a finely shaped chalice decorated with a falcon bearing a shield and a stylized rose tree. These were the badge of Anne Boleyn and this her cup, made two years before she was beheaded. It became the property of her daughter Elizabeth, who gave it to her physician, Dr. Richard Master, a propertied gentleman granted the abbey at Cirencester after the monasteries were dissolved. He, in turn, gave the cup to the parish church. Nearer the door, a less regal reminder of times gone, a big-headed, middle-age-faced schoolboy, hat in one hand, open book in the other, wearing the blue coat of a charity schoolboy, a figure who once solicited money for a school founded early in the eighteenth century.

The best view of the tower is from the abbey lawns to the north. It sits serenely on the supporting buttresses, in no way betraying its bloody begetting. During the struggle for the throne in the last years of the fourteenth century and the first of the fifteenth, the earls of Kent and Salisbury aligned themselves with the forces that tried to restore the throne to Richard II. They were arrested and beheaded in Cirencester's market place. Henry IV took over the throne to which he was not surely entitled, a common enough event in the histories of kings. In his first pleasure and to show his gratitude, the town was given the strong boxes of the defunct earls and with that money the abbey tower was built.

Cirencester's Roman life, medieval ecclesiastical and business life, English Renaissance life, Georgian life, seems to have left her a bit slap-happy, a bit blowsy, and quite *simpatica*. It is not easy to tear oneself away, particularly if the super-ebullience of the Friday market is coming up, or the big sheep fair on the first Monday of September (on the Tetbury Road), or the jollity of fairs in early October, whose carousels and booths supplanted ancient hiring fairs. But above all other people, the

tourist has miles to go before he sleeps, and numerous choices
to make. How many more honeyed Cotswold villages? Content
oneself with those surrounding Stroud? Taste among the villages off the direct road to Gloucester or those toward Malmesbury? Or a sampler sewn of a few?

On the way to Gloucester: the gate, not too aggressive, that
opens on the endless avenue of trees in Cirencester Park and
on to **Sapperton,** an exquisitely polite, bird-loving village which
asks that you close the church door with, OF YOUR CHARITY
WOULD YOU PLEASE CLOSE THE DOOR TO PREVENT THE BIRDS FROM
FLYING IN AND TRAPPING THEMSELVES. The church has its eccentricities as rows of slim herms living uneasily in linenfold
carving, one Indian, one Asian, and most of the others classic
grotesque. The monuments are large, explicit, and colorful, but
the best of the church is the view of steep falls of green and
patches of velvety shade that open to green, then blue, then
gray, gently contoured hills; the design is repeated and recom-
posed endlessly, always harmonious and serene, lifting to one
village, sloping to another. **The Duntisbornes—Rouse, Leer**, and
Abbots—a place of broad fields, satisfied houses and horses,
conduct one toward coarse, moorlike land and heavy woods
and into **Miserden,** a village of sharp-eaved, gray, large Victorian houses sitting in Cotswold panoramas.

Whiteway lives in an emptiness of endless high fields flowing
from a sprinkling of isolated houses. The cottages may still
hold some of the idealists who came here about fifty years ago
to live in a non-violent, non-money, non-governmental coopera-
tive colony. The early rigidities had to be modified to a degree
but the neighbors say that there was no private ownership of
property, and aggression, personal or political, was held in
contempt. What happens in the land-greedy seventies is probably another matter altogether. At one side, a tall hill that
follows you toward the Gloucester road and on the other,
farms, a small reservoir, and small houses climbing toward
woods. Half-hidden by hay stacks you will find a sign: ANCIENT
MONUMENT—ROMAN VILLA. At the end of the road indicated there
is a farm house which acts as custodian of the keys of the
area, closed off to guard it from the vandalism that molested
the ruins for the last hundred years. A young son of the house
(a tactfully offered tip will not be taken amiss) and visiting
relations will point out the bases of several enormous rooms

and traces of building which could not hold the hill and slid down to shatter on the slope. The boy will also show you mosaics of sea-animals that usually adorned a room used for baths, adjoining pipes for heating the water, and the thermal room itself. Whose villa this was no one knows; there is still much excavation to be done. Whoever he was, general or successful merchant, he undoubtedly lived Romanly well in his country villa on the majestic site overlooking a measureless fan of lea and copses.

If you are ready for a northward journey and westward to the Welsh border, the departure point of Gloucester is at hand. For more Cotswold villages, head southward on the A46 (which has a ROMAN VILLA sign, if you've missed the other) to the distinctive town of **Painswick**. It, too, speaks of the gone wool days, expressed in a great house, elaborately bayed, at the end of the churchyard and medieval houses later dignified with classical porticos, noble window frames, and plasterwork. A good example of these changes can be seen in a bookshop (also a National Trust office) on the High Street whose interior is medieval, the outside later glorified. Painswick coils and mounds itself on itself but not exaggeratedly, turning with dignity to present substantial houses, many antique shops, a fine manor house near the Cheltenham road, and a solid church. As elsewhere, the whole equals more than its aggregate parts in Painswick and a memorable, stately whole it is.

Coming down to **Stroud** watch out for ponies who give ground to no one and nothing, including large machines, as they stand like their own monuments on the roads. Watch too for old red locomotives mounted on tractor wheels used in these fields and for signs thickly sprinkled through the country indicating footpaths that occasionally spew heedless hikers. The verdant rise from Painswick to Stroud ends in dusty Victorian meeting halls, an underachieving factory, a basic railroad bridge and its station, and vestiges of mill at the river which once supplied the power for innumerable early textile establishments. The city is not large, though, and soon releases one to fly out under long shadows that dig into the hills and an immense low curtain of sky painted with swags of pinkish-gray clouds. Hamlets scramble up to strange hills that rise and rise, threatening an immediate drop off a silent world. Suddenly, a wide plateau, frothing with summer weekenders practicing golf shots on the bitten green, kicking footballs, picnicking under the feet of hikers and mildly curious cows; it is as if one had awakened from a strange dream to the noisy, mundane reality of children's kites and Cadbury's chocolate. (The best way to negotiate this journey is to ask in Stroud for directions to the Bear Hotel.)

A steep climb on Chalford's "Old Neighborhood" road to **Chalford Vale** brings one to sharp-roofed houses that peg gardens which might otherwise fall down the hills. Higher hills turn and separate from the curving road and flatten to grazing land on the approach to **Bisley,** a compilation of rows of clothiers' houses whose gray stone warms to pale gold in sunlight. The church trails a wooded path off its south side and a set of steps to five wells now dressed in Victorian elaborations.

The church features a portrait of Queen Isabella (east window) who killed Edward II, next to her, with the help of Roger Mortimer. He owned much of Bisley and gave an extensive piece of property to the poor as common land (much later sold off), possibly an act of expiation, although medieval royal murders were not often accompanied by guilt or regard for Church and peasantry. The church holds a few other distinctions; the carved wood in the ceiling near the tower; a bearded Saxon head near the organ; a medieval lady of considerable beauty in a corbel at the north side of the church; on the same side, very old corbel figures of grotesques, angels who are musicians and some who are warriors.

Like its neighbors Bisley has, besides its richness of views, "antiques" to sell, but a better measure of its present economy are the shops slotted into old cottages. They hold a little of everything in timid desperation—children's clothing, shoes, a few toys, a few household objects, some chemists' supplies, almost anything commonly needed and cheaply salable. And like people who have to count pennies they urge, when you buy a pen for 5 pence, that you try it before you pay, and charge up a hill, calling urgently, if you leave an inexpensive pair of sunglasses on a counter.

With time and curiosity to spare you might inquire at Bisley for the way to **Nether Lypiatt** and its "haunted house." On a road that crests noble views and is utterly silent except for the occasional clip-clip of horses mounted by bloom-faced country

girls, you should be startled, in the emptiness, by an attractive
house of the late seventeenth century standing behind a remarkable set of ironwork gates. There is a Palladian–Inigo
Jones look about the house: the splayed set of stairs that
mounts to a doorway with a rounded pediment; the placing of
chimneys that suggest classical pilasters; the shape of the
house repeated in miniature pavilions at its corners. No ghosts,
however. Because the house is square and well windowed, the
afternoon light seems at times to float through and out again,
creating an eerie, insubstantial quality, as if the house were
nothing but spectral light.

Back to Bisley now for cheese, bread, and ale at its Bear
Inn, which daubs gray stone with brilliant flowers? Or possibly
southward to Stroud if you are headquartering there, tracing
loops in and around **Nailsworth** and landing in **Minchinhampton** for another set of narrow streets with close gray weavers'
cottages striving for the creamy. They stray from a pleasant
market square with its cross and meeting hall raised on pillars, a few of them still the same hardworking beams hewn
in the seventeenth century. The High Street and its tangents
show classical porticos (one is helped out by sturdy country
wood) and a late-seventeenth-century house stippled with bits
and pieces of classical antiquity. The pride in these, the Gothic
lettering for "Public Conveniences," the number of souvenir
shops and those that serve teas, and the general refinement
hold at the crest of the village and then the High Street and its
cottages lose all decorum to tumble wildly into hillocks and
piles of luxuriant country green.

With enough time one might swing down to linger with
good-looking **Tetbury** and in and out of the semi-tamed wilder-
nesses around **Wotton-under-Edge,** slowly leaving the Cotswolds for **Berkeley Castle,** to the northwest.

Dusty rose crenellations, turrets round and square, tall and
short, a stutter of chimneys. It looks like a drawing of a medieval castle whose design has strayed from the artist's hand.
There is nearly a millennium of vivid, historical reasons for the
disturbed, seductive shape. Supposition, unconfirmed but ir-
resistible, makes the site the primitive keep of the father of
King Harold who succumbed to William the Conqueror. After
the Conquest it was handed over, together with vast stretches

of adjoining lands, to William Fitz Osbern as an eminently useful place for guarding the Severn River against Welsh raiders. A crude fortress was built, then destroyed during a local uprising late in the eleventh century and rebuilt by an agent of Fitz Osbern, Roger de Berkeley. A short line of Rogers held the lands and fortress until 1153, when they were dispossessed by the Henry who became the II. He, in turn, gave the holdings to a Robert FitzHarding. Lost and found again, through backing the wrong or right powers, the castle grew in size and enough in importance to be the site of Edward's murder in 1327, to send a Lord Berkeley to an early Parliament, to be mentioned by Shakespeare, to be erased and restored to royal favor and embroiled in border wars and battles for succession for many years. King Charles II graced the family with the title of Earl in 1679, some decades after Cromwell's forces had besieged the castle for three days, during which they blasted a break in the wall, left unrepaired by government decree—a sort of national monument in negative.

The struggles for succession reached a high point in the House of Lords, in 1811, when it had to examine and decide the rights of a number of contending brothers. It appears that the fifth earl had fallen in love with a local commoner, lived with her, and had children by her but didn't officially marry her until 1796. There was supposedly a secret marriage eleven years before but the Lords ruled the older progeny illegitimate and decreed the first of the legitimate sons Earl of Berkeley, while the eldest of the first crop was given the castle and the title of Lord FitzHarding. Both titles have disappeared but the present Mr. Berkeley traces his ancestry to a forebear of the mid-twelfth century, an incumbent in the favor of Henry II.

Because Berkeley Castle is still basically medieval, some areas one moves in are small, almost intimate, enhanced by the modern perquisites of souvenir shop and outdoor eating tables, set in a closely walled court of the Middle Ages. Walking under the maze of turrets, Gothic-windowed walls, and vestiges of Norman lifting shapely Tudorish chimneys, one is enfolded in the antique atmosphere, less and less a traveler from a far century, more and more a contemporary visitor to a friend or foe of the early Henrys and Edwards. Gracious ladies with precise speech usually conduct one to the King's Gallery, hung with regal portraits and cut by an ancient, rough doorway and a barred hole. The latter is the dungeon into which putrefied corpses of livestock were thrown to asphyxiate prisoners thrown in with them. The prisoner-king, Edward II, was allowed to sit in the small room (very much smaller than the present gallery) breathing the hellish odors from the pit below and hopefully to die of an ensuing infection. He didn't and was murdered, instead, by his guards. It is still in question whether or not there was complicity on the part of the Thomas, Lord Berkeley, who was the king's host, but it is difficult to credit the possibility that he could have been ignorant, and thus innocent, of the regicide.

Passing through and skirting twelfth- and fourteenth-century walls, the visitor moves into more luxurious centuries, implied by Brussels tapestries, royal and family portraits, fine rugs and embroideries, and a diversity of furniture that ranges from a sturdy fifteenth-century oak chest through heavily turned and carved ebony (pieces brought from the then Portuguese West Indies by the Portuguese wife of Charles II, Catherine of Braganza) into lighter furnishings of the early eighteenth and nineteenth centuries. If the crowds are large—and they can be during the summer holidays—the guiding ladies go rather briskly. Don't let them deny you early, plain portraits of an almost Byzantine strictness, more effective than the ubiquitous Knellers and Lelys, and the graceful heroism of a Berkeley admiral as painted by Gainsborough. Look for the plain, patient face of Elizabeth Drax (wife of the fourth earl), whose likeness as seen by Reynolds hangs near an ornate Chinese chest at the head of an early-seventeenth-century stairway. Remembering the controlled face, it will not surprise you to know that it was she who, over a number of years, covered the gilded furniture in the Long Drawing Room with petit-point designs of family shields embedded in flowers.

Try to find an enticing fifteenth-century virgin sitting in a medieval niche; linger, if you can, on tapestries designed by Raphael in the Morning Room; on Van de Velde sea paintings; on George Stubbs's sleek horses and a tall Tompion clock. Wherever you are guided, look at ceilings and window arches of several early periods. The timbers of the Morning Room, for instance, bear the faint incision of lines from Revelations translated into the commonly spoken Norman French by a fourteenth-century cleric; a fourteenth-century ship may have supplied the wood for the Small Drawing Room ceiling. The Great Hall has a wooden canopy of straight and arched timber that may date from the mid-fourteenth century or a revision of the late fifteenth, and above the immense fireplaces, sinks, spits, and ovens of the kitchen a web of beams copied from spiders' designs.

Out of the mélange of centuries into quiet walks among flower beds, the peaceableness of the village, and back to the church and the inhabitants of its yard. A boxlike monument tells us that the Earl of Suffolk kept a fool who died at sixty-three in 1778, a rather anachronistic date, one might think, for court jesters. An earlier tomb enjoys the free spelling and word play of the Elizabethans:

> *Here Lyeth Thomas pierce whom no man taught*
> *Yet he in Irone Brasse & Silver wrought*
> *He Jaks [?] and clocks and watches (with Art) made*
> *And mended too when other work did fade*
> *Of Berkeley five tymes Major this artist was*
> *And yet this Major, this Artist was but Grasse*
> *When his owne Watch was Downe on the last Day*
> *He that made Watches had not made A Key*
> *To Winde it up, but Uselesse it must lie*
> *Until he Rise A Gaine no more to die.*

NOTES

HOURS: Berkeley Castle is open only April 1 to September 30, weekdays except Mondays, 2:00 to 5:30 (Bank Holidays, open 11:00 to 5:30); open Sundays only in October, 2:00 to 4:30.

Gloucester is a busy market town, not too different from others you've seen and, like others, once dominated by an enterprising abbey. But it may be that **Cheltenham's** Regency charms are more to your taste at this point. They speak of it as "poor, proud and pretty." Proud? With the exception of decayed Midlands villages, choked and darkened for too many years to care anymore, English places are usually proud. Poor? Not desperately, but obviously not the place it was when George III came to take the water cures and was followed by the retired India-hands with ruined digestions and the fashionable, who made a spa of Cheltenham that almost equaled the popularity of Bath. Pretty? Though the luster is dimmed, a gorgeous dome collapsed, a wide arch abandoned and left without meaning, it is still pretty in the becurled, beribboned style of a town planned for fun, games, flirtation, display, and the indulgences of spa life. Like Bath, Cheltenham was designed in parades, terraces, promenades, and crescents that curve off a few straight streets and roads in an organic design that suggests flowers held on sturdy stems.

The primary magnet, the Pump Room designed early in the nineteenth century, is north of the town, in Pittville Park, now a large recreation area of modern play equipment, well-kept cricket grounds, pools, and a gay little pavilion for children's entertainments. The Pump Room is the expected domed and columned building of abundant size, painted inside in floury reds and greens, the coffered ceiling heavy with huge white plaster blossoms. The Pittville water ("the only natural alka-line water in Great Britain," a leaflet says) can be drunk from an elaborate structure, rather like an altar, out of paper cups. The same leaflet says that one large tumblerful should be taken at a time, not too quickly drunk. The salty taste may remind you of the magnesia once—and still?—used as a laxative in many American homes. The Regency was obviously constipated and no wonder, with the gorging by those who could afford it in that carefree, appetiteful time. Portland Street, which leads back toward town, is a tasteful example of the more modest squares, not quite so tall or lacy as the showier. The showiest is the wide Promenade, which opens at one end with Edward VII, dubbed the "Peacemaker" and represented as the kindest and fattest of fat men holding a small, frail child by the hand. He leads off a show of majestic houses, some supported by caryatids, others with shallow ironwork balconies, the rows facing each other across lordly green and flowered space inter-rupted by a complex fountain. One of the most splendid of these rows is arcaded, centered on enormous columns and pilasters that wear curly capitals of faint Wedgwood green and delicate ironwork. These walls built for chinoiserie, frail chandeliers, and brocades are now the offices of information and other municipal services, an insurance company, and a hair-removal by electrolysis establishment. *O tempora* . . .

Take the rows near the Promenade and observe the variations on graceful architectural themes and the habit of lavishing on shops sprinklings of column and festoons, skirts of metal lace, and pagodas. Some rows are white and frilly; some more austere, blue-blooded, and poverty-stricken; some are square, some rounded; one row will wear heavy balconies, others metal drapes over windows. Parabola Road, for instance, contents itself with small, neat versions of the classic, while Landsdown Road keeps large, separate, masculine blocks of houses on one side and feminine trills of grillwork on the other. On Landsdown Court, which melds with Malvern Road, the houses are arranged in units of six, the galleries glassed in, the long front gardens become miniature jungles. Decayed as some of them may be, they are lent dignity and style by the generous spaces between the set-back houses and the long pauses of grass and tree that separate crescent and terrace.

NOTES

HOTELS: Cheltenham offers a good many hotels, some of them in old mansions and therefore driven to improvised modernization, such as a gaily painted coffin of a shower box pushed into the corner of a bedroom. The Queens, on the Promenade, is *the* queen, asking highish rates, breakfast extra. The Carlton, on Parabola Road, throws in breakfast at a charge of about £4.50 a single. The Savoy, Majestic, and George are £1 or more cheaper, breakfast provided.

RESTAURANTS: As in any self-respecting English town, you will find some that are Chinese. Two favorites are an old place and small, Ah Chow, off Clarence Street in the commercial center of town; and at one end of the Promenade the newer and somewhat costlier King's. Occidental meals and snacks with an English flavor, not at all expensive, can be found at the fresh minirestaurants on the Promenade and on Winchcombe Street.

For those eager for more Cotswold views and stone there are the villages north of Cheltenham.

The SCENIC ROUTE, indicated before the juncture with the major 46 road, shows the small spire of **Stanway** hiding in its greenery, and closer to, the gloriously elaborate golden gate of a fine house lording it over modest church. The carefully shored-up cottages that sit at the edge of a thread of stream served as the vicarage once upon a time. The churchyard offers the best view of the house, as well as the proximity of a hugely buttressed, minute-windowed tithe barn, and as if arranged to complete a composition of rural pleasures, white cricket players strolling across lawns, their ladies watching from the shelter of parasols, and a few children playing decorously near the parked cars.

A quarry of the local blond stone that seems to gray, like people, as it ages, introduces paths through the golds of grain splashed with the yellow of mustard greens, through cool gray-green bowers stippled with broken sunlight, past dimpled streams and into the famous allures of **Broadway, Stow-on-the-Wold, Moreton-on-Marsh, Upper Swell,** and other villages that choose to hide from it all—the trippers, the souvenirs, the ice-cream cones, and the sweet wrappers—like **Cutsdean Ford** and its shy relations.

Toward the west, the Malvern Hills concealing the River Severn and the slightly distracted, appealing Tewkesbury. But stop, first, at **Deerhurst,** south of the city, a hamlet hardly more than a place name but in Saxon days the site of the leading monastery in the area. Extraordinarily, it holds two Saxon churches, or rather, one church and one chapel. Despite changes made in later times, the Priory Church of St. Mary is clearly of three (some say four) periods, all predating the year 1000, and shows influences from early Europe, Ireland, northern England, Scandinavia, and even, it has been suggested, Abyssinia. And the stones may have been Roman. Face the west wall and observe the closedness, the mystery of the long narrow stretch broken only by a low, rounded doorway, a high blank niche, a higher blank stone panel, and between them twin sharp-arched openings; at the side of the niche, a small triangular opening. It is an impressive, unyielding abstract design. Was the cut triangle an early squint, a place from which monks or nuns or priests could observe the activities at the altar without being seen? Was the niche built for a primary, special saint or is this the vestige of lines of saints in several niches? Or part of a raised chapel? What was on the blank stone—a holy banner? A cross? A sculptured holy symbol destroyed in anti-clerical disasters? The same mesmeric attraction of the too old to be understood, the forceful, uncommunicative primitive, comes from the rare font, found in a local yard and carefully cleaned up to show its Celtic patterns bound up with the Northumbrian. The base it stands on, also a local find, was once a Saxon cross which wandered in from the south of England. At the apsidal side, two animals' heads terminate the arch; they may be horses (once brightly painted) or the flared nostrils those of a chimera descended from pagan animals. Another pair of heads, maybe wild dogs or wolves whose ears and stiff crests of fur are abstracted as simple floral patterns, have the all-over patterns that remind one of African masks or the features of Northwest Indian totem animals or of ancient Scandinavian ships' heads. Not far from these heads, on the outside, and embedded in the stones of a ruined apse, a wide-eyed angel, a famous piece of Saxon sculpture not too far distant in style from the staring, admonishing Byzantine and the round-eyed protectors of Near Eastern temples before them.

A few paces away, a farm house of patterned timber attached to a small stone barn. Until not too long ago it was used as a barn with bedrooms for farm help, and in no way associated with a significant stone found nearby in the seventeenth century. The Latin message on the stone said that Earl Odda had built a chapel "for the good of the soul of his brother Elfric," who died in 1056. Although the priory church was obviously older, it was taken for granted that the chapel referred to was the church until, in 1885, the disjointed farm house was explored and the stone barn-chapel restored to its original simplicity—or almost. The chapel contains a copy of the dedication stone (the original is in the Ashmolean Museum at Oxford), a fragment of dedicatory altar stone, a head of Jupiter found at the church, a few bits of Norman ornament, a faint sketch of a clock to mark time for Masses scratched on an outer wall, remains of ancient oak and stone. The Conquest overshadowed and even wiped out much of earlier England. Here, a clearly documented entity that brings to life two kinsmen of Edward

the Confessor, and, in combination with the church, presents
one with a testament of pre-Conquest times.

The sacristy door of **Tewkesbury** Abbey is crisscrossed with
metal, like a great shield. The material derives from the famous
Battle of Tewkesbury (see Shakespeare) of 1471; the scattered
armor, after the battle, was beaten into the supporting door
strips. Lancaster lost in this phase of the War of the Roses,
and those who could still move ran to the abbey for safety. The
forces of York managed to follow and the battle continued on,
splashing blood around the bases of the vigorous Norman
columns. Though this was the only time the abbey was steeped
in actual blood, its earlier movers and doers came of blood-
letting lines. An early abbey was sacked and ruined by the
Danes; the founder of the Norman abbey died of battle wounds
in 1107. An early-fourteenth-century inheritor of the estate and
abbey—the family were by then the earls of Gloucester—died
doing battle in Scotland. He was succeeded by his sister,
Eleanor, the wife of Hugh le Despenser, who was ultimately
drawn and quartered by the Roger de Mortimer involved in the
death of Edward II. A Despenser of 1400 found his violent
way to the executioner's block. The male line ended soon
thereafter and the female line, which included the Despenser
woman who married Warwick the Kingmaker, somewhat later.
The extensive estates reverted to the Crown, with only the
Manor of Tewkesbury left for the Kingmaker's daughter. She
had married George, Duke of Clarence, the doubledealing
brother of Edward IV who ended up in the Tower on charges
of treason and there it is said—and who would deny so gaudy
a splash in the pages of history—drowned in a vat ("butt") of
Malmsey wine.

Like its peers, the abbey came up for destruction in 1539.
The monastery was almost totally demolished but the townspeople said the abbey church had always been their parish
church and they were permitted to buy it for the estimated
value of the bells and lead in the roof which, when melted
down, would come to a bit over £450. From this event stemmed
an engaging Tewkesbury tradition: because his ancestors paid
for the church and it is now his, any citizen of Tewkesbury
has a right to sing in the choir, be his voice angelic or bellow-
ingly unstable. A less musically hazardous tradition centers on

the memorial plaque of Edward, the Prince of Wales, killed in the Battle of Tewkesbury and interred below the abbey tower. Those who feel strongly Lancastrian—and there is still fervid partisanship about ancient battles in England—insist that the church was remiss in not protecting him more carefully and in subtle penance someone places near the plaque a small bundle of dark red roses on the dawn of the anniversary of the prince's death. A romantic mystery has been woven about the floral commemoration; it must be a descendant who places the roses but what he or she looks like no one seems to know. Tewkesbury is a sociable, talkative town, everyone loves the abbey for many good reasons, the verger is always around and so is the man who sells booklets and cards and so is the conversational master mason in charge of checking for faults and repairing them, and they seem to like each other and have much to talk about. Could they—or the townspeople who stroll in for a spot of talk or prayer or the pleasure of the abbey's company—never have seen the mysterious mourner? Hardly likely, but they like to maintain the harmless little hoax which gives abbey and local life a small charge of extra zest.

Between Prince Edward and the apsidal chapels clustered in the warm Romanesque style is an enchanted forest of stone ferns and fretwork, shapely stalagmites and stalactites gathered to imitate churches. Stone-curtained beds are the reliquaries for effigies of Despensers and their kin and the abbots who were almost their peers. The tombs, dated from the thirteenth to the fifteenth century, offer not only their own decorative delights but a quick lesson in changing elaborations from the strictness of the Perpendicular to the interlaced spiderwebs and curled fronds of the Flamboyant. Most of the effigies lie in remote medieval calm, feet cushioned on little animals that speak of masculine power or feminine fidelity. A few have a less placid time of resting through the centuries: one abbot is host to a company of crawling grave animals; Edward le Despenser, an early Knight of the Garter and Lord of the Manor in the fourteenth century, chooses to spend his eternity kneeling in a high, airy enclosure of frail columns and spires.

Everything is worth studying—the very early fan vaulting in one of the chapels, the decorated vaulting above the long, thirteenth-century altar made of Purbeck marble brought from

Dorset, the gleaming fourteenth-century windows that give almost equal importance to Old Testament, New Testament, and
armored Despenser knights. Don't miss the bosses of musical
angels and the skillfully massed personae that witnessed events
in the life of Christ, nor the corbels of heads, a few of them
meant to be contemporary portraits, those in the nave especially imposing as they gaze out over the massive Norman
piers. In the sacristy, a rich collection of embroidered, brocaded satin and velvet vestments gathered through several
centuries. Finally, the tower, which you must have seen before
and possibly not quite given its due. You are told that it is the
biggest extant Norman tower, purely Norman except for the
later ornaments at the top. But "largest," "most authentic,"
hardly matter in the presence of these finely etched arches and
windows cut into tawny golden stone, brought across the Channel from Caen in Normandy to create triumphant might.

Below the infinite dignity sits a town made jolly by its very
old inns, merry patterns of timbered, tipsy buildings, by the
sheen of ancient woods in restored antiquities. It has bold, entertaining shop and pub signs, medieval alleys that hide a
variety of surprises, a meeting of rivers, and an active, friendly
population (all eight thousand of them). The Civic Society,
whose office sits on a street across from the abbey (St. Mary's
Lane), is supervised by an elderly, gentle-spoken lady who will
give you a helpful pamphlet or two, and if you show an interest,
considerable information about the problems, failures, and
successes involved in the restoration of monuments, even in
a town listed as a "Conservation Area" (unfortunately too late
to avoid the destruction of many small and very old houses).
A few paces on, toward the river, a recently restored set of
weavers' cottages with the characteristic wide windows that
afforded maximum light for the hosiery looms of the eighteenth
century; nearby, overhung by the tower, a deep-eaved, half-
timbered sixteenth-century house. On the other side of Church
Street, a long, smooth row of shops and houses with beautiful
doors restored to their serene selves, their timbers scraped
clean of paint and plaster and brought to a silvered tone. These
are the Abbey Lawn Trust, built by the church as a business
venture in the late fifteenth or early sixteenth century. They
are Tewkesbury's proudest achievement in restoration to date
and luckier than a contemporary in an alley across Church

Street, Old Baptist Church Court. Derelicts with broken windows, defeated by age and vandalism, lead to the Old Baptist Chapel, small and unadorned, and one of the oldest in the country (1690). Next to it, the Baptist cemetery whose inhabitants include a Thomas Shakespear Hart and a Samuel Jew, whom the dissenting Baptists had to take in because there was apparently no other place for him. Keep peering into alleys and side streets. Mill Street, for one, will take you to the ancient Abbey Mill, old enough to have witnessed the fifteenth-century battle, and the abbey granary, now used as a pottery and art center.

As Church Street splits into Barton and the High Street, an entertaining mélange of anything and everything in architectural styles: authentic half-timbered; tarted-up maquillage of timbering; big columns and pediments; sensible Georgian traces; a mixture gathered in one structure that leans and menaces with a thrust of bulges. Near the big bookshop on the High Street, a path that leads to launches for short trips on the Avon or Severn which meet at Tewkesbury. On Quay Street, which also stems off the High Street, the weir at the confluence of the rivers and a graceful small iron bridge.

The inns, too, call for attention. The Royal Hop Pole was mentioned in *Pickwick Papers*; the Berkeley Arms shares with neighbors what is probably the oldest façade in town, bearing work of the fourteenth century. The Gaiety Restaurant, anciently the Wheatsheaf, has sections which date from the early sixteenth century; the Black Bear is one of the most venerable in the county. A restaurant called The Ancient Grudge (referring to the Houses of York and Lancaster?) has an entrance carved with Tudor animals. On the inns and among them, handsome signs—a key, a lock, a hat of Napoleonic times; big, unabashed, well made. A touching example of acculturation and acquired pride is Luigi's Italian restaurant (near the abbey), which sports the big red rose of Lancaster.

In the course of a conversation with the abbey's master mason, he may suggest you see **Kempley.** "Nothing like it," he adds.

He's right, though he has neglected to tell you that the search for it takes on aspects of a treasure hunt based on obscure clues. But sooner or later you will find the Norman church of Kempley, isolated in its fresh fields. There once was a village here but it moved away from the earth's alternations of flooding and freezing, taking its people to higher ground. The damp, however, little affected the murals of the church, which was sturdily built against nature's vagaries. They succumbed to man in the sixteenth century when the Reformation covered the paintings with whitewash. Thus it stayed, obscure and shrouded, interesting only to aficionados of twelfth- and thirteenth-century architecture, until a vicar of the late nineteenth century detected color seeping through the white and called in experts to revive the ancient shapes and tints that were painted in the chancel in the twelfth century and over the nave a century or two later. The most primitive are the fullest and most evocative, harshly pure, explicit Bible lessons and stern icons worked in red, ocher, brown-black. Overhead, a mandorla of Christ the King, surrounded by St. Peter, the Virgin, angels, and Evangelists, each in his separate, clear space; nothing touches anything else in the hieratic, awesome isolations. Inside the round, dog-tooth ornamented arch, sets of six Apostles, their heads perilously slanted; checkerwork attempts at perspective for the Heavenly City; and two solitary figures, probably the lords of the family who built the church, divested of their armor, wearing the more humble pilgrim's costumes. The murals are not beautiful; they are raw and rigid, tight and narrow; their palette is scant, but they have—of sheer density and unearthly, untouchable asceticism—considerable power.

Beckoning, opening a route to the northwest for skirting the Welsh border in Herefordshire and Shropshire, sits **Ross-on-Wye,** an English siren flatteringly edged by waters. Before you reach her, luring from the height above her river, you may have passed a signpost that felicitously gathers together the names LITTLE MARCLE (the son of Much Marcle), PIXLEY, and TRUMPET, maybe passed a huge topiary peacock that charges out into the road from an otherwise proletarian hedge, the nets and webs of hopfields, and the pink-fenced fields ploughed to red earth.

The parish church of St. Mary the Virgin at Ross-on-Wye is the expected palimpsest, medieval over Norman over Saxon with nothing but the Domesday Book to prove the existence of the latter, and that tenuously. Good alabaster (one tomb carries a piece of Italian exotica, St. Zita, who was lost in prayer while she was supposed to be looking after loaves baking in the oven. An angel rescued her loaves and her job and she became elevated to the saint who watches over maids), a few interesting brasses, a fifteenth-century glass in nineteenth-century tracery, and a number of worthwhile etceteras. An isolated, unused area of the churchyard bears a cross which says: PLAGUE, 1637. BURIALS 315. LIBERA NOS DOMINE; obviously the town's plague pit. But Ross has gayer and greater attractions, mainly her hilly self. The town hero is "The Man of Ross," a benefactor named John Kyrle, who lives in painted signs, in a big plaster portrait at the center of town and in fancy lettering on a set of public conveniences now shut and cobwebbed. From the efficient double-eaved stone market hall, raised on pillars, the town separates, curves, dips, and whips like an octopus. The market hall leaves fruits and vegetables to the splash of market below but saves for itself clothing, baskets, china, ethnic clothing, and books, an intellectual note echoed by the public library located in the upper story of the building. A set of half-timbered houses, whose repeated black and white rectangles look like disjointed piano keyboards, are held up by a contingent of cavaliers with smiling, frowning, or singing carved faces. Near the church, a row of shy almshouses, repaired in the sixteenth century, the earlier façade left untouched. (One comes to see these as the most attractive early multiple dwellings. They were built solidly by men of substance as lasting shows of charity. The daub, wattle, rush, and thatch of the less lucky poor burned easily and frequently, or if they survived fire, slid and melted into the earth. English working-class housing of antiquity has disappeared as thoroughly as the buildings of the Etruscans.)

Clamber and slide anywhere you like in Ross and have tea, perhaps at the Royal Hotel where Dickens planned his American reading tour, so rich in profits and venom, and admire the U-bends in the river. Or, better still, buy some portable lunch and join the picnickers sitting on the long lawns that lift away from the river. Replete with food and scenery, you head for Leominster, by way of oast houses and hills sweeping to additional place names for your collection: **Ocle Pychard**, **Hope-under-Dinmore** (this on the River Lugg), and a sign that says you must be cautious because pedigreed stock pass this way.

Rather shapeless, neither urban nor rural, **Leominster** (pronounced Lemster) has not much to show that does not appear more optimistically elsewhere except eccentric Eye Manor and the contrasting **Croft Castle.** The castle sits at the top of a long slope, combining aesthetics with use as hill fort in prehistoric days, and the stage for Welsh forays in later years. Recorded before the Conquest, its knights fought infidels during the Crusades and rebellious dissidents at home. With the marriage of a member of the family into the powerful Welsh Glendowers and connections with early Tudors, the Crofts had friends at court and wielded considerable influences there when they weren't concerned with forays into the lands of kinsmenfoes near their own terrain.

Surrounded by avenues of majestic trees, Croft Castle is in the tradition of the square castle with four corner turrets. Although these have been considerably patched and improved, the essential elements of the exterior date from the fourteenth to fifteenth centuries. It must once have had more protective elements—moat and walled gateways, surely, since it could never in the warlike old days have left itself vulnerable to assault. Before entering, walk around the house to enjoy its position at the top of sweeps of lawn and the indomitability of its centuries-old trees. The church adjoining the castle sparks one piece of splendor, the tomb of Sir Richard Croft and his wife, Dame Eleanor, both of whom died early in the sixteenth century and both people of importance, due the carved luxury in which they now lie. He had been treasurer to the household of Henry VII and she, in her youth, governess to the royal household.

The interior is quiet, discreetly balanced. Among the family portraits, Queen Elizabeth and one of the Lord Burghleys accompanied by a Croft who was comptroller of Elizabeth's household. The Man of Ross, no relation, distributes his gifts to the poor, and George IV, painted by the atelier of Lawrence, poses as the Lawrentian ideal of pink-cheeked, milk-fed, good-natured male beauty. The Blue Room provides Jacobean paneling of repeated squares—once painted blue, we are told—around gilded roses. The furniture—William and Mary, Queen Anne, and Georgian—is variously attractive, but the major adornment here is an early Gainsborough painting of a Croft wife with clear English schoolgirl features, dressed in dark veiling and heavy pearls, her eyes wise and cold as Circe's. English, Dutch, and Italian paintings follow, and then the library, where we find the literary Crofts: an annotated copy of Johnson's work, books by a Croft medievalist, and, along with two early examples (1760) of the Gothic revival in furniture, a desk–filing cabinet, with lettered sections, that another scholarly Croft designed. A drawing by Lawrence, prints and water colors of the estate and nearby views, and an elaborate chimney surround of the eighteenth century finish the visit.

NOTES

DAYS: Easter Saturday through September, Wednesdays, Thursdays, Saturdays, Sundays, and Bank Holidays; October, Saturday and Sunday afternoons. For opening and closing times, inquire locally.

The insatiable will find more border castles as ruin, manor house, or suggestive place name by consulting detailed maps, *Historic Houses, Castles and Gardens*, and booklets issued locally. Others might head for Wales or, in the company of cows whose udders swing like deep bells and the bounding rumps of sheep, make for **Ludlow,** a classic, loose composition of sheep, fields, hedgerows, and houses pinned together by castle walls and church tower. On the main street, wayward designs of inn (see the Elizabethan Feather Inn, for one) dressed in every sort of pattern that black and white and medallions of heads can make, outshouting the details of calmer houses.

Flowing hills ease one to the once-momentous town of **Shrewsbury** ("Shrozebury" is the way to say it), an accommodating place that combines imaginatively its old and new. It arranges ingenious modern cat's-cradles of ramp, bridge, and tunnel to propel its people in and out of shopping areas that the top of the main street—which changes its name from St. timber houses of the sixteenth and seventeenth centuries. At combine twentieth-century glassy with richly patterned half-

John's Hill to Shoplatch (a family who lived here) to Pride Hill
(another family) and finally Castle Street—stands the restored
medieval border castle, built on a Norman fortress, its glowering past tamed to supply a final flourish to an enterprising,
vivid street whose clothing, shoes, sweets, teas, and sundries
have lived here in one arrangement or another for centuries.

Let us assume that you are in a hotel on the Mount, where
Charles Darwin was born. You breach the upper town by crossing the Welsh Bridge and, negotiating an ingenious set of
modern buttresses that rise from a lake of parked cars, find
yourself inside Woolworth's and then out onto the main streets.
By way of Shoplatch into High Street, and a turn that avoids
both Fish and Milk Streets, find the Information Bureau embedded in a Music Hall dignified by Roman columns and pediment. With the map they supply, peering into alleys and "shuts"
(passages between broader streets) you should come on the
raised, late-sixteenth-century market hall of warm color and
design, surrounded by Georgian dignity and the folksiness of
half-timbering; on its walks, a bench or two for sitting with big
exploding vats of flowers. Lend yourself now to Fish and Milk
and Dogpole, whose meaning is erased by time, and Wyle Cop
(probably a Welsh name), to the curves of brick and timber
that fold and unfold on the churches of St. Mary's (extraordinary glass), St. Alkmund's, and St. Julian's. Ask your way
to Grope Lane, whose upper stories swell toward each other,
cutting out the light, hence the necessity for groping. From
that medievalism into the medievalism of Butchers Row shops
and the "shut" called SEVENTY STEPS, asking your way whether
you really need to or not in order to savor conversation with
the citizens of Shrewsbury.

You cannot miss the Rowley House, a stunning black-and-
white edifice built by a sixteenth-century merchant and now
used as a museum which shows Roman artifacts found locally.
It stands on a spacious market place that fronts modern
shopping arcades as adroitly designed as the approach from
river to upper town. From the combination of late medieval and
modern, turn up Claremont Hill for rows of Georgian houses
crested with three lions and a banner. The banner says FLOREAT
SALOPIA, the "Salop" that means Shropshire, not only the county
of Housman and Darwin but the birthplace of Robert Clive
of India as well. The Clive House, now a small museum, sits in

a beguiling close off College Hill, part of a Georgian sector of town. Then there is what is left of antique St. Chads, sketches of old town wall, the library and museum in a school built early in the seventeenth century, the broad entertainment and recreation field called the Quarry where an annual flower show and music festival are held, so well and profitably that the proceeds have paid for notable town improvements. And there are the more sociable stretches of the Severn River to cross and recross, and prowling for old houses and lanes. Try standing on a corner looking helpless and wait for two or three locals to discuss laughingly where to send you next, then launch into ancient tales and present gossip, leaving you wreathed in their affability but quite unnoticed—for a fair time—as they talk on and on with unhurried pleasure.

Three miles on the way to **Whitchurch** there is a church, seemingly related to nothing but blank earth, immediately off the road. It has well-designed windows whose tracery reveals the styles of several early eras, a spirited tower of the late fifteenth century, a worn Pietà, and a significant row of shields. You are in **Battlefield Church,** built in the first years of the fifteenth century as a chapel for the salvation of Henry IV in his lifetime, for his soul after death and those of the almost three thousand gentlemen who died in the Battle of Shrewsbury. This was the battle, as readers of English history and Shakespeare remember, at which the forces of Percy, the Earl of Northumberland, and his son Henry Hotspur gathered, hoping for assistance from the Welshman Owen Glendower to defeat and depose Henry IV, who had deposed Richard II. Glendower was busy with other marauding and the battle was joined without the Welsh. The Northumbrians were defeated, and Hotspur the Incandescent—at least as Shakespeare recreated him—was killed. After the battle a great burial pit was dug, the several thousand bodies dumped in it. Covered and smoothed over it became the site of Battlefield Church.

A sense of unease follows one to **Oswestry,** close on the Welsh border. A signpost is broken here, another there, and more and more, too many to be accidents or impromptu vandalism. As one approaches the town, a sign that says KEEP OSWESTRY OURS, a reminiscence of ancient border disputes obviously not resolved, now translated into a struggle for Welsh independence. The town is poor and has a frontier roughness; one hesitates

to ask whether "ours" means British or Welsh. The speech is
a lilting Welshness and the vocabulary a bit strange. Off the
big parking lot there are signs that point to VAULTS, stimulating images of caves, crypts, ancient prisons? What does
Oswestry produce or save in sufficient quantity to require
vaults? Vaults, it turns out, are pubs, nothing more. A street
near the parking lot is marked ENGLISH WALLS; a short distance away, a street marked WELSH WALLS. Whether this is an
attempt at peaceable balancing or symptomatic of timeless, angry proximity is not easy to know. No one is impolite, of course,
nor excessively conversational, and possibly neither curious nor
well informed. Ask about directions to **Offa's Dyke**, for instance. "I think I went with a school group as a child but I
don' actually remember"; "No dikes around here I don't think."
A garage attendant is more likely to know: "Go out to Selattyn
and turn off at the sign of the old racetrack on the left."

King Offa of Mercia had the immensely long ditch and em-
bankment made to define clearly the boundary of what was his
and what was Welsh toward the end of the eighth century.
Never a sturdy structure—it did not have to be since numerous border castle-fortresses and the villages that grew with
them protected the terrain—it has been flattened and filled
over many centuries and in many places. At this point it runs
at the side of a field, near a miniature water hole where the
farmer's boy likes to whirl, dip, rise in a boat made of a shallow tub. The Dyke is neither attractive nor communicative, the
bank not very high, the ditch not very deep, their difference
equalized by a thousand winds and oceans of rain. That it exists
at all is exciting, particularly in this superb setting. On the hill
marked RACECOURSE, standing beside a closed-off, square
mound that might be a barrow, one is in an extraordinary
landscape—silent as if never touched by sound, trees and fields
fixed immortally on hills beyond hills of strange shapes and
odd, irregular rhythms.

(You may have wondered whether you were trespassing on
the field of the Dyke. No, the path is signposted and part of an
arduous hiking route that walks with the Dyke for about 60
miles and leaves it for many more, which go through forests,
mountains, across moors and rivers, hugging the north-south
line of Wales. There are youth hostels along the way and short

sections of the hike can be tackled from local villages. Nevertheless, only experienced hikers and woodsmen need apply.)

The layers of hill follow the road in and out of towns hung with bilingual WELCOME TO WALES signs and hotels that prepare "border catering." One town will flourish a very high railroad bridge over its river, another show a banner of new company houses, but soon they all turn mining-black, black churches, black slag heaps; the noses sharper, the faces darker and more pinched, children offering for sale tattered, used comic books.

It all brightens as one crosses the sturdy fourteenth-century bridge over the Dee and bursts into brilliance in the red and cream stones, the overhanging, slatted houses, the arches and ironwork doilies and fancy clock on the main streets of independent **Chester**, which, while clasping the traditional to its capacious, well-dressed bosom, is also willing to chance the chic and trendy.

The Romans, no mean judges of strategic and profitable sites, found the land whose river poured into the nearby Irish Sea good, and where the river made an angle they placed their crude fortress. It became a town called Deva, complete with amenities—temples, barracks, and huge amphitheater, abandoned in the fourth century. The ruined wilderness the Romans left became a battleground of contending local tribesmen and venturesome Danes. Recorded early history—a fact or two dropped into wells of hearsay and tradition (and plagiarism, a common sin of monastic scribes who ran out of material and borrowed events from other counties and kingdoms)—tells us that a daughter of Alfred the Great, with the flannel-chewing name of Aethelflaed, rebuilt the fortress, repaired and lengthened the Roman walls and, on the banks of the river, built a castle. She must have planned well and artistically, making Chester worthy of a royal visit that tradition paints as supremely autocratic: King Edgar of the Saxons sailing down the river on his way to the Church of St. John; the men who ply the oars are not churls but earls, chieftains from the west and across the seas come to offer vows of fealty.

William and his Normans conquered Sussex in 1066, but Chester was not taken until 1070 and then reduced to rubble. The apportioning of lands among Norman knights created a line of earls of Chester with resplendent French names who for

over 150 years ruled it as an autonomous kingdom subject to
no other power. During the reign of Henry III, in the mid-
thirteenth century, the domain fell to a flock of sisters and
their daughters and the king lifted it from them ("lest so fair
a dominion should be divided among women," to quote a local
booklet) and turned it over to his son. Thereafter, the eldest
royal son was not only Prince of Wales but Earl of Chester
as well.

In spite of plague, fires, constant warfare and disorder, the
city grew rich and became a major port, the Liverpool of its
day. In its medieval prosperity it saw shipping of a wide variety
of goods and produce to and from a meshwork of far-flung
ports. In the fifteenth century the waters to the sea choked up
and Chester fell apart again, but not so completely that it didn't
continue to pull its wagonloads of mystery plays through the
town until the late sixteenth century, when they were banned
as being too Popish. Nor was the citizenry so enfeebled that it
stopped fighting the abbey, a common divertissement. Chester,
as usual, maintained its disputes longer than the rest. The
abbey had already been long powerless when town-versus-
Church reared its dissensions again early in the seventeenth
century. The functionary who carried the weighty civic sword,
point upward, in the mayor's processions (often into the heart
of the Cathedral) had died and the church decided to close the
doors to him, his funeral, the mayor, co-workers, family, and
sword. They found another way in and marched to their usual
places, sword point up. The hot issue came to law and the lay
powers won. Mayor and sword-bearer may now proceed, sword
held as it anciently was, into the Cathedral.

The Roman walls were pierced by four gates whose roads
met at the principal government building. Where this *principia*
stood there is now St. Peter's Church; the four Roman roads
are the present Eastgate, Watergate, Northgate, and Bridge
Street, and until Cromwell put an end to the fun, their place
of meeting held the City's High Cross, which stared down at
bear baiting, hangings and whippings, and other forms of
entertainment. At this central point one enters a set of the
unique "Rows," arcaded walks along shops built above street-
level shops. They offer shelter, the nosy pleasures of balconies,
and some of the most attractive—and smart and expensive—
shops in their part of the country. Where space was available,

the Rows extended inward, one area glassed in like a French "passage" of Proust's day, and to those were added a modern terrace café and the inevitable comforting toilets.

From a balcony on Watergate, listen for the shouts of medieval draymen, the slow smack of hooves as burdened nags carry sacks of grain, bundles of skins, and tuns of wine to and from the ships jammed together at the end of the street. Trace the decorative stars and arrows, the arches and darts and the spindles of chimney on the houses of merchants who controlled the traffic below. Passing under the exuberant clock and over, follow the jaunty lines of myriad sharp eaves, brick curves, and knobs, chimneys, and finials chasing each other across the sky. Licking—as the Latins say—the shop windows, you may come on a low coffeeshop which is proud of the fact that its eggs are fried in butter and, more important to the traveler, serves Eccles cakes, a mound of currants clothed in short dough, hot and delectable.

Lined with cakes, you can feast on the carved detail of Bishop Lloyd's house on Watergate. Nearer the walls, the Stanley Palace, much restored, like the rest, and like the rest, riotously patterned; more of the animated same near Bridgegate. Walls to walk now and stops to make at truncated or restored towers, at classical gates, and the Victorian-Gothic wedding cake that is the town hall. The dour Bridge of Sighs conducted condemned prisoners to their last prayers at St. John's before execution. Chester still has its Roman amphitheatre and Roman remains neatly assembled near the Newgate.

The square of the not wholly defunct abbey is a tranquility of weathered stone and green lawn. The Abbey Gateway, overarched by smooth, firm lines of rustication, shares the serenity of dignified old age. In its youth of the fourteenth and fifteenth centuries it opened to the buying and selling, the street entertainers, the drinkers, roisterers, the sharp-eyed for country matters, who gathered for a June fair. During Whitsun, it watched guildsmen and apprentices stop to perform their mystery plays, important in the annals of drama as rivals—in country wit, occasional lyricism, and sharp characterizations—to the famous play cycles of York and Coventry. (As in York, they are still occasionally played, though not in the peripatetic fashion of the Middle Ages.)

Chester Cathedral shares, in large part, the history of its

peers: an Anglo-Saxon chapel dedicated to a saint, here Werburgh, the daughter of a king of Mercia; the founding of a
Benedictine abbey and a new church built in the twelfth and
thirteenth centuries; later changes erased by thoroughgoing
Victorian reconstruction, dominated by the mighty hand of the
ubiquitous Sir Gilbert Scott. Early in this century, the monastic
buildings, in much better shape than most, were patched up
and made usable adjuncts of the church. Ennobled by age,
size, and the very weight of its name, a cathedral is always
imposing and Chester is no exception, although no one, not
even citizen-enthusiasts, would compare it to Lincoln or Ely
or York. Nonetheless, there are the evocative medieval cloisters
clothed in the arches and bosses of the sixteenth century (with
some support by the twentieth), the re-ordered stones of the
twelfth-century baptistry, and the remote height, the rounded
arch and Romanesque archlets of the north transept (the oldest
part of the church) canopied by heraldic bosses. In the refectory, a good-looking door and, in the same Early English style
of the thirteenth century, a set of open arches rising on a
staircase to an angle of pulpit from which one monk read to
others at mealtimes.

Inevitably one finds St. Werburgh's shrine badly smashed, its
many statues in frondy niches gone except for a bundle of
knights or kings. As inevitably, there are stolid monuments
and billowy and tough-faced baby angels holding commemorative plaques. By far the most engaging is that of Thomas
Greene, mayor of Chester in the last years of the sixteenth
century, who stands between his first wife and his second in a
frame that leaves ample room for telling about his accomplishments and goodness. The three figures are of equal height,
hands joined in prayer in precisely the same fashion, all wearing ruffs and mounted on cushions, all six eyes staring out in
restrained misery. One waits for the hour to strike and for
them to turn and follow each other like cuckoo-clock dolls.

It is the choir stalls that matter most. To some degree
copied from Lincoln, they are not quite as exquisite as those,
yet accomplished enough to serve as pinnacles of medieval
wood sculpture. The tabernacles, once simple structures to
guard the monks from the winds that came through openings,
had by the fourteenth century proliferated to fancies of leaves
and brackets, slender pilasters, and barbed minute spires like

the flight of a thousand arrows. Under these elaborations, the famous bench-ends, corbels, and misericords. It is difficult for the non-expert to say what is authentically medieval, what partly fifteenth- and partly nineteenth-century, or is it mostly Victorian? In any case, the old spirit is maintained. A truly fourteenth-century bearded pilgrim with a prophet's profile sits at one bench end as sentinel to an artfully carved Jesse Tree. Elsewhere, animals fighting, a touching Annunciation, and an elephant bearing a castle, a big-headed, wide-eyed, rather slender animal on stumpy legs saved from anonymity by his trunk; an imaginative work considering that a fourteenth-century carver would hardly have had an opportunity to see an elephant and had to create it from bestiaries and remote hearsay. The corbels give you musical angels and saints, a grotesque animal eating a man, a grotesque man eating a chunk of animal, wrestlers, women chasing beasts. The misericords take us to Gawain, to the legend of the unicorn, to Tristan and Isolde, to the miraculous flight of Alexander supported by two monster-birds, and to two favorites—the wily fox and his gullible victims and the corrupt mendicant friar and his foolish flock.

It is a pity that the Victorians took out a few misericords that they thought unseemly, vulgar. They left as compensation political-cartoon corbels in the south transept. One is Gladstone, in a jester's cap, quill pen in mouth, trampling out symbols of Popery. The other is a lion-bodied, curly-maned Disraeli, clutching the crown and sword to fight off a crude-faced dissenter.

NOTES

HOTELS:
Cirencester—The Fleece and the Crown are low-moderate.

Stroud—The Bear of Rodborough, in a fine location, is moderate.

Cheltenham—The Queens is highish; the Savoy, Berkeley, and Carlton are moderate. The town is well supplied with lodging at various price levels.

Tewkesbury—The Royal Hop Pole, Swan, and Tudor House are moderate.

Shrewsbury—The Beauchamp, Abbey Gardens, and Lion are moderate.

Chester proper—The Grosvenor is high; the Chester, Curzon, Mollington, Banastre, Riverside, and Queen are moderate; the Olde King's Head, Dene, and Oaklands are inexpensive. About a dozen miles outside Chester, the Chequers Hotel, which acts like a house, pleased with its ribbed ceilings, sporting and sporty prints, well-appointed bedrooms equipped with TV and comfortable bathrooms, the rooms named for American and English political worthies—Kennedy, Roosevelt, Eisenhower, Churchill. Where there used to be gambling in a former incarnation, there is a large dining room with food highly praised in the locality and, on Saturday night, a band and entertainment. The service at meals is good or odd, depending on whether your waiter is Mediterranean or English, the portions big, and the wine list respectable. High moderate.

And Be Prepared For

It might be of help, if you've never traveled in England before, to round out this exploration with a few hints for meeting some national phenomena. Like every nation—and for that matter, all humanity—England has its tranquilizers, to be respected and coped with in their several ways.

First, the "cuppa" tea, not always the unobtrusive short pause we picture it to be. Often it seems to be a response to a primitive call—like that which urges the flight of bees and the migration of birds—to mystic celebration. Typewriter and vacuum cleaner are silenced, ledgers and vestry doors closed, car and road abandoned. At the tops of the moors, even when earth and sky growl at each other with thunder, the cloth is spread and the ceremonial objects placed. In every reach of the island, the less important aspects of life stop for the liturgy of rattling teacups and anointment in butter and jam. Your role is to wait respectfully as you might through church services foreign to you.

Almost as calming is the conviction that that which has been is good, revealed most overtly in adoration of the old-fashioned innocence of hamlets—an eye of water, six ducks, a church with downcast eyes wearing a whimsical spire, a manicured green scalloped in bow-windowed shops. And since there is never too much of a good thing, a bouquet of ten hamlets with engaging faces is ten times as lovable as one. The same clinging tastes, resistant to mutability, shore up such monstrosities as swollen, pimpled Victorian town halls. Never breathe a word of criticism; be charmed or, at least, polite.

Tranquilizer Three guards the self-image of perfection: a rural chemist who is out of sunglasses says they are bad for your eyes rather than confess that he has forgotten to re-order. A country grocery refuses to slice ham on a Sunday morning. Not that they are too busy, they explain, but the law prohibits it. Don't question the obviously improvised law but consider the strong possibility that face-saving, La Bella Figura, is not an Italian monopoly.

If your time in England is the spring, take a touch of skepticism along to deal with its legendary enchantments. Spring is, in some years, mainly perpetrated by the poets, save the clear-eyed Elizabethans. Sir Philip Sidney says it for them: "Her

[Nature's] world is brazen, the Poets only deliver a golden." Chaucer, a shrewd, practical man, was carried away like any mad poet by the April showers piercing to the root the droughts of March. What droughts in this moist land? Browning wrote, "Oh to be in England now that April's here," in a sunny land, his recollections misted by nostalgia. Collaborators who perpetuate the illusion of immutable golden springtimes are the stalwart English flowers which battle their way through crusts of snow to stand in their rowdy reds and yellows, defying the elements and traffic fumes. (There is a fanciful theory that explains their indestructibility by suggestions that they are really made of pliant steel, painted and pulled up a quarter-inch every night by retired colonels and bony, immortal ladies.) They, too, have caught the English pride in endurance and strive to endure so that they may enhance the poets' picture of boyish sun and girlish April gowned in daffodils. The daffodils *are* there and the "tender crops," but they are better equipped for rain and wind than you; consider carefully whether you should abandon sweater and raincoat just yet. Properly equipped, you should not be dissuaded by weather from tasting many English pleasures. It doesn't impede the English, ever, who should set you an admirable example. And a few damp clouds are little enough to pay for the famous, lovely green they paint the English earth.

You will find that Nanny (Aunty in some regions) still guides much of life, transmuted from the individual nurse-governess to the large tutelary goddess who, among other things, paints the signs NOW WASH YOUR HANDS in public toilets. You and the English are being taught constantly. Directions are always given at least twice, slowly and carefully, and then "Did I make myself clear?" Placards in buses teach, museums teach, churches teach, and radio teaches—and so do television (the BBC is frequently referred to as Aunty) and the newspapers; classes from hat-making to speaking Urdu are invitingly cheap, all under the serious guidance of Nanny. You can't mind because the constant learning and teaching may be responsible in part for the soothing manner and voices of English women, all part-time impromptu schoolteachers whether dealing reasonably with their children or directing you to the Guildhall.

London is too worldly; the south, London's electric-blanket bedroom, is too sophisticated for it. But other areas cling to an insular self-love that is touching. A decayed cloister is claimed by its parishioners and clergy to be as splendid as that of St. Paul's Outside the Walls in Rome; a fourteenth-century church painting is vaunted as every bit as good as Italian painting of the time. Comparable to Duccio, Giotto, Simone Martini? In the voluminous English information about England, every tomb monument is as effective as Bernini's St. Theresa group, each misericord carving a masterpiece of naturalism and humor. Why cavil? Simply read "attractive" for "superlative," "pleasing" for "great," "interesting" for "overwhelming" in descriptive booklets.

An English garden, whether as front-door patch or regal park, is more than you may think it is. Trees and flowers around a house were among the basic appurtenances of a gentleman. Only the poorest, the dwellers of the black Midlands warrens described by de Tocqueville, the gin-soaked inhabitants of London slums portrayed by Dickens, were beyond the seductions of tulips in spring, durable roses throughout several months, a full, carefully clipped hedge. Gardening opens up conversation for the bashful and feeds the vanity of people who eschew the vanities of dress and stylish furnishings. It fills the need to spend all the care and tenderness unused by children and grandchildren gone off to Australia and Canada. It returns discipline in a structured life to the elderly officer removed from India, fills a need for color and design difficult to express in the rural conventions for the neutral and conservative, and provides the decorous excitements of community flower and garden competitions. With tea, telly, *The Times*, and the library, gardening shapes a fairly complete life of employment, aesthetics, sociability, and, for lagniappe, the sense of being lord and lady of the manor. Your contribution will be enthusiastic admiration and, if you can manage it, a few intelligent gardening questions to show your respect for a master.

Finally, remember to drive to the left, to say "petrol" for "gas" and "boot" for "trunk," and that English policemen are truly public servants, eager to help. Now, enjoy yourself and England.

INDEX

As aids to the reader, the page numbers of the map
(or maps) on which English counties are to be found
are given herein; and hotels, inns, and
restaurants (with their location) are indexed by name.

"Aaron the Jew's House" (Lincoln),
63–4
Abbey Gardens (hotel, Shrews-
bury), 308
Abbey Gate (Bury St. Edmunds),
25–6
Abbey Lawn Trust (Tewkesbury),
294–5
Abbey Mill (Tewkesbury), 295
Abbey Park (hotel, York), 106
Abbots, 281
Abelard, Peter, see Bernard of
Clairvaux
Adam, Robert, 117–18, 139, 261
Addison, Joseph, 260
Agricola, Gnaeus Julius, 29, 111
Ah Chow (restaurant, Cheltenham),
289
Akenfield (Blythe), 13, 15, 28, 36
Albany (hotel, Compton Wynyates),
82
Albert, Prince, 89
Alcuin, 101
Aldeburgh, 13
Alfred the Great, King, 209, 218, 303
Alfriston, 196
Allen, Ralph, 260
Allerford, 221
All Saints, Church of (Cocker-
mouth), 154
All Saints' Church (Sudbury), 17
All Saints' parish church (Ilkley),
111
All Saints' parish church
(Odiham), 240
Alnwick, 139, 141–4, 146; Castle,
136–40, 144
Altarnun, 226
Amberley, 197
Ambleside, 158
American Museum (Claverton
Manor), 263–4
Ampneys, the, 276
Anchor (pub, Pyrford), 177
Ancient Grudge, The (restaurant,
Tewkesbury), 295
Angel Corner (Bury St. Edmunds),

30
Angel Hotel (Bury St. Edmunds),
25, 29, 30
Angel Inn (Lavenham), 22
Anglian (restaurant, Norwich), 48
Anne, Queen, 92, 160; court of, 173
Anne of Cleves, 180
Anne of Cleves House Museum,
186–7
Antelope Hotel (Dorchester), 201
Appleby, John, 26
Arles, Council of, 100
Arnold, Matthew, 158
Arpino, Il Cavaliere d' (Giuseppe
Cesari), 256
Arthur, King, 217–18, 224–5, 226, 245,
268–9
Artichoke (pub, Norwich), 47
Art Nouveau, 41, 73, 87, 106, 169
Arundel Castle, 27, 197
Ashmolean Museum (Oxford), 291
Askew, Anne, 68
Assembly Rooms (lunch and tea,
Norwich), 48
Astaire, Fred, dancing shoes, 250
Astor, William Waldorf, 180
Athelstan, King, 85–6, 109
Athenaeum (Bury St. Edmunds),
28–9, 30
Atlantic View Hotel (Treknow), 230
Audrey's Café (St. Colomb Major),
232
Austen, Jane, 213, 244, 258
Avebury, 252–3
Avon, River, 78, 252, 253, 265, 295

Badbury Rings, 211–12
Banastre (hotel, Chester), 308
Baret, John, 27, 28
Barnes, William, 203
Basingstoke, 240
Bassano, Jacopo, 256, 270
Bastard, John and William, 211
Bath, 17, 252, 253, 254, 257, 258–65,
288; Academy of Arts, 257;
hotels and restaurants, 272;
Music Festival, 265

Bathurst, earls of, 278
Battle, 194-5
Battlefield Church (Shrewsbury),
  301
Bear Hotel (Stroud), 283
Bear Inn (Bisley), 284
Bear of Redborough (hotel,
  Stroud), 307
Beauchamp (hotel, Shrewsbury),
  308
Beaufort, Cardinal, chapel, 244
Bebside, 145
Beccles, 37, 38
Becket, Thomas, 114, 196, 265
Bede, the Venerable, 101, 125
Bedlington, 145
Beetle and Chisel (pub, Delabole),
  225
Beggar's Opera, The (Gay), 260
Bell and Steelyard Inn
  (Woodbridge), 32
Bellingham, 136
Bellingham family (Levens Hall),
  161
Belper, 121
Belton, 38
Belton House, 58-61
Benedictine Cathedral Priory
  (Norwich), 39
Bere Regis, 207-8
Berkeley, Roger de, 285
Berkeley (hotel, Cheltenham), 307
Berkeley Arms (Tewkesbury), 295
Berkeley Castle, 284-7
Bernard of Clairvaux, 115
Beverley Minster, xiv, 109-10
Bibury, 276
Bickleigh, 217
Biddenden, 185
Bideford, 221
Bishop Lloyd's house (Chester), 305
Bisley, 283, 284
Black Bear (restaurant,
  Tewkesbury), 295
Black Boys, 189
Black Lion (hotel, Long Melford),
  20, 21
Black Swan (hotel, Helmsley), 107
Black Swan (inn, York), 92
Blake, William, 174
Blanchland, 132
Blandford Forum, 210-11
Blenheim palace, painting of
  (Chartwell), 179
Blood Accusations, 64, 101-2
"Bloody Assizes" (1685), 201-2

Blyth, 145
Blythe, Ronald, 13, 15, 28, 36
Blytheburgh, 35
Bodiam, 189-90, 191
Bodmin, 226-7
Bodmin Moor, 225-6
Boleyn, Anne, 138, 168, 180, 240, 242,
  280
Bonington, Richard Parkes, 162
Borromini, Francesco, 181
Borrowdale, 154-5, 163
Boscastle, 223-4
Bosch, Hieronymus, 173
Bosham, 198
Bothal, 145
Boucher, François, 118
Box Tree (restaurant, Ilkley), 119
Bradford-on-Avon, 257-8
Bradford Pool (Lincoln), 61
Brangwyn, Sir Frank, 156
Brenchley, 182
Brentwood, 155
Breughel, Pieter, 162
Bridges family (Cirencester), 279
Bridwell Museum (Norwich), 42, 43
Brighton, 196
Bristol, earls of, 23-5, 210
British Museum, 33, 58
British Tourist Authority, 3
Briton's Arms (Norwich), 48
Britten, Benjamin, 13
Broads, The (river and canals), 13,
  37, 49
Broadway, 275, 290
Brontë, Charlotte and Emily, 119,
  120-1, 184
Bronzino, Il (Agnolo di Cosimo),
  175, 256
Broughton, 149
Brown, Capability, 210, 254
Browne, Sir Anthony, 195
Browne, Sir Thomas, 41
Browning, Robert, 310
Brownlowe, Richard, 60
Bruno's (restaurant, Bath), 272
Bull Hotel (Long Melford), 20, 21
Burford, 275
Burgh Castle, 38
Burlington, Lord, 91
Burns, Robert, 203
Burwash, 189
Bury St. Edmunds, 23, 25-30, 40, 41
Buttermere, Lake, 154

Cadbury, 217-18
Cambridge, 13, 57, 64

Camelford, 218, 225
Canaletto, Antonio, 139–40, 168
Canova, Antonio, 25
Canterbury, 100, 114, 178; archbishops of, 207; Cathedral, 178
Canterbury Tales, The (Chaucer), 64, 172; see also Chaucer, Geoffrey
Canute, King, 26, 102–3, 129, 198, 244
Caravaggio, Michelangelo Amerighi, 256
Cardinal's Hat (house, Lincoln), 65
Carlton, 119
Carlton (hotel, Cheltenham), 289, 307
Carnegie, Andrew, 153
Castle Acre, 51, 52–3
Castle Howard, 113
Castle Museum (York), 94, 105
Castlerigg Ring (Keswick), 156
Catherine of Aragon, 80, 242–3, 244, 255
Catherine of Braganza, 286
Cattle Market (Bury St. Edmunds), 30
Cavendish, 18
Caxton, William, 69
Cellini, Benvenuto, 150
Cerne Abbas, 208–9
Chalford Vale, 283
Chanctonbury Ring, 197
Charles I, King, 80, 81, 92, 99, 210, 249, 251, 255, 256
Charles II, King, 92, 131, 160, 243, 251, 252, 285, 286
Charles V, Emperor, 245
Chartwell, 178–9
Chatsworth, 121
Chaucer, Geoffrey, 64, 69, 75, 114, 172, 258, 262, 310
Cheltenham, 287–9, 290; hotels and restaurants, 289, 307
Checquers Hotel (near Chester), 308
Cheshire, map, 274
Chester, 61, 95, 303–6; Cathedral, 304, 305–6; earls of, 303–4; hotels, 308
Chesterfield, 75
Chesters (Roman fort), 135
Cheviot Hills, 136
Chichester, 197, 198
Chiddingfold, 171
Chilham, 186
Chippendale, Thomas, 117, 118, 219, 256
Chippenham, 254

Chippings (villages), the, 275
Chiswick, 91
Chiswick Villa (London), 182
Chollerford, 135
Christ College (Oxford), 55
Christian, Fletcher, 154
Churchill, Arabella, 180
Churchill, Winston, 146, 178–9
Church Militant (Durham), 124
Chute, John, 242
Cimabue, Giovanni, 24
Cinque Ports, 193, 194
Cirencester, 277–81; hotels, 307; Park, 281
Civil War (1642–52), 62, 68, 80, 86, 99, 183, 210, 211, 249
Clandon Park, 176
Clare, 18
Claverton Manor, 263–4
Clementi, Muzio, 256
Cleopatra, Queen of Egypt, panels, 219
Clifford's Tower (York), 86, 88, 91
Clifton House (King's Lynn), 56
Clive House (Shrewsbury), 300–1
Clock House (restaurant, Ripley), 177
Clouet, Jean, 180, 251
Clovelly, 221–2
Cluniac Priory (Castle Acre), 53
Cobbett, William, 7, 50
Cobbs Hill (Lincoln), 63
Cobham, 177
Cockermouth, 153–4; Castle, 154
Colchester, 61
Coleridge, Hartley, 156, 158
Coleridge, Samuel Taylor, 120, 149, 153, 155, 156, 157, 221
College Arms (pub, near The Vyne), 243
Colnes, the, 276
Commonwealth, the, 125, 266; see also Cromwell, Oliver
Compton, 169–70
Compton, William, 79–80, 81
Compton Wynyates, 79–82
Congregation Society (Norwich), 39
Coniston, 155
Conquest (Norman), 13, 86, 136, 195, 284, 291–2, 303; see also William the Conqueror
Consett, 131
Constable, John, 12, 14–15, 246
Constantine (Roman emperor), 85, 100, 101, 104
Copper Lodge Hotel (Norwich), 48

Cordell, Sir William, 18, 20
Corinium Museum (Cirencester), 278–9
Corneille de Lyon, 177
Cornsay, 131
Cornwall, xiv, 213, 222–39; Earl of, 224; map, 214; moors of, 225–7, 229, 231
Corpus Christi (guild), 22
Corsham, 254–7
Corsham Court, 254–7
Cortona, Pietro da, 250, 256
Cotman, John Sell, 40
Cotswold villages, 254, 275–84
County (hotel, Compton Wynyates), 82
Court Hall (Winchelsea), 193
Coventry, 77–8, 95; Cathedral, 67, 77–8
Cowdray (house), 195
Cranach, Lucas, 180
Cranbrook, 183
Crediton, 217
Crispe, Elizabeth, 181
Crockham Hill (Kent), 179
Croft, Sir Richard, 298
Croft Castle (Leominster), 298–9
Cromwell, Oliver, 21, 40, 51, 53, 68, 80–1, 114, 227, 240, 285, 304; *see also* Commonwealth
Cross in Hand, 189
Crown (hotel, Cirencester), 307
Crown (hotel, Wells), 272
Crown Inn (Chiddingfold), 171
Crummock Water, 154
Crusades, the, 33–4, 52, 298; Jews during, 101–2
Culloden, Battle of, 95
Cullompton, 218
Cumberland, 149; maps, 148, 130, 137; *see also* Lake District
Cupola House (Bury St. Edmunds), 29
Curzon, George Nathaniel, 70–1, 190
Curzon (hotel, Chester), 308
Customs House (King's Lynn), 56
Cuthbert, Bishop, 124
Cutsdean Ford, 290
Cuyp, Albert, 172, 177

Dahl, Michael, 173
Dalton, John, 153
Da Cortona, *see* Cortona
Da Pietro, *see* Pietro
Darlington, 122
Dart, River, 215–16

Dartington school, 216
Dartmoor, 215
Dartmoor Prison (Princetown), 216–17
Darwin, Charles, 300
Davidstow, 225–6
Da Vinci, *see* Vinci
Dawes, Thomas, 16
Dean Court (hotel, York), 106
Deben, River, 32
Dedham, 14
Dee, River, 303
Deerhurst, 290–2
Defoe, Daniel, 7, 155, 201
De Gaulle, Charles, clock, 178
Deincourt family (Sizergh Castle), 158–9
Delabole, 225
Denbighshire, map, 274
Dene (hotel, Chester), 308
De Quincey, Thomas, 149, 153, 158
Derbyshire, 75; map, 76
Derwent, River, 153, 154
Derwent Reservoir, 132
Derwent Water, 155
Despenser family (Tewkesbury), 292, 293–4
Deva (Roman town), 303
Devon, 213–23; dukes of, 121; map, 214; moors of, 216–17, 219, 220, 221, 223
Devon (hotel, Lyme Regis), 213
Devonshire Hotel (Grassington), 120
Dickens, Charles, 95, 106, 295, 297, 311
Digby, Sir John, 210
Dinas (hotel, Padstow), 239
Disraeli, Benjamin, 307
Dissolution of the Monasteries, 28, 35, 58, 65, 107, 126, 161, 209, 258, 280; *see also* Reformation
Ditchling, 196
Ditchling Beacon, 196–7
Domenichino, Il (Domenico Zampieri), 256
Domesday Book, 13, 39, 86, 136, 269, 296
Doniert, King of Cornwall, 229
Dorchester, 201–5, 212
Dorking, 178
Dorset, 201–12, 222; map, 200
Dorset (Hymas), 203
Dorset Hotel (Lyme Regis), 213
Dove Cottage (Grasmere), 157–8
Dover, 193

Dozmary Pool (Bodmin Moor), 226
Drax, Elizabeth, 286
Dudley, Robert (Earl of
    Leicester), 78
Duke's Head (King's Lynn), 56, 57
Dulverton, 219
Du Maurier, Daphne, 226, 236–7
Dumfries (Scotland), map, 130
Dunkery Beacon, 220–1
Dunster, 219–20; Castle, 219
Duntisbornes, The, 281
Dunwich, 34–5
Durham (city), 44, 122–35; bishops
    of, 138, 146; Cathedral, xiv, 122–7,
    136; map, 123; University of, 127–8
Durham (county), map, 130

Eagle (hotel, Launceston), 226
East Anglia, 13–57, 222; map, 12
East Bergholt, 13, 14–15
Eastgate (hotel, Lincoln), 67, 70
East Looe, 238
East Riding (of Yorkshire), map, 108
Eboracum (Roman fortress, York),
    85
Edenbridge, 179
Edgar, King, 258, 303
Edmund, King, 26, 28, 40
Edward I, King, 29, 65
Edward II, King, 69, 138, 283, 285,
    286, 292
Edward III, King, 56, 69, 255
Edward IV, King, 129, 292
Edward VI, King, 29, 60, 139, 167–8,
    249
Edward VII, King, 288
Edward VIII, King (Duke of
    Windsor), 61
Edward the Confessor, King, 194,
    291–2
Edward the Martyr, King, 207
Edwin, King of Northumbria, 100
Egremont, earls of, 171
Elbow Room (restaurant, Totnes),
    216
Elfrida, Queen, 207
Elizabeth I, Queen, 20, 32, 34, 78, 80,
    129, 139, 159, 167, 168, 179, 180, 183,
    195, 210, 247, 249, 255, 256, 259, 280,
    298
Elizabethan Feather Inn (Ludlow),
    299
Elm Park (hotel, York), 106
Elsdon, 136
Ely, 13, 44, 57
Endicott, Captain, 203

Esk, River, 150
Essex, 14
Etchingham, 189
Ethelred the Unready, 207, 255
Ethelreda, Queen, 132
Etty, William, 98–9
Everard (hotel, Bury St.
    Edmunds), 30
Exe, River, 219
Exeter, 213–14; Cathedral, 213–14
Exford, 220
Exmoor, 220
Eye Manor (Leominster), 298

Fairford, 275, 277
Fairy Cross, 221
Falmouth, 237
Fangdale Beck, 109
Far from the Madding Crowd
    (Hardy), 201
Farnham, 175
Fawkes, Guy, 139, 172
Ferrybridge, 85
Fielding, Henry, 260
Fiennes, Celia, *Through England
    on a Side Saddle*, 7, 41, 155, 233,
    259
Fighting Cocks (pub, Horncastle),
    72
Fishbourne, 197–8
Fisher, Molly, 157
FitzHarding, Robert, 285
Fitz Osbern, William, 285
Fitz Park (Keswick), 156
Flatford, 14
Fleece (hotel, Circencester), 307
Fletcher, John, 191
Flushing Inn (Rye), 191
Folk Museum of Sussex
    Archaeological Society, 186–7
Ford, 221
Fortey, John, 276
Foss, River, 85, 88
Foulkes (restaurant, Totnes), 216
Fountains Abbey, 110, 113, 115–17
Fowey, 238, 239
Fowey, River, 227, 238
Framlingham, 33–4; Castle, 33–4
Francis (hotel, Bath), 272
Frederick II, King of the Two
    Sicilies, 68
Freston tower, 31
Friar's Crag (Keswick), 155
Friar's Restaurant (Sudbury), 17
"Friendly Society of Agricultural
    Workers," 206

Fritton, 37–8
Fulbroke Castle, 81
Fuseli, Henry, 174

Gaiety Restaurant (Tewkesbury), 295
Gainsborough, Thomas, 4, 16, 31, 139, 162, 174, 257, 286, 289–9; birthplace of, 17
Galtries Lodge (hotel, York), 106
Gauguin, Paul, 178
Gaveston, Piers, 138
Gay, John, 260
Gayton, 53
Geoffrey of Monmouth, 224–5
George II, King, 25, 262
George III, King, 288
George IV, King, 298
George V, King, 60
George VI, King, 177
"George" hotels: Cheltenham, 289; Chollerford, 135; Compton Wynyates, 82; Rye, 194
Gibbons, Grinling, 60, 103, 168, 172, 173–4
Gillow (Lancaster craftsman), 162
Giorgione, Il (Giorgio Barbarelli), 81
Giotto di Bondone, 24
Girondin, Le (restaurant, York), 106
Gladstone, William, 307
Glastonbury, 268–9
Glastonbury Tor, 268
Glendower, Owen, 301
Glendower family (Wales), 298
Globe Hotel (Cockermouth), 153
Gloucester, 61, 102, 281, 282, 287; earls of, 292
Gloucestershire, 275–96; maps, 274, 241
Glyndebourne, 187–8
Gobelin tapestries, 118, 139
Godalming, 171
Godiva, Lady, 77, 78
Goes, Hugo van der, 251
Golden Fleece (pub, York), 92
Goldsmith, Oliver, 75, 260
Gonzagas of Mantua, 81
Gooding, Thomas, 46
Goose Fair (Nottingham), 75
Gordo, Enrique el, 81
Gorges, Thomas, 247
Gosforth, 151, 153
Gothic Exchequer Gate (Lincoln), 62

Graham, Colonel James, 161
Granacci, Francesco, 256
Grand (hotel, Lincoln), 70
Grange (restaurant, Salisbury), 272
Grantham, 58; Lords, 118
Grasmere, 157–8, 163
Grassington, 120
Grassington House (hotel, Grassington), 120
Gray, Thomas, 155
Great Bookham, 177
Great Dixter, 191
Great Yarmouth, 38, 55
Greene, Thomas, 306
Greta Hall (Keswick), 156
Greville, Mrs. Ronald, 176–7
Grey, Lady Jane, 248
Greyfriars, the (Lincoln), 65
Grime's Graves, 40, 50–1
Grosseteste, Robert (Bishop of Lincoln), 68
Grosvenor (hotel, Bath), 272
Grosvenor (hotel, Chester), 308
Guide to the Lakes, A (Wordsworth), 155
Guildford, xiv, 167, 175
Guildhalls: Coventry, 78; Lavenham, 21, 22–3; Norwich, 41, 42, 48; Totnes, 216; York, 105
Gulbenkian Museum of Oriental Art and Archaeology (Durham), 127–8
Gunpowder Plot, the, 139, 172
Gutenberg Bible, page from, 139
Gwennap Pit, 237
Gwithian, 234

Haddon Hall, 121
Hadleigh, 15
Hadrian (Roman emperor), 101, 141
Hadrian's Wall, 132, 134–5, 222–3; map, 130
Halfmoon (hotel, York), 106
Halvasso, 237
Hampshire (Hants), 240; maps, 241, 200, 166
Hanseatic League, 88
Harding House (Lincoln), 63
Hardy, Thomas, 201–7 *passim*, 212
Harold, King, 284
Harper, Archibald, 268
Harrogate, 112–13, 119
Hart, Thomas Shakespur, 295
Hartland, 222; Point, 222
Harvey, Mary (Lady), 25
Hastings, 193, 194–5; Battle of,

see Conquest (Norman) *and* William the Conqueror

Hatchlands, 176

Hatton, Sir Christopher, 255

Haunch of Venison (restaurant, Salisbury), 272

Hawker, Rev. Stephen, 223

Hawkhurst, 191

Haworth, 119, 120–1

Hawstead, 23

Headcorn, 185

Helmsley, 107

Henfield, 196–7

Henry, Earl of Surrey, 34

Henry I, King, 224

Henry II, King, 33, 113–14, 158, 265, 285

Henry III, King, 138, 207, 304

Henry IV, Emperor, 55–6, 126–7, 138

Henry IV, King, 126–7, 138, 280, 301

Henry VI, King, 28, 70, 150

Henry VII, King, 207–8, 244, 275, 298

Henry VIII, King, 28, 31, 34, 35, 53, 58, 62, 79–81, 86, 110, 114, 126, 138–9, 174, 186, 195, 207, 240, 242–5 *passim*, 249, 254; BBC TV series on, 270; wives of, *see* Boleyn, Catherine of Aragon, *and* Parr; *see also* Dissolution of the Monasteries; Reformation

Herbert, Henry, 249

Herbert, William, 248–9

Herbert family (Wilton House), 248–50

Herefordshire, 296; map, 274

Hever Castle, 180

Hexham, 132–5; Abbey, 132–5

Higher Bockhampton, 205–6

Hillaby, John, 235, 236

Historic Houses, Castles and Gardens, 4, 119, 131, 299

History of the English Church and People (Bede), 101, 125

Hog's Back (pub, Guildford), 175

Holbein, Hans, 81, 168, 174, 180, 249

Holbourne of Menstrie Museum (Bath), 264

Hole in the Wall (hotel, Bath), 272

Holkham Hall, 56–7

Holy Island (Lindisfarne), 124

Holy Trinity Micklegate, Church of the (York), 94, 95

Holy Trinity Church (Bradford-on-Avon), 257

Honister Pass, 155

Honiton, 213

Hope Anchor (hotel, Rye), 194

Hope-under-Dinmore, 297

Horncastle, 72

Horsehouse, 119

Hotspur, Henry, 138, 140, 141, 301

Hotspur (hotel, Alnwick), 144

Hovingham, 107

Howard, Castle, 113

Howard, Thomas (Duke of Norfolk), 34

Howard family, *see* Norfolk, dukes of

Hudson, George, 93

Hunt, Leigh, 153

Huntingdonshire, map, 76

"Hurlers," the (near Minion), 229

Hyams, John, 203

Hythe, 193

Ickworth House, 23–5

Ightham Mote, 180–1

Ilkley, 110–11, 119

In Britain, 3

Industrial Revolution, the, 39, 233–4

Ingres, Jean Auguste Dominique, 118

Innocent III, Pope, 30

Institute of Historical Research (York), 92

Ipswich, 17, 31

Irish Sea, 149, 303

Isabella, Queen, portrait, 283

Ivy Hatch, 180

James, Henry, 191, 264

James I, King, 34, 81, 125, 167, 168, 210, 279

James II, King, 159, 160, 180, 202, 251

Jarrow monastery (Durham), 125

Jeffreys, Judge George, 201

Jew, Samuel, 295

Jews: in Lincoln, 63–5, 102; in Norwich, 47; in York, 101–2

John, King, 26, 30, 34, 54, 116, 138, 207, 255, 265

John of Gaunt, 69

John Gershom Parkington Memorial Collection (Bury St. Edmunds), 30

Johnson, Samuel, 299

Jones, Inigo, 186, 242, 248, 250, 251, 284

Jonson, Ben, 249

Journey Through Britain (Hillaby), 235

Judge's House (York), 91–2

Keats, John, 149, 156
Keighley, 120
Kempley, 295-6
Kendal, 158
Kent, 21, 167, 177-86; earls of, 280; map, 166
Kersey, 15-16
Keswick, 155-6, 163
Kineton, 79
King's (restaurant, Cheltenham), 289
King's Arms (hotel, Dorchester), 212
King's Arms (hotel, Salisbury), 272
King's Head (hotel, Louth), 73
King's Head (hotel, Wells), 272
King's House (Thetford), 50
King's Lynn, 53-7
King's Manor (York), 99
Kipling, Rudyard, 189
Kirk Collection (York), 88-90, 105
Kirkham (Paignton), 215
Kittlewell, 119
Kneller, Sir Godfrey, 4, 60, 139, 173, 286
Knole, 179
Kyrle, John, 297

Lacock, 253-4
Lake District, the, 144, 149-63; map, 148
Lake District Leisure Pursuits (Windermere), 163
Lamb, Edwarde, 15
Lamplugh, 153
Lancashire (northern), 149; map, 148; *see also* Lake District
Land's End, 235, 236
Langley, Thomas, 126-7
Lanhydrock House, 227-9
Lansdown Terrace (Bath), 260
Launceston, 226
Lavenham, 13, 21-3, 31, 196
Lawrence, D. H., 75
Lawrence, Sir Thomas, 4, 251, 257, 298, 299
Lear, King, 258-9
Leeds, 75
Leer, 281
Leicestershire (Leics), map, 76
Lely, Sir Peter, 4, 60, 172, 251-2, 286
Le Nain, Louis, 173
Leominster, 297, 298
Levens Hall, 158, 160-2
Lewes, 186-7
Leyden, *see* Lucas van Leyden

Lincoln, xiv, 44, 61-70, 85; Art Gallery, 65; bishops of, 65, 68; Cathedral, 61, 62, 66, 67-70, 306; City and County Museum, 65-6; College of Art, 63; Jews in, 63-5, 102, Museum of Lincolnshire Life, 67
Lincolnshire, 58-75; maps, 59, 76, 108
Lindsey, 16
Lion (hotel, Shrewsbury), 308
Lion Reserve (zoo, Longleat), 269-70
Lippi, Fra Filippo, 256
Liskeard, 229
Little St. Hugh of Lincoln, 64, 69
Lizard Point, 236-7
London (pub, Padstow), 231
London House (restaurant, Norwich), 48
Longfellow, Henry Wadsworth, ancestors of, 111
Longhi, Pietro, 271
Longhirst, 145
Longleat, 252, 269-72
Long Melford, 18-21, 31
Lord Leycester Hospital (Warwick), 78-9
Lorrain, Claude, 172
Losely House, 167-9
Lotto, Lorenzo, 250, 270
Louth, 72-4
Loveless, George, 206
Lowestoft, 37; porcelain, 40
Loweswater, 154
Lozinga, Herbert de (Bishop of Norwich), 55
Lucas van Leyden, 251
Luccombe, 220
Ludlow, 299
Lugg, River, 297
Luigi's Italian (restaurant, Tewkesbury), 295
Lung Chu (restaurant, Louth), 73
Luttrell Arms (hotel, Dunster), 219
Lyme Regis, 213
Lynmouth, 221
Lynn Cathedral (King's Lynn), 55-6
Lynton, 221
Lyon, *see* Corneille de Lyon

Macpherson, James, 173
Magna Carta, 26, 30, 69, 255
Maiden Castle, 205
Maid's Head (hotel, Norwich), 47-8
Majestic (hotel, Cheltenham), 289
Malmesbury, 281; Abbey, 254
Malvern Hills, 290

Manor House Museum (Ilkley), 111
Mansion House (York), 91
Marazion, 236–7
Margaret, Queen of Scotland, 242
Margaret of Anjou, 28
Marie Antoinette, Queen of France,
    fireplace fittings, 60
Mark, King, 225, 238
Marlborough, 252
Martineau, Harriet, 158
Mary (sister of Henry VIII), Queen
    of France, 28
Mary I, Queen, 34, 139, 244, 249
Mary Magdalen, Church of
    (Launceston), 226
Mary Queen of Scots, 34, 129, 139,
    153, 171, 197
Master, Dr. Richard, 280
Matsys, Quintin, 177
Maumbury Rings (earthworks,
    Dorchester), 204–5
Maurier, *see* Du Maurier
Mayflower (ship), 39
Mayor of Casterbridge, The
    (Hardy), 202
Medici, Catherine de', enamels, 140
Melford Hall (Long Melford), 18,
    20–1
Melton Grange (Woodbridge), 33
Merchant Adventurers' Hall (York),
    87–8, 105
Merchant Taylor's Hall (York), 92,
    105
Mereworth, 181–2; Castle, 182
Mermaid (hotel, Rye), 194
Methuen, Paul, 254–5
Methuen family, 256
Metropole (hotel, Padstow), 238–9
Mevagissey, 237
Michelangelo Buonarroti, 24, 118,
    256
Midhurst, 171
Midlands region, 75, 287–8, 311
Milton, John, 66, 158
Minack Theatre (Porthcurno),
    235–6
Minchinhampton, 284
Minehead, 221
Miner's Arms (Trevallas), 232–3
Miner's Arms (Yorkshire), 110
Minion, 229
Miserden, 281
Mollington (hotel, Chester), 308
Monet, Claude, 178
Monmouth Rebellion, 201–2
Montague, Lord, 196

Montfort, Simon de, 138, 207
Montgomery, Earl of, 249
Montefeltre, Federigo da, 242
Moore, Henry, 247
Moors, *see* Cornwall; Devon;
    Yorkshire
More, Sir Christopher, 167–8
More-Molyneux family, 167
Moretonhampstead, 217
Moreton-on-Marsh, 290
Morris, William, 118, 204, 218, 228,
    229, 276
Morte D'Arthur (Malory), 225
Mortimer, Roger de, 283, 292
Morton, Cardinal, 207
Morwenstow, 223
Mount Royal (hotel, York), 106
Mousehole, 236
Muddle Green, 189
Muggleswick, 131
Muncaster Castle, 149–51
Mystery plays, 95–6, 304, 305

Nab Cottage, 158
Nailsworth, 284
Nain, *see* Le Nain
Napier, Robert, 202
Napoleon I, 24, 162, 204, 240
Napoleon III, china, 178
Napper's Mite (Dorchester), 202
Nash, John, 254–5
Nash, Richard "Beau," 259–60, 262
National Park system, 155, 163;
    Devon, 216; Lake District, 149;
    Northumberland, 137
National Portrait Gallery (London),
    120, 170, 184, 250
National Trust, 4, 22, 24, 70, 159,
    176, 178, 190, 205–6, 227, 231, 240,
    253, 282
Nelson, Horatio (Lord), 40
Nelson Hotel (Norwich), 48
Nether Lypiatt, 283–4
Nether Wallop (restaurant,
    Glyndebourne), 187
Neville, Richard, *see* Warwick the
    Kingmaker
Neville family (Durham), 125–6, 129
Newby Bridge, 149
Newby Hall, 117–19
New Inn (Winchelsea), 194
Newlyn, 236
Newmarket, 57
Newquay, 232
Newton, Sir Isaac, 175

Nicolson, Sir Harold, 184
Nightingale, Florence, 250
Nonconformity, 39, 45, 46, 87
Norfolk, 13, 38–57; dukes of, 26, 34;
    map, 12
Northampton, earls of, 80
Northamptonshire, 146; map, 76
Northleach, 276–7
North Riding (of Yorkshire), map,
    108
North Tyne River, 135
Northumberland, 136–46; dukes of,
    136–40; earls of, 124, 171–2, 173,
    301; maps, 137, 130; National
    Park, 136
Norwich, xv, 38–49; bishops of, 55;
    Cathedral, 44–5, 47, 55; City Hall,
    41; Jews in, 101; Music House, 47
"Norwich Players," 43
Norwich school of painting, 40
Nottingham, 75–7, 126
Nottinghamshire, maps, 76, 59
Notyngham, John, 27
Noverre Theatre (Norwich), 48

Oaklands (hotel, Chester), 308
Ockham, 177
Ocle Pychard, 297
Odda, Earl, 291
Odiham, 240
Odo, Bishop, 195
Offa's Dyke, 302–3
Old Baptist Church (Tewkesbury),
    295
Old Clergy House (Alfriston), 196
Old Cross (pub, Alnwick), 141–2
Old King's Head (hotel, Chester),
    308
Old Ship Inn (Padstow), 231, 239
Old Tea House (Lavenham), 22
Oldway (house, Paignton), 215
Openwoodgate, 121
Oswestry, 301–2
Otley, 112
Otterburn, 136
Oulton, 37
Ouse, River, 54, 85, 93, 94
Oxford: Christ College at, 55;
    Jews in, 64
Oxford House (Lavenham), 22

Pack of Hounds (pub, Lamplugh),
    153
Padstow, 231; hotels, 238–9
Paignton, 215
Paine, Thomas, 50

Painswick, 282
Palladio, Andrea, 23–4
Palmer, Alice, 186
Palmer, John, 260
Par, 238
Parham House, 197
Parr, Catherine (or Katherine),
    159, 168, 248, 255
Paul V, Pope, portrait, 256
Peasants' Revolt, 18
Peasemarsh, 191
Peeping Tom, 77
Pegswood, 145
Pembroke, earls of, 249, 250, 251
Pendragon, Uther, 224–5
Pennines mountains, 9, 131
Pennington family (Muncaster
    Castle), 150
Penobscot, Mrs. (of Maine tribe),
    243
Pensanooth, 237
Penshurst, 179–80
Pentewan, 238
Penzance, 236
Percy family (Northumberland),
    138–41, 171, 172, 301
Perranporth, 232
Peruzzi, Baldassare, imitation of,
    270
Petworth House, 139, 171–5
Pevensey, 196
Philip II, King of Spain, 244
Pickwick Papers, The (Dickens), 295
Pietro, Da (restaurant, Bath), 272
Pilgrims, the, 203
Pilgrim's Restaurant (Hastings),
    195
Piombo, *see* Sebastiano del Piombo
Piper, John, 67
Pittville Park (Cheltenham), 288–9
Plough (hotel, Alnwick), 144
Plymouth, 238
Polesden Lacey, 176–7
Polperro, 238
Polyphant, 226
Pont l'Evêque, Archbishop Roger,
    113
Pop In (restaurant, Louth), 73
Porlock, 221; Hill, 221
Port Graverne Hotel (Port Isaac),
    239
Porthcurno, 235–6
Port Isaac, 230, 231, 239
Port Quin, 230–1
Portscatho, 237, 239

Postbridge, 216
Post House (hotel, York), 105
Potter, Beatrix, 149
Poussin, Nicolas, 250
Praa, 237
Pratts (hotel, Bath), 272
Praxiteles, head by?, 173
Preservation Trust (King's Lynn), 54–5
Prideaux family (Padstow), 231
Princetown, 216–17
Pritchett, V. S., quoted, 13
Provençal French (restaurant, Salisbury), 272
Puddletown, 206
Pull's Ferry (Norwich), 47
Pump Room (Cheltenham), 288–9
Pyrford, 177

Quantock Hills, 221
Queen (hotel, Chester), 308
Queen (hotel, Lincoln), 70
Queens (hotel, Cheltenham), 289, 307

Raby Castle, 129–31
Raeburn, Sir Henry, 177
Railway Museum (York), 93–4, 105
Raleigh, Sir Walter, 172, 210, 231, 243
Raphael Sanzio, 286
Ravenglass, 149
Red Lion (hotel, Salisbury), 272
Red Mount Chapel (King's Lynn), 56
Redruth, 227, 237
Reformation, the, 68, 72, 88, 92, 103, 110, 126, 127 280 296; *see also* Dissolution of the Monasteries
Rembrandt van Rijn, 40, 60, 250, 251
Rendlesham, 33
Reni, Guido, 256
Restoration, the, 81, 92
Restronguet, 237
Revere, Paul, and lantern signal, *see* Dawes
Reynolds, Sir Joshua, 4, 60, 139, 173, 174, 251, 257, 286
Ribera, José, 248
Richard I, King, 102, 255, 265
Richard II, King, 18, 86, 92, 129, 138, 255, 280, 301
Richard III, King, 129
Richard II (Shakespeare), 69
Richmond, 119
Rievaulx Abbey, 107–8

Ripley, 177
Ripon, 119; Cathedral, 113–15
Ritson, Jonathan, 173
Riverside (hotel, Chester), 308
Robartes family (Cornwall), 227–8
Roche, 227
Rock Inn (Roche), 227
Roman Baths (Bath), 262–3, 264
Romano, Giulio, 81
Romney, George, 257
Romney, 193
Romsey, 245–6
Roosevelt, Franklin D., figure of, 178
Rose and Crown (hotel, Long Melford), 20, 21
Rosehill Theatre (Whitehaven), 163
Roseland House (hotel, Portscatho), 239
Rose Villa (Salisbury), 246
Rosevine House (hotel, Portscatho), 239
Ross-on-Wye, 296–7
Rothbury, 136
Rother, River, 189, 193
Rouse, 281
Rowley House (Shrewsbury), 300
Royal (hotel, Norwich), 48
Royal Baths (Harrogate), 112
Royal County (hotel, Durham), 128
Royal Crescent (hotel, Bath), 272
Royal Hop Pole (inn, Tewkesbury), 295, 308
Royal Hotel (Bideford), 221
Royal Hotel (Ross-on-Wye), 297
Royal Station (hotel, York), 106
Royal York (hotel, Bath), 272
Rubens, Peter Paul, 60, 162, 250
Rufus, *see* William II
Ruisdael, Jacob van, 177
Ruskin, John, 155, 170
Rutland, map, 76
Rydal Mount, 158
Rye, 189, 191, 193, 194

Sackville-West, Vita, 184
St. Acca, 132–3, 134
St. Agnes, 233–4
St. Aldhelm, 257
St. Alkmund's Church (Shrewsbury), 300
St. Andrew, 132
St. Andrew, Church of (Norwich), 42
St. Andrew's Church (Bothal), 145
St. Andrew's Church (Cullompton), 218

St. Anthony's Hall (York), 92
St. Austell, 238
St. Bede (the Venerable), 101, 125
St. Bees, 153
St. Breock, 231
St. Buryan, 236
St. Catherine, 256, 280
St. Cecilia, 277
St. Chads (church, Shrewsbury),
  301
St. Christopher, 134, 280
St. Cleer, 229
St. Colomb Major, 232
St. Cuthbert, 124–5, 126
St. Cuthbert's parish church
  (Bath), 268
St. Edmund, 25, 26, 29, 40
St. Ethelbert's Gate (Norwich), 44,
  48
St. George, figure of, 68
St. George's Church (Wrotham), 181
St. George's Guildhall (King's
  Lynn), 56
St. Gregory, Church of (Sudbury),
  17–18
St. Helen's Church (York), 92, 105
St. Hugh, Little, of Lincoln, 64, 69
St. Ia (of Ireland), 234
St. Issy, 231
St. Ives, 234, 236, 239
St. James Cathedral (Bury
  St. Edmunds), 27
St. James parish church (Louth), 72
St. Jerome, painting of, 248
St. John, Church of (Chester), 303,
  305
St. John the Baptist, Church of
  (Cirencester), 279–80
St. John's Church (Keswick), 155
St. Julian's Church (Shrewsbury),
  300
St. Just, 235
St. Lawrence, Church of
  (Bradford-on-Avon), 257
St. Lawrence, Church of
  (Mereworth), 182
St. Leonard's Hospital (York), 98
St. Mabyn, 231
St. Margarets, Church of (King's
  Lynn), 53, 55
St. Martin's Micklegate Church
  (York), 94–5
St. Mary, Church of (Fairford), 275
St. Mary, Priory Church of
  (Deerhurst), 290–1
St. Mary Magdalen with St. Paul

in the Bail (Lincoln), 62
St. Mary the Virgin parish church
  (Ross-on-Wye), 296–7
St. Mary's Abbey (York), 95, 98, 99;
  Hospitium of, 96–7
St. Mary's Church (Bury
  St. Edmunds), 27–8
St. Mary's Church (Cerne Abbas),
  208
St. Mary's Church (Shrewsbury),
  300
St. Mary's Church (Warwick), 78, 79
St. Mary's Church (Woodbridge), 32
St. Mary's Lodge (house, York), 98
St. Mawes, 237, 239
St. Merryn, 231
St. Michael, Church of
  (Framlingham Castle), 34
St. Michael's, Church of (Coven-
  try), 77
St. Michael's Mount, 236
St. Nicholas Chapel (King's Lynn),
  56
St. Nicholas Chapel (Winchelsea),
  194
St. Olave's Church (York), 98
St. Osmund, 248
St. Oswald, 124
St. Patrick, 268
St. Peter, 125, 296
St. Peter Hungate Church
  (Norwich), 44
St. Peter Mancroft Church
  (Norwich), 41
St. Peter's Church (Chester), 304
St. Peter's Church (Dorchester),
  202, 203
St. Peter's Church (Sudbury), 16
St. Sebastian, 26
St. Theresa, 248
St. Tudy, 231
St. Werburgh, 306
St. Wilfrid, 114, 132–3, 134
St. William's College (York), 92–3
St. Zita, 296–7
Salisbury, xiv, 44, 245, 246–8;
  bishops of, 210, 247; Cathedral,
  246, 247–8; earls of, 159, 280;
  hotels and restaurants, 272;
  Plain, 252
Sandwich, 193
Sandys, Francis, 24, 28
Sandys, Sir William, 240–3 passim
Sapperton, 281
Saracen's Head (restaurant, Bath),
  272

Sargent, John Singer, 179
Savernake Forest, 252
Savoy (hotel, Cheltenham), 289, 307
Sawley, 110
Saxtead, 34
Scott, George Gilbert, 227–8
Scott, Sir Gilbert, 27, 306
Scott, Sir Walter, 153, 157
Seaton Delaval Hall, 145
Sebastiano del Piombo, 140, 256
Seckford, Thomas, 31, 32–3
Seckford Hall (Woodbridge), 32–3
Septimus Severus (Roman
   emperor), 85, 101, 133
Sestro, Cesare da, 251
Sevenoaks, 178, 179, 180
Severn, River, 285, 290, 295, 301
Shaftesbury, 210
Shakespeare, William, 18, 56, 75, 95,
   96, 150, 249, 258, 285, 292, 301
Shelley, Percy Bysshe, 149, 156
Sherborne, 209–10; Castle, 210;
   School, 209
Shere, 175–6
Sheridan, Richard Brinsley, 176, 260
Shire Hall (Woodbridge), 32
Shrewsbury, 299–301; Battle of, 138,
   301; hotels, 308
Shropshire, 296; map, 274
Sidney, Sir Philip, 172, 180, 249,
   309–10
Silenus, figure (mythology), 204
Silkstede, Prior, 244
Singer, Isaac Merritt, 215
Sissinghurst, 183; Castle, 183–5
Sizergh Castle, 158–60, 162
Skell, River, 116
Skelton, Tom, 150
Slingsby, 107
Small Dole, 197
Smarden, 185
Smollett, Tobias George, 260
Smyth, Jankyn, 27
Snape, 13
Snitter, 136
Solway, River, 135
Solway Firth, 152
Somersby, 66
Somerset, 219, 238, 252; dukes of,
   173; maps, 214, 241
Sompting, 197
South Acre, 52, 53
Southey, Robert, 153, 155, 156, 157
Southwold, 35–7
Spa (hotel, Ripon), 113
Spence, Sir Basil, 77–8

Spenser, Edmund, 249
Spinning Wheel (inn, Hadleigh), 15
Staffordshire, map, 274
Stanley Palace (Chester), 305
Stanway, 290
Star (hotel, Wells), 272
Stephenson Locomotive Society, 94
Stevenson, Robert Louis, 153
Steyning, 197
Still, John, 266
Stinsford, 205
Stoke d'Abernon, 177
Stokesley, 109
Stonehenge, 252
Stour, River, 14, 15
Stow-on-the-Wold, 290
Strangers' Hall (Norwich), 43
Stratford-upon-Avon, 78, 79
Strickland family (Sizergh Castle), ·
   159–60
Stroud, 281, 282–3, 284; hotels, 307
Stubbs, George, 286
Stump Cross Caverns, 110
Sudbury, 16–18, 41
Suffolk, 13–38, 57; dukes of, 28;
   earls of, 287; map, 12
Suffolk (hotel, Bury St. Edmunds),
   30
Suffolk Summer (Appleby), 26
Surrey, 21, 167–77; earls of, 34; map,
   166
Sussex, 167, 186–98; maps, 166, 192
Sussex Archaeological Society,
   Folk Museum of, 186–7
Sutton, 33
Sutton Hoo burial mounds, 33
Swaffham, 51–2
Swan (hotel, Bath), 272
Swan (hotel, Lavenham), 22
Swan (hotel, Tewkesbury), 308
Swift, Jonathan, 152
Swynford, Katherine, 69

Tadcaster, 85
Talbot Hotel (Ripley), 177
Tamar, River, 226
Tame, John, 275
Tateshales, Robert de, 70
Tattershall Castle, 70–2
Tavern on the Town (restaurant,
   York), 106
Teniers, David, 172, 173, 250
Teniers the Younger, David, 177
Tennyson, Alfred, 66–7, 170
Terborch, Gerard, 177
Terry, Ellen, 170

Terry's (restaurant, York), 106
Tetbury, 284
Tewkesbury, xiv, 290, 292, 294–5;
  Abbey, 292–4; Battle of, 292, 293;
  hotels, 308
Thetford, 39, 49–50
Thoresby, Thomas, 55
Thoresby College (King's Lynn), 55
Three Tuns (hotel, Durham), 128
Thropton, 136
Through England on a Side Saddle
  (Fiennes), 41, 155, 233, 259
Tin mining (Cornwall), 233–4
Tintagel, 218, 224–5
Tintoretto, Il (Jacopo Robusti),
  60, 140, 256
Titian (Tiziano Vecelli), 60, 81, 140,
  173, 180, 270
Tiverton, 218–19
Toadmoor, 121
Toby Cottage (restaurant, Ripley),
  177
Tocqueville, Alexis de, description
  by, 311
Tolpuddle, 206–7
Tom Jones (Fielding), 260
Torquay, 215
Totnes, 215–16
Trade-union movement, beginnings
  of, 206–7
Treasurer's House (York), 93, 105
Tredaule, 226
Treen, 236
Tregadilett, 226
Treknow, 230
Trent, River, 61
Tresillian, 237
Trethevy Quoit, 229–30
Trevallas, 232–3
Trewoofe, 236
Trianon (restaurant, York), 106
Trinity Guildhall (King's Lynn), 56
Tristan and Isolde, 224–5
Truro, 237
Trust House hotels, 6
Tudor House (hotel, Tewkesbury),
  308
Tudor Rosa, La (restaurant,
  Norwich), 48
Turberville (D'Urberville) family
  (Dorchester), 201, 207
Turner, Joseph Mallord William,
  40, 66, 154, 156, 171, 174, 175, 213
Twynnoy Hannah, 254
Tybald, Simon, 18
Tyne, River, 135

Udimore, 191
Ulpha, 149
Undercroft Gallery (York), 101–3
Unicorn (hotel, Ripon), 113
Upper Swell, 290
Usher Gallery (Lincoln), 66

Valley Gardens (Harrogate), 113
Value Added Tax (VAT), 6
Vanbrugh, Sir John, 145
Van der Goes, see Goes
Van der Weyden, see Weyden
Van de Velde, see Velde
Van Dyck, Sir Anthony, 60, 140, 172,
  175, 250, 251, 256
Vane, Sir Harry, 129–31
Van Gogh, Vincent, 178
Vanishing Cornwall (du Maurier),
  236–7
Van Leyden, see Lucas van Leyden
Velde, Willem van de, 251, 286
Venus, head of, 240
Veryan, 237
Vespasian (Roman emperor), 85
Victoria, Queen, 67, 89, 112, 122, 126
Victoria (hotel, Compton
  Wynyates), 82
Victoria and Albert Museum, 24
Victoria Art Gallery (Bath), 264
Vigée-Lebrun, Madame, 25
Viking (hotel, York), 93, 105
Vinci, Leonardo da, 251
Vyne, The, 240–3

Walberswick, 35
Waldron, 188
Walpole, Sir Robert, 174–5
Walton, Isaak, 244
Wark, 136
Warkworth Castle, 144
Warminster, 271
Warrenne, Earl of, 52
Wars of the Roses, 71, 138, 189, 208,
  292
Warwick, 78–9; earls of, 78, 129
Warwick the Kingmaker, 129, 292
Warwickshire (Warcs), maps, 76,
  274
Wash, The, 54
Washington, George, 145–6, 159
Washington Old Hall, 145–6
Watchet, 221
Wateringbury, 182
Watts, George, 67, 169–70
Watts Gallery (Compton), 169–70
Wat Tyler rebellion, 18

Wayneflete, Bishop, 244
Wear, River, 124
Webb, John, 249
Weddell, William, 117–18
Wellington, Duke of, 162
Wellington Mine (Whitehaven), 152
Wells, 44, 252; Cathedral, 265–8;
  hotels and restaurants, 272
Wensley, 119
Wesley, John, 122, 229, 237
Wessington, de (family), 159;
  see also Washington, George;
  Washington Old Hall
Wessyngton, see Washington Old
  Hall
West Farleigh, 182
West Looe, 238
Westminster Abbey, 19, 205
Westmorland, 146, 149; Countess of,
  129; earls of, 182; map, 148; see
  also Lake District
West Riding (of Yorkshire), map,
  108
Weyden, Rogier van der, 173
Weymouth, Viscount, 271–2
Wharfe, River, 111, 119–20
Wharton, Edith, mansion, 58
Whatstandwell, 121
Whitby, 89
Whitchurch, 301
White, Rev. John, 203
"White Hart" hotels: Bath, 272;
  Lewes, 187; Lincoln, 70; Salisbury,
  272
White Hart Inn (Launceston), 226
Whitehaven, 151–2, 153; Rosehill
  Theatre in, 163
White Swan (hotel, Alnwick), 144
White Swan (hotel, York), 106
Whiteway, 281–2
Widecombe-in-the-Moor, 216
William II (Rufus), King, 86, 101,
  243–4, 259
William IV, King, 167
William the Conqueror, 34, 52, 69,
  70, 86, 101, 136, 194, 207, 218, 255,
  284, 303; see also Conquest
  (Norman)
William of Malmesbury, 257
Wilmington, 196
Wilton Abbey, 249
Wilton Diptych, the, 250
Wilton House, 248–52

Wiltshire, 252; map, 241
Wimborne Minster, 211
Winchcombe, Henrie, 277
Winchelsea, 189, 191–5
Winchester, xiv, 39, 44, 102;
  Cathedral, 243–5; College, 244–5
Windermere, 163
Windermere, Lake, 158
Windsor, Duke of (Edward VIII),
  61
Wint, Peter de, 66
Witham, River, 61, 70
Withies, The (restaurant,
  Compton), 170
Wolsey, Cardinal, 35, 65, 243
Wood, John, 260
Wood, John, the Younger, 263
Woodbridge, 31–3
Woolfardisworthy, 221
Worcestershire, map, 274
Wordsworth, Dora, 158
Wordsworth, Dorothy, 149, 153, 155,
  156, 157–8, 221
Wordsworth, William, 149, 153–4,
  155, 156, 157–8, 221
Workington, 152
Wotton-under-Edge, 284
Wren, Christopher, 60, 69, 117
Wrotham, 181
Wrotham, Richard de, 181
Wroxham, 49
Wycliffe, John, 44
Wye, 185–6
Wykeham, Bishop, 244
Wyndham, Charles, 171
Wyndham family, portraits, 172

Yalding, 182
"Ye Olde"-s, 5
York, xiv, xv, 39, 41, 44, 61, 85–106;
  Art Gallery, 98–9, 105; Cathedral
  (Minster), 85, 87, 100–5; Festival
  for Jesus, 87; map, 84; University
  of, 99; Yorkshire Museum, 96,
  97–8, 105, 120
York, Richard, Duke of, 95
Yorkshire, 85–121; maps, 108, 59;
  moors of, 109, 119; Rides, map, 108
Yorkshire Museum (York), 96, 97–8,
  105, 120
Ypres Tower (Rye), 191

Zennor, 234–5

A Note on the Type

The text of this book was set on the Linotype in
Aster, a typeface designed by Francesco
Simoncini (born in 1912 in Bologna, Italy) for
Ludwig and Mayer, the German type foundry.
Starting out with the basic old-face letterforms
that can be traced back to Francesco Griffo
in 1495, Simoncini emphasized the diagonal stress
by the simple device of extending diagonals to
the full height of the letterforms and squaring off.
By modifying the weights of the individual
letters to combat this stress, he has produced a
type of rare balance and vigor. Introduced
in 1958, Aster has steadily grown in popularity
wherever type is used.

Composed by Cherry Hill Composition
Pennsauken, N.J.
Printed and bound by The Colonial Press, Inc.
Clinton, Mass.

Maps by David Lindroth

Typography and binding design by
Virginia Tan